Islamophobia and Free Speech

Steven Greer

Islamophobia and Free Speech

Steven Greer

Academica Press
Washington

Library of Congress Cataloging-in-Publication Data
Names: Greer, Steven (author)
Title: Islamophobia and free speech | Greer, Steven.
Description: Washington : Academica Press, 2026. | Includes references.
Identifiers: LCCN 2025943381 | ISBN 9781680533767 (paperback)

To Aster, Penny, Rowan, and Alice

May their world be fairer, more tolerant, and more sustainable than ours

'When you come across people who speak with scorn about Our revelations, turn away from them until they move on to another topic', Qur'an 6:68.

'To apostatize and proselytize, to offend and embrace, to accept and reject: these are the dualities that uphold the essence of liberty', Ed Husain.

'We refuse to renounce our critical spirit out of fear of being accused of "Islamophobia," a wretched concept that confuses criticism of Islam as a religion and stigmatization of those who believe in it', *Manifesto – Together Facing the New Totalitarianism*, signed by 12 prominent writers including Sir Salman Rushdie.

'In order to advance their warped and malign cause, militant Islamic fundamentalists eagerly exploit confusion about the difference between the expression of anti-Muslim prejudice and responsible critical engagement with the faith and its followers. This splendid book calls their bluff by drawing the distinction with authoritative precision. It should be required reading for all Muslims as well as those of other religions and none'.
— Dr Taj Hargey, Imam of the Oxford Islamic Congregation and Provost of the Oxford Institute for British Islam.

'With problematic "anti-Islamophobia codes" being enforced in many ways, accusations of Islamophobia being weaponised to silence legitimate criticism of Muslim beliefs, practices, and conduct, and the government considering an official definition, we are perilously close to the introduction of an Islamic blasphemy law in the UK. It is, therefore, great to see Professor Steven Greer bringing his erudite skill and pointed legal analysis to bear in an authoritative and persuasive study which anyone who cares about free speech should urgently read'.
— Tim Dieppe, Head of Public Policy, Christian Concern, and author of *The Challenge of Islam*.

'Steven Greer's new book is a valuable, scholarly, and accessible examination of the conflict between "Islamophobia" and free speech. Unique in its scope and written by a man who knows all too well whereof he speaks this book is essential reading for all those who wish to understand one of today's most vexing issues'.
— Daniel Sharp, Editor, *The Freethinker*.

'Professor Greer's excellent study comes at a critical juncture as confusion mounts about how to distinguish between, on the one hand, legitimate criticism of Islam and its followers and, on the other, escalating anti-Muslim hatred and prejudice. It not only provides much needed clarity on where this line should be drawn; it should also be essential reading for anyone who cherishes the increasingly endangered right to freedom of speech'.
— Hardeep Singh, Deputy-Director for the Network of Sikh

Organisations, Assistant Editor of The Sikh Messenger, and author of '*Islamophobia*' *Revisited*.

'This welcome and authoritative study demonstrates how false accusations of Islamophobia, and the fear of being denounced as an Islamophobe, are censoring lawful and legitimate debate in Britain and elsewhere. Greer powerfully and eloquently argues that, in the UK context, people should be able to voice the same kind of criticism of Islam and its adherents as can legitimately be made in respect of any faith or ideology and those who subscribe to it. Required reading for anyone concerned about the free speech crisis sweeping the west'.
— William Makesy, Director, Alumni for Free Speech.

'In our topsy-turvy age, supposedly "liberal" forces in the West are not only silent when it comes to the suppression of legitimate criticism of Muslims and Islam but have linked arms in furthering it. This splendid book's compelling message could not be simpler: neither Muslims nor Islam are above criticism and indeed cannot be. Its publication also serves as a grim and much-needed reminder that, by failing to uphold freedom of expression in this and other ways, the West risks destroying itself'.
— Rahul Sur, former UN Chief of Peacekeeping Evaluation, former Inspector General of Police in Maharashtra and Deputy Commissioner of Police in Mumbai, India.

'This book provides a timely, unflinching, and authoritative examination of one of the most emotive issues of our age. Reviewing the history and teachings of Islam, providing copious studies of recent controversies, and linking theoretical discussions with their practical – and particularly legal – implications, the author highlights the urgent need to address conflicts between faith, identity, and fundamental rights in our diverse society. A must-read for policymakers, scholars, activists, and anyone interested in the current debate'.
— Stephen Evans, Chief Executive Officer, National Secular Society, UK.

'Amongst many other things, Steven Greer's excellent book breaks the wall of silence concerning the risks posed to liberal democracy by "political Islam" which seeks to shield itself from scrutiny by penetrating western public institutions and dominating public discourse. Indispensable reading for experts and the wider public alike'.

— Achilles Skordas, Emeritus Professor, University of Bristol, and Senior Research Affiliate, Max Planck Institute for Comparative Public Law and International Law, Heidelberg, Germany.

'This timely and fascinating book reminds us that we are at a critical juncture in our political life. The author's forensic and penetrating analysis warns us that we can either elevate "causing any offence to religious sensitivities" into a "right" policed by violence and intimidation, or we can defend the ideal of freedom of expression as a centre piece of democracy and human rights. Greer makes an unanswerable case for the latter'.

— Pragna Patel, Director of Project Resist and former Director of Southall Black Sisters.

Contents

Glossary

Abrogation – Islamic doctrine according to which any inconsistency found in the Qur'an, which cannot otherwise be eliminated, can and should be resolved by the later revelation taking precedence over the earlier.

Ahkam al-jihad – collection of the most authoritative statements about jihad.

Ahl al-suffa, 'the people of the *suffah* or the bench' – refers to the impoverished devotees of Mohammad who used to gather at the *suffah*, a sheltered raised platform outside his home in Medina.

Ahmadiyya (or Ahmadi) – peace-loving, 'heretical', Muslim sect founded in India in 1889 by Mirza Ghulam Ahmad who claimed to be the Messiah, the Prophet Mohammad, and/or an incarnation of the Hindu God Krishna, which now numbers 170 million worldwide.

Al-'adl, 'the justice of God'.

Alawites/Nusayrites, 'worshippers of Ali' – offshoot of Shia Islam dating from 9th century, historically confined to Jebel Alawi on the Syrian coast, but now numbering 2.6 million worldwide.

Al-Fatiha, 'the Opening' – the first chapter of the Qur'an consisting of seven verses praying for guidance and mercy.

Allah, 'the God' – the principal deity of the traditional Arab pantheon and the sole God of Islam.

Allahu akbar, 'God is Great!' – Muslim call to prayer and to arms.

Al-Lat – one of Allah's three daughters in traditional Arab pantheon.

Al-Manat – one of Allah's three daughters in traditional Arab pantheon.

Al-Shabab – jihadi terrorist organization operating in East Africa.

Al-Uzza – one of Allah's three daughters in traditional Arab pantheon.

Al-wala wa al-bara – loyalty to the umma and hostility towards everyone else.

Aqida – rigid and ruthless enforcement of the sharia, particularly against blasphemy, apostasy, and criticism of the faith from both insiders and outsiders.

Ash'arite – 9th/10th century movement advocating subordination of reason to the Qur'an and sunnah.

As-salāmu 'alaykum, 'peace be upon you' – traditional greeting throughout Muslim world.

Ayah – a verse from the Qur'an.

Ayatollah – honorific title for high-ranking Shia clergy in post-Islamic revolutionary Iran.

Bara'a – excommunication of heretics, including killing other Muslims deemed to have become bandits, rebels, apostates, and/or to be involved in decadent or corrupt pro-western Muslim governments

Barelvi – Sunni revivalist movement founded in late 19th century seeking a return to Islamic orthodoxy.

Boko Haram – jihadi terrorist movement based in Nigeria.

Burqa –head-to-toe body cover, including the eyes, worn by some Musim women as an act of modesty, piety, or in obedience to husbands, fathers, brothers, or sons.

Caliph, 'God's representative on earth' – title of Mohammad's successors as leader of the ummah and supreme governor of Caliphate.

Caliphate – an Islamic state governed by a Caliph.

Dar al-Aliftaa-al-Misriyyah – Egyptian government agency issuing 5,000 fatwas per week in response to questions.

Darvish (Persian), 'Islamic mystics' – from which the English word 'dervish' derives.

Deobandi – Sunni revivalist movement founded in Deoband, India, in 1850s to defend traditional Islam from modernism and secularism.

Dhimmi, 'protected person' – historic formal subordinate legal status for non-Muslims, particularly Jews and Christians, in Muslim states.

Druze/Muwahhidun, 'Unitarians' – 680,000–strong sect, widely regarded as heretical and found mostly in mountainous parts of contemporary southern Lebanon, which broke away from Shia Islam in 10th century.

Eid al-Adha, 'feast of sacrifice' – celebrates Abraham's willingness to sacrifice his son Isaac.

Eid al-Fitr – feast following end of daily dawn-to-dusk fast of Ramadan.

Eid Mubarak, 'blessed feast/festival' – traditional Muslim greeting anticipating or during Eid al-Adha or Eid al-Fitr.

Emir –historically a war lord or military leader later also referring to those with high social status and holders of high office, including ceremonial, in the Muslim world.

Ex-Muslims – increasingly high-profile movement of those who have renounced their Muslim faith.

Faqir, plural *fuqara*, 'the poor' – from which the English words 'fakir' derives.

Fard – religious duty commanded by God.

Fatwa – an opinion about Islamic law delivered by a Muslim legal scholar.

Fiqh – Islamic jurisprudence.

Fitna –Arabic for trial, affliction, distress, conflict, or strife particularly within the ummah.

Five Pillars of Islam: the 'shahadah' – the two testimonies that 'there is no God but Allah and Mohammad is his prophet'; 'salat', praying five times a day; 'zakat', a voluntary 'tax' or charitable obligation for the relief of poverty; 'sawm', fasting during Ramadan; and 'hajj', the pilgrimage to Mecca during the month of Dhu-al-Hijah.

Ghuraba, 'strange or weird' – the sense Muslims have of being perceived as strangers or outsiders by non-Muslims.

Hadd – severe punishments including beheading for murder and attempted murder, amputation of the right hand for theft, stoning to death for blasphemy and apostasy, and severe flogging for adultery, false accusation of adultery, and drunkenness.

Hadith, 'remnant' or 'effect' – anecdotes about the life and sayings of Mohammad some of which mainstream Islam recognizes as creating religious obligations (*sunnah*).

Hajj – annual Muslim pilgrimage to Mecca during the month of Dhu-al-Hijah.

Hakimiyya – Islamic governance.

Hamas – jihadi movement based in Gaza and dedicated to destruction of Israel.

Hanafi – the oldest and most widely-followed of the four schools of Sunni jurisprudence.

Hanbali – one of the four schools of Sunni jurisprudence.

Haram, 'forbidden' – in the case of Islam, by God.

Hashemite – a member of the House of Hashim, part of the powerful and wealthy Quraysh tribe into which Mohammad was born. Also refers to the contemporary Jordanian royal family.

Hezbollah, 'Party of God' – Iran-backed Shia jihadi terrorist organization based in Lebanon, dedicated to the destruction of Israel.

Hijab – scarf covering head, but not face or neck, worn by some Muslim women as an act of modesty, piety, or in obedience to husbands, fathers, brothers, or sons.

Hijra, 'severing of ties of kinship or association' – refers in Islam to flight of Mohammad and the first Muslims from Mecca to Yathrib (later known as Medina) in 622 CE.

Hikma – the secret knowledge of the Druze found in the Book of Wisdom.

Hisbah – enjoining good and forbidding wrong.

Hizb ut-Tahrir, 'Party of Liberation' – an international jihadi terrorist organization founded in 1953, dedicated to the establishment of a global Islamic caliphate governed by the sharia.

Houri – a young, beautiful, virginal woman available to faithful Muslim men in paradise.

Hudud, 'borders, boundaries, limits' – refers to punishments under Islamic law believed to be mandated and fixed by God for unlawful sexual intercourse, false accusations of unlawful sexual intercourse, drinking alcohol, highway robbery, and some forms of theft.

Ibadites/Ibadism, 'The People of Truth and Integrity' – a marginal Muslim sect claiming adherence to the most pristine version of the faith, said by some to be the last remnant of the Kharijites.

Ijma, 'consensus' – referring in Islam to consensus on points of Islamic law.

Ijtihad, 'physical or mental effort' – refers in Islam to independent reasoning by Islamic scholars.

Imam – a spiritual and community leader in Sunni Islam and, for Shias, a spiritual authority descended from the family of the Prophet.

ISIS – Islamic State of Iraq and Syria (DAESH in Arabic), a Salafi jihadi terrorist movement which briefly established a brutal, genocidal Caliphate from 2014-19 in northwestern Iraq and eastern Syria.

Islam, 'submission to the one true God' – second largest religion in the world after Christianity, founded by the Prophet Mohammad in the first half of the 7th century.

Islamofauxbia – slang term referring to false accusations of Islamophobia.

Islamophobia – irrational prejudice against Muslims and Islam.

Islamophobia-phobia – the excessive fear of being accused of Islamophobia.

Isnad – chains of authority by which hadith have been transmitted.

Isra and Mi'raj – the two-stage Night Journey Mohammad is said to have taken, first from Mecca to Jerusalem, and then from Jerusalem to heaven.

Jahiliyyah, the 'Age of Ignorance' – term used by Muslims to refer to pre-Islamic Arabia and to criticize un-Islamic conduct in the Muslim world.

Jam'iat Ihyaa Minhaaj Al-Sunnah (JIMAS), 'Movement of the Revival of the Prophet's Way' – a UK-based conservative Muslim charity dedicated to improving understanding of Islam, particularly among young people.

Jihad, 'exerting', 'striving', or 'struggling' particularly with respect to a praiseworthy aim – in Islam this includes combatting one's own un-Godly impulses (the 'greater', inner struggle), and/or 'striving in the cause of Allah' (the 'lesser', outer struggle) by either 'jihad of the pen/tongue' (debate or persuasion) or 'jihad of the sword' (armed conflict).

Jinni, plural *jinn* – a pre-Islamic Arabian and Islamic shape-shifting fiery demon, potentially good but more commonly evil, and capable of inter-breeding with humans.

Jizya – a type of taxation historically levied on non-Muslim subjects of an Islamic state.

Kaaba – stone building in the centre of the Masjid al-Haram mosque in Mecca, which Muslims believe was constructed by Adam, rebuilt by Abraham, defiled by Arab polytheism, and restored to the original worship of Allah by Mohammad.

Kafir (plural *kuffar*) – someone who does not believe in the Muslim faith.

Kalam – scholastic, speculative, or rational study of Islamic theology using a form of dialectical doctrinal reasoning.

Kharijites, 'successionists' – 7th century radically egalitarian Islamic sect advocating rebellion against corrupt and sinful Caliphs, branding Muslims who deviated from their uncompromising interpretation of Islam as unbelievers deserving to be killed unless they repented.

Liberal/progressive Islam – interpretation of Islam sympathetic to western conceptions of human rights, democracy and the rule of law.

Mahdi, 'chosen one' – a figure in Sunni and Shia eschatology, not mentioned in the Qur'an but prophesized by various hadith to appear at the 'End of Times', shortly before the return of Jesus, and the final elimination of evil and injustice.

Makruh/makrooh, 'detestable', 'abominable', or 'disliked' – in Islam meaning 'discouraged' or 'disapproved', one of five types of conduct from 'obligatory' to 'forbidden'.

Maliki – one of the four schools of Sunni jurisprudence.

Maqasid al-Sharia – Islamic doctrine referring to the goals or objectives of the *sharia*, divine law.

Maslaha, 'public interest' – a concept in sharia denoting prohibition or permission of that which serves the public interest of the ummah.

Meccan verses – refers to the verses of the Qur'an delivered in Mecca prior to the Hijra.

Medinan verses – refers to the verses of the Qur'an delivered in Medina during the war between the Muslims and the Meccans. Much more marshal and belligerent than their Meccan counterpart.

Messenger of God – Islam acknowledges only three Messengers of God – those who transmit directly received Divine revelation – Moses, Jesus, and Mohammad.

Mihna, 'ordeal of Quranic createdness' – religious persecution in Abbasid Caliphate from 833-851 CE of those opposed to Mu'tazila doctrine.

Millet system – legal independence pertaining to 'personal law' granted to Jews and Christians in Ottoman empire.

Misyar marriage – type of marriage observed by some Sunni Muslims in which the couple continue to live separately as before and only see each other to fulfil their sexual needs.

Mohammad, 'Highly Praised'.

Mozarab, 'Arab wannabe' – medieval non-Arabs who admired Arab culture and civilization.

Mu'tazilites, 'those who separate or withdraw from' – an early Muslim sect which emphasised the importance of reason as a route to spiritual truth.

Mubah, 'permitted'.

Mufti – an Islamic jurist.

Mujahid – scholars trained in Islamic law.

Mujahideen, 'those engaged in jihad' – came to prominence in 1980s during and after Soviet occupation of Afghanistan.

Murji'ah, 'those who postponed judgment' – a sect in early Islam which maintained that those who observed the sharia and did not challenge the Caliph's authority should be regarded as Muslims unless and until God declared otherwise on the Day of Judgment.

Muslim – one who submits to the will of Allah as revealed in Qur'an.

Mustahabb, 'beloved thing' – refers in Islam to that which is recommended or favoured.

Niqab – veil for the face, but not the eyes or the rest of the body, worn by some Musim women as an act of modesty, piety, or in obedience to husbands, fathers, brothers, or sons.

Orthodoxy – orthodox belief.

Orthopraxy – orthodox practice.

Qadi – a magistrate or judge of a sharia court, who also exercises extrajudicial functions such as mediation, guardianship over orphans and minors, and the commissioning and supervision of public works.

Qisas – tit-for-tat retaliation.

Qiyas, 'analogy' – the process of deductive analogy in which the meaning of hadith are compared and contrasted with the Qur'an in order to arrive at a solution to a novel legal problem.

Qur'an, the 'recitation, 'lecture', 'discourse' – the published collection of the allegedly comprehensive and complete orally delivered Divine revelations of the Prophet Mohammad.

Raisail al-Hikma – the book containing the secret knowledge of the Druze.

Riba, 'usury' – putatively unjust, exploitative gains made in trade or business.

Riddah wars/wars of apostasy – brief but brutal wars conducted shortly after the death of the Prophet against rebellious Arab tribes some proclaiming alternative versions of Islam.

Safa, an Arabic word for purity and cleanliness,

Salafism – revivalist movement in Sunni Islam seeking to return the faithful to the beliefs and life-styles of the *salaf*, 'pious predecessors', the Prophet Mohammad and the first three generations of his disciples.

Salat – the obligation to pray five times a day.

Satanic verses – revelations said to have been received by Mohammad authorizing prayer to the three daughters of the traditional Arab pantheon which, claiming to have been misled by Satan, Mohammad rapidly rescinded. Also the title of a novel by Salman Rushdie.

Sawm – abstinence, including fasting, during Ramadan.

Shafi – one of the four schools of Sunni jurisprudence.

Shahabad, 'similar' – juridical concept meaning application of rule or principle in one set of circumstances to those which are similar.

Shahadah – affirmation that 'there is no God but Allah and Mohammad is His prophet'.

Sharia, 'path', 'way', 'well-trodden path', 'the way to a watering place', 'that which is prescribed' – Islamic law based upon the Qur'an, hadith, and sunnah.

Shaykh/Sheikh, 'elder' – refers to a tribal chief, a particularly distinguished Muslim scholar, a member of the royal family of some Arab countries.

Shia Islam – minority branch of the Islamic faith which affirms that the leadership of ummah passed down Mohammad's blood line.

Shirk – unforgivable idolatrous 'sin of association', comparing Allah to other gods, or to humans claiming to represent Him.

Shura, 'consultation' – term for collective decision-making by representative institution such as a council, or process such as a referendum.

Sira, 'the way' – traditional biography of Mohammad.

Soof/suf – refers to the course woollen clothing worn by Sufis in preference to the lighter cotton typically chosen by early Muslim ascetics.

Sufism – mystical interpretation of Islam more interested than other traditions in the subordination of the ego to the Will of God and the primacy of love over intellect, tradition, doctrine, and dogma as routes to authentic spirituality.

Sultan – governor of Muslim territory.

Sunni Islam – majority Muslim tradition asserting that leadership of ummah should be by popular acclaim not Mohammad's blood line.

Surah – chapter of Qur'an.

Takfir – excommunication of one Muslim by another on the grounds of alleged apostasy.

Talaq – divorce available to husbands by declaring, three times, 'I divorce you'.

Taqiyya, 'prudence' – doctrine permitting a degree of strictly defined dissimulation, secrecy and dishonesty about beliefs in the face of extreme persecution.

Taqlid, 'conformity' or 'imitation' – denotes doctrinal continuity in Islamic scholarship.

Tatarrus – willingly causing collateral damage to 'human shields' allegedly used by a military adversary.

Tawhid – the oneness and unity of God.

Ulama, 'the learned' – collective term for Muslim clerics/Islamic scholars.

Ummah – the global Muslim community.

Uqqul, 'sages' – custodians of the secret knowledge of the Druze.

Wadribuhunna, 'to go away from', 'beat', 'strike lightly' or 'separate' – used in Qur'an 4.34 to refer to legitimate admonishment of a disobedient wife by her husband.

Wahhabism – puritanical Sunni reformist movement aimed at purging Islam of 'un-Islamic' superstitious beliefs and practices.

Yathrib, name given to Medina before Islamization of Arabia.

Zakat – Islamic voluntary 'tax' or charitable obligation for the relief of poverty.

Chapter 1

Overview

Introduction

Tackling prejudice, hatred and discrimination, whatever the substance or source, is both laudable and necessary. However, this noble cause has spawned another, much less worthy corollary – the increasingly widely-held assumption in Britain and elsewhere, that little if any criticism of Muslims and Islam should be permitted.

As this study will show, an unholy alliance unites some very disparate elements taking this view. One is a minority of 'militant', 'fundamentalist', or 'extremist' Muslims and 'Islamists', who shrewdly recognise that their antagonism towards the west can be advanced by castigating even lawful and legitimate criticism of Muslim beliefs, practices, and conduct, as proof of a western conspiracy to destroy Islam. Some, but by no means all, other Muslims, including community leaders, have jumped on the bandwagon for various reasons. These may include the assumption that any criticism of Islam is blasphemous and that contesting it signals enduring fidelity and honour to family and clan, notwithstanding the physical and cultural distance from the taken-for-granted norms of ancestral lands. A third faction consists of far-left activists who regard the militant Muslims as allies in the struggle against a perceived common enemy – western, neo-colonial, neo-liberal, capitalism – despite the fact that their respective visions of what should replace it are radically different. This cohort has been joined by other paternalistic and very badly-informed non-Muslims including some 'critical social scientists'. Believing that Muslims are universally repressed and persecuted by western states and societies, they maintain that the faith and its adherents should be shielded from most, if not all, criticism in order to prevent additional offence and further anti-Muslim prejudice. Whether or not powerful institutions such as universities endorse this view, they also actively seek to silence legitimate and lawful criticism of Muslims and Islam. Avoiding possible financial loss and other negative consequences, including potentially violent repercussions, is also a compelling motive. As Sir Salman Rushdie has observed, 'fear is being disguised as respect', with responses tending to seek resolution 'through compromises and ceding' when the opposite should be the case.[1]

It is, however, highly unlikely that there would be a debate in the west about 'Islamophobia' in general and 'Islamophobic expression' in particular had it not been for five factors. The first two primed the controversy while the rest have fuelled it: the visceral reaction of some Muslims and others to the publication of Salman Rushdie's novel, *The Satanic Verses* in 1988; the onset of jihadi terrorism, and its consequences, particularly since 9/11 in 2001; the explosion of 'cancel culture' in the west over the past decade or so; the growing public controversy in the UK about immigrants and asylum-seekers, most of whom come from the predominantly Muslim countries of Pakistan, Afghanistan, Iran, Bangladesh and Syria; and the sharp rise in anti-Muslim and antisemitic hatred since the wars in the middle east erupted in the aftermath of the invasion of Israel by Hamas on 7 October 2023. Without these drivers, non-white Muslims would certainly have been exposed to colour-based racism. But this is unlikely to have been framed in religious terms any more than prejudice against non-white Sikhs, Hindus, or Christians is referred to as 'Sikhophobia', 'Hinduophobia', or 'Christianophobia'.

A campaign against Islamophobia has not only developed over the past thirty or so years; it suffers from a host of problems. These include: a lack of consensus about what the term means; confusion about related concepts and ideas; questionable assumptions and conclusions; widespread ignorance about authentic Muslim beliefs and practices, centuries-old exchanges of opinion, and relevant legal and human rights frameworks; plus reluctance to specify how prejudice against Muslims and Islam, on the one hand, and legitimate and lawful criticism on the other should be distinguished and what should follow as a result. The primary purpose of this study is to expose all of this, to address it, and to defend the right critically to appraise Muslims and Islam in the same manner, and subject to the same conditions, as that regarding any faith or ideology and its adherents. There are three main reasons.

First, any public allegation of Islamophobia, whether true or false, is likely to have serious consequences for those accused. These may include

---

[1] 'Salman Rushdie says the world learned the 'wrong lessons' from his Iran fatwa', *Agence France-Press*, 22 July 2015.

murder, other physical harm, vilification, cancellation, ostracism, disciplining or dismissal by employers, and irreparable damage to employment, career, and reputation. Self-censorship has been the inevitable consequence. Second, censuring the expression of lawful criticism of any system of beliefs, and/or those who hold them, is unlawful in liberal democracies by definition because it constitutes a violation of the fundamental right to freedom of expression. Third, in the cosmopolitan environments which characterize virtually every contemporary western state, singling out any ideology for privileged treatment – as the stigmatization of 'Islamophobic expression' inevitably does – is more likely to increase resentment, division, and social disharmony than to dispel it.

Towards conceptual clarity

Before considering in depth the distinction between legitimate and illegitimate criticism of Muslims and Islam, we need to begin with an attempt to clarify some other core issues and concepts.

Faith and race

A key issue in the debate about Islamophobic expression concerns the distinction between race and religion. Prima facie, 'race' is a matter of biology and ancestry typically rooted in DNA and manifested, though not straightforwardly, in skin colour and other physical characteristics. 'Religion', by contrast, concerns ideas about a range of issues including cosmology, ontology, theology, politics, ethics, and the 'meaning of life'. While both race and religion are, to a degree fluid and contingent, one of the key differences is that it is impossible for anyone to change their race, while changing religion is, in principle, simply a matter of abandoning one set of beliefs and possibly exchanging them for another. As we shall see, the failure to draw this distinction is central to the confusion surrounding anti-Muslim hatred and 'Islamophobic expression'.

Belief, practice, and conduct

For the purposes of this study, 'belief' concerns faith-based ideas, particularly those ostensibly held by the bulk of 'mainstream' or 'orthodox' Muslims, 'practice' refers to faith-related activity, eg fasting during Ramadan, while 'conduct' is behaviour attributable to at least some Muslims linked, though less directly, to their faith, eg publicly protesting against the inclusion of LGBT+ issues on school curricula.

Islam, Islamism, orthodoxy, heterodoxy, and heresy

The debate about legitimate and illegitimate criticism of Muslims and Islam would also benefit from a better appreciation of the differences between Islamic orthodoxy, heterodoxy, and heresy, and between 'Islam' – a complex worldwide religion – and 'Islamism' – the much more specific political project of reviving the historic Caliphate, ideally on a global scale – a vision which the majority of Muslims do not endorse.

A spectrum of non-Muslim attitudes and behaviour

Nor, in the current debate, is it as clear as it should be, that non-Muslim attitudes towards Muslims and Islam span a spectrum. At one end we find visceral anti-Muslim hatred while at the other there is 'Islamophilia', uncritical admiration. More neutral positions in between include ignorance, indifference, or a mixture of informed positive and negative attitudes. While it is important to draw these distinctions as sharply as possible, grey areas between the many possible positions can never be fully eliminated.

A wide range of terms, such as 'animosity', 'antagonism', 'aversion', 'contempt', 'dislike', 'distaste', 'hatred', 'ill-will', 'hostility', 'intolerance', 'resentment', 'spite', and 'unfriendliness' can be used to describe negativity towards anything, including Muslims and Islam. But these do not lie in a clear hierarchy. And they can all be held with varying degrees of intensity and/or commitment. 'Hatred', probably the strongest, may stem from fear, insecurity, pain, or from feeling threatened, powerless, or wronged. A wish to harm may be implied. But this need not necessarily be the case. Arguably the weakest is 'unfriendliness'. By definition, 'anti-Muslim hatred' means hatred of Muslims because of their faith. Not because of their race. Not because of their nationality. Not because of their country of origin. And not because of any feature of their culture unrelated to their religion. However, in practice these elements may be difficult to disentangle. Hostility towards Islam, however, concerns antagonism towards a body of ideas. The current debate would benefit from greater attention to this distinction. Although tenable in theory, it can nevertheless be difficult to draw in practice.

While attitudes are one thing, conduct is another. Not all attitudes manifest in behaviour, including speech, at all. Negativity may be expressed in various ways from murder and physical assault at one end to mild impoliteness at the other.

Behaviour may also be underpinned by 'prejudice', or 'pre-judgment', a favourable or unfavourable opinion about, or attitude, towards anything, including people, beliefs, social practices, and/or conduct, typically arrived at without proper evaluation of relevant evidence or the giving of cogent reasons. By contrast, a 'judgment' is a view reached following consideration of such evidence referenced to a discernible and credible standard. Some negative prejudices, particularly those based upon ignorance, may be dispelled by education. However, those which manifest in stubborn hatred can be difficult if not impossible to dislodge.

Attributing anything discreditable – such as crime, terrorism, dishonesty, untrustworthiness, and so on – to 'all Muslims', would clearly constitute anti-Muslim prejudice. But determining whether it is a prejudice against Islam to assert that the faith is, for example, 'evil', 'violent', 'oppressive', 'inhumane', 'stupid', 'nonsensical' etc., will depend upon context, form, tone, intentions, any possible contribution to public debate, likely consequences, and the extent to which any such claim is grounded upon reliable evidence. It would, for example, be entirely appropriate to describe a loud angry mob barracking a mosque as manifesting unlawful anti-Muslim hatred. But an evidence-based claim in an academic journal that Islam, in whatever form, is hostile to human rights and, therefore, out of step with international standards of right and wrong, would not.

However, it does not necessarily follow that regarding Islam as 'evil' 'violent', 'oppressive', 'inhumane', 'stupid', 'nonsensical' etc, includes those who believe in it. In principle it may be possible to maintain that, although the faith has these characteristics, most Muslims are merely 'mistaken', 'deceived', or 'ignorant' about the 'true' character of their own religion, possibly as a result of having been misled by Islamic scholars and clerics. 'Hate Islam – love Muslims' is, in fact, the position adopted by some Christians. However, expressing 'hatred' for, rather than criticism of any lawful belief system may, amount to incitement to hatred, at least in certain circumstances. It would, therefore, be much wiser for such opinions to be expressed without using the term 'hate' at all.

The campaign against 'Islamophobic expression' tends to manifest in three principal ways: signalling virtue by verbally 'standing up for the Muslims'; manufacturing false charges of Islamophobia ('Islamofauxbia'); and, motivated in most cases by the excessive fear of being denounced as an Islamophobe, attempting to suppress lawful critique rather than defending those falsely accused ('Islamophobia-phobia').

Discrimination and disadvantage

The term 'discrimination' also has both positive and negative connotations. To say, for example, that someone has 'discriminating taste' in wine, food, literature, music or whatever, means they are deemed to have experience and insight into what counts as quality. Insofar as it relates to people, in its negative sense, 'discrimination' means treating some less favourably than others without good reason or just cause. However, prejudice may not necessarily lead to discrimination. And discrimination may not always be based upon prejudice, at least not directly. A prejudiced person may, for example, rarely if ever, be in a position to act upon their prejudices. But where prejudice exists, the risk of discrimination arises. Conversely, discrimination does not necessarily require prejudice on the part of the party directly responsible. It is possible, for example, for someone to be treated less favourably by an adherent to their own religion or a member of their own race seeking to pander to somebody else's prejudices or unreasonable preferences, such as those of the discriminating party's employer for example.

A 'disadvantage', on the other hand, is a negative differential between individuals or groups regarding access to goods and benefits – including income, employment, education, health care, opportunities, and life chances – which may be the result of circumstance but not discrimination. For example, as a result of the lack of skills necessary for better paid jobs, newly arrived immigrants may suffer economic disadvantage in the land to which they have migrated. But it is only if unfair obstacles prevent, or continue to prevent, them from acquiring and benefiting from such skills, that the initial disadvantage will become discriminatory. It should also be noted that perceptions of disadvantage and discrimination, no matter how firmly held, may not always tally with the objective reality which may also be difficult to prove or disprove.

Blasphemy against Islam or Islamophobic expression?

It should also be noted that there has been some confusion in the debate about the concepts of 'blasphemy against Islam' and 'Islamophobic expression'. The term 'blasphemy' refers to contempt, disrespect, or lack of reverence for that which is deemed sacred, particularly a deity, a divine messenger/saviour, and/or a divine message: in Islam – Allah, Mohammad, and the Qur'an respectively. Blasphemy is, therefore, fundamentally a religious notion while, by contrast, the concept of prejudice against a faith and/or its adherents is secular and neutral about the alleged sacredness of the core elements in question. Of vital importance for the issues under discussion is that debates have raged for centuries about where to draw the line between insult and legitimate debate, and what to do about the former particularly whether it should be tolerated or outlawed and, if the latter, what form this should take.

Islamophobia by act, omission, and word

'Islamophobia-by-act-or-omission' may be defined as unjustified discrimination against Muslims, for example, in the allocation of goods and benefits and in abrasive encounters with officialdom, physical attack, and murder. 'Islamophobia-by-word', or 'Islamophobic expression', on the other hand, refers to the oral and/or written presentation of deliberate, antagonistic negativity about the Islamic faith, and/or towards those who follow it, derived largely or entirely from myth or the misrepresentation of genuine Muslim beliefs, practices, and/or conduct. Muslims unquestionably suffer from prejudice and discrimination in all these senses in the UK and elsewhere. But this is not the experience of them all, all of the time. And, in any case, this book deals with the narrower, though nonetheless vital questions of how legitimate and illegitimate criticism can be distinguished and what does, and should, follow as a matter of public policy.

While clear in principle, the distinction between Islamophobia-by-act-or-omission and Islamophobia-by-word is nevertheless often blurred in practice. This is because public controversies about the former tend to give rise to accusations that anyone who expressly denies this is, by definition, guilty of the latter. It has, for example, been alleged that anyone who defends Britain's counterterrorist strategy, Prevent, is racist and Islamophobic because these are said (wrongly) to be the key characteristics of the programme itself.

Orientation

My own knowledge of Muslims and Islam was fairly rudimentary until the Islamic Revolution in Iran in 1979 and the events of 9/11 in 2001 and their aftermath. This was deepened when, in the mid-2000s, I began preparing to teach undergraduate and postgraduate units on Human Rights in Law, Politics and Society (HRLPS) at the University of Bristol. However, the primary impetus to explore more fully the distinction between anti-Islamic and anti-Muslim prejudice, on the one hand, and legitimate critical appraisal of the faith and those who believe in it, on the other, was a potentially life-threatening public campaign to have me sacked on maliciously confected allegations of Islamophobia in 2021. After a five-month inquiry I was unequivocally officially exonerated. Amongst many other things, my accusers – the University of Bristol Islamic Society (BRISOC) – falsely alleged that Islam had been 'singled out' for criticism while other faiths and ideologies had been ignored. This experience is reviewed in Chapter 10. My response to anyone tempted to criticize this study on similar grounds would be along similar lines. I was singled out for vilification by a bunch of intolerant Muslims students. Had I been demonized by a different constituency I would have written a very different book.

In view of my own bitter personal experience, few if any would be surprised if I were more inclined to attack than to defend Islam and its adherents. But this is not the case. In spite of what has happened, I remain committed to serious, balanced, impartial, and reflective study. Of course, what counts as 'positives and negatives', 'pros and cons', 'pluses and minuses', or 'strengths and weaknesses' with respect to the faith and its followers is not self-evident but value laden. I should, therefore, make clear the core methodological and substantive values which underpin this monograph and indeed all my teaching, research, writing, and reflection over the past 45 years or so.

The methodological dimension has two components. One, the 'scientific method', insists upon the systematic, non-prejudiced, and comprehensive assembling and neutral analysis of relevant data in as clear a conceptual framework as possible. The other, 'scientific language', refers to the cautious and measured expression of the conclusions which emerge, coupled with the circumspect admission that only those capable of being supported by the data are justified, that they may be limited and unclear, and that they will always be provisional until authoritatively confirmed or disproved.

The 'substantive values' to which I adhere might be called 'ethical individualism'. This is the view that every human being in the world is prima facie of equal inherent moral worth and that global, national, local, and other institutions should be designed and should function in a manner which reflects this. For the record, I should also perhaps add that, although Research Director at the Oxford Institute for British Islam – an independent progressive Muslim think-tank – I am not a Muslim but a lapsed Irish Methodist who inclines towards Buddhism.

The core thesis of this book is that any measured comment, critical or otherwise, relating to an authentic aspect of Muslim belief, practice or conduct cannot, by definition, be 'Islamophobic'. The debate about Islamophobic expression should, therefore, rest upon the authoritative specification of what these are. But here we encounter two problems. First, the campaign against Islamophobic expression has conspicuously failed to provide it. Second, authoritatively summarizing the essentials of any globally significant ideology is not straightforward. And this is particularly the case for contemporary mainstream Islam – let alone the various ultra-orthodox, heterodox and heretical alternatives – because the foundational sources are ambiguous and have been interpreted in various ways, including by violent exponents of competing versions.

The following chapter offers a brief history of the Islamic faith and its reception. This includes its origins, its imperial institutionalization, the decline and fall of the Ottoman empire, the post-Second World War era, and the various debates conducted by internal and external critics and sympathizers over the course of its checkered history. The principal conclusion relevant to this book which emerges is that, in common with every other significant faith and ideology, Islam has, since the outset, both inspired admiration and provoked criticism from both insiders and outsiders.

Noting the principal bones of contention, but resiling from siding with any particular view about which is right or wrong, Chapter 3, 'Foundations of the faith', discusses the Qur'an, the hadith, sunnah, sharia and fatwas, and the discussions to which they have given rise. Sharing these objectives, Chapter 4, 'Muslim beliefs and practices', considers the core metaphysical elements of orthodox Islam – God's nature and purpose, prophesy and revelation, the day of judgment, the afterlife, and religious observance. It also surveys the central beliefs about temporal issues, particularly concerning governance, the economy, sex, marriage and the family, the position of women, crime and punishment (especially for blasphemy and apostasy), rights, and jihad. Chapter 5, 'Dissenting voices', observes that, as with most other ideologies, Islam has generated ultra-orthodox, heterodox, and heretical interpretations. As far as the issues discussed in this book are concerned, two of the most important are the views of 'liberal' or 'progressive' Muslims and of those who have renounced the Islamic faith, most, if not all of whom share the legitimate criticisms of mainstream orthodoxy which, when made by non-Muslims, are typically denounced as Islamophobic.

Chapter 6, 'Rights and law', observes that international human rights law and UK law permit the criticism of any creed or ideology, including Islam, providing it does not incite violence or hatred, cause public disorder, or violate other rights. However, it notes that this is not always as coherently respected as it might be, especially by the European Court of Human Rights.

Chapters 7-9 consider the most prominent and well-documented false accusations of Islamophobic expression, primarily in the arts, in contemporary public debate, and in the academy and education. Chapter 10, 'Defining Islamophobic expression', critically reviews discussion about this issue in the UK. Chapter 11, 'Islamophobia and free speech', summarizes and integrates the conclusions of previous chapters.

Finally, I would like to thank the following for their generous assistance and support for this project in a multitude of ways. Needless to say none necessarily endorses the views expressed: Hannah Baldock, Simon Baughen, Graham Child, Sue Cohen, Taj Hargey, Declan Henry, Stan Houston, Sir John Jenkins, Alistair Lawrence, Megan Manson, Collin May, Liz Mooney, Patrick Nash, Lars Nitschke, Paul Stott, and as always, my ever-loving family, Susan, Peter, Elma, Jack, Cara, Lucy, Joe, Jake, Hope, Aster, Penny, Rowan and Alice.

Chapter 2

Debating Islam – a history

Introduction

According to reliable estimates, Islam has between 2.0-2.05 billion adherents worldwide, about 25-26% of the global population.[1] It is not only the world's second-largest religion, after Christianity, but is also the world's fastest growing faith. About 70% of Muslims live in Asia, 20% in the Middle East and North Africa, 15% in Sub-Saharan Africa, and 5% elsewhere. Of the world's 195 countries, 49 have Muslim majorities. Between 35-40 of these incorporate Islam to some degree in their national institutions, law and politics. In 23, Islam is the official state religion.

Islam is also the second largest religion in several western states including the US and the UK. An estimated 26 million Muslims were living in Europe in 2017, a figure projected to rise – primarily as a result of immigration and a higher Muslim than non-Muslim birthrate – to 58 million (8%) by 2050.[2] Some parts of Europe have had Muslim populations for centuries while others have received significant numbers only since the end of the Second World War.

Although, by definition, Muslims share core beliefs and practices, there is also considerable diversity in how these are understood and observed. In common with all the world's globally significant religious and secular ideologies, both the Islamic faith and those who believe in it have had a very checkered history. We, therefore, need to proceed by exploring this and the debates to which it has given rise. While not devoid of controversy, the central features have been identified and discussed by reputable scholars for centuries.

---

[1] Pew Research Centre, *How the Global Religious Landscape Changed from 2010 to 2020*, June 2025.

[2] Pew Research Centre, *Europe's Growing Muslim Population*, 29 November 2017.

A distinction should first be drawn between the core of the historic Muslim world (the middle and near east, central Asia, and north Africa), the periphery (south-east Asia particularly in what is now Malaysia and Indonesia), and the diaspora (especially in the modern west). Islam began in the core as a persecuted faith, heretical with respect to traditional Arab pantheism. It was then beset by war between Muslims and other Arabs, and between its adherents and each other. This was followed by a series of glittering civilizations – established and consolidated by war, conquest, imperialism, slavery, servitude, and the subordination of minorities – then multiple crises, fragmentation, destruction, and restoration, culminating in imperial decline and fall. Although unwelcome to many Muslims, and in spite of claims to the contrary, it is not Islamophobic merely to note any of these historical facts or to explore the details and their contemporary implications.

In their heyday, many of the Muslim empires, particularly the Abbasid, were the most advanced civilizations in the world, excelling in virtually every field of human endeavour, including agriculture, architecture, astronomy, engineering, geography, mathematics, medicine, philology, philosophy, and science. However, some commentators, including Muslims, have argued that this was more in spite of their Islamic character than because of it. For example, Akyol, a devout Turkish Muslim, maintains that these achievements peaked before Islamic orthodoxy had been fully consolidated.[3] And, according to Rosenthal: 'The indisputable fact remains … that Islamic civilization as we know it would simply not have existed without the Greek heritage'.[4]

By contrast, in the periphery, Islam spread from the 12th century onwards, more by trade than conquest. As a result, it adapted to pre-existing non-Muslim environments more readily than in the core, a feature arguably shared with the contemporary diaspora in the west. Several other layers – including western colonization and military intervention in 'Muslim lands', contemporary violent conflict between Muslims in many parts of the world, jihadi terrorism, and the continuing global spread of Islam – have also been added to the mix.

Needless to say, the debate about Islam to which both Muslims and non-

---

[3] M. Akyol, *Reopening Muslim Minds: A Return to Reason, Freedom and Tolerance* (Forum, 2022), p. 58. See also Ibn Warraq, *Why I Am Not a Muslim* (Prometheus Reprint, 2003), p. 1.
[4] F. Rosenthal, *The Classical Heritage in Islam* (Routledge, 1992), p. 14.

Muslims have contributed, has taken various forms in the millennium and a half or so in which it has been in progress. Two, less well-known aspects, are, however, particularly relevant to the current controversy about Islamophobic expression. First, while many of the non-Muslim contributions have been critical and often hostile, more than a few have been appreciative and sympathetic. Second, during its early history, and at least equally surprising, is the fact that several influential and celebrated critics of Islam emerged from the Muslim community (*ummah*) itself.

A brief history of the faith

The word 'Islam' is Arabic for 'submission to the will of the one true God', while 'Muslim' means 'one who submits' to it. According to the mainstream orthodox tradition, the religion was established by the Prophet Mohammad (570-632 CE), an allegedly illiterate merchant from Mecca in Arabia. At the time, the peninsula was an anarchic region, dominated by an aggressive macho culture practising human sacrifice and female infanticide, venerating tribal loyalty, bravery in battle, wealth, generosity, fame, and a multiplicity of gods, plus the possession of many wives, concubines, and children.[5] It was, in fact, so afflicted by caravan raiding, war, and vendetta that four sacred months were traditionally set aside each year for peace.

Origins

From 610 to his death, Mohammad (which means 'Highly Praised') claimed to have received, through the medium of the Archangel Gabriel, a series of revelations from *al-lah* – literally 'the God', the creator deity of the traditional Arab pantheon – containing His final, flawless, and unalterable will for humanity. The Prophet also claimed that this was the last instalment of the truths offered by the other two preceding monotheistic Abrahamic faiths, Judaism and Christianity, whose adherents he saw as 'people of the book' following authentic, though less complete, religious insight. Mohammad's revelations, considered more fully in the following two chapters, were delivered and initially received in a piecemeal oral and unwritten form.[6]

---

[5] P. Hitti, *History of the Arabs: From the Earliest Times to the Present* (Palgrave MacMillan, revised 10th edn., 2002), Ch. VII.

[6] M. Cook, *The Koran: A Very Short Introduction* (Oxford University Press, 2000), p. 127.

In essence Mohammad's message was that Allah is the one and only true God who will judge humanity at the end of time, rewarding, with eternal paradise, those who obey Him and punishing, with eternal torment in hell, those who do not.[7] Opinion over the authenticity of these revelations is said immediately to have divided Mohammad's own tribe, the Quraysh. Some became believers. But most regarded him as a dangerous heretic, threatening traditional polytheistic Arab religion and values which had also already been exposed to Judaic and Christian influences.[8]

Some sources claim that, at the time, Mecca was a 'boiling cauldron of discontent and strife ... between the newly prosperous merchant class and the older artisans' and that there was a 'growing rift between the rich and the poor'.[9] Others dispute this.[10] It has even been suggested that the traditional narrative which sites Mecca as the origin of Islam is a myth concocted by later Muslim historians in order to relocate the early history of their faith in Arabia and to affirm its distinctive non-Jewish identity.[11] However, according to the traditional account, over a fifteen-year period, without retaliating, the first Muslims endured harsh persecution in Mecca from their own kith and kin. As Akyol observes, since 'in today's terms, early Islam was guilty of "offensive speech" and "blasphemy" against traditional Arab polytheism ... what an irony ... that today it is often Muslims who are most eager to ban "offensive speech" and "blasphemy."'[12]

In 615 about 100 of Mohammad's followers are said to have sought sanctuary in the neighbouring Christian kingdom of Abyssinia across the Red Sea in Africa. Then, in 622, having learned of a plot to kill him, Mohammad is reputed to have led his followers, in an event known as the Hijra, to Yathrib (later re-named Medina), a date-producing oasis city, 300km to the north of Mecca occupied by other Arab tribes, including Jews and Christians. Some commentators have, however, argued that, rather than simply delivering the

---

[7] Ibid., p. 113.

[8] Hitti, *History of the Arabs*, pp. 60-62, 89, 97-102, 107.

[9] D. Morgan, *Essential Islam: A Comprehensive Guide to Belief and Practice* (Praeger, 2009), p. 115; C. Horrie & P. Chippendale, *What Is Islam?* (W.H. Allen, 1990), p. 14.

[10] P. Crone, *Meccan Trade and the Rise of Islam* (Wiley-Blackwell, 1987), pp. 234-45.

[11] P. Crone and M. Cook, *Hagarism: The Making of the Muslim World* (Cambridge University Press, 1977).

[12] Akyol, *Reopening Muslim Minds*, p. 168.

faithful from persecution, the migration was, in fact, a strategic move intended to establish a military base from which to conduct hostilities against the Quraysh.[13] Having previously arbitrated in a Medinan tribal dispute, Mohammad had little difficulty in forging an alliance with his new neighbours.

In order to survive, the nascent Muslim community is said to have resorted to two long-established Arab traditions – tribal warfare and caravan-raiding. Though frequent in Arabia, each was traditionally conducted according to informal codes which sought to limit bloodshed and generally to avoid killing.[14] But by engaging in them in this new environment, Mohammad and his followers broke a core Arab taboo; the targets of the Muslims were members of their own tribe. The Quraysh retaliated and a cycle of violence ensued. The war, which had begun primarily for material motives, became fiercely religious as the Quraysh attempted to exterminate rather than merely defeat their Muslim enemies. In turn the Muslims, supported by some of their non-Muslim Medinan allies, and allegedly betrayed by some of the Jewish tribes, defended themselves ferociously and retaliated aggressively. While retaining a 'tribal mentality … based on commerce and power',[15] they also re-calibrated their identity in religious rather than kinship terms as a community of believers, the 'ummah'. After each significant battle against the Meccans, Mohammad is reputed to have punished the Medinan Jews by death, enslavement, or exile, allegedly including those who had remained officially neutral.[16] During this crisis Mohammad also claimed to have received fresh revelations from God, indicating amongst other things, how the Muslims should deal with the hostile environment in which they found themselves. The distinction between the 'Meccan' and 'Medinan' revelations – with the latter marking a distinctively more militant defence of the faith and the ummah – is universally acknowledged by Muslim and non-Muslim commentators.[17] The implications are considered further in the following two chapters.

---

[13] N. Sinai, *The Qur'an: A Historical-Critical Introduction* (Edinburgh University Press, 2017), p. 196; T. Holland, *In the Shadow of the Sword: The Battle for Global Empire and the End of the Ancient World* (Little Brown, 2012), p. 21.

[14] Hitti, *History of the Arabs*, pp. 25, 87; Sinai, *The Qur'an*, p. 192.

[15] Adonis, *Violence and Islam: Conversations with Houria Abdelouahed* (Polity Press, 2016), pp. 19, 28, 36, 61.

[16] Morgan, *Essential Islam*, p. 125.

[17] Sinai, *The Qur'an*, Ch. 8; R. Firestone, *The Origin of Holy War in Islam* (Oxford University Press, 1999); Adonis, *Violence and Islam*, p. 95; Cook, *The Koran*, p. 130.

The Muslim counter-offensive against the Quraysh was hugely successful.[18] As Kelsay puts it, the result was nothing less than a cultural revolution in Arabia replacing tribal loyalties with a communal submissiveness to God. The traditional pantheon of patron deities, machismo and associated virtues, fame and reputation, plus heroic stories about ancestors, was replaced by the Qur'an, the example of the Prophet, piety, obedience to God and His Messenger, and the promise of resurrection, judgment, and eternal paradise.[19] By 630 the Muslims had completed their conquest of Mecca, with its defeated inhabitants said to have received magnanimous treatment unparalleled in late antiquity. Although it is likely that, by the time of Mohammad's death, fewer than a third of the inhabitants of Arabia had converted to the new faith, the entire peninsula, nevertheless, came under an uneasy *Pax Islamica*.[20] But this did not last. The short reign of Mohammad's immediate successor, Abu Bakr (632-634), was dominated by the so-called wars of succession/apostasy (*riddah*) in which those professing a different interpretation of Islam were ruthlessly crushed. As Akyol observes: 'with the riddah wars, Islam's marriage with power was consolidated – not as a temporary adaption in Medina due to extraordinary circumstances, but as a permanent system – a system that would prove, frankly put, both aggressive and coercive, imposing religious observance upon Muslims as a matter of law'.[21]

Imperial institutionalization

The faith not only weathered these early crises; it flourished. Abu Bakr, who died as a result of illness in 634, was succeeded as Caliph – 'God's representative on earth' also later translated as 'Mohammad's successor' – by his nominee, Umar ibn al-Khattab, who rapidly conquered Syria, Palestine, Egypt, and parts of north Africa. By all accounts this, together with the professed egalitarianism of Islam, was initially welcomed by the mostly

---

[18] Hitti, *History of the Arabs*, pp. 117-8.

[19] Morgan, *Essential Islam*, pp. xxv-xxvi; J. Kelsay, *Arguing the Just War in Islam* (Harvard University Press, 2007), p. 27; G. von Grunebaum, 'The Sources of Islamic Civilization' in P. Holt, A. Lambton & B. Lewis (eds.), *The Cambridge History of Islam: Volume 2B, Islamic Society and Civilisation* (Cambridge University Press, 2008).

[20] Morgan, *Essential Islam*, p. 141.

[21] Akyol, *Reopening Muslim Minds*, p. 175.

Christian inhabitants of the region who resented the heavy tax burden imposed by their former Byzantine rulers. Umar insisted that Arab armies, but no other settlers, should colonize these territories. As a result, a military caste living in camps outside the principal towns and cities was created with no function other than to loot and extract tribute from conquered lands on condition that the Caliph took his share.

As Akyol states:

'According to the jihad doctrine, whose details would be perfected over time, Muslims had the right to conquer any non-Muslim territory by giving its inhabitants three choices: either convert to Islam and join the caliphate as full citizens; or preserve your religion (unless it is Arab polytheism) but accept Muslim supremacy by paying the jizya, or "poll tax"; or face the sword, with consequences such as death, slavery and expropriation'.[22]

Acting upon this principle, within a few decades of Mohammad's death, the first Caliphate – the territory governed by the Caliph – had become an empire stretching from the Iberian peninsula to the Himalayas, the two regional superpowers, Byzantium and Persia, having been defeated in the process. This was achieved, in the first instance, as a result of war and conquest motivated primarily by the quest for material acquisition rather than to spread the new faith. As Holland puts it: 'the story of Islam has been one of storming military triumph'.[23]

Rather than nominating a successor himself, Umar, who was stabbed to death by a disgruntled Persian bureaucrat in 644, had opted to entrust the succession to a six-man council (*shura*). Ali ibn Abi Talib ibn Abd al-Muttalib was offered the position on condition that he did not establish a Hashemite dynasty based on his own clan within the Quraysh tribe. He declined. So, Uthman ibn Affan ibn Abi al-As, who was appointed instead, thereby became the third post-Mohammad incumbent in this the first, al-Rashidun Caliphate – the regime from 632 to 661 which included the four caliphs succeeding Mohammad who were also his blood relatives.

a) The Caliphate

As Caliph, the Prophet Mohammad exercised a distinct form of 'imperial

---

[22] Ibid.
[23] Holland, *In the Shadow of the Sword*, p. 24.

absolutism', embracing religious, political, military, and judicial spheres of authority. This was believed to have been delegated by God on sacred trust for the welfare of all, but especially Muslims. Lacking any conception of the separation of religion from other public domains, there was also little room for a distinction between civil society and the state, and no scope for formal constitutional limits on the exercise of public power.[24] In common with all traditional societies, the key normative concept in mainstream orthodox Islam was, and remains, 'obligation' rather than 'rights'.[25]

In several senses the power of the Caliph was, nevertheless, relatively rather than strictly absolute. First, as time passed, the authoritative interpretation of the faith was increasingly monopolized by the *ulama*, (literally 'the learned', or more loosely, 'Muslim clerics' or 'Islamic scholars'), to whom the Caliphs generally deferred. Second, since orthopraxy (orthodox practice) has always been valued by Muslims more than orthodoxy (orthodox belief), Islam has historically been more tolerant of diverse interpretations of the faith than Christianity, with dissent generally only suppressed, though not infrequently, when considered a political threat.[26] Third, traditional Islamic societies have always been governed by a combination of the *sharia* (the holy law discussed further in Chapter 3), political expediency, tribal and client-patron systems, plus local law and custom. Governance was also delegated to regional warlords (*emirs*) or regional governors (*sultans*) some of whom became sufficiently powerful to challenge the Caliph himself, particularly when the latter was personally weak or beset by crisis.[27]

According to the celebrated writer, V. S. Naipaul, 'the Arabs were the most successful imperialists of all time; since to be conquered by them (and then to be like them) is still, in the minds of the faithful, to be saved'.[28] And, as Ibn Warraq remarks: 'Bowing toward Arabia five times a day must surely be the ultimate symbol of this imperialism'.[29] However, the Muslims saw imperial expansion less as an exercise in the subjugation of others and much

---

[24] M. Ruthven, *Islam: A Very Short Introduction* (Oxford University Press, 2012).

[25] J. Schacht, 'Law and Justice', in Holt et al (eds.), *Islamic Society and Civilization*, p. 541.

[26] Holt et al (eds.), *Islamic Society and Civilization*, p. xv.

[27] Hitti, *History of the Arabs*, p. 27; G. von Grunebaum, 'Sources of Islamic Civilization', Holt et al (eds.), *Islamic Society and Civilization*, p. 531.

[28] B. King, *V.S. Naipaul* (Red Globe Press, 2nd edn., 2003).

[29] Ibn Warraq, *Why I Am Not A Muslim*, p. 199.

more as the liberation of people living in ignorance and submission to false religions and illegitimate political authority. The rapid success of the imperial endeavour was also taken as clear evidence of divine favour and Arab racial superiority.[30]

On account of their decadent and corrupt pursuit of wealth, power, and pleasure – including excesses of sex, alcohol, and luxurious living in preference to the stern austerities of the spiritual life – many Caliphs, especially the Umayyads, made unconvincing 'representatives of God on earth'. Abd al-Malik ibn Marwan is, for example, reputed to have said at his coronation: 'I swear that I will behead anyone who expects me to be pious'.[31] Wilkinson maintains that the separation of the secular authority of Muslim rulers from the gradually declining authority of the ulama, resulted in Muslim states being deprived of responsible constraints upon the exercise of public power. It also opened the door to self-appointed exponents with distorted interpretations of the faith as traditionally conceived.[32]

b) Slavery, servitude, and dhimmi status

Slavery was adopted by the first Muslim empire of the late-7th century not merely in materially convenient imitation of the near universal global practice at the time. On the contrary, the Qur'an expressly endorses it as a God-given right.[33] From the early years of the Umayyad empire it was also sustained by a vast slave trade including regular supplies as a form of tribute from vassal states.[34] This 'enabled the Arabs to live on the conquered land as a rentier class and to exploit the potential of the rich Fertile Crescent'.[35] Black slaves had a particularly lowly status in early Muslim society.[36]

Manning maintains that slavery increased as a result of the expansion and

---

[30] Kelsay, *Just War in Islam*, pp. 38-9; von Grunebaum, 'Sources of Islamic Civilization', pp. 472, 475.

[31] Adonis, *Violence and Islam*, p. 49.

[32] M. Wilkinson, *The Genealogy of Terror: How to distinguish between Islam, Islamism and Islamist Extremism* (Routledge, 2018), pp. 35-7.

[33] Qur'an, 4:3, 23:6, 16:77, 30:28, 33:50-52, 70:30.

[34] J. Marozzi, *Captives and Companions: A History of Slavery and the Slave Trade in the Islamic World* (Allen Lane, 2025).

[35] J. Black, *Slavery: A Brief History of Slavery* (Robinson, 2011), pp. 11, 27-35, 72-74, 184-5; C. Bosworth, *The New Islamic Dynasties: A Chronological and Genealogical Manual* (Edinburgh University Press, 2004), p. 6.

[36] Ibn Warraq, *Why I Am Not A Muslim*, p. 204.

consolidation of the great Muslim empires,[37] while Lewis has argued that the Islamic prohibition against Muslims enslaving other Muslims led to a massive increase in the enslavement of non-Muslims.[38] It has also been observed that, by contrast with the west, the Muslim world never produced its own indigenous anti-slavery movements. This was not least because the institution was deeply rooted in the Qur'an and sharia and because Mohammad had himself been a slave owner and trader. Nevertheless, in Islam, liberty has always been regarded as the norm and slavery as the exception. The humane treatment of slaves is also mandated, including a prohibition on the forced prostitution of female slaves. The use of alms for manumission, and the freeing of slaves as atonement for sin, were also recommended. Some slaves also had high status in Islamic history as, for example, administrators or army officers. In the middle ages, the Mamluks, originally taken into slavery from southern Russia, even established their own dynastic Shia Fatimid sultanate in Egypt and Syria. However, it was not until the end of the 20th century that, largely as a result of external pressure, slavery was finally abolished in Muslim lands. Until ISIS/DAESH revived the practice in the 2010s, Mauritania was the last Muslim-majority country formally to ban it in 1981. Although slavery is currently condemned by most Muslim scholars as inconsistent with Islamic morality, the fact that the Qur'an sanctions it and that Mohammad and his successors benefitted from it remain thorny issues.

According to orthodox Islam, around 622, Mohammad drafted the 'Constitution of Medina' in an attempt to unite the city's fractious pagan, Christian, and Jewish tribes, and their new Muslim neighbours. In essence this document – or set of documents, no copies of which survive – recognized the equal rights of Muslims and non-Muslims including freedom of religion, the obligation of non-Muslims to take up arms to defend the ummah, and the commitment of each not to betray the other. However, from their earliest days, the first Muslim empires not only depended upon slavery but also upon servitude and the taxation of Jewish and Christian *dhimmi* ('protected person'), a formal legal distinction between Muslims and non-Muslims, conferring different rights, freedoms and obligations.

Originally the status of dhimmi applied only to 'people of the covenant',

---

[37] P. Manning, *Slavery and African Life: Occidental, Oriental, and African Slave Trades* (Cambridge University Press, 1990), p. 28.

[38] B. Lewis, *Race and Slavery in the Middle East: An Historical Enquiry* (Oxford University Press, 1990) p. 10.

Christians, Jews, and Sabians, the latter a mysterious non-Abrahamic faith, mentioned three times in the Qur'an about which very little is known. But as the empire expanded, Zoroastrians, Sikhs, Hindus, Jains, and Buddhists were also included. Under the sharia, in exchange for protection from the state, dhimmis were forbidden from building new places of worship, repairing existing ones, ringing church bells, sounding the Jewish *shofar* (a type of musical horn), carrying weapons, or riding either horses or camels. They were also prohibited from testifying in court against a Muslim. Non-Muslim families which could not afford to pay the dhimmi tax, the *jizyah,* were also obliged to hand over their children to the state instead. In the Ottoman empire their male offspring became an elite miliary corps, the Janissaries, ultimately disbanded after violent unrest provoked by their arrogant isolation and abuse of power and status. Muslims and dhimmis were not allowed to inherit from each other, nor could the houses of the latter overlook those of the former. While dhimmis were forbidden from proselytizing under pain of severe penalties, Muslims were encouraged to convert them. Accusations of blasphemy against dhimmis were also frequent.[39]

The fortunes of the dhimmi waxed and waned throughout history. They enjoyed both periods of tranquility and toleration and also suffered bouts of popular and official persecution including bloody massacre particularly of Jews. For example, hundreds of Jews were killed near Córdoba between 1010 and 1013, 6,000 were massacred in Fez in 1033, and in 1066 the entire 4,000 strong Jewish population of Granada was put to the sword.[40] Armenian Christians also suffered from particularly severe Muslim persecution.[41] At other times, Jews were confined to ghettos and, as means of identification, were required to dress in particular ways and to mark their homes with distinctive symbols. Nevertheless, in the middle ages they generally received much better treatment in the Islamic world than in Christendom. And when, in the 15th century, Jews and Muslims were expelled from the Iberian peninsula, they were each welcomed with open arms by the Ottoman Sultan.

The Ottoman 'millet system' also permitted dhimmi courts to settle legal disputes between members of a given religious minority. But this did not include capital or public order offences, or issues involving those from outside the specific community. Jewish and Christian Arabs were also often granted

---

[39] Ibn Warraq, *Why I Am Not A Muslim*, p. 229.
[40] Ibid., p. 228.
[41] Ibid., pp. 233, 238.

legal privileges over non-Arab Muslims who were subject to a 'kind of apartheid'.[42] At some points Jews and Christians even held high office in Islamic states. For example, Arab Christians became governors of non-Arab parts of the empire 'which caused huge resentment amongst local Muslim populations'.[43] Non-Arab Muslims 'were regarded as inferior and subjected to a whole series of fiscal, social, political, military, and other disabilities'.[44]

c) Schism

Uthman, the third Caliph, was accused of corruption, nepotism, and of seeking to establish a dynasty centred on his own Umayyad clan. Opposition was strongest amongst the most fanatical of Mohammad's original followers, the *Kharijites* ('successionists') who regarded the Umayyads as mere opportunists and fortune seekers with no genuine commitment to the faith. However, lacking a uniform and coherent body of doctrine, it is difficult to establish precisely what else the Kharijites believed. They are, nevertheless, known for their uncompromising insistence upon governance according to strict conformity with a literal interpretation of the Qur'an, their denunciation of non-Kharijites as *kuffar*, 'fake Muslims', and their willingness to enforce compliance with their vision by violence, especially against other adherents to the faith whom they deemed deviant and apostate.[45]

Regarded by some as evincing anarchist tendencies, the Kharijites also subscribed to a radical egalitarianism, virtually unknown anywhere else in the world at the time. They maintained, for example, and pious male Muslim with the requisite leadership skills could become Caliph. They also disavowed privilege based on ethnicity, embraced the equality of women, and scrupulously respected the dhimmi status of non-Muslims. Some rejected the authority of the hadith, including the punishment of adultery by stoning prescribed by other schools of Islamic jurisprudence. In the 8th and 9th centuries, Kharijites also contributed to several theological debates, asserting, for example, the primacy of determinism over voluntarism, a view which eventually took root in orthodox Islam. Many were also gifted orators and poets whose favourite themes were piety and martyrdom. On account of their eagerness for deposing Muslim rulers by force, the Kharijites were ruthlessly

---

[42] Ibid., p. 202.
[43] Horrie & Chippendale, *What Is Islam?*, p. 70.
[44] B. Lewis, *The Arabs in History* (Oxford University Press, 2002), pp. 37-38.
[45] See E. Husain, *The House of Islam: A Global History* (Bloomsbury, 2018), Ch. 11.

suppressed by their more powerful opponents. Contemporary orthodox Islam regards them as heretics or apostates and claims that their Islamist offspring include ISIS/DAESH, al-Qaeda, and the Muslim Brotherhood, a designation rejected by these groups themselves. Noting the differences in their respective socio-political backgrounds, more independent commentators regard the putative resemblances between these movements and the Kharijites as superficial.[46]

Uthman rejected Kharijite doctrine in favour of that of a rival sect, the *Murji'ah* ('those who postpone judgment'). The latter maintained that the question of who was, and who was not, a genuine Muslim could only be settled by God on the Day of Judgment. And that, while those who violated the sharia should be punished, the putative Muslim identity of anyone who outwardly observed the Caliph's authority and did not challenge it, should not be called into question. The Kharijites declared Uthman a *kafir*, demanded that he be overthrown and declared war upon him and his supporters. In 656 he was killed in Mecca by a Kharijite mob and the shura immediately appointed Ali ibn Ali Talib, Mohammad's cousin and the husband of his daughter, Fatima, as the fourth Caliph. This was welcomed by all, including the less extreme Kharijite factions.

However, pledging to avenge the death of his cousin Uthman, to overthrow Ali's Kharijite-backed Caliphship, and to destroy the Kharijites themselves, Mu'awiya, the Umayyad governor of Mecca, launched a savage war against Ali, the new caliph and his supporters, declared himself Caliph, and conquered most of the empire within three years. In 661, while at morning prayer, Ali was himself assassinated by a dissident Kharijite and in 670 his eldest son Hassan died, allegedly having been poisoned. By the end of the 8th century, Mu'awiya had persecuted the Kharijites almost out of existence. They survived only in isolated Bedouin communities in remote desert areas where their descendants, the *Ibadites*, continue to adhere to the Kharijite version of the Islamic faith unaltered since the original revolt of the 650s. The Kharijite policy of 'holy murder' was later revived by the Shi'ite Nizari Ismaili Order of Assassins (1090-1275) founded by Hasan-i-Sabbah. The word 'assassin', found in various forms in several European languages, was

---

[46] J. Kenney, *Muslim Rebels: Kharijites and the Politics of Extremism in Egypt* (Oxford University Press, 2006).

once said to derive from the hashish taken by devotees when embarking upon a murderous escapade. But this has recently been discredited.[47]

The protracted struggle over the imperial succession also resulted in a rift between what became known as Sunnis and Shias, creating 'a crisis of authority that has never been resolved'.[48] While the Sunnis favoured succession by acclamation, a form of 'charismatic' rather than democratic selection, the Shi'as (or 'party of Ali') favoured a hereditary alternative. The schism reached the point of no return when Ali's second son, Husayn, Mohammad's grandson, was killed in 680 by Umayyad forces at the Battle of Karbala as he travelled to Baghdad expecting to be installed as Caliph. Sunnis and Shias subsequently developed different legal traditions recognizing different customary norms. This historic and enduring split has not, however, been the only source of division in the ummah. In common with Protestantism, Buddhism, and Hinduism, Islam lacks any universally recognised ultimate institutional authority, apart from the Caliph himself, to interpret the faith. As a consequence, it has spawned many sects and traditions. Typically, these have been, and continue to be, inspired by charismatic preachers linking their insights with, or against, tribal leaders and/or warlords, often in pursuit of power and control over territory and people in complex and fluid political environments.

The Umayyads, who as already noted, had 'little enthusiasm for religion and generally despised the pious and ascetic',[49] are said to have 'regarded their Empire first and foremost as Arab' and 'effectively turned Islam into a religiously decadent political tool for expanding Arab rule'.[50] By 650, as the rate of imperial expansion slowed, looting was increasingly replaced by taxation. Though outstandingly successful from the outset, the fledgling Muslim empire nevertheless also suffered several early setbacks including, for example, defeat at the Battle of Tours/Poitier in 732 when the French king, Charles Martel, permanently stopped its expansion from the Iberian peninsula into France.

In the historic core, a series of Muslim empires followed the Sunni/Shia schism. In addition to the Umayyad Caliphate with its capital in Damascus

---

[47] F. Daftary, *The Ismailis: Their history and doctrines* (Cambridge University Press, 1990), p. 13.
[48] Ruthven, *Islam*, pp. 59-60.
[49] Ibn Warraq, *Why I Am Not A Muslim,* p. 70.
[50] Horrie & Chippendale, *What Is Islam?*, p. 70.

from the mid-7th-mid-8th centuries the principal others were: the Abbasid (capital – Baghdad), mid-8th-mid-13th centuries; the Seljuk, (capitals – Nishapur, Merv, and Shahr-e-Rey), 11th-14th centuries; the Safavid (capitals – Tabriz, Qasvin and Isfahan), 16th–18th centuries; and the Ottoman (capital – Istanbul), 1299-1920.

Critical appreciation

Debates about Islam, with positive and negative contributions from both the Muslim and non-Muslim worlds, have ebbed and flowed since the inception of the faith in the 7th century.

Late antiquity

Not surprisingly Christian and Jewish commentators were among the earliest non-Muslim critics of Islam. Noting that Muslims honour Jesus as a prophet but deny his divinity, John of Damascus (675/6-749), a Christian Syrian Arab monk, priest, hymnographer, apologist, and a secretary in the Umayyad Caliphate, maintained, for example, that Islam was a Christian heresy.[51] Most Christian theologians in the European 'Dark' and Middle Ages either agreed or saw the faith as a form of Judaism rather than a new religion.

Yet, there were also countervailing trends. Appreciation of Islamic civilization in non-Muslim Europe appeared hot on the heels of the Islamic revolution as its distinctive aesthetic – including architecture, calligraphy, illustrated manuscripts, ceramics, glass, and metal work – were admired and copied. Textiles from the Muslim world were, in particular, often used for church vestments, shrouds, hangings, and expensive clothing, while everyday pottery was preferred to home-produced European counterparts. The fact that, in England, Offa, the Anglo-Saxon Christian King of Mercia from 757-96, minted gold coins bearing his name and the Arabic inscription 'there is no god but God', also testifies to the positive impact of Islam in some far-flung parts of the non-Muslim world.[52] In the mid-9th century, the Christian priest and Theologian, St Eulogius of Córdoba, concluded that the Prophet Mohammad had been 'seduced by demonic delusions, devoted to sacrilegious idolatry'

---

[51] Morgan, *Essential Islam*, pp. xx-xxii.
[52] Husain, *House of Islam*, pp. 296-7

and was, in fact the Anti-Christ.[53] However, a contemporary commentator and sharp critic of Islam, Paulus Alvarus, observed that: 'All the talented young Christians read and study with enthusiasm the Arab books' not to refute their philosophers and theologians 'but to form a correct and elegant Arabic'.[54] Christians fascinated by Muslim culture were dubbed *Mozarab*, 'Arab wannabes', by their more conservative co-religionists.[55] Islamic architecture also influenced styles particularly in Christian southern Italy and Sicily, reflected even in some Templar churches in the Middle East, and some European cathedrals such as that in Aachen. In the 10th century Nicetas of Constantinople claimed that the Qur'an was a 'coarse booklet' expounding a 'mythical and barbarous belief' and that Mohammad was 'by nature perverse and talkative or rather stupid and bestial, a coward too, quick to anger, distrustful and arrogant'.[56]

Under the Sunni Abbasid caliphate, 'dozens of heterodox religious sects also emerged, debating theology and law and trying to impose some order on the doctrinal chaos and legal arbitrariness inherited from the Umayyads'.[57] This included two principal critical traditions: rationalism and scepticism. Amongst the most celebrated of the first exponents of Islamic rationalism were the *Mu'tazilites* – 'those who separate themselves or withdraw from', a reference to 'withdrawal' over a theological disagreement from a study circle by Wasil ibn 'Ata, the movement's founder. Having remained neutral in the Sunni/Shia schism, the *al-mu'tazilah* had, by the 10th century, developed a distinctive Islamic school of speculative theology (*kalam*) based around three fundamental principles: the oneness (*tawhid*) and justice (*al-'adl*) of God, human freedom of action, and the creation of the Qur'an by God rather than its co-originality with Him. Setting a particularly high premium upon reason, though faithful to core Islamic assumptions about the existence and character of God, prophethood, and revelation, the Mu'tazilites were influenced by ancient Greek philosophy and were sceptical about the authority of many if not all hadith, traditions about what Mohammad had said and done

---

[53] J. Tolan, *Saracens: Islam in the Medieval European Imagination* (Columbia University Press, 2002), p. 87.

[54] Z. Karabell, *People of the Book: The Forgotten History of Islam and the West* (John Murray, 2007), p. 67.

[55] M. Akyol, *Islam without Extremes: A Muslim Case for Liberty* (W. W. Norton & Co, 2013), pp. 77-8.

[56] Morgan, *Essential Islam*, p. xxi.

[57] Horrie & Chippendale, *What Is Islam?*, p. 72.

without claiming to have been divinely inspired. Believing that reason was itself a gift from God, the Mu'tazilites saw it as integral to justice, human freedom, and the Divine plan.

The movement flourished in various parts of the Abbasid empire at different times, reaching the height of its power and influence during the *mihna*, an 18-year period (833–851) of religious persecution, instituted by the Caliph al-Ma'mun, involving the imprisonment and execution of those who rejected Mu'tazilite doctrine. However, traditional *Ash'arite* theology, nevertheless, dominated Sunni Islam from the 11th century onwards. Named after its principal exponent, Abu al-Ḥasan Ali ibn Isma'il ibn Ishaq al-Ash'ari (874–936), in stark contrast with the priorities of the Mu'tazilites, the Ash'arites argued for the subordination of reason to the Qur'an and sunnah. Later, Al-Ash'ari's hierarchy of sources of the faith fostered the emergence of four distinctive legal traditions in Sunni Islam – the Maliki, Hanafi, Shafi and Hanbali. Although originating at the very birth of the faith, another sect, Sufism – a peace-loving contemplative interpretation of Islam considered more fully in Chapter 5 – did not fully crystallize until the 11th century.[58]

Among the Muslim sceptics were the following: Ahmad ibn Habit, executed for heresy in 845 and ostensibly a subscriber to the Mu'tazilite movement, who taught that Jesus was divine and that others had been more virtuous than Mohammad whom he criticized for having so many wives; Abu Isa Muhammad ibn Harun al-Warraq, known as Abu Isa al-Warraq (d. 861/62), an Arab critic of Islam and religion in general from whom the modern critic, Ibn Warraq, takes his pseudonym; Abu al-Hasan Ahmad ibn Yahya ibn Ishaq al-Rawandi, known as al-Rawandi (827–911), a scholar and theologian, once a rationalist Mu'tazilite, who parted company from the movement, became a Shia scholar and, according to most sources, ended life as an atheist; Abu al-'Ala' Aḥmad ibn 'Abd Allah ibn Sulayman al-Tanukhi al-Ma'arri, also known by his Latin name Abulola Moarrensis (973–1057), a blind Syrian philosopher, poet, and writer, regarded as one of the foremost atheists of his time, who described all religions as 'noxious weeds'; and Abu Bakr Muhammad ibn Zakariyya' al-Razi Abu Bakr al-Razi, also known by his Latin name Rhazes/Rhasis (864/5–925/35), a Persian physician, philosopher, and alchemist, widely seen as one of the most important figures in the history of medicine, who also wrote about logic, astronomy, and

---

[58] Hitti, *History of the Arabs*, pp. 433-9.

grammar, and who criticized religion, especially the concepts of prophethood and revelation.

The Middle Ages

From the 11th century onwards, the Crusades and the establishment and consolidation of the Frankish kingdoms of the Levant (1098-1291) greatly soured relations between Islam and Christendom. But it was not until the 12th century – facilitated by the first complete Latin translation of the Qur'an by Peter the Venerable in 1143 – that there was any significant theological engagement with Islam by Christians.[59] Also in the 12th century, European troubadours celebrated in song the noble character of Saladin, Sultan of Egypt and Syria, an enemy of the Crusader states. Some Crusaders even converted to Islam, a phenomenon which had, of course, been occurring since the dawn of the faith, particularly amongst those enslaved or living in territories conquered by the rapidly expanding Muslim empires.

During the 12th century Renaissance, as Arabic texts were increasingly translated into Latin, European interest in the Arab and Muslim worlds also deepened. Córdoba – the capital of the emirate of Al-Andalus, then the largest and most well-managed city in the world – hosted famous debates between the Jewish and Muslim polymaths, Moses ben Maymun and Ibn Rushd, known respectively in the west as Maimonides and Averroes. Maimonides, later physician to Saladin, criticized the politics of Muslim regimes and considered Islamic ethics inferior to their Jewish counterpart, while Ibn Rushd argued for the integration of the Islamic faith with the rationalism of the ancient Greek tradition. Around the same time, the Greek Orthodox bishop, Paul of Antioch, accepted that Mohammed was a prophet but denied the universality of his revelations and maintained that Christian law was superior to its Islamic equivalent.

In 1179 and 1215 the Lateran Councils forbade Christians from working for or dining with Muslims or Jews, and in the mid-13th century Pope Gregory IX decreed that Muslims and Jews must wear distinctive clothing and could not hold office in Christendom or even appear on the streets during Christian holidays. [60] In his seminal study of Judaism, Christianity and Islam,

---

[59] Morgan, *Essential Islam*, p. xvii; N. Smirnov, *Islam and Russia* (Central Asian Research Centre, London, 1956), pp. 36, 48.
[60] Morgan, *Essential Islam*, pp. xxi-xxii.

Examination of the Three Faiths, published in the late 13th century, Jewish philosopher and physician, Ibn Kammuna, maintained that there was no proof that Mohammad was the 'perfect man' and argued that the sharia was incompatible with the principles of justice. He also claimed that men generally only convert to Islam 'in terror or in quest of power, or to avoid heavy taxation, or to escape humiliation, or if taken prisoner, or because of infatuation with a Muslim woman'.[61] Published in the same century, in his epic poem *Divine Comedy*, Dante accused Mohammad of being a Christian schismatic and imagined him condemned in the eighth circle of hell along with his cousin and son-in-law Ali ibn Abi Talib.

By the end of the 12th century the Abbasid empire had degenerated into a loose federation of autonomous emirates exposing it to the merciless and destructive Mongol invasions from the middle of the 1250s to the end of the 13th century. However, in 1295, the Mongols themselves converted to Islam, facilitating, amongst other things, the rise of the Timurid empire in central Asia, the Ottoman empire in the west, plus the Seljuk and Safavid empires further east. The Timurid Empire of Central Asia, the Caucasus, and what is now Iran and Afghanistan, was founded by Timur Lang (1336–1405). Also known as 'Tamerlane' and 'Timur the Lame' on account of a limp stemming from a youthful arrow injury, the emperor in question was a Turco-Mongol conqueror, the most powerful Muslim ruler of his time, one of the last 'great' nomadic conquerors of the Eurasian Steppe, and the great-great-great-grandfather of Babur (1483–1530), founder of the Mughal Empire in India. Undefeated in battle, including by the Khans of the Golden Horde, the Mamluks of Egypt and Syria, the Ottoman empire, and the Delhi Sultanate amongst others, Timur is widely regarded as one of the most successful military leaders in history. His genocidal military campaigns, estimated to have caused the deaths of millions, were also, however, amongst the most cruel and brutal of his, or indeed any, age. While still retaining a positive image in Muslim Central Asia, including recognition as a national hero in Uzbekistan, Timur remains reviled by many in Arabia, Iraq, Iran, and India, where some of his worst atrocities occurred.[62]

---

[61] M. Peremann (trans.), *Ibn Kammuna's Examination of the Three Faiths: A Thirteenth-Century Essay in the Comparative Study of Religion* (University of California Press, 2022), p. 8.

[62] B. Forbes Manz, *The Rise and Rule of Tamerlane* (Cambridge University Press, Reprint edition, 2008).

As the middle-ages progressed, the Iberian peninsula was gradually reconquered for Christendom. However, this was not always a straightforward contest between Christians and Muslims. For example, in the mid-14th century, King Peter I of Castile and Leon fought several wars against rival Christian monarchs, and even assisted the Muslim Sultan of Granada to defeat several incursions and an attempted coup. In the mid-15th century John of Segovia planned a conference of Muslim and Christian scholars to enhance their mutual understanding but died in 1458 before it could take place.[63] In 1460, philosopher and theologian, Nicholas of Cusa, praised the ethics and religiosity of Muslims in his *The Sieve of the Quran*, a thoughtful discussion which the author also claimed could serve as an introduction to the Chrisian Gospel.[64]

Imperial decline and fall

It is generally accepted that the Ottoman empire had peaked by the end of the 17th century and then slid into slow but inexorable, and ultimately, terminal decline. But, before turning to this, several other developments relevant to this study are worthy of note.

a) 16th-18th centuries

By the 16th century the Muslim world had itself become 'increasingly fascinated by European architecture, technology and especially weaponry'.[65] Early in the 1500s, the Pope called for yet another crusade, this time against the Ottoman invasions of Hungary and Austria. However, some German Protestant preachers thought that, compared with Catholicism and the Papacy, the Turks represented the lesser of two evils. Having initially prevaricated, Martin Luther supported the military and spiritual defence of Christendom against the Turks, but not as a crusade. However, he later came to believe that the Ottoman threat was a harbinger of the Last Days as prophesied in the Old Testament Book of Daniel. Conscious that in territories conquered by Muslim armies many Christians converted to Islam, Luther also embarked upon a campaign to warn Christendom of the spiritual peril.[66] Arguing that the

---

[63] Morgan, *Essential Islam*, p. xxii.
[64] Ibid., p. 36.
[65] Ibid., p. xvii.
[66] Ibid., p. 36.

Qur'an was a shameful 'book full of lies' and an 'abomination', and that Mohammad was a false prophet driven by ambition and lust, he endeavoured to make as much information as possible available about Islam by, for example, contributing to a Latin translation of the Qur'an and to the first collection of Latin texts about the faith.[67] In the 16th and 17th centuries several Sikh gurus – including Guru Tegh Bahadur, who refused to convert to Islam in an effort to protect Hindu religious practice – were martyred in the Mughal empire as it oscillated between tolerance and intolerance of non-Muslim faiths.

Other developments in the 16th century included the founding of the first Chair of Arabic in Europe at the Collège de France in 1539.[68] Later, facing a common enemy – imperial Spain – English Queen Elizabeth I, fostered trade and diplomatic relations with Morocco and the Ottoman empire. However, though contemplated, a full-blown military alliance was never achieved. Also in the 16th century, French philosopher Jean Bodin (1530-96), an advocate of religious tolerance, praised 'the great emperor of the Turks' who 'permitteth every man to live according to his conscience'.[69]

Other developments in the 16th and 17th centuries included the enslavement, between 1500 and 1800, of up to 1.25 million Europeans by north African 'barbary corsairs', many of whom subsequently converted to Islam.[70] One of the most unusual was John Ward, said to have been the model for Captain Jack Sparrow in the film series, *Pirates of the Caribbean*.[71] Having been born in Faversham, Kent, around 1553, Ward spent most of his adult life as a poor fisherman. Then, in middle age, he became an Elizabethan privateer and subsequently a seaman in the Royal Navy. Around 1602, he deserted to become a pirate/privateer in the service of Uthman Dey the Ottoman ruler in Tunis. Later, Ward converted to Islam, changed his name to Yusuf Reis, and having acquired vast wealth, lived the life of a sultan in a

---

[67] A. Francisco, 'Martin Luther, Islam, and the Ottoman Turks', *Oxford Research Encyclopaedia* (Oxford University Press, 22 December 2016).
[68] P. Bruckner (trans. by S. Rendell and L. Neal), *An Imaginary Racism: Islamophobia and Guilt* (Wiley, 2018), p. 72.
[69] D. Goffman, *The Ottoman Empire and Early Modern Europe* (Cambridge University Press, 2002), p. 111.
[70] R. Davis, *Christian Slaves, Muslim Masters: White Slavery in the Mediterranean, the Barbary Coast, and Italy, 1500-1800* (Palgrave Macmillan, 2003).
[71] G. Milton, 'Pirate John Ward: the real Captain Jack Sparrow', *BBC History Revealed*, November 2019.

sumptuous palace attended by numerous servants and slaves. He died around 1622 probably from the plague.

In the mid-17th century, relying on a French version, Scotsman Alexander Ross published an English translation of the Qur'an which contained a 'generally objective view of Islam'.[72] And in his *Historical and Critical Dictionary* published in 1697, Pierre Bayle, a French Huguenot philosopher, author, lexicographer, and forerunner of the 18th century *Encyclopédistes*, became one of the first to present Christian criticisms of Islam in a neutral and objective style. He nevertheless concluded that Mohammad had been a lustful abuser of women and that, while Christianity had spread peacefully, Islam had expanded by force.[73] That same year, Humphrey Prideaux, Dean of Norwich, published *Mahomet: The True Nature of Imposture*, which denounced Islam as a fraud and claimed Mohammad's twin dominant passions had been ambition and lust.[74]

The 17th century also saw the founding of chairs in Arabic at the Universities of Oxford and Cambridge, and throughout the west, Islam 'became synonymous with a refined civilization, a countermodel of tolerance compared with medieval obscurantism'.[75] In this era, English architect Sir Christopher Wren, who amongst many other things designed St Paul's Cathedral in London, is reputed to have said that 'the Gothic style should more rightly be called the Saracen style'.[76] A Latin translation of an Arabic manuscript, *Philosophus Autodidactus*, ('The Self-Taught Philosopher'), translated into Dutch and English, also proved a huge hit in Europe, including with Robert Boyle, the father of modern chemistry, and Enlightenment thinkers Spinoza and Leibniz. It is also said to have influenced John Locke, the progenitor of modern political liberalism, and the novelist Daniel Defoe, author of *Robinson Crusoe*.[77]

In the late 17th and early 18th centuries an Arabic novel, *Hayy ibn Yaqzan* (*Alive, the Son of Awake*), written by 12th century Andalusian polymath Abu Bakr Muhammad ibn Tufayl, was translated into Latin and English to

---

[72] Morgan, *Essential Islam*, p. xxii.

[73] T. Khan, *Muslim Actually, How Islam is Misunderstood and Why it Matters* (Atlantic Books, 2022), p. 21.

[74] Morgan, *Essential Islam*, p. 98.

[75] Bruckner, *An Imaginary Racism*, p. 72.

[76] O. Wainwright, 'Looted landmarks: how Notre-Dame, Big Ben and St Mark's were stolen from the east', *The Guardian*, 13 August 2020.

[77] Akyol, *Reopening Muslim Minds*, p. 2.

considerable literary acclaim.[78] It tells the story of Hayy, a boy growing up alone on an uninhabited tropical island, who uses his senses and reason to formulate rational theories of natural science, theology, and ethics. Leaving the island in adulthood he visits an inhabited land, the people of which have a religion, and concludes that the essentials of faith and reason are compatible and complementary. But he also observes that many of those who adhere to religion have a crude understanding of the fundamental principles which underpin both faith and science and that some are hypocrites. Many 17th and 18th century European thinkers, including Spinoza, Leibniz and Locke, admired Ibn Tufayl's conviction that – by applying reason, conscience, and divinely-granted insight – knowledge, virtue, and wisdom could be found either with or without religious faith. The Quakers, a Protestant sect which emerged in the upheavals of 17th century Britain and Ireland, also saw resonance between Ibn Tufayl's perspective and their core doctrine that all human beings have an 'inner divine light'.

In 1705, Dutch orientalist, Adrian Reland, published *De Religione Mohammedica*, which was promptly added to the Catholic Index of Forbidden Books for being too positive about Islam.[79] In 1707 and 1717, Antoine Follant's translation of *The Thousand and One Nights* 'electrified the century of the Enlightenment, which dreamed of this happy sensuality so contrary to Catholic hypocrisy'.[80] Other Enlightenment thinkers expressed admiration for at least some aspects of Islam. According to Ibn Warraq it is impossible, for example, 'to exaggerate the importance' of a sympathetic biography of Mohammad – by Count Henri de Boulainvilliers (1658-1722) published posthumously in 1730 – 'in shaping Europe's view of Islam and its founder' as a wise and tolerant ruler and lawgiver.[81] De Boulainvilliers, who had no knowledge of Arabic and was thus forced to rely upon secondary sources, found the Muslim faith to be reasonable and admired the absence of mysteries and miracles. Combined with a sympathetic view of the apparently tolerant Ottoman empire – which presented a diminishing military threat to Europe as a result of the successful defence of Vienna in 1683 – and the increasing secularism of the European intelligentsia, De Boulainvilliers' book is known

---

[78] M. Akyol, 'The Muslims Who Inspired Spinoza, Locke and Defoe', *New York Times*, 5 April 2021.
[79] Morgan, *Essential Islam*, p. xxii.
[80] Bruckner, *An Imaginary Racism*, p. 73.
[81] Ibn Warraq, *Why I Am Not A Muslim*, p. 19.

to have influenced Voltaire and the eminent historian, Edward Gibbon, amongst others. However, Voltaire seemed to have difficulty making up his mind about Mohammad and Islam. In his tragedy, *Mahomet,* published in 1742, the Prophet was described as an 'imposter'. Yet in 1756, Voltaire commended him in *Les Moeurs et l'esprit des nations,* as an important political thinker, and praised Islam as a rational religion more tolerant of other faiths than Christianity.[82] Adam Smith, the founding theorist of modern capitalist economics, also praised 'the empire of the Caliphs' under which 'the ancient philosophy and astronomy of the Greeks were restored and established', reviving 'the curiosity of mankind'.[83]

In 1734 George Sale produced another English translation of the Qur'an, together with a largely positive *Preliminary Discourse.*[84] Some Enlightenment thinkers also used criticism of Islam as a surrogate for critiques of Catholicism, Christianity, or both. Others were more directly hostile. For instance, denouncing the Qur'an as an 'absurd, obscure, and dishonest book', Diderot (1713-84) concluded that Mohammad was 'the greatest enemy that human reason has ever known', while Kant (1724-1804) regarded Islam as a fantasy and one of many 'illnesses of the head'.[85] The Scottish philosopher David Hume (1711-76) thought the Qur'an was the 'wild and absurd performance' of a 'pretended prophet' who 'bestows praise on such instances of treachery, inhumanity, cruelty, revenge, and bigotry as are utterly incompatible with civilized society', every action 'blamed or praised, so far only as it is beneficial or hurtful to the true believers'.[86] Gibbon (1737-94), admired the Mohammad of the early Meccan years but not that of the later Medinan phase.[87] He also declared that the Qur'an was an 'endless incoherent rhapsody of fable and precept, and declamation, which seldom excites a sentiment or an idea, which sometimes crawls in the dust, and is sometimes

---

[82] Morgan, *Essential Islam,* p. 99; I. Ahmad, 'Islam and the Enlightenment', *Marginalia,* 15 January 2021.

[83] A. Smith, *The Essays of Adam Smith* (Alex Murray, 1872), p. 353.

[84] Morgan, *Essential Islam,* p. 36.

[85] I. Almond, *History of Islam in German Thought: From Leibniz to Nietzsche* (Routledge, 2012), p. 33.

[86] D. Hume, *Enquiries Concerning the Human Understanding and Concerning the Principle of Morals* (Kessinger, 2004), p. 450.

[87] Morgan, *Essential Islam,* p. 99.

lost in the clouds'.[88] By contrast, Goethe (1749-1832) wrote poems praising Mohammad and orientalism.

In the 17th and 18th centuries, various Muslim movements advocated a return to the imagined pristine religion of the first believers both as a remedy for the perceived social degeneration of the Islamic faith and also to stiffen its resolve in the face of increasing western global ascendancy.[89] For example, Shah Wali Allah of Delhi (1703-62), an Indian theologian, was amongst the first to attempt to reassess Islamic theology in the light of modernity.[90] Considered more fully in Chapter 5, a particularly influential movement, *Salafism* – from the Arabic term *salaf* ('predecessors') – also sought to return the faithful to the beliefs and life-styles of the 'pious predecessors', the Prophet Mohammad and the first three generations of his disciples. Also known as *Wahhabism* after its founder, Salafism began in Arabia in the mid-18th century when Mohammad ibn Abd al-Wahhab (1703-91) sought to purge the faith of the many distortions and lapses from orthodoxy to which he believed it had succumbed over the previous millennium.[91] In 1744 Mohammad ibn Saud recognized al-Wahhab and his successors as *imam* (religious leader) in return for the latter acknowledging the former and his successors as emir (political leader). Threatening other Muslims in the peninsula with violent retribution if they resisted, this alliance proved a great success, enduring to this day in what is now known as Saudi Arabia.

The 18th century also witnessed some high profile voluntary conversions of Europeans to Islam, one of the most notable being that of Lieutenant-Colonel James Achilles Kirkpatrick (1764-1805), an East India Company officer and diplomat. Born in 1764 in Madras, and educated in Britain where he learned English, Kirkpatrick spoke Tamil (his mother tongue), Persian and Hindi, and also wrote poetry in Urdu. Enamoured with the Indo-Persian culture at the Nizam of Hyderabad's court, during his initial few months as Resident (a British government official) from 1798 until 1805, Kirkpatrick abandoned European dress in favour of the Persian equivalent. He also wore

---

[88] D. Womersley (ed.), *E. Gibbon, The History of the Decline and Fall of the Roman Empire* (Penguin Classics, 1996,), vol. 5, p. 240.

[89] F. Rahman, 'Revival and Reform in Islam' in Holt et al (eds.), *Islamic Society and Civilisation*, p. 240.

[90] *Ibid.*, pp. 638-9, 642-3.

[91] R. Leiken, *Europe's Angry Muslims: The Revolt of the Second Generation* (Oxford University Press, 2012), p. 70.

Mughal-style attire at home, smoked a *hookah*, chewed betelnut, and maintained a small harem. In 1800, he married a local Hyderabadi Sayyida noblewoman, Khair-un-Nissa, converted to Islam, and became a double agent working for the Hyderabadis against the East India Company.

b) 19th century

The 19th century produced various kinds of western interest in the Islamic world and significant changes in the latter itself. When Napoleon invaded Egypt in 1798 he famously announced – 'I respect God, the Qur'an, and Mohammad' – and is said to have made a favourable impression upon scholars from Cairo's Al Azhar 'university mosque' whom he invited to a discussion.[92] As the century progressed, the Ottoman empire declined, the global power of the west increased, and the Islamic world came under increasing pressure to modernize and to eliminate formal inequalities including dhimmi status. The latter eventually disappeared in spite of short-lived attempts by militants to reimpose it. The Ottomans also embarked upon an ambitious programme of modernization and liberalization which included affirming the equal citizenship of all the Sultan's subjects, permitted apostasy, and established an elected parliament with some legislative powers. Nevertheless, as Akyol notes: 'Today almost two centuries after the first Ottoman reforms, it is hard to argue that equal citizenship is fully established in the Muslim world. While there are brighter spots, such as Bosnia, Morocco, or Tunisia, most Muslim-majority states discriminate, either explicitly or implicitly against their non-Muslim citizens ....'[93]

In the 1850s, France and the UK joined the Ottomans in the Crimean War to counter Russian imperial expansion. Mid-century, home furnishings from the Muslim world, such as carpets, silks, and embroidered tapestries, also became fashionable amongst the wealthy in Britain.[94] Queen Victoria, who developed a close friendship with her servant, Munshi Abdul Karim, is said to have been 'obsessed with Muslims' to the point of learning Urdu, writing with the Arabic alphabet and studying Muslim poets, the Quran and the Sufis'.[95] However, violent and indiscriminate Turkish reprisals during and

---

[92] Morgan, *Essential Islam*, p.xxiii.
[93] Akyol, *Reopening Muslim Minds*, p. 223.
[94] Husain, *House of Islam*, p. 296.
[95] Ibid., p. 294.

after the Bulgarian independence uprising of April and May 1876, provoked western outrage, including in Britain.

The suppression of the 1857 'Sepoy Mutiny' or the 'First War of Independence',[96] which brought the Mughal empire of northern India to an end, was also a significant moment in the development of modern Muslim political consciousness. A decade later, a centre for Islamic Studies was established in Deoband, near Delhi, from which two very different movements with enduring relevance emerged. One, *Tabligh Jama'at* aims to revive Islamic influence through the cultivation of spirituality, while the other, the Taliban, governed Afghanistan in the late 1990s, briefly hosted Al Qaeda facilitating the 9/11 attacks on the US, and returned to power when the western coalition left in 2021. Also in the 19th century, admirers of al-Afghani (1838/9–1897) – political activist and Islamic ideologist who preached pan-Islamic unity against the British in India and Afghanistan – advocated the violent prosecution of this cause. In the 1890s al-Afghani also emerged as a key player in resistance to increasing British influence in Iran.

The 19th century also saw the emergence of a salacious fascination with the allegedly decadent and sensual character of the Muslim Middle East. Amongst other things this inspired adventurers, such as Sir Richard Francis Burton, to translate *The Book of One Thousand and One Nights* into English and to publish *A Personal Narrative of a Pilgrimage to Al-Medinah and Meccah*, an account of his visit in disguise to both cities during the Hajj. Another motive for increased interest in the Muslim world at this time was the need to train more culturally aware civil servants as administrators for those parts of expanding and/or consolidating European empires with significant Muslim populations. There can be little doubt that, while this was also typically accompanied by the desire to prove the superiority of the West over the East, there was also genuine curiosity as well.

As the 19th century unfolded, a new academic discipline, sociology, (the 'scientific study of society') developed, which generally regarded religion as integral to social, economic, and political processes rather than, as the exponents of any given faith including Islam maintain, derived from an external supernatural or spiritual realm. For example, Weber regarded Islam as a 'warrior religion' in which 'the quest for salvation through inner-worldly

---

[96] Other terms include, the 'Indian Mutiny', the 'Great Rebellion', the 'Revolt of 1857', and the 'Indian Insurrection.'

asceticism' was, 're-directed towards land acquisition and imperial expansion'.[97] For Karl Marx, it was one of several products of the 'oriental mode of production' which, he believed, would ultimately be replaced by atheistic global communism.

Recognizing that Islam was the younger sibling of Christianity, and sharing its opposition to materialism, rationalism, atheism, scepticism, and secularism, some 19th century Christian scholars increasingly realised that both stood or fell together. This produced fresh sympathetic appraisals of the Islamic faith. For example, Catholic theologian, Adam Möhler, praised Mohammad for his 'original piety' and 'touching devotion' reflected in the 'quite characteristic religious poetry of the Qur'an'.[98] Christian theologian Philip Schaff (1819-93) also admired the Qur'an for its poetic beauty, religious fervour, and wise counsel, but also considered it to be mixed with 'absurdities, bombast, unmeaning images, and low sensuality'.[99]

According to Ibn Warraq, an essay taken from the book, *Sartor Resartus: And on Heroes, Hero-Worship and the Heroic in History* – first published in 1844 by Scottish polymath and hugely influential Victorian essayist, historian and philosopher, Thomas Carlyle (1795–1881) – was the 'first truly sympathetic portrait' of Mohammad 'by a Western intellectual'.[100] However, in the following chapter of his book, Carlyle also expressed some very negative opinions about the faith. For example, he dismissed belief in prophets as indicative of a primitive stage in social development, characterized the Qur'an as a 'wearisome confused jumble' of 'crude, incondite ... endless iterations' and 'long-windedness', amounting to 'insupportable stupidity', and a 'stupid piece of prolix absurdity'.[101] Also referring to Mohammad as 'uncultured' and a 'semi-barbarian',[102] he predicted the eventual decline of the Islamic faith as history progressed. Carlyle's sentimental glorification of violence, cruelty, extremism, irrationality, anti-Benthamite utilitarianism, and anti-materialism, have been regarded by many subsequent critics as proto-fascist.

---

[97] B. Turner, 'Max Weber and the Sociology of Islam' (2016) 276 *Revue internationale de philosophie*, 213 -229.

[98] H. Küng, *Islam: Past, Present and Future* (One World Publications, 2007), p. 75.

[99] P. Schaff, *History of the Christian Church, Volume IV: Mediaeval Christianity, A.D. 590-1073* (Scribner's Sons, 1910), p. 174.

[100] Ibn Warraq, *Why I Am Not a Muslim*, p. 22.

[101] T. Carlyle, *Sartor Resartus: And on Heroes, Hero-Worship and the Heroic in History* (MacMillan, 1927), pp. 299, 344. See Morgan, *Essential Islam*, p. 26.

[102] Morgan, *Essential Islam*, p. 99.

The methods adopted by critical Biblical scholars in 19th century Europe, particularly Germany, were also of seminal importance for the informed western intellectual debate about the Qur'an and Islam.[103] Modern scholarly Islamic studies were founded in Europe at this time by Theodor Nöldeke, Christiaan Snouck Hurgronje, and particularly by Ignáz Goldziher (1850–1921), a German-speaking Hungarian Jew also renowned for his groundbreaking exegesis of the Hebrew Bible. Amongst other things, Goldziher concluded that Mecca was not the birthplace of Islam and that most *hadith* (anecdotes about the life of Mohammad) were fraudulent concoctions which sought to project on to the Prophet, arguments and positions advocated by competing factions which emerged as the faith and Muslim society evolved. However, as clearly indicated by the following extract from the diary in which he recorded his travels, daily activities, and reflections, Goldziher was far from being an Islamophobe. He writes that, in Cairo, forehead against the floor of the mosque during Friday prayers …

'I truly entered into the spirit of Islam to such an extent that ultimately I became inwardly convinced that I myself was a Muslim, and judiciously discovered that this was the only religion which, even in its doctrinal and official formulation, can satisfy philosophic minds. My ideal was to elevate Judaism to a similar rational level. Islam, as my experience taught me, is the only religion, in which superstitious and heathen ingredients are not frowned upon by rationalism, but by orthodox doctrine'.[104]

Nevertheless, notwithstanding his affection for the Islamic faith, Goldziher remained a devout Jew all his life, a decision which, in spite of the many academic honours he received, deprived him of the full German university professorship for which only Christians were then eligible.

In the late 19th and first half of the 20th centuries the celebrated 11th century Persian polymath, Omar Khayyam, inspired a virtual cult movement in Europe, particularly in the Anglo-sphere. Although outwardly an observant Muslim, Khayyam's religious and philosophical outlook has been variously described as a combination of religious scepticism, rationalism, materialism, pessimism, nihilism, Epicureanism, fatalism, atheism/agnosticism, and Sufi

---

[103] Holland, *In the Shadow of the Sword*, pp. 34-51.
[104] https://hadith.net/en/post/49796/ignaz-goldziher/.

mysticism.[105] Some of his poetry was translated into Latin by Thomas Hyde in 1700, into German by Joseph von Hammer-Purgstall in 1818, and into English by Gore Ouseley in 1846. But it was not until the 1860s, when Whitely Stokes popularized Edward Fitzgerald's 1859 book, *Rubaiyat of Omar Khayyam*, that a 'cult of the Rubaiyat' (named after one of Khayyam's poems) developed. Amongst its many manifestations were admiration by the Pre-Raphaelite artistic movement in Britain, translations of Khayyam's work into many languages, the rekindling of interest in his native Iran, and the establishment of Omar Khayyam clubs throughout the English-speaking world. In the 20th and 21st centuries, monuments and other memorials were erected to Khayyam in Iran, Austria, Italy and the US. And, as a result of Fitzgerald having rendered Khayyam's name 'Tentmaker', in the late 19th and first half of the 20th centuries, the term 'Omar the Tentmaker' featured in novels and other expressions of popular culture in the English-language. This even included nicknaming Second World War US general Omar Bradley (a non-Muslim), 'Omar the Tent-Maker'.

Prominent conversions of westerners to Islam continued in the 19th and into the 20th century. The most famous Englishman to do so, William Henry Quilliam (1856-1932), changed his name to Abdullah Quilliam and was also known as 'Henri Marcel Leon' and 'Haroun Mustapha Leon'.[106] Born in Liverpool to a wealthy local family, Quilliam, raised as a Methodist, spent most of his childhood in the Isle of Man, and was a firm proponent of temperance. He qualified as a solicitor in 1878 and married Hannah Johnstone the following year. Having visited Morocco to recover from an illness, he converted to Islam in 1887. As the result of a donation from Nasrullah Khan, Crown Prince of the Emirate of Afghanistan, Quilliam purchased some property in Brougham Terrace, Liverpool, which became the Liverpool Muslim Institute in 1889. Hosting educational classes covering a wide range of subjects, and including a museum and science laboratory, the Institute became the first functioning mosque in Britain. Quilliam also opened a boarding school for boys, a day school for girls, and a home for the children of non-Muslim parents who, unable to look after them themselves, agreed that

---

[105] A. Tikkanen, *Omar Khayyam: Persian poet and astronomer* (Encyclopaedia Britannica, 2023); M. Aminrazavi, *The Wine of Wisdom: The Life, Poetry and Philosophy of Omar Khayyam* (Oneworld, 2007).
[106] R. Geaves, *Islam in Victorian Britain: The Life and Times of Abdullah Quilliam* (Kube Publishing, 2010).

their children should be raised in the Islamic faith.

In 1889, Quilliam first published *The Faith of Islam* followed by *The Crescent*, a weekly newssheet for Muslims in Britain, and *Islamic World*, a monthly publication with a worldwide readership. It is estimated that, as a direct result of his work, around 600 people in Britain, including a number of prominent figures, converted to Islam. Travelling extensively in the Muslim world, Quilliam received many honours from its leaders. Abdul Hamid II, the Ottoman Sultan, granted him the title 'Shaykh al-Islam for the British Isles' and the Emir of Afghanistan recognised him as the 'Sheikh of Muslims in Britain'. He was also appointed Persian Vice Consul in Liverpool by the Shah. On account of these associations some regarded Quilliam as a traitor. Having been struck off the Roll of Solicitors for unprofessional conduct in 1908, he returned to the Isle of Man and the Institute in Liverpool was sold. Without it, Quilliam's influence and funding, the Muslim community in the city dispersed. Following his death in London in 1932, Quilliam's legacy is principally maintained by the Abdullah Quilliam Society founded in 1996. 'Quilliam', originally 'The Quilliam Foundation', a separate think-tank challenging extremist Islamist ideologies, was launched in 2008 but went into liquidation in 2021.

c) 20th century

In the early 20th century western scholars in Arabic, Islamic studies, and related disciplines, were broadly sympathetic to Islam. One of the most celebrated was Montgomery Watt (1909-2006), a Scottish Orientalist, historian, academic, Anglo-Catholic priest and, from 1964 to 1979, Professor of Arabic and Islamic studies at the University of Edinburgh. Watt believed that, though not infallible, the Qur'an had been divinely inspired and that Mohammad was similar to an Old Testament Prophet preaching the oneness of God, social justice, and fair dealing. An unusually prescient perspective was, however, also provided by G. K. Chesterton in his 1914 novel, *The Flying Inn,* which imagines a Muslim take-over of Britain, facilitated in the first instance, by naïve British liberals who regard it less as surrender than 'a beautiful fusion' of the best of East and West.[107]

However, the prevailing view among most Europeans at the time was that

---

[107] A. Doyle, *The End of Woke: How the Culture War Went Too Far and What to Expect of the Counter-Revolution* (Constable, 2025), p. 178.

the perceived inflexible nature of Islam stifled innovation and impeded social, political, and technological progress in the Muslim, and particularly Arab, worlds. Following the First World War the component parts of the defeated Ottoman empire were parcelled out to the victorious allied powers under the League of Nations' mandate system ostensibly for modernization and development. While this was welcomed by some Muslims, it was deeply unsettling for most because 'military defeat was defeat not only in a worldly sense; it also brought into doubt the truth of the Muslim revelation itself'.[108] The most thorough-going version of the view from inside the Islamic world that it needed secularization and modernization was Kemel Ataturk's post-First World War conception of a secular, democratic, nationalist, modern Turkey, in military and other alliances with the west.[109] The discovery of oil in Iran in 1908 also greatly increased western interest there and led to support for the pro-western secular Pahlavi dynasty installed by coup d'etat in 1921.[110] The emergence of communism and fascism in the early-to- mid-20th century also offered Islamists an alluring model for achieving their vision by mobilizing small, militant, highly-disciplined, and ideologically committed activists. The decolonization and partition of India in the mid-1940s added a further ingredient to the mix. Islamists were divided over the creation of Pakistan, not least concerning its Islamic character,[111] and a substantial Muslim minority remained in the new Indian state.

On the ideological plane, the 20th century saw further developments, including significant contributions from Islamist thinkers such as, amongst others, Hassan al Banna (1906-1949),[112] founder of the Muslim Brotherhood in Egypt, Mawlana al-Mawdudi (1903-1979),[113] and Sayyid Kutb (1906-1966),[114] the intellectual forbearer of Al Qaeda. Their vision, which continues

---

[108] B. Lewis (ed.), *The World of Islam* (Thames & Hudson, 1976), p. 322.

[109] B. Lewis, *The History of Modern Turkey* (Oxford University Press, 3rd edn., 2001).

[110] E. Abrahamian, *A History of Iran: Revised and updated* (Cambridge University Press, 2nd edn., 2018), Ch. 3.

[111] I. Talbot & G Singh, *The Partition of India,* (Cambridge University Press, 2009).

[112] A. Moussalli, 'Hassan Al-Banna' in J. Esposito & E. Shahin (eds.), *The Oxford Handbook of Islam and Politics* Oxford University Press, 2016); Wilkinson, *Genealogy of Terror*, pp. 158-61; Leiken, *Europe's Angry Muslims*, pp. 83-4.

[113] J. White and N. Siddiqui, 'Mawlana Mawdudi' in Esposito and Shahin (eds.), *Islam and Politics*; Wilkinson, *Genealogy of Terror*, pp. 155-8.

[114] S. Akhavi, 'Sayyid Qutb', in Esposito and Shahin (eds), *Islam and Politics*; Wilkinson, *Genealogy of Terror*, pp. 162-70; Leiken, *Europe's Angry Muslims*, pp. 84-5.

to dominate debates amongst Islamists to this day, is typically expressed in the binary godliness of Islamism and its negation in every other alternative. One such issue concerns the implications of the view that the Qur'an and sunnah provide an inexhaustible and infallible guide for every feature of life including personal matters and those of law, state, and politics. Another relates to the characteristics of Islamic states seeking to realise this vision on earth. This has included, amongst other things, discussion about how such regimes should be established – particularly the role of violence in their creation, defence, and extension – the conditions for political participation by non-Muslims, and the relationship between such states and the west.

Although hostile to western notions of democracy, 20th century Islamist thinkers were, nevertheless, generally in favour of consultative decision-making, underpinned by the belief that professional Muslims, not members of the traditional ulama, also had the right to seek to understand and to apply the sharia, an idea with a particular appeal to the rising Muslim middle classes. A significant exception was Iran, where inspired by Ayatollah Khomeini (1902-1989), the Iranian revolution of 1979-82 demonstrated the popular appeal of Islamization directed and governed by mullahs, imams, and the ulama.[115] Modern Islamist liberation movements have also sought to oppose and expel foreign interlopers, while also, nevertheless, incorporating some of their key contributions – for example, nationalism, scientific thinking, and improvements in both political representation and the position of women.[116] It has been argued, however, that, in spite of this, they nevertheless remain 'essentially a continuation of the pre-Modernist reform movements' whose roadmap to the future lies in invoking an imagined pristine past.[117]

The 20th century also began with the sense in the west that the fall of the Ottoman empire would have the same corrosive impact upon Muslim beliefs, practices, and conduct as the demise of feudalism had had upon Christianity in Europe particularly from the 17th century onwards. Islam also seemed increasingly peripheral and irrelevant to the great ideological struggles of the time, dominated as they were by multi-dimensional conflicts between nationalism, liberalism, fascism, communism, and capitalism.

---

[115] M. Mahdavi, 'Ayatollah Khomeini' in Esposito and Shahin (eds.), *Islam and Politics*.
[116] Rahman, 'Revival and Reform in Islam', pp. 641-56.
[117] Ibid., pp. 641-2.

But, in the aftermath of the Second World War, this all began to change in several ways. To assist with post-war economic reconstruction, a number of states in Europe, including the UK, France, Germany, the Netherlands and others, encouraged foreign immigration, often from decolonized territories including 'Muslim lands'. Three further complications followed in the Cold War: oil was discovered throughout the middle east, the state of Israel was established, and demands for Palestinian freedom and statehood spread throughout the Arab and Muslim worlds. However, popularized in the 1950s and 1960s particularly by Nasser's Egypt and Ba'athism in Syria and Iraq, an experiment with secularism and modernization – pan-Arab national socialism – conspicuously failed. This maintained that, opposing western intervention, cultivating close relations with the Soviet bloc, adopting the technological achievements of both sides in the Cold War, and acting in a spirit of pan-Arab solidarity and cooperation, each Arab country should develop its own socialist economy, state, and society ultimately leading to a single Arab state straddling north Africa and the middle east.[118] However, regimes based on this model failed to generate prosperity and also limited, and/or dissolved, legislatures whenever they chose. They also had a semi-detached relationship with Islam. In Egypt, for example, the faith was recognised as the official religion. Though effectively circumscribed in the context of marriage and divorce, the sharia nevertheless, also became the primary source of legislation. In spite of being officially acknowledged as equal under the law, Coptic Christians and other minorities were also subject to restrictions upon both religious observance and material opportunity. The appeal of the pan-Arab nationalist vision and the strongman-dominated military regimes it produced, were fatally discredited by the victory of Israel over Egypt, Jordan, and Syria in the Six Day War of 1967.

In 1962 the Vatican Ecumenical Council conceded that Islam had provided valuable truths about God, Jesus, and the Prophets. By contrast, in the 1970s a wave of sceptical scholarship challenged a great deal of the received wisdom in western Islamic studies. Agreeing with the German sceptics of the 19th century, those concerned argued that the historic Islamic tradition had been greatly corrupted in transmission, and that a reconstruction of its early history from other arguably more reliable sources, such as coins,

---

[118] Y. Choueiri, *Arab Nationalism – A History: Nation and State in the Arab World* (Blackwell, 2000).

inscriptions, and non-Islamic texts, was required. Noting unconventional verse orderings and rare styles of orthography in the 'Sana'a manuscripts' – part of a sizable cache of Quranic and non-Quranic fragments discovered in Yemen during restoration of the Great Mosque in 1972 – scholars suggested that some of the parchments may have been palimpsests, pieces of written material on which later writing had been superimposed, indicating that the text had been altered over time.[119]

Salafi-Jihadi ideology also gained currency as a result of a series of mostly post-Cold War international events. Two of these, the Soviet invasion of Afghanistan and the Islamic revolution in Iran, occurred in 1979. Acting in support of a fraternal communist regime which had come to power in a revolutionary coup the year before, the former plunged the country into civil war. The west regarded as natural allies, the *mujahideen* ('those engaged in jihad'), who took up arms against the infidel invader. Together with Arab nations and other parts of the Muslim world, the US and others provided the resistance with substantial material support. From 1979 to 1989 between half a million and two million Afghans were killed, around two million were displaced and just under 14,500 Soviet troops died, nearly 54,000 were wounded, and almost half a million fell ill. The human impact and costs to the USSR, both in terms of resources and international reputation, contributed significantly to the demise of the Soviet system itself.[120] In 1989 the Berlin Wall fell, and later the USSR withdrew from Afghanistan leaving competing factions – particularly the Taliban and the secular, western-sponsored Northern Alliance – to continue the struggle.

The collapse of the Soviet Union also revived dormant ethnic and religious conflicts involving Muslims in various parts of the former Soviet-influenced world, including Bosnia, Kosovo, and Chechnya. Islamists were not slow to capitalize on the opportunities this presented. Meanwhile, between 1980 and 1988, Iraq and Iran, each overwhelmingly Muslim majority nations, fought a vicious, bloody and inconclusive war, resulting in over a million fatalities, deepening the pre-existing hostility (*fitna* – 'discord') between Sunni Arabs and Iranian Shia and their respective allies.

There were several other developments in the 1990s. In secular post-

---

[119] G-R. Puin, 'Observations on Early Qur'an Manuscripts in Ṣan'ā', in S. Wild (ed.), *The Qur'an as Text* (Brill, 1996), pp. 107–111.
[120] A. Saikal, W. Maley & A. Saikal, *The Soviet Withdrawal from Afghanistan*, (Cambridge University Press, 2009).

colonial Algeria the prospect of the Islamic Salvation Front winning the 1991 general election on a 'one person, one vote, once only' platform, precipitated a military coup catapulting the country into almost a decade of civil war between the regime and Islamist rebels. This claimed between 40,000 and 200,000 lives before it ended with the defeat and 'repentance' of the latter.[121] Also in 1990, Saddam Hussein's Iraq invaded neighbouring Kuwait prompting the deployment of a massive US-led international coalition to Saudi Arabia. Kuwait was liberated in the swift and, for the allies, remarkably blood-free Gulf War which followed. But Saddam's regime was left in power. The terms of surrender included a 'no fly zone' over the northern Kurdish and southern Shia regions, ostensibly intended to prevent Iraqi forces from continuing the massacres and other brutalities which followed their defeat in the war. The US and its allies also maintained a military presence in the region, including in Saudi Arabia, to ensure, amongst other things, that these and other conditions were met. Meanwhile, in 1995 the Taliban, now the enemy of the west on account of its Islamist programme, entered Kabul and declared Afghanistan an Islamic Emirate. Amongst other things, this established a safe haven for Al Qaeda which, together with its affiliates, had already launched several attacks on US targets around the world including a fatal bomb attack on the World Trade Centre in New York in 1993. The stage was, therefore, set for 9/11.

In the late 20th century – in spite of the fact that they had acutely different visions about what should replace it – elements of the European left also began to express approval and support for radical Islam on the grounds that they each regarded global capitalism as their principal enemy. For example, several iconic figures of the French left, such as Michel Foucault, Jean Baudrillard, and Simone de Beauvoir, supported the Islamic revolution in Iran.[122] Former official philosopher of the French Communist Party, Roger Garaudy (1913-2012), also became a Muslim. In 1994, in a long and highly influential article entitled 'The Prophet and the Proletariat', Chris Harman, leader of the Socialist Workers' Party – a tiny British Trotskyist organization – offered a rationale for what became known as 'Islamo-leftism'.[123] Harman argued that Islamism is the result of a deep social crisis which it is incapable of resolving. Although he thought some of its features were regressive, others such as the

---

[121] P. Nesser, *Islamist Terrorism in Europe: A History*, (Hurst & Co., 2015), Ch. 3.
[122] P. Bruckner, *An Imaginary Racism*, pp. 39-46.
[123] https://www.marxists.org/archive/harman/1994/xx/islam.htm

jizyah tax which only the rich are expected to pay, were not. The fundamentalists, he claimed, were less wedded to turning the clock back to the 7th century than in seeking to blend traditionalism with modernity through the medium of a regenerated religious faith which embodied the egalitarian ideals of early Islam. According to Harman, 'many of the individuals attracted to radical versions of Islamism could be influenced by socialists – provided socialists combine complete political independence from all forms of Islamism with a willingness to seize opportunities to draw individual Islamists into genuinely radical forms of struggle alongside them'. Harman concluded that although 'the Islamists are not our allies', where they are in opposition 'our rule should be "with the Islamists sometimes, with the state never."'

d) 21st century

In addition to the US-led international invasion of Afghanistan, the events of 9/11 prompted US President George W Bush to announce an ill-defined 'war on terror', a term never officially endorsed by other states including the UK. Indeed, even the Pentagon itself preferred 'the long war' instead.[124] Since then Salafi-Jihadi groups such as the Taliban, ISIS/DAESH and Boko Haram in west Africa have also increasingly made their presence felt.[125] Amongst other things, this has included attempts to institutionalize particularly brutal and uncompromising forms of Islamic law involving routine torture, execution, and the systematic violation of a whole raft of other human rights, such as the enslavement of non-Muslim women and girls, and, at best, intolerance of non-Muslim minorities and other Muslim traditions.[126] The pursuit of these goals has often been complicated and compromised by tribal and sectarian rivalries in regional or national contexts and conflicts, including wars in Syria, Iraq, and Yemen, global friction between Sunnis and Shia, and competition between Saudi Arabia and Iran for regional domination.[127] A complex mixture of rivalry and collaboration also emerged between Islamists and anti-authoritarian movements during the short-lived Arab spring which

---

[124] 'Pentagon says "long war" could last decades', *Irish Times*, 4 February 2006.

[125] K. Willsher, 'Europe faces new wave of terrorism as jihadis return, says Interpol head', *The Guardian*, 20 December 2018.

[126] J. Stern and J. Berger, *ISIS: The State of Terror*, (William Collins, 2015); H. Solomon, *Terrorism and Counter-Terrorism in Africa: Fighting Insurgency from Al Shabaab, Ansar Dine and Boko Haram*, (Palgrave Macmillan, 2015); R. Meijer (ed.), *Global Salafism: Islam's New Religious Movement*, (Hurst, 2009).

[127] Leiken, *Europe's Angry Muslims*, pp. 87-88.

flourished for a few years from 2010, before in most cases, being overwhelmed by tyranny or anarchy.

In the west, the events of 9/11 and their aftermath also produced three principal reactions towards Islam relevant to the issues discussed in this book. First, a genuine curiosity was reflected in newspaper articles, books, other platforms of public debate and in the establishment of various study centres and degree subjects/programmes. Second, hostility towards Muslims and Islam also increased, as evidenced amongst other things, by recorded hate crime incidents. Third, by contrast, a 'paternalistic Islamophilia' also developed, one of the most high-profile examples of which was when, in 2008, the Archbishop of Canterbury, Rowan Williams, declared that the introduction of sharia law for Muslims in the UK was 'unavoidable' and would help facilitate integration.[128] Others have also maintained that the 'war on terror' has turned the Muslim diaspora in the west into a repressed, 'suspect', or 'securitized' community suffering from pervasive social and official Islamophobia. One of the key characteristics of this view is a readiness to condemn as Islamophobic those who criticise Muslims and Islam and to avoid any critique of the faith or its adherents themselves. As Jacques Ellul, eminent French philosopher, sociologist, lay theologian, Christian anarchist, university professor, and prolific writer states: 'In France it is no longer acceptable to criticize Islam or the Arab countries',[129] a view shared, with respect to the UK, by best-selling author Douglas Murray.[130]

As these, and other developments have unfolded, several differences between Al Qaeda and ISIS/DAESH, the most prominent and notorious jihadi movements, have been noted by observers.[131] Prior to 9/11, Al Qaeda was primarily a 'company headquarters'[132] for a predominantly anti-western-imperialist organization, offering funding and training for its highly autonomous franchises throughout the middle east and elsewhere. Its attention was focused upon attacking the 'far enemy', namely the US and its allies at home and abroad, occasionally involving cooperation with Shiites whom other Salafists regard as heretics. By contrast, ISIS/DAESH was primarily

---

[128] R. Butt, 'Archbishop backs sharia law for British Muslims', *The Guardian*, 7 February 2008.

[129] https://dhimmitude.org/books/Preface.html.

[130] D. Murray, *Islamophilia: A Very Metropolitan Malady* (Self-published, 2013).

[131] Leiken, *Europe's Angry Muslims*, pp. xv-xvii.

[132] Ibid., p. xv.

interested in establishing, defending, and extending a territorial caliphate and destroying the 'near enemy', the allegedly apostate regimes of, in particular, Egypt, Joran, Iraq, Lebanon, Iran, and Saudi Arabia. While it has not prioritized attacks upon the west, it has, nevertheless, encouraged free lancers to do so wherever they have the opportunity. Unlike al Qaeda, ISIS/DAESH also embraces *takfir*, denouncing other Muslims as apostates with all this implies about the brutal treatment, including murder, they are then deemed to deserve. Also unlike al Qaeda, ISIS/DAESH also believes the prophesied millennium, discussed in Chapter 3, is at hand, with the imminent return of the *Mahdi* (Messiah) and the final segregation of the righteous ('true Muslims') from everybody else including other Muslims.

The 21st century also saw the brief establishment of an ISIS/DAESH 'Caliphate' in parts of Syria and Iraq from 2014-18, and the further consolidation of Hezbollah in Lebanon and Hamas in Gaza. In 2016 the Turkish regime's repressive response to a botched Kemelist coup – which it blamed on the pro-western, pro-democracy, Sufi-inspired Gülen movement – seemed to confirm a more hard-line trend in what had hitherto been widely regarded as President Erdogan's 'liberal Islamism'. The war between Israel and Hamas in Gaza, which began with a violent incursion by Hamas militants into Israel in 7 October 2023, has resulted in tens of thousands of Palestinian and over a thousand Israeli fatalities and has also significantly weakened Hamas and Hezbollah. Deep anti-Israeli sentiment across the Muslim and wider worlds has also been re-energized, prompting record levels of both antisemitism and Islamophobia in many places.

Two further issues of particular importance to the issues considered in this book concern how non-Muslims regard Muslims, and how Muslims living in the west have come to see themselves and their non-Muslim social, political and cultural environment. The picture is complex, multidimensional, and characterized by contrary and competing trends on both counts. The attitudes of non-Muslim Europeans towards Muslims vary from state to state. A 2019 study found, for example, that the countries with the highest percentages of negativity were Slovakia (77%), Poland (66%), and the Czech Republic (64%) and those with the lowest were Ukraine (21%), Russia (19%), and the UK (18%).[133]

---

[133] Pew Research Center, *European Public Opinion Three Decades After the Fall of Communism — 6. Minority groups*, 14 October 2019.

And, while Muslim immigrants have integrated into European society to a degree, it is widely accepted that this has not yet been as fully achieved as it could be. Part of the problem lies in the fact that the mainstream interpretation of Islam, considered more fully in the following two chapters, encourages the belief that the faithful should be governed by eternal and unchangeable rules laid down in the distant past, which bind all believers, take precedence over secular law, and which are open to only one interpretation.

This has produced conflicting trends within the European ummah. A recent study found, for example, that two-thirds of those surveyed agreed that religious rules are more important than civil laws, 75% thought there was only one possible interpretation of the Qur'an, and almost 60% thought Muslims should return to their Islamic roots. The same study found that 64% of Muslims in the UK identified as 'highly religious', followed by 42% in Austria, 33% in France, and 26% in Switzerland.[134] And while perceived discrimination is a marginal predictor of religious Islamic conservatism, the perception that western governments are inherently hostile towards Islam is common in European Muslim communities. However, this also tends to vary according to age, education, and international events. The study also found that Belgium – which has comparatively generous policies towards Muslims and immigrants in general – had a relatively high level of Islamic conservatism, while this was less the case in France and Germany which have more restrictive policies.

As Chapter 5 discusses more fully some, particularly the second and third generation offspring of immigrants, maintain an uneasy equilibrium between their orthodox Muslim faith and the liberal assumptions of the wider society. Others lose their faith and maintain only minimal levels of visible observance if any. This may include indulging in 'decadent' western pleasures, such as alcohol, extra-marital sex, dancing, and drugs, which their faith traditionally abhors. Yet others have abandoned their religion altogether, either quietly or more publicly.

Conclusion

Some of the issues raised in this chapter will be revisited in subsequent parts of this study as the debate about Islamophobic expression is explored.

---

[134] "'Islam shouldn't culturally shape Germany," Alexander Dobrindt claims', *Deutsche Welle*, 11 April 2018.

However, for now, the following conclusions can be drawn. To begin with, no observation about the history of the Muslim faith can be Islamophobic if it is at least adequately supported by fact and/or informed opinion. According to this criterion, it is clear that the west has not been uncompromisingly hostile to Islam since it first appeared. The arrival of this distinctive religion prompted impassioned debates. But this was not conducted in simple binary terms with non-Muslim hostility towards Muslims and Islam, on one side, parallelled by uncritical Islamic apologetics from Muslims on the other. The western view has, admittedly, been dominated by criticism and suspicion. But there have also been significant counter-currents of sympathy and admiration. Nor is it true to claim that western negativity towards Islam has always been irrational ('phobic'). For one thing, from the late 7th century onwards, the Muslim empires in question undeniably posed both a military and ideological threat to Europe and elsewhere, albeit more acute at some times than others. And, although often exaggerated, and certainly far from existential, the same is true of the current challenge presented by violent Islamism.

There could be no more fitting way in which to end this chapter than by illustrating that it is possible to be simultaneously an admirer and critic of Islam. As Pascal Bruckner states:

'All that is admirable about classic Islamic civilization – the beauty of the Arabic language chanted or recited, the art of gardens, the geometric anticipation of the paradise to come, the symmetry of believers bowed down by an implacable clock at prayer times, the metaphysical vehemence tempered by a culture of compromise and syncretism, in Asia as in Africa, the grace of slender minarets reaching for the sky, the sumptuous calligraphy evading the ban on representation, the divine message's power of attraction, the hospitality and warmth of its believers – all that has been swept away, annihilated over the past thirty years by the abuses perpetrated by Allah's pious mercenaries'.[135]

---

[135] Bruckner, *An Imaginary Racism*, p. 103.

Chapter 3

Foundations of the faith

Introduction

The following chapter seeks to summarise core mainstream Muslim beliefs and practices. But, first, we must consider the formal sources of the faith from which these are said to derive.[1] In common with most other ideologies, Islam also bears the hallmarks of several informal influences. While Muslims acknowledge the legacy of its sibling Abrahamic faiths – Judaism and Christianity – there is much less official recognition of the contributions made by Zoroastrianism, ancient Greek philosophy and, most controversially, pre-Islamic Arab spirituality and culture which Muslims dismiss as integral to *Jahiliyyah*, the Age of Ignorance.[2] Nevertheless, it has been argued that traditional Arab virtues – such as manly courage, heroism, dignity, nobility of spirit, loyalty, honour, oath-keeping, fierceness in battle, retaliation to insult, revenge, perseverance, patience, generosity, and hospitality – survive in Islam, particularly in its Arab heartlands. This is also said to be the case with respect to certain metaphysical assumptions, including fatalism, and social practices such as polygamy, instant divorce, modest dress, circumcision, and ceremonial cleanliness.[3] Indeed, Holland maintains that, 'far from spelling the end of what had gone before', Islam 'seems in many ways to have been its culmination'.[4] Contemporary intolerance of criticism of their beliefs, practices and conduct, on the part of some Muslims, could also be traced to the transfer, by the Islamic revolution, of traditional Arabian

---

[1] See, eg, D. Morgan, *Essential Islam: A Comprehensive Guide to Belief and Practice* (Praeger, 2010); P. Stewart, *Unfolding Islam* (Garnet, 2nd edn., 2008); C. Horrie & P. Chippendale, *What Is Islam?* (W.H. Allen, 1990).

[2] T. Holland, *In the Shadow of the Sword: The Battle for Global Empire and End of the Ancient World* (Abacus, 2012), pp. 54-62.

[3] Morgan, *Essential Islam*, pp. xxv-xxvi.

[4] Holland, *In the Shadow of the Sword*, p. 51.

cultural norms, particularly concerning retaliation to insult, from their original personal and tribal focus to the faith itself.

For most religions, particularly those with contemporary global significance, formal sources tend to fall into the following three categories – the revelations or insights of a charismatic visionary or visionaries, recorded in a sacred text, and interpreted and practiced by an interpretive community typically dominated by a priesthood or other authoritative interpreters. In Islam these take the form of the revelations of Mohammad assembled in the Qur'an; religious norms *(sunnah)* derived by Islamic scholars (the *ulama*) from the Qur'an and other sacred sources including the *hadith* (anecdotes about Mohammad's life and sayings); Islamic law (the *sharia*); and the opinions of specific Islamic scholars delivered in response to particular queries or concerns *(fatwas)*.

The precise historical origins of the sharia and fatwas are, arguably of less importance to the authenticity of Islam than are the history of the Qur'an and the sunnah-imposing hadith upon which the entire faith is said to depend. And here we encounter a critical problem, awareness of which has been developing since the mid-19th century: the historical sources are either non-existent or very unreliable. As Holland observes, there are no Muslim records from the age of Mohammad itself, nor for a considerable time thereafter – 'not a single Arab account of his life, nor of his followers' conquests, nor of the progress of his religion, from the whole of the near two centuries that followed his death'.[5] Far from Islam having been born 'in the full light of history', Holland adds that, 'its birth was shrouded in what has appeared, to an increasing number of scholars, an almost impenetrable darkness'. It is 'as though we had no eye witness accounts of the Protestant Reformation, or the French Revolution, or the two World Wars'.[6]

The purpose of this chapter is not exhaustively to explore every feature of the formal sources of the mainstream faith, nor to resolve relevant controversies about them. Its objective is simply to provide a broad overview of the former, to note the main contentious issues, and to affirm that it is not Islamophobic to do either.

---

[5] Holland, *In the Shadow of the Sword*, p. 42.
[6] Ibid., p 44.

The Qur'an

According to mainstream Islam, in adulthood the Prophet Mohammad developed a keen spirituality. For three years before he received the revelations which became the Qur'an, he would retreat to Mount Hira outside Mecca for periods of prayer and meditation lasting days or weeks. On one of these occasions, in 610 CE, he is said to have been thrown into terror by the sudden appearance of an apparition which demanded 'Read!' or 'Recite!', an experience he immediately thought was a sign of madness, possession, or, in his opinion worst of all, receiving the gift of poetry. He ran home to Khadija, his wife, who covered him in a sheet and held his hand all night. The apparition, later allegedly identified as the Archangel Gabriel, is said to have reappeared and Khadija convinced Mohammad that he was not mad or possessed but was being granted an authentic revelation from God. Muslims believe that, from 610 until his death in 632, Mohammad then received a series of further revelations which became the Qur'an (the 'recitation, 'lecture', 'discourse').

All Muslims regard the Qur'an, the foundational first of the Five Pillars of the faith discussed more fully in the following chapter, as the uniquely authentic source of God's final revelation of His nature and purpose for humankind. Even the suggestion that it is merely the 'inspired' rather than the 'literal' Word of God is likely to be regarded by most as dangerous heresy.[7] Indeed, the Qur'an proclaims itself to be 'peerless, divine, infallible, inerrant, and incorruptible'.[8] An early controversy amongst the faithful concerned whether the Qur'an is timeless or was created before Mohammad received it. According to Holland, 'it would take six hundred long years of bitter and occasionally murderous argument' before scholars finally agreed that it was 'eternal, not created, and divine, not a reflection of God'.[9]

Believers have typically sought in several ways to prove that the Qur'an is the literal word of God. One is that it accords with authentic human intuition and reason. Another is that the text is so incomparably beautiful it could not have been composed by a single human author or even a team.[10] According to

---

[7] Morgan, *Essential Islam*, pp. 34-5; Horrie & Chippindale, *What Is Islam?*, p. 16.

[8] Morgan, *Essential Islam*, p. 30.

[9] Holland, *In the Shadow of the Sword*, p. 33.

[10] '10 Reasons Muhammad Could Not Have Authored the Qur'an', *IlmFeed.com*, 20 March 2014.

some, this is especially the case because Mohammad was illiterate. But others, Muslims included, maintain that, as a merchant from a privileged background, he would almost certainly have been able to read and write.[11] Another argument, employed particularly in the early days, was that the staggering worldly success of the new faith would not have been possible without God's assistance and approval.[12]

Structure and style

The text of the Qur'an is non-narrative, non-chronological, and non-systematic. There is no clear organization of themes. It is assembled according to the length of *surahs* (chapters), rendered in an allusive, rhythmic, rhetorical, and elliptical style, and addressed to people already familiar with its message.[13] According to tradition, the full canon containing 114-surahs varying in length from three to 286 verses – with a total of 6,616 verses, 77,439 words and 323,015 letters – had been collected by 650 CE. However, other versions were also in circulation and the final orthodox edition was not fully assembled until 933, almost exactly three hundred years after Mohammad's death.[14] Eighty-six surahs have subheadings indicating they were received in Mecca while twenty-eight state they were revealed to Mohammad in Medina. For reasons explained in the previous chapter, it is also acknowledged that the principal distinction, reflecting the respective contexts, is that the former are more pacific and the latter more marshal.

According to the celebrated German Islamic scholar, Theodor Nöldeke (1836-1930), aesthetically considered, the Qur'an:

> '…is by no means a first rate performance… Indispensable links, both in expression and in the sequence of events, are often omitted … there is a good deal of superfluous verbiage and nowhere do we find a steady advance in the narration … The connexion of ideas is

---

[11] Morgan, *Essential Islam*, p. 108.

[12] Kelsay, *Just War in Islam*, pp. 38-9; G. von Grunebaum, 'Sources of Islamic Civilization', in P. Holt, A. Lambton & B. Lewis (eds.), *The Cambridge History of Islam: Volume 2B, Islamic Society and Civilisation* (Cambridge University Press, 2008), pp. 472, 475.

[13] Morgan, *Essential Islam*, p. 24-8; M. Cook, *The Koran: A Very Short Introduction* (Oxford University Press, 2000); Holland, *In the Shadow of the Sword*, p. 31.

[14] Morgan, *Essential Islam*, p. 32-3; Cook, *The Koran*, p. 6, 119; P. Hitti, *History of the Arabs: From the Earliest Times to the Present* (Palgrave MacMillan, revised 10th edn., 2002), p. 123.

extremely loose, and even the syntax betrays great awkwardness …
there is no great literary skill evinced in the frequent and needless
harping on the same words and phrases … Mahmet in short, is not in
any sense a master of style'.[15]

Interpretation and content

As far as interpretation is concerned, Jafar al-Sadiq, an 8th century Shia
scholar, claimed that the Qur'an could be understood on four levels: 'literal'
(for the common folk), 'allusion' (for the scholars), 'hidden meaning' (for the
so-called Friends of Allah), and 'spiritual truths' (for the Prophet and Imam).[16]
But it is difficult to sustain these distinctions across the entire text.

This claim aside, two principal types of interpretation can be
distinguished for any text including the Qur'an. One concerns exegesis, the
task of determining what the words, taken more or less at face value, mean.
For the faithful, the primary purpose is to identify and to follow God's
commands.[17] However, over the centuries, as the previous chapter showed,
many non-Muslims have engaged in this exercise out of scholarly curiosity
without necessarily ascribing any divine origin to the subject of their inquiry.
For them, knowledge of the wider social, political, economic, ideological, and
relevant historical backgrounds in which the text was both delivered, and in
which the standard interpretations later became institutionalized, are also
important, as are reflections upon what it might mean for the contemporary
world.

Exegesis also includes, for example, distinguishing between the literal
and allegorical, and between those passages which are intended to be timeless
and universal and those which may be historically and context specific. But
as Morgan observes, there is no agreement 'precisely on *which* verses are to
be taken literally and which should be understood allegorically, or even
between just which verses are supposed to be "clearly understood" and those
which are not'.[18] And as Akyol points out, the orthodox tradition regards
certain elements of the Qur'an as *prescriptive*, for example 'men are

---

[15] T. Nöldeke, 'Koran', in H. Chisholm & F Hooper (eds.), *Encyclopedia Britannica*,
(Horace Everett Hooper, 11th edn., 1910-11), Vol. 15, pp. 898-906.
[16] Morgan, *Essential Islam*, p. 34.
[17] Ibid., p. 18.
[18] Ibid., p. 31 (italics in original).

maintainers of women', when they may be merely *descriptive*.[19] The Qur'an also includes certain commands – for example regarding the months in which armed conflict is forbidden, disrobing indoors during the heat of the day, and owning slaves – 'that are clearly inapplicable today'.[20] It has also been claimed that it refers to many issues – including the Big Bang, antimatter, rotating stars, nuclear fusion, tectonic plates, and the ozone layer – which have only recently been confirmed by modern science. But, as Morgan puts it: 'In some cases, it may appear that a great deal of imagination has been applied to these "parallels."'[21]

The second kind of interpretation is, however, more thorough-going and critical. It concerns, not just what the text of the Qur'an means, but whether or not the orthodox account of its Divine nature and origins is credible. The purpose here may be 'neutrally intellectual'. But it may also be allied to contesting the challenge Islam poses to other world views particularly Christianity and secularism. Several elements of this critique can be distinguished. First, atheists reject and agnostics doubt, the core Qur'anic assumption – the existence of the supernatural Abrahamic God in which Jews, Christians, and Muslims believe. Some Jews and Christians accept the authenticity of some of Mohammad's revelations not least because they are similar to elements of their own faiths. But those who do, nevertheless, dispute the idea that God revealed Himself to Mohammad in the manner claimed. Other religions, including Hinduism and Buddhism, do not easily accommodate and may in fact dismiss, the notion that an anthropomorphic God has revealed Himself, word-for-word, to anybody.

As for content, most non-Muslim scholars agree that the message of the Qur'an is largely a redaction of the Judeo-Christian and Apocryphal scriptures infused with elements of Zoroastrianism and the assumptions of traditional Arab spirituality. As Dashti (1897-1982) – an Iranian journalist, author, and student of Islam, Arabic, and Persian – argues, it 'contains nothing new in the sense of ideas not already expressed by others'. All its moral precepts, he says, 'are self-evident and generally acknowledged … Confucius, Buddha, Zoroaster, Socrates, Moses and Jesus had said similar things'. The stories in it are also 'taken in identical or slightly modified forms from the lore of the Jews and Christians'

---

[19] M. Akyol, *Reopening Muslim Minds: A Return to Reason, Freedom and Tolerance* (Forum, 2022), p. 162.
[20] Ibid., p. 160.
[21] Morgan, *Essential Islam.*, p. 18.

and 'many of the duties and rites of Islam are continuations of practices which the pagan Arabs had adopted from the Jews'.[22]

However, it has been argued, that even if we admit the possibility that the Qur'an contains some kind of Divine revelation, there are significant problems with the proposition that it is God's perfect and timeless Word. This is particularly the case concerning the doctrine of abrogation, the so-called Satanic verses, plus problems with alleged historical editing, comprehensibility, grammar, the inclusion of voices other than that of God, apparent confusion about elements of Judaism and Christianity, and a strangely personal denunciation of one of Mohammad's enemies.

Abrogation

According to the controversial orthodox Muslim doctrine of 'abrogation', certain verses of the Qur'an 'abrogate', or annul, those delivered earlier.[23] Surah 2:106 states: 'If we ever abrogate a verse or cause it to be forgotten, we replace it with a better or similar one. Do you not know that Allah is Most Capable of everything?'. Quoting this, Qur'anic scholars maintain that abrogation pertains only to jurisprudence or practical matters that can change over time but not to essential principles of faith or doctrine.[24]

But some have argued that it is not easy to understand why God would either change His mind over His own perfect revelation, or knowingly reveal Himself in one way only to revise it later. Nor can scholars agree about exactly how many, or to which, verses this applies. But it is said to be around 200.[25] Almost all of these are Meccan or early Medinan, allegedly cancelled by the narrower, less tolerant, and more privileged sense of being Muslim found in the Medinan verses themselves, which also tend to endorse a much more militant, aggressive and binary relationship between Muslims and others.[26] Punishment for adultery provides an example. Surah 24:2 states that an adulterous woman should be shut up in her home until she dies or until Allah ordains a 'different way'. By contrast Surah 4:15-16 stipulates 100 lashes.

---

[22] A. Dashti, *Twenty-Three Year: A Study of the Prophetic Career of Mohammad* (Mazda, 1994), p. 56.
[23] Ibn Warraq, *Why I Am Not A Muslim* (Prometheus Reprint, 2003), pp. 114-115.
[24] Morgan, *Essential Islam*, p. 23.
[25] Ibid., p. 115.
[26] A. Afsaruddin, *Contemporary Issues in Islam* (Edinburgh University Press, 2015), p. 191.

The Satanic Verses

Another controversial issue in the history of Mohammad's revelations concerns the so-called 'Satanic Verses'. According to contemporary sources, in despair that the Meccans would ever embrace his message, and eager for the military support of a particularly powerful clan, Mohammad claimed to have received a revelation that the three daughters of Allah recognised by the traditional Arab pantheon, Al-Lat, Al-Uzza, and Al-Manat, could also intercede between humanity and the Almighty.[27] Rapidly realizing that this constituted a huge compromise with his robust monotheism, Mohammad claimed this concession was the result of having been deceived by Satan. No reference to the three goddesses can be found in the Qur'an and most Muslims believe this story is simply a fictitious attempt to undermine the credibility of Mohammad's revelations. But if the episode is true, it raises a disturbing question: how do we know that other Qur'anic revelations were not also the result of Satanic deception? The enduring capacity of this controversy to ignite violent dispute, even after a millennium and a half, was graphically revealed by reaction to Sir Salman Rushdie's novel *The Satanic Verses*, considered further in Chapter 7.

Other alleged problems

It has also been alleged that at least some of the Qur'an is simply incomprehensible, or that its meaning is not at all clear. According to Crone and Cook, the text is: 'frequently obscure and inconsequential in both language and content, perfunctory in its linking of disparate materials and given to the repetition of whole passages in variant versions'.[28]

Many non-Muslim scholars agree and also share Burton's view that the traditional accounts of its history and formation are 'a mass of confusion, contradiction and inconsistencies'.[29] Most have also pointed out that, given the considerable time lag between the oral delivery of Mohammad's revelations, and the publication of the first authoritative version of the Qur'an in 933, there can be no reliable way of knowing how much of the text was altered or even if it was entirely manufactured. Bell and Watt conclude that

---

[27] S. Ahmed 'Ibn Taymiyyah and the Satanic Verses' (1998) 87 *Studia Islamica*, 67–124.
[28] P. Crone & M. Cook, *Hagarism: The Making of the Islamic World* (Cambridge University Press, 1980), p. 18.
[29] J. Burton, *The Collection of the Qur'an* (Cambridge University Press, 1977), p. 225

unevenness in style suggests that many alterations were, in fact, made in successive drafts,[30] while Crone and Cook maintain that 'it can be plausibly argued that' it 'is the product of the belated and imperfect editing of materials from a plurality of traditions'.[31]

More specifically it has been claimed that some verses in earlier versions were omitted in later renditions and others subsequently added. For example, according to the Shiites, for political reasons Uthman deleted verses sympathetic to Ali from his authorized edition. It has also been alleged that verses 36-8 of Surah 42 were added to justify the elevation of Uthman and to denigrate Ali.[32] The medieval Christian Arab, Abd al-Masih ibn Ishaq al-Kindi (not to be confused with the Muslim philosopher Abu Yusuf ibn Ishaq al-Kindi) also claimed that in the Qur'an, 'histories are all jumbled together and intermingled; an evidence that many different hands have been at work therein, and caused discrepancies, adding or cutting out whatever they liked or disliked'.[33]

Some scholars also point out that 'the Quran contains incomplete utterances not fully explicable without commentary, unfamiliar Arabic, foreign words, bad grammar, and other linguistic snarls that suggest a more human origin'.[34] According to Morgan, the text 'is filled with missing phrases that have since been supplied by translators and commentators'.[35] Dashti also maintains that:

> '... the Qur'an contains sentences which are incomplete and not fully intelligible without the aid of commentaries; foreign words, unfamiliar Arabic words, and words used with other than the normal meaning; adjectives and verbs inflected without observance of the concords of gender and number; illogically and ungrammatically applied pronouns which sometimes have no referent, and predicates which in rhymed passages are often remote from the subjects ... To sum up, more than one hundred Qur'anic aberrations from the normal rules have been noted'.[36]

---

[30] R. Bell & W. Watt, *Introduction to the Quran* (Edinburgh University Press, 2nd edition, 1995) p. 93.

[31] Crone & Cook, *Hagarism*, p. 18.

[32] Ibn Warraq, *Why I Am Not A Muslim*, p. 112.

[33] Cited in A. Rippin, *Muslims: Their Religious Beliefs and Practices, Vol. 1, The Formative Period* (Routledge, 1990), p. 26.

[34] Morgan, *Essential Islam*, p. 25.

[35] Ibid., p. 26.

[36] Dashti, *A Study of the Prophetic Career of Mohammad*, p. 50.

Others have commented upon the lack of dots distinguishing certain letters from others and the absence of certain letters from certain words, with the result that readers have to supply the missing information and may arrive at different meanings.[37] For example, Surah 4:162 includes the following clause: 'But those among them who are well-grounded in knowledge, the believers, … and the performers of the prayer, and the prayers of the alms tax…' The word 'performers' is said to be in the accusative case while it should be nominative as it is for 'well-grounded', 'believers', and 'prayers'. In Surah 9:49 – 'If two parties of believers have started to fight each other, and make peace between them' – the verb for 'have started to fight' is rendered in the singular whereas it should be plural. It is also said that the Qur'an contains between 100 and 275 foreign words from Aramaic, Hebrew, Syriac, Ethiopic, Persian, and Greek.[38]

Nor does it take an expert to observe that some Surahs are rendered in the voice *of* God, whereas others, such as the opening Surah known as the Fatihah, are clearly addressed *to* Him. This states:

'In the name of the Merciful and Compassionate God. Praise belongs to God, the Lord of the Worlds, the merciful the compassionate, the ruler of the day of judgment! Thee we serve and Thee we ask for aid. Guide us in the right path, the path of those Thou art gracious to; not of those Thou art wroth with, nor of those who err'.[39]

Another Surah is universally acknowledged to have been uttered (allegedly) by angels: 'We come not down but by command of thy Lord; to him belongs what is before us and what is behind us and what is between that ….'[40]

According to Morgan, the Quran also 'lays certain charges against Jews and Christians that betray an inadequate understanding of their beliefs'.[41] For example, it states that the Jews regard Ezra as the son of God, a claim Judaism has never made.[42] Scholars have also noted differences between the Biblical and Qur'anic accounts relating, for example, to Adam and Eve, Abraham, Noah, Cain and Abel, Joseph, Moses, and Jesus, plus confusion about the

---

[37] Ibn Warraq, *Why I Am Not a Muslim*, pp. 108-9. Morgan, *Essential Islam*, p. 27.
[38] Ibn Warraq, *Why I Am Not a Muslim*, p. 108.
[39] Qur'an 1:1-7.
[40] Qur'an 19:64.
[41] Morgan, *Essential Islam*, p. xvii.
[42] Qur'an 9:30.

Christian doctrine of the Trinity.[43] Of course Muslims are likely to claim that any differences between the Bible and the Qur'an are easily resolved because the latter simply corrects errors in the former. However, the Qur'an also allegedly confuses Mary, the mother of Jesus, with Mary, the sister of Moses and Aaron, and it is said that its accounts concerning Saul and Gideon are also mistaken.[44] As Obermann states:

> 'Not only the Hebrew original, but any sort of translation would surely have precluded the gross discrepancies, inaccuracies and delusions ... (Mohammad) ... exhibits, almost invariably, when his revelation involves data from the Old Testament; or for that matter from the New Testament'.[45]

And according to Bell, Mohammad…

> 'had very little idea of Christian teaching, or of what the Christian Church was. In fact, he never did acquire very intimate knowledge of these things. As Nöldeke pointed out long ago, the man who made such a stupid story of the chief Christian sacrament, as that in surah v. 11 Iff., one of the latest parts of the Qur'an, could not have known much about the Christian Church'.[46]

It has also been noted that the Qur'an's excoriating denunciation of Abu Lahab, Mohammad's uncle and one of his fiercest critics, a personally vindictive inclusion unusual in what is said to be a universal message for all humankind:

> 'The hands of Abu Lahab shall perish, and he shall perish. His riches shall not profit him, neither that which he has gained. He shall go down to be burned into flaming fire, and his wife also, bearing wood having on her neck a chord of twisted fibres of a palm tree'.[47]

The hadith and the life of Mohammad

The hadith are anecdotes about the life and sayings of the Prophet

---

[43] Ibn Warraq, *Why I Am Not a Muslim*, pp. 55-59, 61, 63, 131-53, 161.

[44] Ibid., p.158.

[45] J. Obermann, 'Islamic Origins: A Study in Background and Foundation' in N. Faris (ed.), *The Arab Heritage* (Hyperion Press, 1981), p. 94.

[46] R. Bell, *The Origins of Islam in Its Christian Environment* (Routledge, 1968), p. 156.

[47] Qur'an 111:1-5.

committed to writing many years after his death. Allegedly ranging from tens of thousands to at least a million, the precise number is unclear. Some, but not all, are said to give rise to recommended or mandated norms of proper Islamic conduct (sunnah).[48] Hadith which do not give rise to sunnah are, nevertheless, widely respected by Muslims as sources of insight and inspiration.[49] The authenticity of some hadith is disputed by some Muslims, certain Islamic traditions acknowledge some hadith but not others, and some are unclear or difficult, if not impossible, to reconcile with each other. Non-Muslim scholars are generally very sceptical about the authenticity of the hadith. Humphreys, for example, notes that Goldziher 'demonstrated that a vast number of hadith accepted even in the most rigorously critical Muslim collections were outright forgeries from the late 8th and 9th centuries – and as a consequence, that the meticulous *isnads* … (chains of transmission) … which supported them were utterly fictitious'.[50] Most Muslims accept the hadith as legitimate components of the Islamic faith. However, a minority reject them in their entirety, relying exclusively upon the Qur'an as the only authentic source of religious truth.[51]

For the purpose of this study, there are two principal problems with the hadith. First, their sheer number, coupled with doubts about their authenticity, consistency, and interpretation, make it difficult if not impossible to state with certainty that any controversial proposition said to derive from them is in fact a genuine feature of Islam. As a result, it is impossible to determine whether or not any such claim is an 'Islamophobic' distortion or a faithful reference to an authentic component of the faith.

Given its profile in the Islamic faith, the life of Mohammad (the 'Praised One') is of considerable importance, not least because controversies about it are relevant to the debate about where the line between Islamophobic expression and legitimate critical appraisal of Islam should be drawn.

A challenge common to accounts of the lives of all seminal historical figures, particularly those from the distant past, concerns the reliability of sources. The first published biography of Mohammad, by Ibn Ishaq – which

---

[48] J. Schacht, 'Law and Justice', in P. Holt, A. Lambton & B. Lewis (eds.), *Cambridge History of Islam*, pp. 543-4.

[49] Morgan, *Essential Islam*, pp. 169-73.

[50] R. Humphreys, *Islamic History: A Framework for Inquiry* (Princeton University Press, 1991), p. 83; Ibn Warraq, *Why I Am Not a Muslim*, p. 153; Holland, *In the Shadow of the Sword*, pp. 37-41.

[51] See Ch. 5.

no longer survives – did not appear until 750, over a century after Mohammad's death. Ibn Hashim (d. 833/4), who edited it, admits leaving out certain passages in order to avoid causing 'distress'.[52] The problem affecting the authenticity of sources regarding Mohammad's life is further compounded by the fact that the orthodox tradition has a long history of suppressing, often violently, any deviation from the official account on the grounds that it amounts to blasphemy. However, this has not silenced criticism from both Muslims and non-Muslims. Some of the latter have concluded, for example, that Islam emerged much later than the orthodox account claims, that Mohammad was largely or entirely a fiction based on Moses, concocted in order to unite the Arabs and to justify their imperial conquests, and that the hadith have all been fabricated to suit certain viewpoints and interests.[53] However, most scholars accept that Mohammad did in fact exist.[54] Some also accept that, although when he received his revelations he genuinely thought they came from God, they may have instead been the result of altered mental states with no divine origin.[55] According to Morgan:

> '… recent linguistic, historical, textual, and cultural research has cast doubt on some of the most widely accepted and deeply held facts about Muhammad, including the date of his birth, events of his life, and sayings attributed to him. However, this work is still emerging and most scholars agree that his traditional biography *sira* (literally "the way") is basically factually correct'.[56]

While this study takes no side in this debate, it nevertheless, categorically asserts that the points of view expressed in it should be presented so that anyone with sufficient interest can make up their own minds, and that it is not Islamophobic to do so.

The orthodox account of Mohammad's life goes something like this.[57] Mohammad ibn Abdullah, the perfect man and a model for all believers, was

---

[52] Morgan, *Essential Islam*, pp. 100-01.
[53] Crone & Cook, *Hagarism*; J. Wansborough, *Quranic Studies: Sources and Methods of Scriptural Interpretation* (Oxford University Press, 1977); Morgan, *Essential Islam*, p.172.
[54] Holland, *In the Shadow of the Sword*, p. 44.
[55] See, eg, R. Dawkins, *The God Delusion* (Bantam, 2006).
[56] Morgan, *Essential Islam*, p. 98.
[57] See K. Armstrong, *Muhammad: A Western Attempt to Understand Islam* (Victor Gollancz, 1991).

born in Mecca around 570 into the declining Banu Hashim clan which claimed descent from the Biblical Abraham and Ismail. Some members were Jewish or Christian. The Hashemites were also part of the powerful and wealthy Quraysh tribe which controlled Mecca, including the Kaaba, the idol-festooned shrine devoted to the worship of the Arab pantheon. Mohammad's father, Abdullah ('Servant of God'), a caravan merchant, died before Mohammad was born. The life of his mother, Aminah ('Peaceful'), came to an end just over six years later. Having himself been orphaned, in later life Mohammad was particularly sympathetic to others who had suffered a similar fate. Following the deaths of his parents, Mohammad was raised by his grandfather, Abd al-Muttalib, reputedly a saintly, handsome man, mayor of Mecca, and guardian of the Kaaba.

Many miracles, beginning in his childhood, have been attributed to, or associated with, Mohammad. For example, when he was five years old it is said he fell over in a field shouting that two angels had slit open his abdomen, looked for something inside, and left having cleansed his heart with snow. At the age of twelve he is also reputed to have been recognised by Bahira, a Syrian Christian monk, as Shiloh, a non-Jewish prophet foretold in the book of Genesis. Mohammad is said to have taken this very seriously. In later life he was also 'revered as a man able to foretell the future, to receive messages from camels, and palm trees, and joints of meat; and to pick up a soldier's eyeball, reinsert it, and make it work better than before'.[58]

Prior to Mohammad reaching the age of maturity, Abd al-Muttalib, then aged 82, also died. As a result, his grandson was taken in by a gentle but impecunious uncle, Abu Talib, head of the Banu Hashim. Mohammad began working for him as a camel driver before becoming manager of a caravan owned by a distant relative, the rich and twice-widowed, Khadija bint Khuwaylid ibn Asad ibn Abd al-Uzza ibn Quasyy, also a member of the Quraysh tribe. A reputation for trustworthiness later enabled Mohammad to become a merchant in his own right. At her instigation, Khadija, then 40, married Mohammad then aged 25. By all accounts, the marriage was a happy one. In addition to two sons who died in infancy, the couple had four daughters, the most famous of whom was Fatimah (605-32). Although polygamy was very common in Arabia at the time, it was not until Khadija died, in 619, that Mohammad took other wives.

---

[58] Holland, *In the Shadow of the Sword*, p. 27.

Since Mohammad is alleged to have declared that any representation of human beings or animals is impious because it risks being tempted into idolatry, no contemporary picture of him exists. As we shall see in Chapter 7, a controversy about the allegedly Islamophobic character of artistic depictions of Mohammad arose when, in January 2023, a US art professor was effectively sacked for having presented in class an iconic medieval portrait by a Muslim artist. According to tradition, Mohammad is said to have been a stocky man of medium height with brilliant white teeth, thick, wavey, shoulder-length hair, a curly black beard reaching his chest, and a lurching walk. He is also said to have owned only one set of clothes – a white shirt, trousers, and a turban which he wore with one end hanging loose. Though not particularly talkative, he was reputedly very polite, mended his own clothes, undertook housework, went shopping, spent more on perfume than victuals, and enhanced his large dark eyes with kohl, an ancient eye-liner. He liked cleanliness (particularly that of his own teeth and those of others), children, cats, honey, cucumbers, dates, and pumpkins, but disliked lizards, windy and cloudy days, artists, expensive textiles, and the smell of garlic and onions. Muslims regard Mohammad's insistence on kindness to all animals – including dogs for which he had no particular fondness – as an Islamic obligation.

In addition to his revelations, one of the most important events in Mohammad's life, the Night Journey (*Isra* and *Mi' raj*), is said to have occurred around 621. He was allegedly awakened by the Archangel Gabriel who slit open his chest, washed his heart in a golden basin (or in the well of Zamzam next to the Kaaba), and filled it with 'belief', before returning it to where it belonged. A white winged beast called Buraq, with a woman's face and between the size of a horse and a donkey, then took the Archangel Gabriel and Mohammad, via Mt Sinai and Bethlehem, to Jerusalem. There, a ladder appeared enabling Mohammad to ascend to heaven. The Dome of the Rock mosque, built on the putative site in 691, is said to preserve Mohammad's footprint at the point of departure. In the various levels of heaven, Mohammad is then said to have met Adam, Jesus, and several Old Testament prophets before encountering God who commanded him to instruct his followers to pray 50 times a day. On his way back to earth Moses allegedly advised Mohammad to renegotiate the number, first to ten and then to five. Muslims disagree about whether the Night Journey was literal or is merely allegorical.

One of the most controversial aspects of Mohammad's life, relevant to the historic and contemporary debate about Islamophobic expression, concerns his sexual activity. Nothing is reported about this prior to his marriage to Khadija. But following her death in 619, when he was 49, Mohammad then had at least 13 wives, not all simultaneously, and an unknown number of concubines. Most of the marriages were concluded for political or social reasons. Several offered protection to the widows of fallen comrades, at least two were to Jews, and another was to a Christian. Although the Qur'an is generally interpreted as limiting the number of permitted contemporaneous wives to four, it also 'made lawful' for Mohammad 'to have' more or less as many consenting wives as he chose, plus 'the slave-girls whom Allah has given you as booty'.[59]

The most controversial, yet also the most celebrated marriage was to Aisha, Mohammad's favourite wife, the only virgin amongst his brides, and the daughter of Abu Bakr, his friend and successor as leader of the faithful. According to some Muslim sources, Aisha was between six and ten years old when she married Mohammad, and that the marriage was consummated when she was between nine and twelve and he was in his 50s.[60] Other sources claim Aisha was in her late teens when she married Mohammad.[61] In the middle of the first millennium CE, marriages between young girls and older men were common amongst the Bedouins. Whatever the truth about her age when she married Mohammad, Aisha was, by all accounts, a formidable and well-educated woman who became a jurist in her own right, was fiercely loyal to her husband, and became a key figure in the early history of Islam particularly in the Sunni-Shia schism.

Another controversial marriage was to Zaynab bint Jahsh, the wife of his adopted son and former Christian slave, Zayd ibn Haritha. Mohammad was said to have walked in on her when she was naked and subsequently received a revelation that she and her husband should divorce and that she should marry him instead.[62] Aisha, who was not pleased, is alleged to have said: 'It seems to me that your Lord hastens to satisfy your desire'.[63] A quarrel between two

---

[59] Qur'an 33:50.

[60] See, eg Imam Ahmad Al-Bukhari, *Hadith of the Prophet*, Vol. 5, Book 63, nos. 3894 & 3896; Vol. 7, Book 67, no, 5133, 5134, & 5158.

[61] M. Ali, *Muhammad the Prophet* (Ahamadiyya Anjuman Ishaat Islam, 1997), p. 150.

[62] Qur'an 33:37.

[63] Morgan, *Essential Islam*, p. 136.

of his wives, Hafsah and Mary the Copt, over Mohammad having bedded the latter when it was the former's turn, was also resolved, according to tradition, by another revelation the meaning of which would otherwise have been utterly obscure. This warned that: 'Haply if he put you both away, the Lord will give him in exchange other wives better than you....'[64] Mohammad was also divorced several times and not always at his own instigation.

From the Hijra (the flight from Mecca) to the end of his days, Mohammad is said to have lived in Medina in a simple hut with walls of unbaked clay and a thatched roof of palm leaves and camel skin. Furniture consisted of a rope cot, a pillow stuffed with palm leaves and an animal skin for a rug. There were no chairs. When he died, in Aisha's arms at the age of 62, his only possessions were said to have been a white mule, a few weapons, a parcel of land, and some barley. His last request was said to have been for a toothbrush.

David Margoliouth, Laudian Professor of Arabic at the University of Oxford from 1889 to 1937, summarizes an unflattering picture of the Prophet written by Ibn Ishaq (704–767) in the following terms:

> 'He organizes assassinations and wholesale massacres. His career as tyrant of Medina is that of a robber chief, whose political economy consists in securing and dividing plunder ... He is himself an unbridled libertine and encourages the same passion in his followers. For whatever he does he is prepared to plead the express authorization of the deity. It is, however, impossible to find any doctrine which he is not prepared to abandon in order to secure a political end ... Even though Ibn Ishaq's name was for some reason held in low esteem by the classical traditionalists of the third Islamic century, they make no attempt to discredit those portions of the biography which bear hardest on the character of their Prophet'.[65]

The sharia

The sharia ('path', 'way', 'well-trodden path', 'the way to a watering place', 'what is prescribed', 'Islamic law'), derives from the Qur'an, the hadith, the sunnah, *ijma* (consensus amongst Muslims), *qiyas* (reasoning by analogy), and *fiqh* (Islamic jurisprudence).[66] Its purpose is to cultivate the

---

[64] Qur'an 66:1-9.

[65] D. Margoliouth, 'Mohammad' (1915) 8 *Encyclopedia of Religion and Ethics* 878.

[66] K. Abou El Fadl, 'The Shari'ah' in J. Esposito & E. Shahin (eds.), *The Oxford Handbook of Islam and Politics* (Oxford University Press, 2013).

Islamic virtues of, particularly, patience, forbearance, truthfulness, fair dealing, kindness, keeping promises, justice, and humility before God. The expectation is that this should be coupled with correct ritualistic and other conduct, especially prayer, fasting, chaste behaviour, and charity.

The sharia seeks to achieve these objectives according to five categories of behaviour – that which is forbidden (*haram*), discouraged (*makruh*), neutral (*mubah*), recommended (*mustahabb*), or obligatory (*fard*). Fard covers the Five Pillars, while haram includes all the prohibitions mentioned in the Qur'an and Old Testament. Failure to observe that which is either obligatory or forbidden is both sinful and criminal and may be punished by a sharia court. The encouragement or discouragement of certain conduct derives mainly from the hadith. Although discouraged, some behaviour – mostly embracing manners, charitable giving, and personal habits – though not sinful, may be criminal and thus also punishable. The most significant of the issues covered by *mustahabb*, which would be governed by civil law in the West, concern marriage and family life considered in the following chapter. The different schools of jurisprudence recognised as legitimate by Sunni and Shia Islam, largely concern divergent conclusions about legal details rather than significant differences in paradigms, frameworks, or juridical method.

The sharia is rooted in pre-Islamic Arabian conceptions of patriarchy, personal status, family, inheritance, tribal blood feuds, and the discretionary application of custom by arbitrators (common in post-Islamic Arabia and elsewhere) by state-appointed *qadis* rather than professional judges.[67] It has been said that it 'represents the core and kernel of Islam itself and, certainly, religious law is incomparably more important in the religion of Islam than theology'.[68] However, while the sharia retained some pre-Islamic elements, it simultaneously transformed their content and function. For example, while the pre-Islamic structure of the family survived, ancient Bedouin tribal organization was dissolved. An attempt was also made to eliminate the blood feud, restrict private vengeance and retaliation, improve the position of women, orphans, the weak and vulnerable, strengthen marriage, and control degeneracy by restricting sexual licence and banning alcohol and gambling.[69]

Over time the sacred law became strongest in the fields of the family, inheritance and the settling of endowments for public or private purposes, and

---

[67] Schacht, 'Law and Justice', pp. 547-9, 556-9.
[68] Ibid., p. 539.
[69] Ibid., p. 542.

weakest or non-existent with respect to punishment, taxation, the exercise of public power, and the conduct of war. The law of contracts and obligations stands somewhere in between.[70] Uncompromisingly individualistic in its focus, there is no sense that corporate entities are, or should be, governed by the sharia.[71] Nor is it entirely clear whether, or if so to what extent, it provides flexible principles or inflexible rules. Of particular importance is the fact that its open texture, particularly as far as the sunnah are concerned, facilitated the formation of the ulama, a body of experts who effectively became, not just interpreters, but law makers.[72] According to traditional Islam, the Qur'an, sunnah, and sharia provide an exhaustive body of legislation. Although, in theory, the Caliph could not legislate, he could, nevertheless, issue administrative regulations which both interpreted and subtly modified existing law.

By the middle of the 9th century, four distinctive legal traditions had emerged in the Sunni world – the Hanafi, Maliki, Shafi, and Hanbali – named after their founders, Abu Hanafi (d. 767), Malik ibn Anas (d.795), Abu Abdullah Muhammad ibn Idris al-Shafi (d. 820), and Ahmad ibn Hanbal (d. 855). Each offered distinct, though not always different answers to challenging legal questions. To this day they remain the principal sources of Sunni law. The Hanafi is regarded as the most liberal and flexible with the Hanbali the most conservative and traditional.

Goldziher describes the debates between Islamic jurists as 'lost in absurd sophistry and dreary exegetical trifling … and hair-splitting … joined with the boldest and most reckless flights of fancy'. For example, a problematic case for the sharia is 'how to deal with the progeny from a marriage between a human being and a demon in human form'.[73]

According to Schacht, by the beginning of the 10th century, the point had been reached when scholars of all schools of Islamic jurisprudence:

'felt that all essential questions had been thoroughly discussed and finally settled, and a consensus gradually established itself to the effect that, from that time onwards, no one might be deemed to have the necessary qualifications for independent reasoning in law, and that all future activity would have to be confined to the explanation,

---

[70] Ibid., p. 565.
[71] Ibid., p. 563.
[72] Ibid., p. 540.
[73] I. Goldziher (trans A. Hamori & R. Hamori), *Introduction to Islamic Theology and Law*, (Princeton University Press, 1981), pp. 63-64.

application, and, at most, interpretation of the doctrine as it had been laid down once and for all'.[74]

Akyol maintains that:

'Today few issues about Islam are as controversial as the Sharia … The reason is obvious. Sharia, as interpreted by the traditional jurisprudence (*fiqh*), has serious conflicts with modern standards of human rights. These include harsh verdicts for "apostasy" or "blasphemy" … legal discrimination against women or non-Muslims … (and) … corporal punishments such as flogging, stoning, amputation of hands, and beheading'.[75]

He also claims that, over time, Sunni theology underwent significant decline and marginalization: 'Instead jurisprudence became the primary discipline. As a result, Islamic culture became a "legal culture" focusing on proper behaviour rather than proper belief', and entailed a 'plenitude of does and don'ts'.[76] According to Turkish theologian, Ali Bardakoğlu, a 'lack of virtues and morals is rampant' in the whole Muslim world because Islamic jurisprudence has become a 'pile of rules' from which 'morality has evaporated'.[77] And, as Abou El Fadl, puts it: 'the average Muslim projects the burden of morality onto the law'.[78]

The sharia remains central to the legal systems of a minority of Muslim-majority states, including Saudi Arabia, Iran, Sudan, and Afghanistan, but has been abolished, modified, or marginalized by most. However, sharia courts, offering a form of Alternative Dispute Resolution outside the official legal system for those who engage with them either voluntarily or under pressure from their families and/or communities, have been growing in significance in a number of western countries. According to an investigation conducted by *The Times* in 2024, with some 85 such institutions, the UK has become 'the western capital' for the administration of traditional Islamic law. Staffed almost exclusively by panels of male Islamic scholars and dealing mostly with family-related matters, they typically dispense a particularly conservative interpretation of the sharia potentially applying to 100,000 Muslim marriages

---

[74] J. Schacht, *An Introduction to Islamic Law* (Clarendon Press, 1982), pp. 70-71.

[75] Akyol, *Reopening Muslim Minds*, p. 72.

[76] Ibid., p. 12.

[77] Ibid., p. 46.

[78] A. Fadl, *Reasoning with God: Reclaiming Shari'ah in the Modern Age* (Rowman & Littlefield, 2014), p. 201.

many unregistered with the civil authorities.[79] Critics have argued that sharia courts enable men to oppress women in the guise of religious piety. Some advocate their abolition. Others have called for more effective regulation including the provision of enforceable codes of conduct.

According to Ibn Qayyin al-Jawziyya (1292-1350):

'Sharia is all about wisdom and achieving people's welfare in this life and the afterlife. It is all about justice, mercy, wisdom and good. Thus, any ruling that replaces justice with injustice, mercy with its opposite, common good with mischief, or wisdom with nonsense, is a ruling that does not belong to the sharia, even if it is claimed to be so according to some interpretation'.[80]

Taking their cue from this conception, a team of US-based Muslim academics annually ranks the countries of the world in the 'Islamicity Indices' according to what they take to be the core underlying values of the sharia, such as safety, security, socio-economic justice, health care, and the business environment. Those states which consistently score highest are New Zealand, Sweden, the Netherlands, and Ireland, not Saudi Arabia, Iran or Afghanistan. In fact, no Muslim majority country has yet appeared in the top forty.[81]

Fatwas

While not strictly sources of law, fatwas are the non-binding legal opinions of respected individual Muslim jurists and scholars (*muftis*)— typically triggered by specific events or requests for guidance from those seeking to lead a Godly life. While the most well-known in the recent past was the death sentence imposed upon Sir Salman Rushdie by the Ayatollah Khomeini for the alleged blasphemy contained in the former's novel *The Satanic Verses*, most are a lot less controversial. In fact, many deal with surprisingly trivial matters such as the permissibility of showering while standing, appearing naked in front of animals including birds, which finger to start with when cutting finger nails, and how to conceal oneself from jinn

---

[79] D. Kennedy, 'Britain revealed as "western capital" for use of sharia courts' and 'Polygamous husbands hold wives to ransom with sharia', *The Times*, 19 December 2024.
[80] Quoted in J. Auda, 'Realizing Maqasid in the Shariah', in I. Nassery, R. Ahmed & M. Tatari eds., *The Objectives of Islamic Law: The Promises and Challenges of the Maqasid al-Sharia* (Lexington Books, 2018), p. 35.
[81] https://islamicity-index.org/wp/.

(demons) when using the toilet.[82] Before delivering a fatwa, Sunni Islamic scholars refer to the Qur'an, hadith, sunnah, sharia, qiyas, ijma, and fiqh. From the 15th century, Ottoman muftis were increasingly integrated into a semi-official bureaucracy. In contemporary Muslim majority states, they are often incorporated in powerful official institutions. The Egyptian Dar Aliftaa al-Misriyyah, for example, issues some 5,000 fatwas per week. These include high-profile ones delivered by its head, the Grand Mufti, in person, with more mundane ones routinely provided by subordinates, sometimes over the phone or via the internet. The opinions of the Grand Mufti of Egypt are very influential throughout the Arab and Islamic worlds.

Conclusion

Mainstream Muslim beliefs and practices – considered more fully in the following chapter – remain embedded in the traditional formal sources of the Qur'an, hadith, sunnah, the sharia, (as interpreted by the various schools of Islamic jurisprudence), and the fatwas of individual Muslim jurists. Doubts about the reliability of these sources have been raised by responsible and thorough scholarship. This book does not seek to adjudicate between any of the competing claims. It simply maintains that those which are supported by serious scholarship cannot be regarded as Islamophobic. In the west, other faiths and secular ideologies, including Christianity, liberalism, capitalism, communism, populism, and feminism, are also routinely subject to critique regarding their alleged intellectual, moral, political, and other flaws. There are no good reasons why Islam should be any different.

---

[82] Akyol, *Reopening Muslim Minds*, pp. 49-50.

Chapter 4

Muslim beliefs and practices

Introduction

Apart from the Qur'an, there is no consensus amongst Muslims about the authority of any of the traditional sources of the faith. Nor is there universal consensus about precisely how essential beliefs should be derived from any of the traditional sources, core practices observed, and other conduct approved or otherwise. This is the case for several reasons.

First, while all religions recognise intuitive experiences of God, the ineffable, or 'ultimate reality', they must, nevertheless, seek to convey their distinctive understandings in human language. And all languages are inherently imprecise and open to interpretation, a characteristic magnified with respect to any creed, including Islam, which first appeared long ago in an unsystematic oral rather than written form. Furthermore, no ideology has ever emerged fully formed from a vacuum. All belief systems, including Islam, have arisen in specific historical, cultural, social, and political contexts. Not only do they typically absorb features of the milieus in which they first appeared; they also tend to take on some of the characteristics of those to which they later migrate. For example, as noted in the previous chapter, at its birth, Islam bore many of the hallmarks of Zoroastrianism, Judaism, Christianity, and pre-Islamic Arabian culture and religion. It is also said that, as the Sufi branch developed, it was influenced by Buddhism and Hinduism into the bargain.[1] Indeed, Mohammad himself claimed that Islam was not a new religion but merely the revival, purification, and completion of Abraham's original monotheistic faith.

Interpretations of any given ideology will also tend to favour specific social and political perspectives. And those which prevail over their competitors tend to further both the particular interpretation which triumphs

---

[1] See Ch. 5.

and also the material interests this serves. It is, therefore, difficult if not impossible to identify the 'pure' or 'pristine' version of any belief system, including Islam, which has not been affected by these and other factors. Interpretations of any ideology also tend to range from the ultra-orthodox ('fundamentalist') to the heretical, with orthodoxy (the 'mainstream') and heterodoxy in between, distinctions considered more fully in the following chapter.

These issues become even more complex when a given ideology or faith has, like Islam, no stable and enduring institution – other than the majority of those who regard themselves as its most faithful adherents – recognised as having the authority to distinguish between orthodoxy, heterodoxy, and heresy. Furthermore, as with any other religion or secular ideology, belief in Islam spans a spectrum. At one end lies fanatical insistence upon observance of the minutest detail, and at the other, 'nominalism', including failure to comply with even the most central elements. The boundary between nominalism and apostasy is not clear cut either. For example, some Muslims, particularly in the west, have limited interest in their religion and give it little thought. While not formally renouncing their faith, and possibly still passively identifying as 'Muslim', 'secular' or 'cultural' Muslim, some eat pork, drink alcohol, and have sex outside marriage, including gay sex.[2] Notwithstanding this, they may, nevertheless, continue to believe in the transcendent Abrahamic God but not much else in the Islamic tradition. It is also a moot point whether any self-identifying Muslims who regard Mohammad's revelations as, at best, divinely-inspired rather than divinely-dictated, have taken themselves outside the ummah altogether. But, if they keep quiet about it and maintain minimum levels of visible conformity, who will know in any case?

It should also be noted that it is not uncommon for more reflective Muslims to accuse their co-religionists of having a poor grasp of their own faith, often attributed to the obscurantism of Muslim scholars and clergy.[3] As Akyol, a devout Turkish Muslim, puts it, a key feature of the 'mainstream

---

[2] D. Henry, *Voices of Modern Islam: What it Means to be Muslim Today* (Jessica Kingsley, 2018), pp. 42, 45, 184, 205-15.

[3] See, eg, T. Hargey, 'Introducing the Oxord Institute for British Islam', in S. Greer & T. Hargey (eds.), *British Islam: A Vision for the Future* (Oxford Institute for British Islam, 2023), pp. 1-2; T. Khan, *Muslim Actually, How Islam is Misunderstood and Why it Matters* (Atlantic, 2022), p. 10.

religious mindset in broad parts of the Muslim world today' is a 'soldier-like obedience to religious texts'. For conservative scholars, the 'true expression of Muslim piety' lies in the slogan: "We hear and we obey, whether we understand or not."[4] This view is echoed by many others, including British Muslim Tawseef Khan who describes his upbringing in the following terms:

'As I got older, the limits imposed on my relationship with Islam became clearer. I wasn't supposed to question doctrine; God had supposedly determined every aspect of our religious practice. To critique Islam, therefore, was to be a bad Muslim who was destined for hell'.[5]

Bearing all of this in mind, this chapter seeks to identify and to discuss core Muslim beliefs and practices found in the mainstream tradition of, particularly orthodox Sunni Islam to which the majority of the world's Muslims subscribe.[6] Needless to say, this will be far from comprehensive. Nor, in spite of the best endeavours of any author could it be entirely free from controversy either. It is virtually inevitable that somebody will say about some element of this account: 'I'm a devout Muslim and I don't believe in what you claim I should!'

It can, nevertheless, be authoritatively stated that the mainstream orthodox tradition is based upon the Five Pillars of Islam: the 'shahadah' – the two testimonies that 'there is no God but Allah and that Mohammad is his prophet' – the sincere declaration of which, ideally in the presence of two witnesses, is all that is required to become a Muslim; 'salat', praying five times a day; 'zakat', a voluntary 'tax' or charitable obligation for the relief of poverty; 'sawm', fasting during Ramadan; and 'hajj', the pilgrimage to Mecca during the month of Dhu-al-Hijah which all Muslims are expected to make at least once in their lifetime if they are physically capable and can afford it.

From these, a number of 'spiritual' or 'metaphysical' beliefs can be identified, plus those regarding the temporal sphere including personal and social life. The former concern Allah, particularly His 'Oneness' and the destiny He has decreed for the cosmos, individuals, and humanity as a whole,

---

[4] M. Akyol, *Reopening Muslim Minds: A Return to Reason, Freedom and Tolerance* (Forum, 2022), p. 27.
[5] Khan, *Muslim Actually*, p. 1.
[6] See, eg, P. Stewart, *Unfolding Islam* (Garnet, 2nd edn., 2008); D. Morgan, *Essential Islam: A Comprehensive Guide to Belief and Practice* (Praeger, 2010),

angels and other supernatural beings, prophesy and revelation, the day of judgment, and the afterlife of heaven and hell.[7] Norms governing personal conduct include such things as the prohibition upon drinking alcohol, how to kill animals for human consumption (and which to avoid for this purpose), ritual cleanliness prior to worship, how to drink a glass of water, which foot should enter the bathroom first, how to treat physical copies of the Qur'an, and how to behave when it is being read aloud. Needless to say, not all Muslims treat these with equal respect. The mainstream tradition also has distinctive implications for, amongst other things, governance, the economy, sex, marriage, family life, the position of women, rights, and armed conflict which are of central importance for the debate about the distinction between the expression of anti-Muslim prejudice and legitimate critique of Muslims and Islam.

As with the issues discussed in the previous chapter, much of this has been subject to vigorous debate and criticism over the centuries, by and from Muslims and non-Muslims. And, as already indicated, it is not the purpose of this study to claim that any of the perspectives which have emerged is right or wrong. Instead, both this chapter and this study in general, simply seek to demonstrate that well-grounded doubts and criticism have been made about core Muslim beliefs by responsible Muslim and non-Muslim scholars alike which cannot plausibly be regarded as 'Islamophobic'.

The metaphysical realm

The most fundamental of Muslim beliefs relate to the metaphysical or supernatural realms which broadly concern the putative reality behind the observable material world – particularly the nature and purpose of God and associated spiritual issues which have no direct or obvious implications for public policy, other than that their peaceful expression is not hindered. As Chapters 7-9 demonstrate, they do not, therefore, feature prominently or at all in the Islamophobia debate. However, in the interests of completeness, they are briefly reviewed here.[8]

---

[7] Morgan, *Essential Islam*, p. 1.

[8] Eg, P. Holt, A. Lambton & B. Lewis (eds.), *The Cambridge History of Islam* (Cambridge University Press, 1970); C. Horrie & P. Chippendale, *What Is Islam?* (W.H. Allen, 1990); K. Armstrong, *Islam: A Short History* (Phoenix, 2001); M. Ruthven, *Islam: A Very Short Introduction*, 2nd edn., (Oxford University Press, 2012);

The nature and purpose of God

The bedrock of Islam, enshrined in the shahada, is the assumption that there is only one true God (Allah) and that the mission of Mohammad, and all true prophets who preceded him, has been to bring humanity to this realization, to urge them to act properly upon it, and to warn them of the dire consequences of failing to do so. To reject the oneness and unity of God (*tawhid*) by comparing Him to other gods, or to humans claiming to represent Him, is idolatrous and constitutes the unforgivable 'sin of association' (*shirk*). According to the orthodox Islamic tradition this is committed by, amongst others, Buddhists, Hindus, Sikhs and Confucianists as well as by atheists, agnostics, humanists, and Marxists. The doctrine of the trinity also puts Christianity at risk of falling on the wrong side of the line. While representations of Allah are not prohibited by the Qur'an, they are generally regarded as dangerously close to idolatry and are, therefore, strongly discouraged.[9]

In addition to His Oneness, Allah is said to have several other characteristics, generally acknowledged by the wider Abrahamic tradition. He is Infinite, Eternal, Omnipotent, Omniscient, Ever-present, perfectly Righteous, Merciful, and the Creator of all that exists, has ever existed, and will ever exist. He demands unquestioning devotion, obedience, and worship and can do anything that is logically possible, a self-imposed restriction to make the Universe function coherently.

Supernatural beings

In addition to God, the Qur'an also acknowledges the existence of Satan and two other kinds of supernatural being – angels and *jinn* (singular *jinni*). There are said to be billions of the former with at least one residing inside the skull of everyone on earth. Some angels have particular responsibilities, including moving the sun and moon around the sky, delivering thunderbolts, recording everyone's thoughts, words and deeds as evidence for the Day of Judgment, making sure we each die when Allah has ordained it, and liaising between Him and each of us. Angels are incapable of sin or error and, lacking free will, have no choice but to obey God.

D. Morgan, *Essential Islam*; E. Husain, *The House of Islam: A Global History* (Bloomsbury, 2018).
[9] Morgan, *Essential Islam*, pp. 3-4.

However, when God created Adam, Satan – King of the Angels – is said to have done just that. Out of jealousy for the special relationship God had established with humanity, he is alleged to have rebelled against God, refused to serve humankind as God commanded, and as a result, was ejected from Heaven. Bitter and spiteful, we are told he has since vowed to destroy humanity by leading people into sin, including through false prophets and false 'divine' revelations. According to the orthodox Islamic tradition, the only way to be protected from these deceptions is for the faithful to fill their hearts and minds with the worship of God leaving no room for Satan to lead them astray.

Jinn, who are made of fire and tend to live in desolate and unclean parts of the earth, have some free will, are born, procreate, and die, and will also be judged on the Last Day. Few will end up in heaven. While some leave humans alone, others plague them with temptation to do wrong and are also responsible for sterility, mental illness, and epilepsy. Mostly invisible, they can nevertheless assume the form of humans, snakes, scorpions, and lizards. Having spied upon angels, they can also influence fortune-tellers, astrologers, Tarrot card readers and the like without their knowledge. While some of the information they provide about the future might be true, most is false.

Prophesy and revelation

Mainstream Islam distinguishes between 'Messengers', who have received a scripture from Allah, and 'Prophets', who have given themselves completely to God and to spread His word. For Muslims, Prophets have three functions: to receive divine revelations, to live exemplary lives, and to teach others to do likewise. While all Messengers are Prophets, not all Prophets are Messengers. Mohammad claimed to be the last in a long line of 124,000 Prophets of Islam. Twenty-five of these – all from the Judeo-Christian tradition from Adam to Jesus including Abraham and Moses – are mentioned in the Qur'an. However, orthodox Muslims acknowledge only three Messengers – Moses, Jesus, and Mohammad. Jesus – whose virgin birth, miracles, and crucifixion Muslims accept, but whose death on the cross and whose divinity, resurrection, and atonement are denied – is nevertheless revered as the greatest of all Messengers preceding Mohammad. Since the orthodox Islamic tradition regards the Qur'an as God's final and perfect revelation to humanity, any discrepancy between it and anything found in other books of revelation such as the Torah and the Gospels must be resolved in its favour.

The Day of Judgment, heaven and hell

At the time of Mohamad's revelations, Jewish and Christian tradition each calculated that the world was approximately 5,500 years old. Christians traditionally believe that God will end it all when He judges the living and the dead, and decides who to send to hell and who to paradise.[10] Initially, Muslims thought this would occur at the beginning of the 12th century, some 6,000 years after creation. When it did not happen, a theological crisis occurred, resulting in sectarian fragmentation further to that which had already taken place.

According to the mainstream Islamic tradition, the Day of Judgment will be preceded by the Last Days, the details of which are foretold by various hadith. This era will begin with Islam splitting into many rival sects and the sharia being ignored or overthrown. Anarchy, violence, crime and inhumanity will be rampant. God will then send the 'chosen one', the Messiah (*Mahdi*) to lead an army of the faithful from Mecca to Jerusalem where, installed as ruler of the world, he will restore order, peace, justice, and the Qur'anic rule of law.

However, the reign of the Mahdi will last for less than a decade after which the one-eyed anti-Christ will appear, legalizing sin, healing the sick, providing food and material comfort for everyone, and performing pseudo-miracles. But just as he is about to destroy the last surviving minority of true Muslims, Jesus will appear in armour and will defeat the anti-Christ at the battle of Armageddon ('Mount Megiddo') in Palestine, inaugurating an era of peace and plenty. But this will not last either. Jesus will die and Allah will destroy the earth and initiate the Day of Judgment.

The Qur'an is replete with lurid descriptions of the suffering of the damned in hell, including being flayed alive on a daily basis with fresh skin rapidly growing in order for the whole process to repeat for eternity. By contrast, heaven is depicted as a sensual male paradise with, for example, unlimited but non-intoxicating wine,[11] and 'damsels with swelling breasts for companions',[12] where the saved with be waited upon by 'young boys ... as

---

[10] Horrie & Chippendale, *What Is Islam?*, p. 31.
[11] Qur'an 46:10-22,
[12] Ibid. 31-33.

fair as virgin pearls'.[13] It is not clear if these delectable waiters and waitresses are also available for sex with either men or women. However, the Qur'an contains no express female sexual fantasies.

According to the orthodox tradition, pious Muslims martyred in defence of the faith, do not die but are suspended in a state of bliss until the Day of Judgment from whence they will enter paradise, richly rewarded, without having to be judged. There is some debate about whether or not they will have exclusive sexual access to virgins. But the Qur'an certainly does not promise 72, a tradition derived from the hadith.

Thorny questions for all Abrahamic faiths, and indeed for some secular philosophies as well, arise from assumptions about the apparently deterministic character of existence. Deriving from deeply rooted Bedouin fatalism, Islam faces two particular challenges. One concerns the source of evil. If Allah is all-powerful and nothing happens against His will, where does evil, including the unforgivable sin of idolatry, come from? If He did not create sin, is He therefore, not responsible for the existence of a significant feature of reality? If so, this appears to mean that He is not omnipotent after all. But if He did create sin, is He not responsible for the very behaviour which will ultimately consign sinners to hell?

The problem is compounded by another central Islamic belief. If God knows everything about the past, present, and future, there is no such thing as 'chance', and nothing can happen against His will. Therefore, no matter what we do, we have no prospect of ensuring that we go to heaven and avoid going to hell because, one way or the other, Allah has already willed it. Yet, if this is the case, how can it be reconciled with God's compassion, mercy, and commitment to perfect justice? And if this is true, would it not simply be more efficient to send everyone directly to their eternal destination when they die, without a trial which cannot possibly affect the outcome anyway, or to send them there from birth, or create them in the respective realms in the first place? In its turn, this raises several other questions. For example, unlike the angels who have no choice in the matter, why would God create humanity – with the freedom to choose whether or not to worship Him – having foreordained that this will make no difference to where they spend eternity? While some Muslim scholars have insisted upon the consistency of free will with the

---

[13] Ibid. 52: 24.

omnipotence of God, most have settled for determinism.[14]

It has often been observed with respect to any faith which endorses it, that the threat of eternal damnation and the promise of eternal paradise provide very powerful incentives for the institutions of state and religion to enforce obedience to their authority here on earth.

Prayer, worship, and other rituals

The Five Pillars include three of the core orthodox Islamic religious rituals – obligatory prayer in the direction of Mecca preceded by ritual cleansing, fasting during Ramadan, and the hajj to Mecca. Other norms, derived from the hadith and sharia, deal with the finer details. As already indicated in the previous chapter, the orthodox tradition regards the obligation to pray at least five times daily as the result of negotiation between Mohammad and the Almighty on the Night Journey of 621. Communal prayer is also obligatory for men on Friday afternoons. No particular building is required for either prayer or worship. A clean space sufficiently large for prostration is sufficient.

In order to deepen their spiritual awareness, during the 30-day month in which Ramadan is observed, the ninth in the Islamic lunar calendar, the mainstream tradition expects Muslims to refrain from eating, drinking (including water), smoking, and having sex, from sunrise to sunset. There are exemptions for the sick, nursing mothers, and travellers. The Qur'an permits a particularly large breakfast before dawn. And the month-long fast ends with the feast of *Eid al-Fitr*. Muslims living in the far north or south, face a particular challenge when Ramadan falls in mid-summer and daylight can last for almost twenty-four hours. The feast of *Eid al-Adha*, which lasts for four days during Dhu al-Hija, the tenth month in the Islamic calendar, celebrates Abraham's willingness to sacrifice his son Isaac. On both occasions Muslims traditionally greet each other with the phrase *Eid Mubarak*, meaning 'blessed feast/festival'.

At least once in their lifetime, if they are physically capable and can afford it, every Muslim is expected to make a pilgrimage (*hajj*) during the month of Dhu al-Hija to the Kaaba – a cube-shaped stone building in Mecca. Muslims believe this was built by Adam for the exclusive worship of Allah but subsequently degenerated into a shrine to what became the Arab pantheon. In

---

[14] Morgan, *Essential Islam*, pp. 5-9, 11.

addition to other elements, pilgrims circumambulate the structure seven times, typically attempting to touch a large black stone, about a metre square, said to have been inserted in one corner by Mohammad.

There is no specified form of clothing in mainstream Islam. Both men and women are expected to dress modestly and to keep their heads covered at all times, a sign of respect for the angels said to live inside everyone's skull. The items of clothing traditionally worn by Muslim women – including the *hijab* (head scarf), *niqab* (face veil) and *burqa* (full head-to-toe covering including a mesh for the eyes) – derive from the hadith and are not prescribed by the Qur'an. The various legal traditions also take different views on the matter.[15] Adherents to the orthodox tradition also observe specific funeral rites, wedding ceremonies, and other customs most of which stem from a fusion of religious and cultural norms.

The temporal sphere

In common with all religions, Islam has implications for the temporal as well as the spiritual dimension. For two reasons, these are the most controversial issues in the debate about where the line between Islamophobic expression and legitimate critical appraisal of Muslims and their faith should be drawn. First, they raise issues, such as the position of women and human rights more generally, central to policy debates in the west. Second, there is also a great deal of confusion about what precisely the policy implications of orthodox Islam are, not least because many of these are disputed by Muslims themselves.

Governance

Apart from being required to comply with the Qur'an, there is no systematically articulated theory of legitimate governance in mainstream Islam. Broadly speaking, over the past millennium and a half, the faith has taken two principal political paths, one in the core and the other in the periphery. As already intimated in Chapter 2, from the mid-7th century to the end of the Ottoman empire in the early 20th century, 'imperial absolutism' dominated the Muslim empires of north Africa, the Mediterranean, the middle east, and central Asia. The Caliph exercised absolute power, unlimited except

---

[15] Ibn Warraq, *Why I Am Not A Muslim* (Prometheus Reprint, 2003), p. 315.

by the orthodox sources of the faith which, guided by the ulama (the community of Islamic scholars), he alone had the ultimate right to interpret and apply. However, given the vast territorial reach of the imperial dominions, the Caliph was compelled to delegate his authority to local war lords (*emirs*) and governors (*sultans*), some of whom harboured ambitions to become Caliph themselves. In the 19th century the Ottomans began to experiment with liberalization and a limited degree of democratization. But apart from this, there has been little of either in the entire history of the Muslim world.

Several features of the mainstream Islamic faith militate against representative government. First, the very essence of the former is that God commands and the faithful submissively obey. There is no scope for negotiation about basics or details, much less for collective, legislative self-governance. Indeed, since the Islamic idea of God resembles that of 'cosmic absolute emperor', it would have been difficult if not impossible for orthodox Islam to have generated a model for temporal governance based on significantly different assumptions. Second, mainstream Islam provides little or no room for the separation of religion and state. Each is inextricably an expression of the other. Third, the entire institutional and legal framework is set in stone for all time with no scope for change. The key institution of governance is, therefore, not an executive accountable to a democratically-elected legislature supervised by independent courts, but the ulama, the community of Islamic scholars which claims to be able to discern the implications of every Divine command in minute detail. As Ibn Warraq puts it:

> 'autocracy and Islam are far more natural bedfellows than Islam and democracy. Democracy depends upon freedom of thought and free discussion, whereas Islamic law explicitly forbids the discussion of decisions arrived at by the infallible consensus of the ulama'.[16]

Fourth, in the 7th and 8th centuries, few Muslims or anybody else considered if public power should be more democratically accountable. Although Arab tribal leaders could consult a tribal council, particularly before making difficult decisions, there was no mechanism in traditional Arabia for any significant democratic control over executive decision-making. At the dawn of the Islamic revolution, the ancient Greek democracies had long since been conquered by Rome, and Greece itself was then at the heart of the Byzantine

---

[16] Ibid., p. 181.

empire. Although the Muslim world discovered the ideas of ancient Hellas a few centuries later, it is doubtful if much, if anything, was known about ancient Greek political theory in Arabia or elsewhere in the 7th century, including in Greece itself. In any case, even if the Arabs had been more aware of the Greek experience, as polytheistic societies Mohammad and his companions are unlikely to have regarded them with much, if any, sympathy.

The other political path concerns what happened in the 'periphery', principally south Asia. As already indicated in Chapter 2, things were more complicated here because Islam spread into this region much more gradually through trade and conversion rather than armed conquest. Prevented from assuming an imperial form it was compelled, therefore, to make various compromises with other civilizations, cultures, and religions.[17]

No reliable social scientific estimate considers any Muslim majority state in the contemporary world to be 'fully democratic'. The Economist Democracy Index 2023 nevertheless judged three – Albania, Indonesia, and Malaysia – to be 'flawed democracies'.[18] Based on 60 democracy-related indicators, the Index classes 167 of the UN's 193 states as either 'full democracies', 'flawed democracies', 'hybrid regimes' or 'authoritarian regimes'. 'Full democracies' are those where civil liberties and fundamental political freedoms are protected by effective systems of government including by functioning institutional checks and balances, decisions enforceable by independent courts, a diverse and independent media, plus a political culture which actively supports democratic principles. In 'flawed democracies' elections are fair and free, and civil liberties are generally well protected. But weaknesses may include the functioning of governance, infringements upon media freedom, minor suppression of political opposition and critics, an underdeveloped political culture, and low levels of political participation. Of the Muslim majority nations, Malaysia ranks 40th in the full league table, Indonesia 54th and Albania 64th, all in the same category as Greece (25th), the US (30th), Italy (34th), and Belgium (36th).

All other states with Muslim majorities are ranked as either 'hybrid' or 'authoritarian' regimes. Typically, as a result of electoral fraud, widespread corruption, harassment of political opponents, official pressure on the media, a lack of judicial independence, a weak rule of law, and other difficulties more

---

[17] S. Aljunied (ed.), *Routledge Handbook of Islam in Southeast Asia* (Routledge, 2022).
[18] https://www.eiu.com/n/campaigns/democracy-index-2023/.

profound than those in flawed democracies, 'hybrid regimes' do not have free and fair elections. Although 'authoritarian regimes', typically absolute monarchies or dictatorships, may have some superficially democratic institutions there is no, or very limited, political pluralism, elections are not free and fair, the judiciary is not independent, there are widespread abuses of civil liberties especially with respect to criticism of the regime, and the media is often owned by the state or by those closely allied with it.

Economy

Mainstream Islam has three specific implications for economic activity. It must conform with the sharia, taxes – particularly the poverty-relieving zakat – must be paid, and it must avoid the charging of interest on loans (*riba*). It has been argued that the result is a mixed economy, or a 'third way' between socialism and capitalism which encourages entrepreneurial activity, enhances prosperity for all, narrows the gap between rich and poor, discourages the speculative hoarding of wealth particularly food, protects lenders from risk through profit-sharing and venture capital, and discourages unlawful confiscation of land and other activities Islam regards as sinful.[19]

Akyol maintains that the concept of a 'religious' or 'moral' police of the kind that is integral to the enforcement of Sunni Islam in Saudi Arabia and Iran's Shia Islam, grew out of the initially limited responsibilities of overseer or inspector of the market originally appointed by the Prophet to ensure fair commercial dealing.[20] However, over time, the role was expanded – ostensibly to fulfil the Qur'anic injunction to 'command right and forbid wrong' (*hisbah*) – because it provided an attractive means of social, moral, and religious control, including the confiscation and destruction of wine, the silencing of music, the enforcement of prayer and fasting, and the separation of the sexes in public.

Akyol argues that this has had two very negative consequences for contemporary Muslim states and societies. First, it legitimizes the imposition on all Muslims of a single, and possibly disputed, interpretation of the faith. The second concerns the hypocrisy and resentment this tends to engender. In such places, the hypocrisy in question manifests in the recruitment and

---

[19] K. Ishaque, 'Islamic Approach to Economic Development' in J. Esposito (ed.), *Voices of Resurgent Islam* (Oxford University Press, 1983), pp. 268–276.
[20] Akyol, *Reopening Muslim Minds*, p. 180-188.

promotion of state employees on the basis of professed piety, which may be manufactured and insincere, rather than upon professional competence. This naturally breeds resentment and cynicism on the part of others, particularly those with more appropriate skills.[21]

Sex, marriage, and the family

The attitude of orthodox Islam to sex has been the subject of much debate. Some commentators have contrasted its allegedly less prudish outlook with the putatively more negative and censorious Christian view. Others have claimed that it embodies a quintessentially masculine vision which regards women as fundamentally subservient.[22]

The Qur'an forbids celibacy for men, and while seeking to regulate sex, neither glorifies nor demonizes it. Orthodox Islam assumes that sex should ideally be practiced only between husbands and wives and regards marriage as a civil contract rather than a sacrament. Although generally arranged by the parents of the intended spouses, the consent of both parties is, nevertheless, required. Chastity is expected outside marriage, including between fiancés.

Both the Qur'an and hadith permit men to have up to four wives simultaneously. However, this does not include slave concubines upon which there is no stipulated limit.[23] At any given time, a woman may only have one husband, and he must be Muslim. As verse 4:3 of the Qur'an states, polygamy is conditional:

> 'If you fear that you may not deal justly with the orphans, then marry [other] women that you like, two, three, or four. But if you fear that you may not treat them fairly, then [marry only] one, or [marry from among] your slave-women. That makes it likelier that you will not be unfair'.

This stipulation reflects both a pre-Islamic Arab convention and the fact that, as a child, Mohammad was himself an orphan. It also served to provide for those whose fathers, and those whose husbands, had been killed in jihad. In practice the vast majority of Muslim men today have only one wife.[24] And,

---

[21] Ibid., pp. 192-4.
[22] Ibn Warraq, *Why I Am Not A Muslim*, p. 291.
[23] Qur'an 4:3.
[24] Pew Research Center, *Religion and Living Arrangements Around the World*, 12 December 2019, pp. 84-5.

if they have a second, the reason is usually that the first has been unable to bear children. The marriage contract may also prohibit the husband-to-be from marrying other women. Sunni, though not Shia, men are permitted to marry Christian or Jewish women. Marriage is also allowed between first cousins. The Qur'an also 'made lawful' for Mohammad to have more or less as many consenting wives as he chose, plus 'the slave-girls whom Allah has given you as booty'.[25] It also permits military victors to take as wives 'the captives that your right-hand possesses'.[26]

Shia Islam permits temporary marriage which may last for as little as a single night or a few hours.[27] Children born as a result are considered legitimate, have equal legal status with the siblings of more permanent marriages, and may inherit from either or both parents. When a temporary marriage ends, women must observe a period of celibacy in order to identify the father of any child thus conceived. Some, particularly young Muslims in the west, find temporary marriages an attractive way of having multiple sexual partners without feeling guilty about, or being accused of, promiscuity. Sunni Islam also recognises another type of marriage, *nikah misyar*, conducted through the normal contractual procedure, in which the couple continue to live separately as before, seeing each other only to fulfil their sexual needs in a legally permissible manner. While most Islamic scholars accept the practice, others regard it as legal but immoral.[28]

According to the sharia a man may divorce his wife by simply saying three times, 'I divorce you', while a woman can only divorce her husband through formal legal proceedings. Although the classical jurists did not require the husband to provide a justification or evidence, much less to obtain official approval, they, nevertheless, required a compelling cause, such as the impossibility of cohabitation due to irreconcilable conflict. Certain other conditions must be satisfied for valid repudiation. For example, the declaration must be made in clear terms and the husband must be of sound mind and not coerced.

Homosexuality is prohibited by the Qur'an upon pain of expulsion from the ummah.[29] The Qur'an also requires 'indecency' – which is not defined but

---

[25] Qur'an, 33:50.

[26] Ibid., 4:3.

[27] Morgan, *Essential Islam*, p. 207.

[28] A. Tago, 'Misyar now "a widespread reality,"' *Arab News*, 12 October 2014.

[29] Qur'an 4:15-16; 7: 80-84; Morgan, *Essential Islam*, p. 202.

appears to mean intimacy between people of the same sex which goes beyond expressions of friendly or familial affection – to be punished. The penalty is more severe for women (being confined to their homes 'until death takes them or Allah appoints' an unspecified 'way') than for men (being punished and 'if they repent and make amends, then suffer them to be'), also unspecified.[30] In several contemporary Muslim-majority states, homosexual acts are punishable by death, though such sentences are rare, and even when passed, are not often carried out.[31] However, in practice Islamic civilization has tolerated both homosexuality and wine-drinking for centuries.[32] A review of survey research conducted in 2018 about Muslims in Britain found that, although attitudes amongst the youth were more liberal than their older co-religionists, 52% of all those surveyed did not agree that homosexuality should be legal.[33]

The position of women

It is widely, though not universally recognised that, by comparison with both pre-Islamic Arabia and with other then contemporary societies, the emergence of Islam in the 7th century greatly improved the position of women particularly regarding property, inheritance, divorce, the prohibition of female infanticide, and the reduction in the number of wives to which any man was entitled. However, most commentators who take this view also agree that progress on this front soon stagnated and that, as a result, 'in general women have an inferior place in Islamic culture' by comparison with the modern west.[34] For example, Ascha claims that 'Islam is the fundamental cause of the repression of Muslim women and remains the major obstacle to the evolution of their position'.[35] However, others argue that, across the Muslim world, there are significant differences in how women are treated.[36]

The Qur'an itself assumes that men and women have different social roles

---

[30] Qur'an 4:15-16.

[31] ILGA, *7 countries still put people to death for same-sex acts*, 29 October 2009.

[32] Ibn Warraq, *Why I Am Not A Muslim*, p. 2; Husain, *House of Islam*, p. 75.

[33] Ipsos MORI Social Research Institute, *A Review of survey research on Muslims in Britain: Research report of the Aziz Foundation, Barrow Cadbury Trust, the Joseph Rowntree Charitable Trust, and Unbound Philanthropy* (Ipsos MORI, 2018), p. 63.

[34] Morgan, *Essential Islam*, p. 199; Husain, *House of Islam*, Ch. 15.

[35] G. Ascha, *Du statut inférieur de la femme en Islam* (L'Harmattan, 1987), p. 11.

[36] See, eg, G. Brooks, *Nine Parts of Desire: The Hidden World of Islamic Women* (Doubleday, 1994).

and, although equal before God, women are and should be, subordinate to men in both private and public spheres.[37] Surah 4 states, for example:

> 'Men are in charge of women by [right of] what Allah has given one over the other and what they spend [for maintenance] from their wealth. So righteous women are devoutly obedient, guarding in [the husband's] absence what Allah would have them guard. But those [wives] from whom you fear arrogance – [first] advise them; [then if they persist], forsake them in bed; and [finally], strike them. But if they obey you [once more], seek no means against them. Indeed, Allah is ever Exalted and Grand'.[38]

The original Arabic term *wadribuhunna* can be translated as 'to go away from them', 'beat', 'strike lightly', or 'separate', itself an illustration of the lack of precision in the text.[39] This has led some scholars to conclude that, since the purpose of 'striking' wives in these circumstances is to express frustration rather than to injure or cause pain, only a twig or leaf should be used. The problem, however, is not simply that the Qur'an appears to endorse wife beating but that its ambivalence offers a possible excuse for those Muslim husbands who might seek to justify their own conduct in this respect.

Some Muslim traditions, ostensibly on the borderline between orthodox and ultra-orthodox, prohibit or discourage female education, including basic literacy.[40] Many hadith also affirm that the role of women is to stay at home, to be at the beck and call of their fathers, husbands, and sons, to obey their husbands without question and to provide them with tranquility and sexual fulfilment upon demand. For example:

> 'The woman who dies and with whom the husband is satisfied will go to paradise'; 'A wife should never refuse herself to her husband even if it is on the saddle of a camel'; 'Hellfire appeared to me in a dream and I noticed that it was above all peopled with women who had been ungrateful'; 'Three things can interrupt prayers if they pass in front of someone praying: a black dog, a woman, and an ass'.[41]

---

[37] Qur'an 4:1.
[38] Ibid., 4.34.
[39] A. Chaudhry, *Domestic Violence and the Islamic Tradition*, (Oxford University Press, 2013), p. 106; N. Ammar, 'Wife Battery in Islam: A Comprehensive Understanding of Interpretations' (2007) 13 *Violence Against Women* 519–23.
[40] Ibn Warraq, *Why I Am Not A Muslim*, p. 317.
[41] Ibid., pp. 298-9, 301.

Amongst other things, the fourth Caliph, Ali (600-61), Mohammad's cousin and son-in-law, reputedly said: 'The entire woman is an evil and what is worse is that it is a necessary evil!', and 'You should never ask a woman her advice because her advice is worthless'.[42]

Women's testimony in matters requiring witnesses is formally equal to half that of a man. According to the Qur'an:

> 'When you deal with each other in transactions involving future obligations in a fixed period of time, reduce them to writing (and) … if the party liable is mentally deficient, or weak, or unable himself to dictate, let his guardian dictate faithfully, and get two witnesses, out of your own men, and if there are not two men, then a man and two women, such as ye choose, for witnesses, so that if one of them errs, the other can remind her….'[43]

Some jurists maintain that this applied only to financial transactions which, in Mohammad's day, would have been dominated by men, and that in other circumstances, a woman's testimony was, and remains, fully equal to that of a man. It should not be forgotten, however, that the Prophet's first wife, Khadija, was a successful business woman in her own right.

The Qur'an also permits women only half the inheritance of a man: 'Allah instructs you concerning your children: for the male, what is equal to the share of two females'.[44] However, women are allowed to spend or to save whatever they inherit as only men are required to support their spouses and families financially. Communal prayers on Friday afternoons are optional for women. But if they choose to participate, it must be in a part of the mosque separate from the men. Orthodox Islam does not permit women to lead Friday prayers.

A hadith also claims that there will be many more women than men in Hell because, as Mohammad is alleged to have observed, they curse frequently, are ungrateful to their husbands, and lack common sense.[45] Mainstream Islam does not formally endorse female circumcision, a tradition practiced by some Muslim communities in Egypt, Mali, Guinea, and Sudan but not in Iran, Iraq, or Saudi Arabia. Although mentioned in a hadith, the custom is not referred to in the Qur'an.

---

[42] Ibid., p. 299.
[43] Qur'an 2:282.
[44] Ibid., 4:11.
[45] Morgan, *Essential Islam*, pp. 199, 211.

Ibn Warraq sums up what orthodox, and particularly ultra-orthodox, Islam forbids women from doing:

> '(1) be a head of state; (2) be a judge; (3) be an imam; (4) be a guardian; (5) leave her house without permission of her guardian or husband; (6) have a tête-a-tête with a strange man; (7) shake a man's hand; (8) put on makeup or perfume outside the house; (9) uncover her face for fear of "temptation" ; (10) travel alone; (11) inherit the same amount as a man – she must make do with half; (12) bear witness in cases of hudud … and accept that her testimony is worth only half that of a man; (13) perform the religious rituals when menstruating; (14) choose where she will live before she is ugly or old; (15) marry without permission from her guardian; (16) marry a non-Muslim; and (17) divorce her spouse'.[46]

While none of these is enforceable in states which are not governed by the sharia, in other contexts they may, nevertheless, remain matters of variable cultural expectation, with the violation of some attracting more censure than others.

It is not difficult to find, in mainstream British Islam, evidence of traditional attitudes towards the roles of men and women which do not sit well with contemporary western standards.[47] Ipsos MORI's 2018 review found, for example, that close to half of Muslim men and a third of Muslim women agree that 'wives should always obey their husbands'.[48] A British sharia council also permits men to divorce their wives by simply telling them three times, on a single occasion or on several, 'I divorce you', a traditional Islamic practice now banned by many Muslim-majority states. Seeking to encourage compliance with traditional Islamic legal norms, an app is now available in the UK with a drop-down menu enabling men to indicate how much they wish to bequeath each of their wives up to a total of four. Fathers are also reminded that daughters are entitled to only half that of sons.

More extreme attitudes are also prevalent. For instance, one of the most prominent sharia courts in the UK was established by radical preacher, Haitham al-Haddad, who said in an online lecture that 'a man should not be

---

[46] Ibn Warraq, *Why I Am Not a Muslim*, p. 320.

[47] See M. Manson, *Mission and misogyny: Religious charities promoting sexism, patriarchy and violence against women* (National Secular Society, September 2025).

[48] Ipsos MORI Social Research Institute, *Review of survey research on Muslims in Britain*, p. 66.

questioned why he hit his wife because this is something between them' with which outsiders should not interfere.[49] In September 2024, a similar view was expressed in a sermon delivered by Mahamed Abdur Razaq at a mosque run by Birmingham's An-Noor Masjid and Community Centre (a registered charity) and uploaded to YouTube. The preacher told his audience that, providing a wife has been advised and admonished about her marital obligations, forsaken in bed, and no bruising is caused nor any bones broken, a husband may hit and shake her for refusing sex. He added that wives should agree to sex 'straight away' without 'delaying', showing 'dislike', or giving any indication that they had been 'forced to do it'. Those who refuse to comply should, he said, also forfeit their right to *nafaqa*, the husband's financial support. The Charity Commission, to which the National Secular Society reported the matter, said that Abdur Razaq had been suspended and that, having given the mosque 'regulatory advice and guidance', it regarded the case closed.[50] However, Raza was said to have subsequently been hosted by Birmingham's Green Lane mosque which had also received advice from the Charity Commission with respect to similar remarks made by another preacher.[51]

Crime and punishment

As already indicated orthodox Islam distinguishes between that which God mandates, encourages, permits, discourages, and forbids. In the forbidden category a distinction is drawn between sin and crime, the former a matter exclusively for divine sanction and the latter for temporal Islamic authorities. Some conduct may, however, be both. According to a widely accepted hadith, Mohammad is alleged to have regarded the following as the seven most 'destructive major sins': worshipping others in addition to Allah, practicing sorcery, wife-murder, benefitting from usury/interest or the wealth of an orphan, fleeing the battlefield, wrongly accusing believing women of adultery.

However, the Qur'an's principal contributions to criminal justice involves

---

[49] D. Kennedy, "'I feel like I have to pay ransom to get out of my marriage,'" *The Times*, 18 December 2024.

[50] F. Hamilton, 'Mosques "preaching misogyny" while being granted tax perks', *The Times*, 29 September 2025; 'Charity watchdog chided for letting off mosque accused of misogyny, *The Times*, 21 March 2025.

[51] Hamilton, 'Mosques "preaching misogyny."'

listing several particularly serious, *hadd*, offences – unlawful intercourse, false accusations of unlawful intercourse, theft, consuming alcohol, and highway robbery.

Providing greater detail, the sharia has two principal characteristics in the criminal justice and penal fields. First, reflecting the Islamic vision of harsh eternal punishment for the damned in hell, it is generally based upon 'an-eye-for-an-eye-and-a-tooth-for-a-tooth' retribution which offers little opportunity for repentance and rehabilitation. Second, it seeks to replace the typically inter-generational pre-Islamic Arabian blood feud with a highly discretionary state-sponsored alternative administered by arbitrators (*qadis*) rather than by professional formally-trained judges.

The Qur'an is silent about stoning adulterers, punishing those who drink alcohol, and killing those who abandon or insult Islam. Nor does it mention an Islamic state, global caliphate, or religious police which might exact these penalties. The hadith also advise sparing resort to the severe *hudud* punishments – beheading for murder and attempted murder, amputation of the right hand for theft, stoning to death for blasphemy and apostasy, and severe flogging for adultery, false accusation of adultery and drunkenness. Accusations of adultery typically create difficulties both in obtaining judgment and in the consistency of verdicts. As a result, confession or the testimony of four eyewitnesses of unimpeachable moral character is formally required. When the Muslim world succumbed to European colonialism, particularly from the 19th century onwards, more formal legal codes and systems were introduced either in tandem with, or instead of the sharia. In the mid-to-late 20th century some Muslim states, such as Saudi Arabia, Pakistan, and Iran, either retained or re-introduced the hudud punishments, while others, such as Turkey, Tunisia, and Niger excluded the sharia altogether from their legal systems.

Orthodox Islam regards rape as a serious offence. But it is not clearly defined. Proving it can also be difficult because the victim is not allowed to testify. An accusation of rape is also very hazardous for the victim because false accusations of any kind of sexual impropriety, the standard defence of anyone so accused, may also be severely punished.

a) Apostasy

The most serious offence for mainstream Islam is apostasy. According to the sharia this can be committed in several ways in thought, word, or deed.

An express renunciation of the faith is not required. Examples include: mocking God, the prophets, the faith, or the faithful; disrespecting the message of the Qur'an; worshipping in a Christian church; doubting the truth of Islam; converting to another religion including Christianity or Judaism; asserting that Mohammad or any other prophet was an imposter; denying the existence of God; idol worship; rejecting the sharia, or permitting behaviour forbidden by it; eating forbidden foods; drinking alcohol. In theory, orthodox Islam affirms that everyone is born Muslim. Nevertheless, adhering to another faith in adulthood, without ever having been aware of a post-natal Muslim identity, does not count as apostasy.

There is a difference of opinion in mainstream Islam about how apostasy should be addressed. Significantly, although discussing the matter no less than twenty times, the Qur'an itself decrees no earthly punishment at all. In fact, the verse – 'There is no compulsion in religion' – tends to suggest the opposite. However, more than a millennium ago, the mainstream Islamic tradition 'abrogated' this to – 'there shall be no compulsion in religion (in becoming a Muslim)'.[52] A string of hadiths then provided the authority for execution. Other Muslim traditions distinguish between 'minor' and 'major' apostasy, the former referring to loss of faith, which does not merit execution, and the latter to active antagonism towards Islam which does. Equating apostasy with treason, the majority of Muslim scholars take the view that, at least for adults of sound mind, apostasy should be punished by death preceded by imprisonment for a few days to allow time for repentance. In those contemporary Muslim-majority countries, where this is the case, executions are, however, rare. Denunciation as an apostate has also proven to be a very convenient way for Muslim rulers, and contemporary Islamists, to deal with political opponents. It has also been argued that fear of being denounced as an apostate hindered the development of learning, particularly philosophy and the natural sciences, in the Muslim world. As Akyol states:

> 'the punishment of apostasy is the zenith of the coercive tradition within Islamic law. Accordingly, if a Muslim openly renounces his faith, to adopt another religion or no religion, he must be seized and asked to recant. If he doesn't recant, he must be executed. All the four Sunni schools of jurisprudence, along with their Shiite counterparts, unanimously agree on this grim verdict… Worse, these verdicts do

---

[52] Akyol, *Reopening Muslim Minds*, p. 197.

not remain buried in classical books of jurisprudence but shape the laws of more than a dozen contemporary Muslim states'.[53]

A particular contemporary problem with the crime of apostasy is that punishment for changing religion is incompatible with the human right to religious freedom as provided by, for example, Article 18 of the Universal Declaration of Human Rights 1948. Some contemporary Islamic jurists, argue that, for Muslims, changing religion should not be punishable or only under restricted circumstances. However, according to Yohanan Friedmann,

> 'The real predicament facing modern Muslims with liberal convictions is not the existence of stern laws against apostasy in medieval Muslim books of law, but rather the fact that accusations of apostasy and demands to punish it are heard time and again from radical elements in the contemporary Islamic world'.[54]

For example, over 60% of Egyptians and Pakistanis are said to believe that apostates should be executed and adulterers stoned.[55]

b) Blasphemy

As with apostasy, the Qur'an warns about Divine punishment for blasphemy in the afterlife but does not prescribe any specific sanction in this one. In fact, it even cautions against a violent or aggressive response to barefaced insult. As it says: 'When you come across people who speak with scorn about Our revelations, turn away from them until they move on to another topic'.[56]

Orthodox Islam, therefore, regards blasphemy by word or deed – eg casting insulting aspersions upon God, Mohammad, the faith, or the faithful, or mistreating the Qur'an – as a cardinal sin. But, as with apostasy, opinions differ over what to do about it.

In jurisdictions where blasphemy is a criminal offence, obtaining a fair trial is a particular problem because for witnesses, lawyers, judges, reporters and others to repeat what the defendant is alleged to have said, is itself blasphemous. But, as Akyol observes, if this is a correct understanding of the

---

[53] Ibid., pp. 195-6.
[54] Y. Friedmann, *Tolerance and Coercion in Islam: Interfaith Relations in the Muslim Tradition* (Cambridge University Press, 2003), p. 5.
[55] Akyol, *Reopening Muslim Minds*, p. xxii.
[56] Ibid., p. 206.

offence, 'the Qur'an is also full of blasphemy. In fact, outrageous blasphemy'. This is because it repeats the blasphemous reposts from the Meccan polytheists to Mohammad's attempts to convert them.[57] For example, the Meccans are reputed to have said about Mohammad's ministry – 'Receiver of this Qur'an! You are definitely mad. Why do you not bring us the angels if you are telling the truth?'. They also proclaimed that 'this is clearly sorcery' and that 'he has invented it himself', and referred to Allah as being 'tight fisted' and to having fathered a child.[58]

Though not often invoked, mainstream Islamic jurisprudence, which remains influential in some thirty Muslim-majority countries, nevertheless, prescribes death for blasphemy, particularly for insulting the Prophet.[59] However, in common with apostasy, some sources distinguish between the bare verbal offence, on the one hand, and, on the other, blasphemy accompanied by active physical hostility towards Muslims and Islam, which is said to deserve death more than the former.[60]

In Muslim majority countries, whether or not blasphemy is a capital offence, violent mobs may nevertheless impose their own lethal punishment, often on the basis of entirely spurious charges. This is, for example, what happened to Farkhunda Malikzada, a devout 27-year old female Muslim religious teacher murdered by an angry mob outside a mosque in Kabul, Afghanistan.[61] On 19 March 2015, Malikzada confronted mullah Zainuddin for selling good luck amulets, a practice frowned upon by mainstream Islam. Zainuddin retaliated by publicly accusing Malikzada of having burned a copy of the Qur'an. An angry crowd quickly gathered. The police took Malikzada to the roof of another mosque ostensibly for her own safety. But, pelted with missiles, she fell off into the hands of the marauders who bludgeoned her and ran her over in a car. The police, who did nothing to intervene, merely directed traffic away from the scene. Many spectators filmed the brutal murder and shared the footage widely on social media. The mob then dragged Malikzada's body to the banks of the Kabul river where they made an unsuccessful attempt to set it alight. In the immediate aftermath of this horrific event, public opinion was solidly against Malikzada. But it changed to anger

---

[57] Ibid., p. 204.
[58] Ibid.
[59] Ibid., p. 210.
[60] Ibid., pp. 208-9.
[61] BBC, 'Farkhunda: The making of a martyr', 11 August 2015.

and shame when an investigation showed that she had not burned the Qur'an after all. Forty-nine suspects were tried. Some, including Zainuddin, received long prison sentences. Eleven police officers were also convicted but were each sentenced only to a year's imprisonment.

Akyol argues that contemporary Muslims who are eager to punish or silence blasphemy are 'jurisprudentially speaking' on 'shaky grounds', and 'rationally speaking, they are out of their minds'.[62] There are three main reasons. First, they tend to confirm the common complaint against Islam – that it is an intolerant and violent faith. Second, seeking to silence blasphemy tends only to invite more of it. And, third, punishing it enfeebles Muslim societies by thwarting the development of the kind of culture of reasoned and civil responses to criticism which the faith urgently needs.

Rights

In common with all pre-modern moral codes, traditional Islam affirms the primacy of duties over rights and of revelation over reason. Like most moral codes, mainstream Islam also expressly values, amongst other things, life, justice, peace, social order, prosperity, private property, human welfare, and the protection of the weak and vulnerable.

Three positions can be distinguished in the expanding literature on the relationship between mainstream Islam and the human rights paradigm. One, held only by some Muslims, is that Allah revealed to Mohammad a conception of human rights derived from Divinely imposed duties long before the western version appeared. But it is not clear precisely what these rights are, nor what their limits might be. And, according to this view, whatever rights people may have can be rescinded by the Almighty with respect to humanity as a whole or any individual, if ever and whenever He chooses. Nor has traditional Islam sought to provide effective mechanisms for victims to secure remedies for rights violations. Although some contemporary Muslim majority states have made progress in this direction, others – particularly those governed by the sharia – have not. A second perspective is that the contemporary international human rights ideal does not fit a Muslim context at all well. This view differs from the first mainly in that it may be held by both conservative Muslims and some non-Muslim commentators. As already indicated, several areas of friction between the contemporary human rights ideal and mainstream Islam

---

[62] Akyol, *Reopening Muslim Minds*, p. 210.

have been identified – the outlawing of apostasy and blasphemy particularly when enforced by capital punishment, weak recognition of the rights of women and minorities, and the harsh punishments of the more uncompromising interpretations of the sharia.[63]

A third view is that Islamic and non-Islamic approaches to human rights, though different, are not inherently irreconcilable although significant gulfs remain.[64] Under pressure from external sources, the Muslim world has relatively recently, for example, sought to address the human rights challenge.[65] The Arab Charter of Human Rights 2004 – a less conservative attempt than its two predecessors, the Universal Islamic Declaration on Human Rights 1981 and the Cairo Declaration of Human Rights in Islam 1990 – is, of course, 'Arab' rather than 'Muslim'. But some of its distinctive characteristics derive from the influence of the faith. Several achievements have been widely recognised. It is a milestone in the formal recognition of human rights by at least one branch of Islam. Internationally respected experts and NGOs were consulted. It faithfully reproduces many international human rights and establishes monitoring processes similar to those found in UN human rights treaties.

Commentators nevertheless attribute most of its alleged shortcomings to its Islamic influence. It omits several central international human rights or reproduces them in a manner which conflicts with international standards. For example, there is no obligation on states to provide effective national remedies. Some core economic and social rights are limited to citizens. States are obliged to protect from torture, inhuman or degrading treatment, but not punishment, and there is no prohibition on the use of statements extracted by torture. Gender equality is also subordinated to the sharia and to national legal limitations, with the result that women's freedom of movement can be significantly limited as, for example, in Saudi Arabia.

---

[63] A. E. Mayer, *Islam and Human Rights: Tradition and Politics* (Westview Press, 5th edn., 2012); K. Dalacoura, *Islam, Liberalism and Human Rights* (I.B. Taurus, 3rd edn., 2007).

[64] E. Karagiannis (ed.), *The New Political Islam: Human Rights, Democracy and Justice* (University of Pennsylvania Press, 2018); A. Saeed, *Human Rights and Islam: An Introduction to Key Debates between Islamic Law and International Human Rights Law* (Elgaronline, 2018); D. Johnston, 'Islam and Human Rights: A Growing Rapprochement?' (2015) 74 *American Journal of Economics and Sociology* 113-48.

[65] M. Rishmawi, 'The Revised Arab Charter on Human Rights: A Step Forward?' (2005) 5 *Human Rights Law Review* 361-376.

Jihad

The vast majority of Muslims are likely to regard their faith as inherently peaceful, life-affirming, universally valid for all humankind, and promising not only personal peace between the believer and the Almighty, but concord between individuals and peoples as well. Indeed, the Arabic salutation, *As-salāmu ʿalaykum* ('peace be upon you'), has been adopted as an every-day greeting by Muslims in many parts of the non-Arab world. However, as Holt et al maintain, two of Islam's principal institutions, Holy Law (*sharia*) and Holy War (*jihad*), are intertwined because the latter is waged to defend the former from its internal and external enemies.[66] The term 'jihad' – which means 'to strive', and in the Muslim context, particularly 'in the cause of Allah' – refers to both internal and external struggle. However, in its most controversial sense, it concerns waging war on Allah's behalf.

According to Morgan, 'the Qur'an contains over 100 verses commanding believers to fight against unbelievers.[67] The dozen or so better-known ones about violence and killing, rendered during the Medinan period, include the following.

'Fight for the cause of God, those who fight you, but do not transgress, for God does not love the transgressors'.[68] 'Jihad (holy fighting in Allah's Cause) is ordained for you (Muslims) though you dislike it, and it may be that you dislike a thing which is good for you and that you like a thing which is bad for you. Allah knows but you do not know'.[69] 'When the sacred months are over, slay the pagans wherever you find them. Capture, besiege, and ambush them. If they repent, perform prayers and pay the religious tax, set them free. God is All-forgiving and All-merciful'.[70] 'Fight those who do not believe in Allah, nor in the latter day, nor do they prohibit what Allah and His Messenger have prohibited, nor follow the religion of truth, out of those who have been given the Book, until they pay the tax in acknowledgment of superiority and they are in a state of subjection'.[71]

---

[66] Holt et al, *Islamic Society and Civilization*, p. xiv.
[67] Morgan, *Essential Islam*, p. 89.
[68] Qur'an 2:190.
[69] Ibid., 2:216.
[70] Ibid., 9:5.
[71] Ibid., 9.29. See also ibid. 4:74; 5:33-34; 9:12; 9:36; 22:39.

A famous lengthy sunnah also contains the following commands from Mohammad himself: 'Fight in the name of God and in the path of God … Do not cheat or commit treachery and do not mutilate anyone or kill children'.[72]

While these and related texts clearly endorse violence, fighting, warfare and killing, a feature of mainstream Islam shared with many other faiths, certain conditions are required. However, since these are not entirely clear, they need to be interpreted to determine what they might imply for the contemporary world. Together with appeals to deeper and wider features of the Islamic faith, this involves such techniques as *ijtihad* (the expenditure of effort and application of relevant sources, especially the sunnah), *ijma* (recourse to precedents which command consensus among Muslims), *qiyas* (reasoning by analogy), *shabah* ('similarity'), *'illa* (appeal to a common principle), *maslaha* (the attempt to discern that which is conducive to the public interest), *taqlid* (imitation), and *kalam* (a form of dialectical doctrinal reasoning). For Muslims, the most persuasive opinions are those which command consensus among believers.[73]

Not surprisingly, reflection upon the legitimacy of armed conflict began very early in the history of the faith. Indeed, the notion of a just war is part of its foundational narrative.[74] Although most of the standard authoritative judgments pertaining to it (*ahkam al-jihad*) originated when Muslim political power was at its height between 750 and 1400, these nevertheless continue to provide the key point of reference for a distinctive Islamic doctrine of 'just (or holy) war', including that relating to jihadi terrorism today.[75]

According to Sinai, violent militancy has also been regarded as 'an integral component of the Medinan vision of piety … not just a circumstantially necessary measure of defence'.[76] Some commentators also argue that the Medinan endorsement of holy war was a response to the unexpected delay in the dawning of the Day of Judgment, with the result that since the Almighty had seen fit to defer the final reckoning, Muslims had to bridge the gap themselves. There is evidence that this conclusion might also

---

[72] J. Kelsay, *Arguing the Just War in Islam* (Harvard University Press, 2007), pp.100-01.

[73] Ibid., p. 125.

[74] Ibid., pp. 97.

[75] Ibid.

[76] N. Sinai, *The Qur'an: A Historical-Critical Introduction* (Edinburgh University Press, 2017), p. 191.

have been influenced by the contemporaneous development of militant piety in Christianity in late antiquity which also invoked a 'narrative of victimhood', framed violent conflict in religious terms, and also promised heavenly reward for the martyred. This was, however, generally confined to personal assault and intercommunal rioting.[77]

The western just war doctrine distinguishes between the legitimacy of resorting to arms (*jus ad bellum*) and how hostilities should be lawfully and morally conducted (*jus in bello*). A similar distinction can also be drawn in the Islamic context. In both cases (with any distinctively Islamic interpretation in brackets) the doctrine of jus ad bellum includes the principles of legitimate authority (spiritual leadership), just cause (defending the authority of Allah), right intention (to restore Islamic peace and order), at least a reasonable prospect of success, and as a last resort. Proportionate cause features in the western, but not in the Islamic conception.[78] A particular feature of the Islamic version, not found in its western equivalent, is the prohibition upon pre-emptive attack which the Prophet stipulated in order to avoid violence by converting the enemy, their migration, or payment of tribute.[79]

Although ill-defined, the Islamic notion of limits to hostilities and legitimate targets also reflects historic constraints upon pre-Islamic Arabian tribal conflict, including the prohibition of fighting in the traditional sacred months and magnanimity in response to the submission of, and repentance by, adversaries. These are embodied in the following elements of the traditional Islamic understanding of *jus in bello*: minimum force; avoidance of unnecessary harm to (particularly Muslim) non-combatants, with children, slaves, women, old, blind, lame and hopelessly insane people generally immune from direct and deliberate attack unless they themselves participate in hostilities; and prohibition upon depriving the enemy of food or water.[80] Orthodox Muslim thinkers have also been willing to grant a wide discretion to commanders in the determination of appropriate means but with no concept of prohibited weaponry.[81] As in the western tradition, unintended yet unavoidable damage, collateral but proportional to that which is otherwise

---

[77] Ibid., pp.192-4.
[78] Ibid., pp. 101, 102.
[79] Ibid., pp. 101, 102, 105, 113.
[80] Morgan, *Essential Islam,* p. 90.
[81] Ibid., pp. 106, 104, 108, 114; S. Maher, *Salafi-Jihadism: The History of An Idea* (Hurst, 2016), pp. 46-9.

required for a legitimate military objective, has also, therefore, been deemed acceptable.

Although the orthodox mainstream Islamic tradition abjures terrorism in nearly all circumstances, elements of the ultra-orthodox variant, considered further in the following chapter, do not. According to Husain, contemporary jihadis advocate departure from the traditional constraints according to five principles: embracing *ghuraba*, the sense of being a minority of righteous 'strangers' or outsiders with respect to sinful global majorities; *al-wala wa al-bara*, loyalty to the umma and hostility towards everyone else; *takfir*, declaring other Muslims *kuffar* ('non-believers'), and, therefore legitimate targets for lethal attack; the religious obligation to restore the Caliphate, God's government on earth; and commitment to the view that, until this happens, all Muslims are living in sin.[82] Providing this is adequately acknowledged, it is not 'Islamophobic' for the relationship between Islam and jihadi terrorism to be raised and debated.

Leiken maintains that the 'crisis' or 'revolt' of the second generation' is a particularly potent factor in drawing a tiny minority into jihadi terrorism. Key elements include a clash between the generally prosperous, urban, hedonistic, secular, individualist, educated, and liberal cultural milieu of their own generation in the west, and the much more religious, puritanical, family-and-community-oriented, rural, and much less materially prosperous, experience of their parents.[83] As Leiken graphically puts it, the jihadis are 'marginal men … outsiders in the land of their birth and strangers in the land of their forbears'.[84] Only jihad against the west appears to offer redress for the lack of fulfilment, personal, socio-political and/or religious injustice (real or imagined), the conflicting identities they feel, and the truth, meaning, belonging, identity, and shared purpose they crave. For others, domestic jihad may offer adventure and a vehicle for the expression of the ultimate form of youthful rebellion.[85]

---

[82] Husain, *House of Islam*, Ch. 10.

[83] Leiken, *Europe's Angry Muslims*, pp. xx, 69-74.

[84] Ibid., pp. 102, 265; R. Pantucci, *'We Love Death as You Love Life': Britain's Suburban Terrorists* (Hurst, 2015), pp. 57-66, 74-5.

[85] Pantucci, *Britain's Suburban Terrorists*, pp. 8-17; Q. Wiktorowicz, *Radical Islam Rising: Muslim Extremism in the West* (Rowman & Little, 2009); I. Burrell, 'BBC's Newsbeat reprimanded for letting Isis fighter compare jihad to Call of Duty', *The Independent*, 10 November 2014.

Conclusion

It cannot, by definition, be 'Islamophobic' for anyone, Muslim or otherwise, accurately to report genuine mainstream Islamic beliefs, practices, or conduct even if some Muslims may not welcome what this reveals. Since any bona fide observation will concern the complex terrain of the Qur'an, hadith, sunnah, sharia, and fatwas, there may be room for debate about whether or not it does, in fact, accurately represent the authentic mainstream tradition. But it is not Islamophobic to engage in it. Nor can an honest mistake, particularly about any of the finer details, be Islamophobic either. Finally, the question of when, if ever, robustly critical comment upon Muslim beliefs, practices, and conduct crosses the line between lawful and legitimate critique on the one hand, and the unlawful and illegitimate expression of anti-Muslim prejudice on the other, is a matter considered more fully in subsequent chapters.

Chapter 5

Dissenting voices

Introduction

Interpretations of any ideology tend to range from the ultra-orthodox – a particularly extreme, uncompromising, 'radical', or 'fundamentalist' version of orthodoxy – to the heretical, an interpretation which those who subscribe to orthodoxy regard as a mortal threat to their beliefs, identity, power, and other interests. Orthodoxy (the mainstream) and heterodoxy (an unorthodox though non-heretical interpretation) lie in between. These distinctions typically depend upon complex doctrinal debates and power struggles between adherents to any given faith or ideology, often driven by both internal and external processes. And, though clear enough in principle, in practice they also tend to be fluid, unstable, and revisable. For example, some Sunnis regard Shia Muslims as heretics while others see them as misguided Muslims, but Muslim nonetheless.

Needless to say, the various positions, who subscribes to them, and the implications, are contested to varying degrees by Muslims themselves. As already noted in previous chapters, about 80% of Muslims in the contemporary world are Sunni and 20% Shia. This broad-brush statistic, however, obscures the fact that each of these traditions harbours numerous sects. There are also several marginal ones outside both. The Qur'an says: 'As for those who divide their way of life and break up into sects, you have no part of them at all. Their affair is with Allah. He will tell them the truth of what they did in the end'.[1] Nevertheless, Mohammad is reputed to have predicted that his followers would eventually divide into 73 sects, two more than he claimed were found in Judaism and one more than in Christianity.

These facts are typically not recognised in the debate about Islamophobic expression. Yet they raise some intriguing and relevant questions. For

---

[1] Qur'an 6:159.

example: will an allegedly 'Islamophobic' criticism of mainstream Muslim belief, practice, or conduct have this status only if expressed by a non-Muslim but not by a Muslim?

As the title suggests, this chapter is concerned with dissent or 'unorthodox' versions of the mainstream faith. It is a moot point whether this should include ultra orthodoxy, of which there is more than one variety. But, since such interpretations deviate from the mainstream they ought to be considered somewhere in this study and they do not belong more comfortably anywhere else. Also included are heterodoxy, the most relevant manifestation of which for present purposes is liberal or reformist Islam, and finally the principal fringe sects, and prominent individuals, typically regarded as heretical/apostate by the Muslim mainstream. It should be noted, however, that some or even many mainstream Muslims may regard anything but the orthodox interpretation of their faith as heresy.

Ultra-orthodoxy

One of the key elements of ultra-orthodox Islam has been, and remains, 'literalism'. More a feature of the Sunni than the Shia tradition,[2] this affirms that the Qur'an contains an easily accessible answer to every issue confronting Muslims and humanity in all ages including the contemporary one. The most prominent contemporary forms are Salafi-Wahhabism, Islamism, and Salafi-Jihadism.[3] As observed in Chapter 2, Salafism – from the Arabic term *salaf* ('predecessors') – seeks to return the faithful to the beliefs and life-styles of the 'pious predecessors', the Prophet Mohammad and the first three generations of his disciples. Also known as Wahhabism after its founder, it began in Arabia in the mid-18th century when Mohammad ibn Abd al-Wahhab (1703-91) sought to purge Islam of the many distortions and lapses from orthodoxy to which he alleged it had succumbed over the previous millennium.[4] A return to the Qur'an and the sunnah – with respectful but not blind adherence to the scholarship and tradition accrued over centuries – was recommended. A particularly austere interpretation of the faith, a philosophy

---

[2] D. Morgan, *Essential Islam: A Comprehensive Guide to Belief and Practice* (Praeger, 2010), p. 34.

[3] M. Wilkinson, *The Genealogy of Terror: How to distinguish between Islam, Islamism and Islamist Extremism* (Routledge, 2018).

[4] R. Leiken, *Europe's Angry Muslims: The Revolt of the Second Generation* (Oxford University Press, 2012), p. 70.

of 'progression through regression'[5] was the result.

Amongst other things, Salafi-Wahhabism abjures mysticism and any whiff of compromise with the oneness of God (*tawhid*), such as the cult of saints found in some Sufi and Shia traditions. It also insists upon strict doctrinal purity (*aqida*), rigid and ruthless enforcement of the sharia (particularly against blasphemy, apostasy, and criticism of the faith from both insiders and outsiders), generally favours the veiling of women in the public sphere, and disparages music, television, photographs of living things, and in order to avoid the sin of pride, men's trousers and robes which cover the ankles. Salafi-Wahhabis regard Sufis and Shia as heretics, apostates, and polytheists. Saleh al-Fawzan – a leading Saudi Wahhabi cleric, popular TV presenter, professor at a government university in Riyadh, and author of school textbooks – has, for example, even declared that: 'slavery is part of Islam. Slavery is part of jihad, and jihad will remain for as long as there is Islam'. He has, therefore, denounced Muslims who oppose slavery as apostates who deserve to be executed.[6]

Several, not entirely discrete, branches of the Salafi-Wahhabi tradition can be distinguished.[7] 'Pietists' are only interested in personal salvation through faith, religious ritual, and strict adherence to the Qur'an and sunnah. 'Political Salafists' or 'Islamists' reject all systems of governance, including those based on democracy, human rights and the rule of 'man-made' law, except an Islamic state anchored exclusively in the Qur'an and sharia.[8] Assuming a fundamental difference and antagonism between 'true' Muslims, 'partial' Muslims, and non-Muslims, they seek a world in which true Muslims are in charge, ideally realized in a sharia-governed global Islamic state.[9] According to Wilkinson, Islamism has arisen as a result of a combination of what, for Muslims, are both 'noxious absences' and 'vicious presences'.[10] The former include the lack, to various extents in the west and elsewhere of: employment status and wealth commensurate with talent, qualifications, and aspirations; civic belonging and empowerment; effective Islamic education

---

[5] S. Maher, *Salafi-Jihadism: The History of an Idea* (Penguin, 2016), p. 6; Leiken, *Europe's Angry Muslims*, pp. 66-9.

[6] E. Husain, *The House of Islam: A Global History* (Bloomsbury, 2018), p. 135.

[7] Wilkinson, *Genealogy of Terror* (Routledge, 2018), pp. 204-05.

[8] Ibid., plates 2-4, pp. 15, 202.

[9] Ibid., pp. 66, 67-70, 201.

[10] Ibid., pp. 204-5.

and educational attainment giving rise to 'us v them' ideologies; and engaged parenting, the lack of which has increased the risk of young people being recruited to the more extreme interpretations of the faith. The 'vicious presences' include political oppression and corruption in 'Muslim lands'; hostility towards Muslims in the west coupled with discrimination in employment etc.; prejudice on the part of 'significant pockets' of Muslims against non-Muslims; wealthy Muslim funders of terrorism plus abundant supplies of arms; Western intervention in 'Muslim lands'; and distorted Islamic narratives on social media, the internet and so on.[11] McCarthy adds another element – a 'conquest ideology' which 'takes well-meaning accommodation as weakness and always demands more'.[12]

A further distinction can be drawn between 'non-violent Islamist extremism' and 'Salafi-Jihadism'. [13] Although sharing the foundational assumptions of Islamism – including the rejection of all other religions and ideologies and an absolute, enduring antagonism between 'true' Muslims and everyone else[14] – the former stops short of advocating violence, particularly terrorism, apart from in exceptional circumstances. By contrast, the core characteristics of Salafi-Jihadism are violent jihad; excommunication of heretics (*bara'a*), including killing other Muslims deemed to have become bandits, rebels, apostates, and/or to be involved in decadent and corrupt pro-western Muslim governments (*takfir*); love of and loyalty to God and all that pertains to Him, plus hatred and disavowal for that which does not (*al-wala'wa-l-bara*); strict monotheism (*tawhid*); Islamic governance (*hakimiyya*); tit-for-tat retaliation – 'as you kill our women and children, we kill yours' (*qisas*); and willingly causing collateral damage to 'human shields' allegedly used by the enemy (*tatarrus*).[15] Allied to these is the novel doctrine of vicarious and collective liability which expands the category of legitimate targets to include the citizens of western democracies held responsible for the alleged crimes perpetrated by their governments against the faithful across the globe. International systems and institutions, regarded as western instruments

---

[11] Ibid., p. 207.

[12] A. McCarthy, *Islam and Free Speech* (Encounter, 2015), p. 25.

[13] Wilkinson, *Genealogy of Terror*, p. 201.

[14] Ibid.

[15] J. Schacht, 'Law and Justice', in P. Holt, A. Lambton & B. Lewis (eds.), *The Cambridge History of Islam* (Cambridge University Press, 1970), p. 543; R. Pantucci, '*We Love Death as You Love Life': Britain's Suburban Terrorists* (Hurst, 2015), p. 10; S. Maher, *Salafi-Jihadism.*

of domination, are also defined as 'enemies of Islam' against which armed action is considered legitimate and necessary. A further distinction can be drawn between those Salafi-Jihadis who confine themselves to attempting to overthrow, through violent revolution, what they regard as un-Islamic regimes in Muslim lands, and those who also pursue this objective through terrorist attacks in the west and elsewhere.

Wilkinson maintains that, as far as issues pertaining to law, governance, social transformation, war and other forms of violence are concerned, 'contemporary mainstream Islam', 'Islamism', and 'Islamist extremism' (both violent and non-violent), have now become fundamentally different bodies of belief and practice.[16]

In a recent research tour around the UK, Ed Husain encountered many progressive Muslims championing causes such as LGBT rights.[17] As he says: 'There is a new Western Islam progressing here; it is just that the people who are quietly developing it are shouting less than the Caliphists'.[18] But he also found ultra-orthodox mosques that discriminate against women, teach a highly literal interpretation of Islam, conduct Islamic weddings without legal registration, and stock books by authors banned as extremist in parts of the Middle East. Husain was also troubled by what he did not find, particularly works by Muslim philosophers, novelists, poets, and scholars extolling the power of reason. In Husain's opinion three distinct trends 'too often insulated from scrutiny … are taking root across Muslim communities in Britain': an increasingly politically conscious affirmation of Islam as the primary identity of Muslims, subordinating other identities such as sect and ethnicity and imposed upon communities by self-appointed leaders who brook no dissent; a 'strange clericalism' with its intolerant cut-and-dried interpretation of the faith which is 'gripping Muslim minds'; and the spread of Caliphism which yearns for the restoration of the sharia-based governance of the Muslim empires of the past, on the grounds that only this can address the flaws and failings of Britain and the rest of the world.[19]

---

[16] Wilkinson, *Genealogy of Terror*, pp. 51-2.

[17] E. Husain, *Among the Mosques: A Journey Across Muslim Britain* (Bloomsbury, 2021); D. Henry, *Voices of Modern Islam: What It Means to Be Muslim Today* (Jessica Kingsley, 2018).

[18] Husain, *Among the Mosques*, p. 184.

[19] Ibid., pp. 186-8.

Heterodoxy

There are many heterodox interpretations of Islam including Shiism and Sufism. But those with the greatest relevance for the debate about Islamophobic expression and free speech are those which concern the social, economic, legal and political, rather than the devotional implications of the faith. And the most distinctive of these is liberal, progressive, or reformist Islam.

Shia Islam

Following Mohammad's death, the Shia ('party of Ali') took a verse from the Qur'an, stating that the family of the Prophet is sinless, to mean that the succession should pass to his daughter, Fatimah, the wife of his cousin Ali, then to their two sons Hasan (d. 669) and Husayn (d. 680), and thence down the blood line. The Shia also believe that, although Ali was Mohammad's legitimate successor, he nobly feigned allegiance to the first three (illegitimate) Caliphs in order to avoid civil war. As already noted in Chapter 2, the Sunni-Shia schism was initially about the succession rather than over fundamental differences concerning doctrine or practice which have, however, developed since.

In spite of being a minority tradition in Islam, Shiism flourished under the Fatimid Caliphate which ruled over various parts of the Maghreb, Egypt and the Levant including briefly Mecca and Medina, from 909 to 1171. It was also declared the state religion of Iran by Shah Abbas of Persia (1587–1629). Shia Muslims remain the majority in Iran, Iraq, and Bahrain. Relentless Sunni persecution over the centuries has also spawned a cult of victimhood and self-denigration. This is graphically dramatized by the brutal public self-flagellation of devotees in commemoration of the killing of Husayn and his associates at the Battle of Karbala by forces of the second Umayyad caliph, Yazid I in 680.

Shia Islam is subdivided into three main factions according to where the line of legitimate succession is believed to have ended.[20] The 'Fivers', or Zaydis, are particularly hostile to other Shia. The 'Seveners', also known as Ismailis, are the second largest faction once represented by the Fatimid dynasty. In the past, they were also known as the 'Assassins' on account of

---

[20] N. Haider, *Shi'i Islam: An Introduction* (Cambridge University Press, 2014).

their fondness, like the Kharijites, for the 'holy murder' of religious and political opponents. However, most Shia are 'Twelvers' who restrict the title of 'Imam' to Ali and his eleven successors and who also believe that Mohammad, and all but the twelfth Imam (the last), were murdered. They maintain that the Twelfth Imam did not die, but having been preserved by God in a state of supernatural suspended animation, will reappear as the Mahdi or Messiah. Many have claimed this role down the ages, but none has yet been able to fulfil other aspects of the prophesy.

Shia Imams are simultaneously political and religious leaders, deemed sinless, infallible and divinely inspired, though not in receipt of direct divine revelation in the manner of Mohammad. Instead of referring to a consensus of the ummah (community of believers) or the ulama (Islamic scholars), the Imams are accorded the right to make binding pronouncements on matters of faith and its implications, and to choose any male descendant as their successor. In the 20th century the leader of the Islamic Revolution, and later Islamic Republic of Iran, Ayatollah Khomeini, advocated a theocracy governed by *mujtahids*, scholars trained in sharia law, the most esteemed of whom would receive the title of 'Ayatollah', a term hitherto virtually unknown to Shiism, or to any other version of Islam.

Shia legal traditions, their call to prayer and ablution rituals also differ from their Sunni equivalents. As Chapter 4 noted, one of the most controversial, 'temporary marriage', has been justified as a moral alternative to promiscuity, a view rejected by many Muslim and non-Muslim critics. Most Shia are also more interested in making pilgrimages to the shrines of the Twelve Imams and their descendants than joining the Hajj.

The status of Shiism in 'mainstream' Islam is, therefore, difficult to state with precision. More liberal Sunnis view it in the same way as many Catholics and Protestants regard each other – as part of the faith albeit a flawed and wayward version of it. However, others see the Shia as inherently untrustworthy.[21] The 'cult of saints', and the fact that deceased Imams and their relatives are believed to be able to intercede with Allah, has also exposed Shiism to accusations of idolatry and *shirk* (compromising the oneness of the Almighty) particularly from ultra-orthodox Sunnis. Shia Muslims can also be sharply critical of Sunnis in ways which would quickly be denounced as

---

[21] D. Toube in E. Webb (ed.), *Islamophobia: An Anthology of Concerns* (Civitas, 2019), p. 104.

Islamophobic if expressed by a non-Muslim. A good example is Sheikh Yasser al-Habib, a Shia cleric jailed in 2003 in Kuwait, his home country, for inciting sectarianism by attacking key figures in Sunni Islam. His Kuwaiti citizenship was also revoked when he described Aisha, the favourite and much-celebrated wife of the Prophet Mohammad, as an 'enemy of God'. Following his release from prison, al-Habib fled to Britain where he set up his own TV channel run from a former church hall in Buckinghamshire. In July 2024 he came to wider prominence with his bid to buy the uninhabited mile-long Scottish island of Torsa, populate it with Muslims governed by the sharia, and build a school, hospital, and mosque there.[22]

Sufism

Although originating at the very birth of the faith, Sufism, did not fully crystallize until the 11th century.[23] 'Absorbing many elements from Christianity, Neo-Platonism, Gnosticism and Buddhism, … passing through mystical, theosophical and pantheistic stages',[24] Sufism is a generally peace-loving interpretation of the faith. Its adherents are also generally more interested than other Muslims, in the subordination of the ego to the Will of God and the primacy of love over intellect, tradition, doctrine, and dogma as routes to authentic spirituality.[25] For the famous 'swirling Dervishes', bedecked with their tall hats, a state of spiritual ecstasy is induced by slowly spinning in a white gown which gracefully opens like a parachute. According to Rahman, next to orthodoxy, Sufism has had the greatest influence upon Islam and has 'posed the biggest challenge to orthodoxy down to the dawn of modern times'.[26] The term 'Sufi' is said to derive from one or more of four sources.[27] Next to the home of the Prophet in Medina was a place known as the *suffa* where the impoverished and most devout of his followers, the *ahl al-suffa*, gathered. *Safa* is also an Arabic word for purity and cleanliness, *soof* or

---

[22] J. Watson, 'Islam McState: cleric wants to turn Scots island into caliphate', *The Times*, 29 July 2024.

[23] A. Knysh, *Sufism: A New History of Islamic Mysticism* (Princeton University Press, 2019); P. Hitti, *History of the Arabs: From the Earliest Times to the Present* (Palgrave MacMillan, revised 10th edn., 2002), pp. 433-9.

[24] Ibid., p. 433.

[25] See Husain, *House of Islam*, Ch. 6; F. Rahman, 'Revival and Reform in Islam' in Holt et al (eds.), *Islamic Society and Civilization*, pp. 633-5.

[26] F. Rahman, 'Revival and Reform in Islam', p. 633.

[27] Husain, *House of Islam*, p. 78.

suf may refer to the course woollen clothing worn by Sufis in preference to the lighter cotton typically chosen by early Muslim ascetics, and *sophia* is Greek for wisdom. Sufis are also sometimes known as 'the poor' – *fuqara*, the plural of *faqir* in Arabic, and *darvish* in Persian – from which the English words 'fakir' and 'dervish' for Islamic mystics in general derive.

The core principles of Sufism include cultivating God-consciousness through right-living; cautiously following the sunnah; indifference to the acceptance or rejection of others; patience and trust in Allah; being reconciled to personal circumstances as His will; gratitude to God in good times and comfort by Him in adversity; and suspicion of the establishment in both Sunni and Shia traditions. Sufis are committed to equality between men and women and have also adopted liturgical forms of worship, fostered a cult of saints whose graves have become sites of pilgrimage, and diffused the use of the rosary among their followers. Skilled in adapting Islam to local culture and customs, since the early days of the faith they have also been deeply involved in missionary work in Africa, Anatolia, Central Asia, India, and Indonesia. The works of the most famous exponent of the celebrated Sufi poetical tradition, Jalal al-din Rumi (d. 1273), are still appreciated even in the west today. Some Sufis also commemorate the Prophet's birthday. With its fraternal lodges or orders, asceticism, and celebration of celibacy, Sufism is also the closest Islam has come to developing a monastic tradition. Although it endorses the essentials of orthodox doctrine, the distinctive interpretation and practices of Sufis have exposed it to the charge of heresy on the part of some other Muslims. Nevertheless, according to Husain, contemporary Sufism has 'hundreds of millions of Muslim followers and mosques spread across the globe' and that 'most of the world's Muslims are either Sufis or at least deeply influenced by Sufism'.[28] But their unassuming profile rarely makes the news headlines.

Liberal reformism

'Liberal', 'progressive', 'modernist', or 'reformist' interpretations of Islam are of particular relevance to the issues discussed in this book, because typically they dispute much of Islamic orthodoxy in ways which, if expressed by a non-Muslim, would almost certainly prompt accusations of Islamophobia. A distinction should first be drawn between 'passive' and 'active'

---

[28] Ibid., pp. 79, 84.

manifestations of this outlook. A good example of 'passive Islamic liberalism' might be the well-educated western Muslim who, to all outward extents and purposes, remains a faithful and observant member of the ummah, but who, nevertheless, privately doubts or who no longer believes in, the central tenets of the mainstream faith. He or she is also likely privately to subscribe to core western liberal values including human rights, democracy, and the rule of law. But, because this position is largely inexplicit and hidden, it is difficult to assess its global profile. The indicators, however, suggest that it is more common in the west than in the rest of the Muslim world, not least because the wider environment here is more propitious.

By contrast, 'active' or 'express' liberal, progressive, modernist, or reformist, interpretations of Islam involve the much more vocal articulation of the perspectives these adjectives suggest. There are, however, significant differences of opinion between the leading exponents. Not all 'modernists' are 'liberal', for example, and 'reformists' do not all agree on the details of what reform requires. Since the orthodox regard these movements with deep suspicion at best, this kind of Islam, therefore, lies in the grey area between heterodoxy and heresy/apostasy. Broadly speaking, liberal, modernist, and reformist interpretations of the faith remain on the heterodox side of this line if they acknowledge that the Qur'an is the literal and infallible word of God dictated word-for-word to Mohammad. However, those who affirm that it was, at best, inspired but not dictated by God are likely to be regarded by most Muslims as having crossed into heresy/apostasy.

Typically, liberal reformists maintain that their goal is to restore the original interpretation of Islam which, they claim, the orthodox tradition has distorted and traduced. Central to this objective is the restoration of the 'proper' relationship between reason and revelation. According to this view, Muslims should endorse any conclusion about the faith supported by reason, provided it is not contradicted by the Qur'an, interpreted where appropriate in a non-literal manner. Nor is this a recent insight. As Chapter 2 notes, this debate has, in fact, been rumbling along since the earliest days of Islam.

Contemporary liberal reformism emerged out of the Islamic revivalist movement of the 18th and 19th centuries in which the Mu'tazilite tradition (see Chapter 2) featured prominently.[29] Jamal al-Din al-Afghani, (d. 1897) argued, for example, that gaps in the interpretive structure of the faith prevented it

---

[29] Wilkinson, *Genealogy of Terror*, pp. 37-42.

from adapting to modernity and needed to be filled by, amongst other things, positive engagement with non-Muslim thinking.[30] His student, Muhammad Abduh (1849–1905), one of the key founding figures of Islamic Modernism who became Grand Mufti of Egypt in 1899, did not refer to himself as a Mu'tazilite. Nevertheless, he contributed to a revival of the essentials of this tradition and became the chief source of inspiration for later modernist and reformist scholars and philosophers. These included Rifa'a al-Tahtawi (1801–1873), Fazlur Rahman (1919–1988), Harun Nasution (1919–1998), Ali Shariati Mazinani (1933–1977), Nasr Abu Zayd (1943–2010), and Farid Esack (born 1959). Modernizers such as these and others, have called for the abandonment of *taqlid* – 'imitation' in conformity with legal precedent – in favour of *ijtihad*, independent reasoning.

Prominent contemporary Muslims advocating the modernization, but not necessarily the liberalization, of their faith include Susilo Bambang Yudhoyono, former President of Indonesia, the world's largest majority Muslim state, and the President of Egypt, Abedel Fattah el-Sisi. In May 2006, opening a summit to discuss how to make the Muslim world more prosperous, Yudhoyono regretfully observed, for example, that amongst nations adhering in varying degrees to Islam, 'there is not one that can be classified as developed according to any criterion. All of them are behind in knowledge, finances, and technologies ... The world associates Islam with backwardness. This makes us angry, but the fact remains that we are backward'.[31] Similarly, in December 2014, addressing the assembled elite of Sunni Islam at the Al-Azhar mosque in Cairo – a cross between a Sunni Vatican and Harvard University – President el-Sisi, said that 'the corpus of texts and ideas, which over many years we have sacralised to the point that departing from it has become almost impossible, arouses the whole world's hostility towards us'.[32] In other words, in the opinion of each of these faithful orthodox Sunni Muslims, non-Muslim hostility towards Muslims and Islam is at least in part the fault of Muslims themselves, a sentiment which, when expressed by non-Muslims, has been roundly condemned as Islamophobic by paternalistic western Islamophiles.

Liberal Muslims embrace not only modernization, but also maintain that

---

[30] Ibid., p. 46.
[31] Quoted in P. Bruckner (trans. by S. Rendell and L. Neal), *An Imaginary Racism: Islamophobia and Guilt* (Wiley, 2018), p. 138.
[32] Ibid., p. 137-8.

'progressive liberal' values – such as the secularization of the state; democracy; the rule of law; gender equality; LGBT+ rights, women's rights, and human rights; religious pluralism; tolerance; freedom of thought, religion, and expression; opposition to theocracy; and the rejection of Islamism and Islamic fundamentalism – are not only consistent with Islam but are much more faithful to its original conception than any other Muslim tradition. They claim that, as a result, Islamic theology, ethics, law, culture, and ritualistic practices need to be revised and updated.

A distinctive strand in this diverse movement, Qur'anism, rejects the hadith and the sharia, and maintains that the Qur'an alone provides the only authentic source of Divine authority. This perspective, therefore, removes at a stroke, many though not all of the obstacles to a more progressive re-interpretation of the Islamic faith. For example, Dr Taj Hargey, Imam of the Oxford Islamic Congregation and Provost of the Oxford Institute for British Islam, an independent progressive Muslim think tank, argues that the conservative Muslim clergy peddles a warped and defective ideology, replete with myths and fairy tales, together with segregationist and concocted supremacist doctrines, not based upon the Qur'an but upon extraneous non-divine sources.[33] He maintains that Muslims who do not fully understand their faith are vulnerable to such manipulation by others who also fail to understand it but who nevertheless find in the mythology a convenient means of asserting their own power and privilege. Non-Muslims also tend to regard such distortions as integral elements of authentic Islam, a double whammy since, according to Hargey, this also makes it more difficult for Muslims fully to integrate and to progress in western societies.

Hargey maintains that Muslim clerics invoke a long-established misconception, to which most Muslims subscribe, that the faith is not to be found in the Qur'an alone but also in the 'toxic trio'– the hadith, sharia, and fatwas – promoted by the 'terrible triplets' of mullahs (religious teachers), mosques, and madrassas (religious schools). According to him, the hadith are unreliable sources of any truth, and the sharia is merely a compendium of hundreds of thousands of medieval legal opinions, crystallizing some 500-600 years after Mohammed died. Nor, he asserts, is it credible to claim, as mainstream Islam does, that all the major jurisprudential questions faced by

---

[33] T. Hargey, 'Introducing the Oxford Institute for British Islam', in S. Greer & T. Hargey (eds), *British Islam: A Vision for the Future* (Oxford Institute for British Islam, 2023), pp.1-4.

Muslims had been settled by the middle ages and that the 'gates of ijtihad' –
independent reasoning by Muslim jurists – have since been closed. For one
thing fresh challenges arise as a result of rapid advances in technology which
jurists and legal systems of all kinds are struggling to meet. According to
Hargey, fatwas are simply the opinions of specific clerics on religious matters,
or their social and other implications, which lack any deeper or wider
credibility or authority. And, as attested by the most notorious fatwa of recent
times – the death sentence passed without trial or evidence on Sir Salman
Rushdie by the Ayatollah Khomeini – this can have catastrophic results, and
not only for those directly condemned. Hargey maintains that the toxic trio
negates the supremacy of the Qur'an as the only authentic source of divine
authority for the faithful. As a result, in addition to numerous other contrived
elements, he argues that the faith has been supplanted by patriarchy, jihad,
polygamy, sexism, and the persecution of alleged apostates and blasphemers.
According to Hargey, without root and branch reform, Islam in the west will,
at best, remain on the periphery of society not at the centre where it belongs.

It follows from this analysis that those Muslims who wish to find a more
authentic interpretation of their faith, which would also equip them to function
better and to integrate more effectively in the contemporary west, must,
therefore, jettison all non-Qur'anic corruptions and adhere solely to Islam's
original principles as found exclusively in its single holy text. Many will be
surprised to hear, Hargey maintains, that political, social, intellectual and
religious freedom and self-empowerment – implying democracy, human
rights, and the rule of law – lie at the very heart of Qur'anic Islam. He,
therefore, encourages Muslims in the west to differentiate more carefully
between creed and culture and between religion and tradition. In his view, and
self-consciously alliterative, an authentic reformed Islam predicated on
adherence to the Qur'an alone, would be a pertinent, pluralistic, progressive
philosophy. It would also be enlightened, egalitarian and erudite, rational,
relevant and reformist, lucid, logical and libertarian, inclusive, integrated and
indigenous and not regressive, ritualistic or reactionary. Nor would it be
beholden to antiquated medieval interpretations, archaic theological concepts,
sectarian beliefs, political baggage, cultural norms or traditional customs from
distant ancestral homelands. It would, therefore, be fully consistent with
western values and more suited to Muslims in the contemporary west than any
other Islamic alternative on offer.

Another contemporary advocate of liberal Islam, Turkish journalist, commentator, and devout Muslim, Mustafa Akyol, maintains that:

> 'When Islam appeared in world history it was a liberating force ...
> Yet today who would really see Islam as such .... Islam is not the
> powerful, creative, sophisticated, beautiful civilization that it once
> was. Quite the contrary; today our lands are among the most
> underdeveloped places in the world. Our wealth is scarce – unless it
> comes effortlessly from oil – as well as our science, knowledge,
> justice, and freedom. We are suppressed by authoritarian regimes,
> whose triumphant rivals often turn out to be new disappointments.
> We are also torn by hateful divisions and violent conflicts, not to
> mention the extremists who do unspeakable evils in our name.
> Certainly, outside powers – colonialists and imperialists – have a
> share in the making of this modern Muslim crisis. But that is often all
> we want to hear and see. We don't want to focus on the only thing
> we can change; our own behaviour, our own mindset, our own
> worldview'.[34]

The solution, he maintains, is to advance an 'Islamic enlightenment' by retrieving the values of reason, freedom, and tolerance buried as 'uncultivated seeds, forgotten paths, or even muted voices' in the Islamic tradition.[35] Arguing that 'we Muslims need to revisit some of the ideas that have been banned to us as "heresy" for about a thousand years',[36] Akyol claims that, far from there being no necessary relationship between Islam and authoritarianism, true Islam positively asserts liberty. Although the Qur'an' 'introduced into Arab society the concept that individuals have inalienable rights', he maintains this did not become a major theme in Islamic law which instead focuses upon duties.[37] Instead, the phrase 'real freedom is slavery to Allah', became an aphorism 'one comes across often in the Muslim universe'.[38] In common with others, Akyol also notes that the Qur'an affirmed the rights of women centuries before the west. But the 'tragedy is that while women's rights peaked in the West in the twentieth century, in Islamdom it

---

[34] M. Akyol, *Reopening Muslim Minds: A Return to Reason, Freedom and Tolerance* (Forum, 2022), pp. 232-3.

[35] Ibid., p. xxiv.

[36] Ibid., p. xvi.

[37] M. Akyol, *Islam without Extremes: A Muslim Case for Liberty* (W. W. Norton, 2013), pp. 52 & 54.

[38] Akyol, *Reopening Muslim Minds*, p. 181.

stagnated for centuries and even declined to its current reprehensible state'.[39] Akyol concludes that Islam 'had produced the seeds of freedom' but they were 'not rooted in fertile soil'.[40]

As he also notes, soon after Mohammad's death, an ideological battle erupted between his followers. The winners were what Akyol calls the 'People of Tradition' who favoured a rigid, dogmatic, and conservative interpretation of the faith which proved very useful for the assertion of the vested interests of the military-bureaucratic, landed, imperial aristocracy. The losers were the 'People of Reason' who advocated a more rational and flexible approach which tended to resonate more with the interests of the urban middle and lower classes.[41] Akyol argues that the faith has yet to recover from the triumph of traditionalism. The principal consequence has been the enduring legacy of ...

> 'an interpretation of Islam that is, by modern standards, authoritarian and intolerant. It manifests itself in laws and institutions that force women to cover their heads, or consider them lesser than men. It jails, flogs, or kills people for criticizing Islam and for even offering alternative interpretations of it. It demonizes Christians, Jews and others, or even fellow Muslims who happen to be from a different sect'.[42]

According to this view, the conservative turn in the history of Islam was much more the result of socio-political and natural than doctrinal factors, foremost being that the Islamic revolution in Arabia rapidly became imperial as a matter of choice rather than necessity. There was no immediate threat from neighbouring states, and as Chapter 2 noted, no motive for expansion other than the quest for loot, tribute, territory, slaves, and dominion. Furthermore, although the Qur'an is silent about the character and structure of political authority, Akyol maintains that the conception of God which emerges is that of cosmic emperor wielding absolute power. Opposition to the Caliph, God's representative on earth, could very conveniently, therefore, be designated as a heretical challenge to the Almighty Himself with all the ruthless severity the appropriate response was deemed to require. The hadith and the ulama also

---

[39] Akyol, *Islam without Extremes*, p. 54.
[40] Ibid., p. 135.
[41] Ibid., p. 124-7.
[42] Akyol, *Reopening Muslim Minds*, p. xxii.

provided a very convenient resource. Those favourable to the Caliph and his regime could be honoured and revered while the others could simply be ignored or denounced as heretical.

As Akyol observes, although local consultative arrangements were common in pre-Islamic Arabia, there were no obvious ways in which they could be applied to the huge centralized Muslim empires which rapidly developed. In his view, the Islamic traditionalists, who frowned upon 'innovation' particularly in matters of faith (except of course their own), also constrained trade between the Muslim world and the wider economic mainstream, with negative repercussions not only for the Islamic economy itself but also for its many cultural manifestations. The unproductive desert terrain also inhibited the emergence of a significant wealthy middle class of the kind that proved so central to the collapse of feudalism in late medieval Europe. Islamic law also made its own contribution. Although having originally stimulated economic activity, around the 10th century the preclusion of private capital accumulation, the formation and regulation of corporations, large scale production, and impersonal exchange, began to act as a drag on development.[43] According to this analysis, it was not until the advent of the Ottoman empire that the tide began to turn, especially as a result of liberalization in the 19th century.

Of particular significance for the debate about 'Islamophobic expression', Akyol shares most of the criticisms of contemporary institutionalized orthodox Islam which have often been denounced as Islamophobic when made by non-Muslims. However, he maintains that the ongoing liberalization of Islam and the secularization of the state in Turkey – which he claims, manifests as an 'ongoing, silent, Islamic reformation'[44] – provide an encouraging model for the rest of the Muslim world. The 'Islamic liberalism' Akyol advocates rests on three pillars: reason – which can and should lead to the systematic reinterpretation of Islamic law in a manner consistent with contemporary notions of freedom and human rights; pluralism – both within Islam and with respect to a 'desacralized' state, necessary in order to avoid the institutionalization of any given interpretation of the faith; and Godliness – which can be cultivated but should not be imposed. He also maintains that a more critical study of Islam's intellectual past is required to move the

---

[43] T. Kuran, *The Long Divergence: How Islamic Law Held Back the Middle East* (Princeton University Press, 2010), p. x, jacket.
[44] Akyol, *Islam without Extremes*, p. 33.

Muslim world beyond defending this heritage 'as though it were our God'.[45] In order to build a liberal Islam, Akyol argues that:

> 'We Muslims need to develop an ethical philosophy of "good" and "bad" according to which we should reinterpret our transmitted religious tradition. To reinterpret the Sharia, in particular, we need to focus on the divine "intentions" behind commandments, rather than their literal wording. We also need a more scientific view of the world, which explains phenomena according to objective facts and laws, not the presuppositions in our minds. And to be able to do all this we should break our self-containment and connect with the rest of humanity so that we can learn from its achievements while also contributing to them. We should even go back to the very core of our faith – the Qur'an – and reconsider the way we understand it'.[46]

Heresy and apostasy

As already indicated, the distinction between heterodoxy and heresy with respect to any faith or ideology is, typically, not clear-cut. But in the case of Islam, as Ibn Warraq observes: 'anyone who denied the unity of God and cast doubt on the prophethood of Muhammad and the divine origin of the Koran was considered beyond the Muslim pale'.[47] The appearance of heresy in the early history of Islam is unsurprising on account of three particular features of this new religion considered in previous chapters. First, the 'wars of apostasy' indicate that, in the immediate aftermath of the Prophet's death, there were multiple competing versions. Second, in spite of the fact that the Qur'an is opaque and, at best, not easy to understand, mainstream Islamic doctrine is, nevertheless, very rigid and uncompromising. Yet, third, many have not been deterred from challenging its typically unforgiving custodians.

The heresy trail is, in fact, littered with outspoken critics from the ummah who refused to toe the orthodox line, some of whom we met in Chapter 2. Others include, for example, Djad ibn Dirham who, in 742/3, became the first Muslim to be executed as a heretic for declaring that Allah had not taken Abraham as a friend, nor had He spoken to Moses. Ibn Dirham also held other unorthodox views, including that the Qur'an had been created and was not co-

---

[45] F. Rahman, *Islam and Modernity: The Transformation of an Intellectual Tradition* (University of Chicago Press, 1982), p. 147.
[46] Akyol, *Reopening Muslim Minds*, pp. 155-6.
[47] Ibn Warraq, *Why I Am Not A Muslim* (Prometheus, Reprinted 2003), p. 239.

eternal with God Himself, a position later associated with the Mu'tazilites. His followers are also said to have accused the Prophet of lying. Abd-Allah ibn al-Muqaffa (d. circa 756) – a philosopher, translator, and bureaucrat of Persian extraction in the Umayyad and Abbasid caliphates – criticized the Muslim deity as unjust, tyrannical, irrational, and malevolent. He was executed in 772 for having accused some of the prophets mentioned in the Qur'an, particularly Abraham and Joseph, of lying, and by his own admission, fabricating more than 4,000 hadith.[48] Bashar ibn Burd (714-783), another Persian with a low opinion of the Arabs, was accused of not praying in the orthodox manner, disrespecting the Hajj, denying the last judgment of the living and the dead, and parodying the call to prayer when drunk. The manner of his death is unknown. Some sources claim he was executed as a heretic, others that he was murdered.

At the end of the 8th century and the first half of the 9th, Khaydhar bin Kawus known as 'Afshin', a prominent Persian general and early Islamic hero for the leading roles he played in the campaigns of Caliph al-Mu'tasim (796–842), 'ridiculed Islamic laws … dreamed of the restoration of the Persian empire and the "white religion," and mocked Arabs, Maghribines and Muslim Turks'.[49] He was eventually tried and executed for disloyalty in 841. According to Goldziher, Afshin was typical of many non-Arabs who joined the Muslim cause for material advantage while hating the Arabs, and particularly in the case of the Persians, for having destroyed their national independence and ancestral traditions.[50]

A 16th century example of heterodoxy which ended in heresy can also be found in the spiritual journey of the third Moghul emperor, Akbar (1542-1605).[51] Increasingly disillusioned with Sunnism from the early 1570s, Akbar came under the influence of pantheistic Sufi mysticism and embarked upon a mission to encourage Sunni-Shia reconciliation and inter-faith dialogue. He even built a special debating chamber at the newly-established city of Fatehpur Sikri, near Delhi, to which renowned theologians, mystics, and thinkers of all religions and none, including atheists, were invited to discuss

---

[48] Ibid., p. 253.
[49] S. Stern (ed.), *Muslim Studies by I. Goldziher*, (State University of New York Press, 1967), Vol. 1, p. 139.
[50] Ibid., p. 140.
[51] I. Mukhoty, *Akbar: The Great Mughal – The Definitive Biography* (Aleph Book Company, 2020)

matters of spirituality, the validity of the Qur'an, the nature of God, and related issues. However, the experiment was abandoned in 1582. Rather than fostering mutual respect and understanding, the representatives of the various participating creeds simply asserted the superiority of their own and denounced everyone else's as false. Rejecting the notion of sacred scriptures and a priestly hierarchy, Akbar then founded his own hybrid religion, *Din-i Ilahi*, derived mainly from Islam and Hinduism with elements of Zoroastrianism and Christianity. This embodied what he took to be the common virtues of all authentic faiths – generosity, forgiveness, abstinence, prudence, wisdom, kindness, and piety. Amongst other things, he also discouraged the slaughter of animals and advocated respect for celibacy and chastity. Akbar died in 1605 and his new religion soon followed.

Historic heretical sects

As already indicated, in common with all global religions, Islam has spawned many sects. The most prominent of those regarded as heretical by the contemporary mainstream, and historically persecuted by other Muslims, are the Alawites, the Druze, and the Ahmadiyya. Indeed, of the four British Muslims murdered since 2010 on account of their faith, Asad Shah and Jalal Uddin were killed by other Muslims on the grounds of their 'heresy' stemming either from their allegiance to a particular sect or from an otherwise innocuous practice endorsed by their particular Muslim community.[52]

In March 2016, Asad Shah, an Ahmadiyya shopkeeper in Glasgow, was murdered by Sunni Muslim taxi driver, Tanveer Ahmed, from Bradford, on account of his alleged blasphemy in claiming to be a prophet. Ahmed was found guilty of murder and sentenced to life imprisonment with a minimum term of 27 years. And, in February 2016, a 71-year-old Bangladeshi imam, Jalal Uddin, was bludgeoned to death by hammer blows to the face in a park in Rochdale, Yorkshire, because he practised *taweez*, a form of Islamic faith healing which involves good luck amulets.[53] Although recognised by the Rochdale Bangladeshi community, ultra-orthodox Muslims regard this as

---

[52] Lord Young, S. Armstrong, F. Attenborough, B. Harris & L. Maby, *Why Labour's Definition of 'Islamophobia' Will Have a Chilling Effect on Free Speech: The Free Speech Union's response to the Government's consultation on a proposed definition of 'anti-Muslim hatred/Islamophobia'*, Free Speech Union Briefing, July 2025, p. 24.
[53] BBC, 'Jalal Uddin murder: Syeedy guilty over Rochdale imam death', 16 September 2016.

'black magic' and an indicator of apostasy. The whereabouts of the alleged murderer, Mohammed Abdul Kadir then aged 24 who promptly fled the UK, remain unknown. His accomplice, Mohammed Hussain Syeedy, a former engineering student then aged 21, who drove Kadir to the park, was sentenced to life imprisonment with a minimum term of 24 years. A third suspect, Mohammed Syadul Hussain, who provided Kadir with £700 to help him escape after the murder, received a jail sentence for assisting an offender. The jury at Syeedy's trial was told that, when the police searched his home following his arrest, a 'large volume' of ISIS-related material was found on his phone and on other devices. In July 2025, the report of a judge-led inquiry – a copy of which, redacted for security reasons, was laid before Parliament – found that, as supporters of Islamic State, counterterrorist officers regarded Kadir and Syeedy as high risk. A 'succession of mistakes' by the police was said to have allowed them to evade detection.[54]

a) The Alawites

The Alawites ('worshippers of Ali') are an offshoot of Islam, concentrated mostly in Syria where they constitute between 10 and 12% of the population with about 2.6 million worldwide.[55] By contrast with the orthodox shahada, the Alawites affirm that 'there is no God but Ali ibn Talib, the one to be worshipped, no Veil but the Lord Mohammad, worthy to be praised, and no gate but the Lord Salman al-Farisi … (one of Mohammad's close companions) … the object of love'. Together with the fact that they also believe Ali taught Mohammad the Qur'an, that Allah has revealed himself as a trinity seven times in human history, and that Mohammad created and sustains the universe, leaves little doubt about their heretical status. Alawites generally have no mosques, do not regard prayer as an obligation, celebrate Christmas and Easter, subscribe to the Hindu doctrine of the transmigration of souls, and retain several pagan Arab practices such as the veneration of arboreal groves. The teaching of their *shaykhs* (leaders) is regarded as the only authentic source of religious authority and insight.

In 1970 General Hafiz al-Assad, an Alawite and Ba'athist pan-Arab secular national socialist, seized power in Syria, became a brutal dictator, and

---

[54] C. Kampfner, 'Imam killed by Islamist fanatics after police blunder', *The Times*, 11 July 2025.
[55] M. Kerr & C. Larkin (eds.), *The Alawis of Syria: War, Faith and Politics in the Levant* (Hurst, 2015).

served as President from 1971 until his death in 2000. During his regime and that of his son, the Alawites became the political and social elite in Damascus. Bassel al-Assad, Hafiz's eldest son and presumed successor, died in a car accident in 1994. His other son, Bashar, a doctor specialising in ophthalmology, was then groomed to fulfil this role. Serving as President from 2000 until being deposed in 2024, his term of office included the bloody Syrian civil war which spiralled out of the Arab Spring of 2010 and thereafter, plus the brief ISIS/DAESH Caliphate which included parts of Syria and Iraq from 2014-18.

b) The Druze

The Druze, who prefer the name *Muwahhidun* (Unitarians), split from mainstream Shiism centuries ago, settling in mountainous parts of southern Lebanon and later in Syria and Jordan, where most of their 680,000–strong community continue to live as farmers and orchardists subsisting on a mostly vegetarian diet.[56] Although without doubt part of the historic Islamic tradition, their highly secretive beliefs and practices, in so far as they are known, are distant from the Shia or Sunni mainstreams. It is said that they originated in the 11th century, when Nashtakin ad-Darazi claimed that the Fatimid Caliph, Al-Hakim, was the Hidden Imam and possibly even an incarnation of Allah himself. Al-Hakim, who reigned from 996-1021, enthusiastically agreed and declared himself the 'cosmic intelligence' for good measure. Amongst other things, he legislated against dogs, banned chess, and prohibited the manufacture of women's shoes in order to keep women indoors. Not surprisingly he is widely regarded as having been insane. He disappeared mysteriously in 1021, possibly murdered.

The Druze are so secretive about their faith that most of their own community are forbidden from knowing all but its most fundamental elements. These can be summarized in seven principles: love of truth, taking care of one another, renouncing all other religions, avoiding the devil and all wrongdoers, accepting divine unity in humanity, endorsing all of al-Hakim's acts and behaving in complete compliance with his will. They also believe in reincarnation, hold their weekly prayer meetings on Thursday evenings, adhere to a modified version of Hanifa law rather than to the sharia, do not

---

[56] J-M. Aractingi, *The Hidden Face of the Druze: 'The Freemasons of the East'* (Independently published, 2021).

fast during Ramadan, promote equality between men and women, refrain from consuming wine, tobacco, and other intoxicants, and do not allow converts in or out of the faith. They also distinguish between the white turban-wearing 'sages' (*uqqul*) – the custodians of a secret knowledge (*hikma*) found in the Book of Wisdom (*Raisail al-Hikma*) – and the 'unenlightened' or 'ignorant', denied access to their six holy texts. Although becoming a sage is technically open to anyone with the requisite skills, in practice it has long been monopolized by certain families.

Although the Druze have been persecuted by other Muslims, when it comes to acts of savagery, they do not have entirely clean hands themselves. For example, in 1860, following the Ottoman Reform Decree of 1856 – which ended the second-class dhimmi status of non-Muslims – they massacred 11,000 Christian Maronites in Lebanon.[57] The Sunni Muslims of Damascus followed suit, destroying churches and monasteries and murdering a further 5,000 Christians. The multidimensional complexity of the turmoil was vividly dramatized by the intervention of Amir Abd al-Qadir al-Jazairi, the celebrated Muslim anti-French Algerian freedom fighter, who saved 4,000 souls from a similar fate.

c) The Ahmadiyya/Amadi

Unlike the Alawites and the Druze, the Ahmadiyya (or Ahmadi) sect, which has also suffered persecution including murder by other Muslims, was founded comparatively recently, in India in 1889, by Mirza Ghulam Ahmad (1839-1908) who claimed to be the Messiah, the Prophet Mohammad, and/or an incarnation of the Hindu God Krishna.[58] He also believed that Jesus survived the crucifixion by feigning death and then lived in India until he was 120 years old. After Ahmad's death, the movement which currently numbers about 170 million world-wide, split into two factions – the Qadiani, who revere the founder as a true prophet, and the Lahore, who regard him only as a reformer. The Ahmadiyya are also associated with several Sufi orders, especially the Egyptian Al-Badawi. Amongst other things, Ahmad taught that jihad should be fought only with the pen and not the sword. As a result, those

---

[57] E. Rogan, *The Damascus Events: The 1860 Massacre and the Destruction of the Old Ottoman World* (Allen Lane, 2024).
[58] D. Henry, *The Lahore Ahmadiyya Movement: The truth will prevail* (Independently published, 2023).

living in the UK have been cultivated by government as allies in the struggle against violent Islamism.

Regarded by other Muslims as heretics, orthodox Sunni hostility towards the Ahmadi has led to attacks on their mosques, publication and distribution of leaflets calling for their murder, the broadcasting of anti-Ahmadi rhetoric, and coordinated boycotts of Ahmadi businesses. For example, in October 2011, Abdul Qadir Jilani, a regular guest on the *Rehmatul Lil Alameen* programme hosted by the Manchester-based channel DM Digital, declared in a live broadcast: 'It is your duty ... to kill those who insult Prophet Mohammad ... Under the guidance from Islamic texts it is evident that if a Muslim apostasizes, then it is not right to wait for the authorised courts: anyone may kill him'.[59] The regulator, Ofcom, later fined DM Digital for broadcasting material likely to encourage or incite crime. Some Muslim organizations, such as the annual *Tajdar e Khatme Nabuwwat Conference*, have even been established with the express objective of persecuting Ahmadis.

Contemporary 'heretics' and 'apostates'

As with their progenitors throughout Islamic history, contemporary progressive Muslims are no strangers to charges of heresy. Even those who accept the oneness of God, and the authority of the Qur'an as His directly dictated Word, are not immune. For example, in her inquiry into threats to social cohesion and democratic resilience, published in 2024, Dame Sara Khan quotes the experience of a Muslim official working for a local authority, regularly targeted by an Islamist extremist organisation.

'I've been labelled a traitor, a lackey to the British, a snake who needs to "watch my back." My children have been harassed and have had to move school. My tyres have been slashed and my house is red-flagged. Threatening terms such as "mushriq, munafiq, murtad" are openly used against me. The police don't understand the inciteful nature of such language, and how such language is creating a climate conducive to violence against other Muslims. Islamist extremists target Muslim practitioners in a way they do not target non-Muslim practitioners. I don't have confidence that either the police or the local authority understand the intra-community abuse I and other

---

[59] A. Meleagrou-Hitchens, *Understanding and Responding to Blasphemy Extremism in the UK* (Commission for Countering Extremism – Rethinking Extremism, 2024), p. 28.

Muslims experience and how frightened we are. This intimidation directly contributes to a climate of fear among local Muslim communities – they are too frightened to challenge Islamist activists'.[60]

And this from an Imam:

'I have regularly received death threats because of my work and because of my religious and academic beliefs which ... (are considered) ... heresy. As a Muslim, I have been repeatedly targeted by Islamist extremists with claims that I am a "threat to Islam." During one incident, I received many death threats which resulted in 18 months of police protection. I was very worried that my home would be firebombed, and my children used to cower underneath the kitchen table out of fear. I have been attacked both physically and verbally with my children by Islamist extremists. The impact on my career has been distressing. I have in effect been silenced. I had to turn down interviews and book deals as I could not cope with the trauma. I have been left traumatised and I know this intimidation has led me to self-censor when I did not want to'.[61]

Two recent cases in the UK – one concerning Paigham Mustafa, a British author, editor, publisher, and Qur'an scholar, and the other, imam and Cambridge educated astro-physicist, Usama Hassan – further illustrate the problem.

a) Pagham Mustafa

Mustafa was born in Pakistan to Muslim parents from the Punjab in India. In 1963, at the age of five, he moved with his family to Huddersfield, West Yorkshire, before settling in Scotland in 1968.[62] Having spent his formative years in Glasgow, he currently lives in Aberdeen. In his teens and early adulthood, paying little attention to anything religious, Mustafa says he was what some might call a 'lapsed Muslim'. But the issues raised by the Qur'an kept haunting him and he felt compelled to find answers. What concerned him most was the difference between what the Qur'an says and how most Muslims practise their faith. Having produced his first newspaper as a pupil at Govan

---

[60] S. Khan, *Threats to Social Cohesion and Democratic Resilience: A New Strategic Response*, March 2024, p. 65.
[61] Ibid., p. 66.
[62] P. Mustafa, *From Greece to Glasgow* (Signature, 2016).

High School, by the mid-1980s Mustafa had established his own successful publishing business. In addition to a regular flow of books from European writers, this included the periodicals (some of which he also edited) *The Tribune Glasgow*, *The Buccaneer*, *CityLife Aberdeen*, *Asian Life*, *Friday Standard*, and *Signs International*, the last of which had a global readership of over 5,000 especially in South Asia. Mustafa has also written for *The Sunday Herald*, *The Sunday Times*, and *The National*, and been interviewed on BBC Radio Scotland. In the mid-1980s, having met some Islamic scholars in Malaysia, he became their publisher.

The Glasgow Muslim clergy strongly objected to Mustafa's published output, particularly its critical scrutiny of some allegedly Islamic religious practices. Denouncing him as a heretic and blasphemer, in 2001 a committee representing 12 leading Glasgow mosques issued a fatwa, endorsed by a fraternity of 16 prominent ulama. Believed to be the only one of its kind in Europe, it remains in force to this day. The three-page document, which carries the imprimatur of *Jamiat ittihad-ul-muslimeen*, the leading organization for Muslims in Glasgow, was reported by *The Herald*, *The Sun*, and *The Times*. It is fully documented in Mustafa's book, *From Greece to Glasgow*.[63] In addition to the accusation and verdict, it compares Mustafa with Sir Salman Rushdie and quotes an extract from *Signs* claiming this proves he insulted the Prophet. But, according to Mustafa, the quotation in question is, in fact, a hadith. Mustafa concedes that, while *Signs* questions the authority of the clergy, he denies that it was ever blasphemous. In contesting the fatwa, Mustafa was supported by **Des Browne, then MP for Kilmarnock and Loudoun who later became Baron Browne of Ladyton.** Although the fatwa stopped short of anything that could be construed as an incitement to violence, Mustafa believes the comparison with Salman Rushdie sent the less-than-subtle message – 'stop what you're saying or you may suffer unpleasant consequences at the hands of others'. He maintains, however, that the denunciation, nevertheless, had a silver lining because it motivated him to press ahead with exposing misguided traditional outlooks, particularly through his new translation of, and commentary upon, the Qur'an.

b) Usama Hasan

Dr Usama Hasan, who comes from an Indo-Pakistani family, is a fellow

---

[63] Ibid.

of the Royal Astronomical Society, consultant in Islamic studies, part-time Imam, Senior Analyst at the Tony Blair Institute for Global Change, and patron of both the Forum for the Discussion of Israel and Palestine (FODIP) and Friends of the Bereaved Families Forum.[64] He was also formerly a planetarium lecturer at the Royal Observatory Greenwich, senior researcher in Islamic Studies at the Quilliam Foundation, and senior lecturer in business information systems at Middlesex University. His speaking engagements include participating in the UK Foreign and Commonwealth Office's, 'Projecting British Muslims' delegations to Egypt in 2008 and to Afghanistan in 2010; delivering a keynote speech at the Anglo-Syrian government-sponsored conference, 'The Message of Peace in Islam', in Damascus in 2009; and speaking at the Google Ideas/Council on Foreign Relations 'Summit Against Violent Extremism' in Dublin in 2011. He has also appeared on BBC and CNN television programmes and has written columns for *The Guardian* and *The Washington Post*.

Although having no formal qualifications in Arabic or Islamic Studies, Hasan was schooled in this field by his father Suhaib Hasan, an Islamic scholar trained in Saudi Arabia. His grandfather, Abdul-Ghaffar Hasan Al-Hindi, was also an Islamic scholar who taught at the Islamic University of Medina at the invitation of the influential Salafi, Al-Albani. Having fought against the Soviet occupation of Afghanistan, Usama Hasan later became a vocal critic of Islamism and jihadi terrorism. In October 2013 he was alerted by counterterrorism police to the fact that, together with other prominent Muslim critics of Islamism in the UK, he had been targeted in a propaganda video by Al-Shabaab. This East African jihadi organization was responsible, amongst other things, for 71 deaths in an attack on the Westgate shopping mall in Nairobi, Kenya, that September.

Hasan has been involved in several other controversies. These have included issuing a fatwa with others in 2014 condemning British Muslims fighting for ISIS,[65] and arguing that during Ramadan, Muslims in the UK should observe a fast shorter than the dawn-to-sunset tradition because daylight at the height of the British summer can last up to 19 hours.[66] In 2012, as one of its trustees, he reported London's *Masjid al-Tawhid* mosque to the

---

[64] BBC Hardtalk, 'Usama Hasan', 30 August 2007.

[65] Z. Boren, 'Isis terror threat: Leading British Muslims issue fatwa condemning terror group', *The Independent*, 31 August 2014.

[66] BBC News, 'Ramadan fast in UK "should be shortened" says scholar', 9 June 2016.

authorities for 'extremism' and stood down with the other trustees to facilitate arbitration. The new trustees then accused him and his relations of having run the mosque as a family affair. Hasan has also received death threats, and his lectures have often been disrupted by hecklers. This has particularly been because of his view that Adam and Eve are purely symbolic figures in the Qur'an and that, not only is Islam compatible with the theory of evolution, but Darwinism was in fact anticipated by Muslim thinkers such as Ibn Miskawayh (932-1030) and Ibn Khaldun (1332-1406).[67]

c) Ex-Muslims

Amongst the most intriguing contributions to the debate about the difference between Islamophobic expression and legitimate critique of Islam and its adherents are those made by ex-Muslims who have publicly renounced their faith, some of whom now actively oppose it, typically from the perspective of secularism or that of another religion.[68] Such a position is, of course, replete with risk in 'Muslim lands' themselves. But, although generally less vulnerable in the west, overt ex-Muslims nevertheless experience various forms of negativity, especially from members of their own families and communities.[69] All faiths and ideologies have powerful mechanisms, particularly ostracism from family, friends, comrades, and fellow believers which discourage renunciation. Many religions, including Islam, reinforce these with the additional threat of divine punishment in this life and/or thereafter. To make a successful transition, the 'apostate', therefore, needs both to meet these challenges and to find viable alternatives to the support and rewards hitherto offered.

In principle, the reasons for 'Muslim apostasy' are not significantly different from those associated with the abandonment of any faith or ideology.[70] Typically, the journey begins with the onset of doubt, triggered by

---

[67] U. Hasan, 'Knowledge regained', *The Guardian*, 11 September 2008.

[68] See https://ex-muslim.org.uk/; M. Namazie, in E. Webb (ed.), *Islamophobia*, pp. 75-80.

[69] Khan, *Threats to Social Cohesion*, p. 61.

[70] M. Khalil & M. Bilici, 'Conversion Out of Islam: A Study of Conversion Narratives of Former Muslims' (2007) 97 *The Muslim World*, 111–124; T. Pauha & A. Aghaee, '"God never existed, and I was looking for him like crazy!" Muslim stories of deconversion', in K. van Nieuwkerk (ed.), *Moving In and Out of Islam* (University of Texas Press, 2018); S. Cottee, *The Apostates: When Muslims Leave Islam* (Oxford University Press, 2015).

a range of factors including a naturally inquiring mind, personal experience, exposure to alternative views as a result of education and/or certain publications or presentations, encounters with persuasive outsiders, and/or dissatisfaction about how doubts regarding the faith have been addressed by those in positions of authority.

A study by Khalil and Bilici, for example, found the following amongst the most important intellectual/ideological reasons for departing the Islamic faith: the subordinate status of women; contradictions between Islamic law and human rights; regarding the Qur'an as the literal word of God and the hadith as reliable sources of religious truth and moral value; the character of the Prophet Mohammad and other Muslim leaders; illogicality in Islamic doctrine; clashes between traditional Islam and modern natural sciences including the theory of evolution; the traditional Muslim expectation that even virtuous non-Muslims will be condemned to eternal damnation; unnecessarily prescriptive commands and prohibitions especially regarding trivial matters; and enduring Arab-centricity rather than genuine ethnic universality. [71] Among apostates with more personal social/experiential than intellectual reasons, the following were noted: unpleasant encounters with bad, cruel and/or oppressive Muslims, alleged Muslim backwardness, a lack of critical self-awareness on the part of Muslims concerning the problems presented by their own faith, and the ill-treatment of women and non-Muslims. However, the authors also observe that ex-Muslims are not necessarily always fully aware of the range of historical and contemporary scholarly Muslim opinion.

According to a recent survey of ex-Muslims conducted by Ben Jones – doctoral researcher at the University of Warwick and Director of Case Management and Outreach at the Free Speech Union – the vast majority of ex-Muslims in Britain are not able to meet openly and most lead secret double lives. The rate of apostasy from Islam, and the extent to which ex-Muslims face persecution in contemporary Britain, are also poorly understood.[72] While only 7% of children raised in the UK will have left the religion by adulthood – a small figure compared with other religions – this is, nevertheless, equivalent to hundreds of thousands. Those whose departure from their faith is known, typically face hostility from family and community. In some cases, their finances may be seized and they may suffer physical abuse. However,

[71] Khalil & Bilici, 'Conversion Out of Islam.'
[72] B. Jones, 'British ex-Muslims, already unfree, face perils of worsening censorship', *National Secular Society*, 21 August 2024.

despite the challenges, social media have enabled them to build substantial networks of support, including informal social groups and formal organizations such as the Council of Ex-Muslims of Britain and Faith to Faithless.[73] Some even become high profile public activists for the ex-Muslim cause. Jones maintains that 'by far the most dangerous threat' to ex-Muslims in Britain is the definition of Islamophobia advanced in 2018 by the All-Party Parliamentary Group (APPG) on British Muslims, discussed in Chapter 10. Among other things, this brands as Islamophobic anyone who makes mendacious, dehumanizing, demonizing, or stereotypical allegations about Muslims. As Jones points out, if adopted in law as the APPG advocates, discussion by ex-Muslims of the persecution and mistreatment they have suffered at the hands of other Muslims would become unlawful.

Several high-profile contemporary ex-Muslims have made particularly strident and uncompromising criticisms of their former faith. One of the most prominent is Ali Ahmad Said Esber – better known by his penname 'Adonis' or 'Adunis' – a prolific Syrian poet, essayist, and translator of Alawite extraction. A perennial contender for the Nobel Prize for Literature, Adonis has been described as the Arab T.S. Eliot and the greatest living poet in the Arab world. In the 1970s he was a leading exponent of the neo-Sufi trend in Arab poetry. But, developing a powerful public critique of Islam as an inherently violent ideology, he later described himself as a 'pagan mystic'. In conversation with the psychoanalyst Houria Abdelouahed, Adonis attributes the wave of violence and war following the Arab spring, to unresolved tensions deeply rooted in the Islamic faith, manifesting principally in its aggressive imperialistic character, the violent intolerance of dissent, the subordination of women, and the many graphic depictions of hell found in the Qur'an.[74] He argues that, if there is to be any hope of peace or progress in the Arab world, a new spirit of inquiry including freedom to interrogate the past and to question cultural norms, must be allowed to emerge.

Referencing 9th century sceptical Arab scholar, Abu Isa al-Warraq, the contemporary Ibn Warraq (literally 'son of a papermaker', a pseudonym adopted by dissident writers throughout Islamic history), is a British Gujarati-born ex-Muslim. Paying homage to Bertrand Russell's famous, *Why I Am Not*

---

[73] Ibid.
[74] Adonis (trans. by D. Watson), *Violence and Islam: Conversations with Houria Abdelouahed* (Polity, 2016).

a Christian, Ibn Warraq's book, *Why I Am Not a Muslim*,[75] systematically criticizes the religion in which he was raised. As he states: 'This book is first and foremost an assertion of my right to criticize everything and anything in Islam even to blaspheme, to make errors, to satirize, and mock'.[76] The result is not, however, an intemperate polemic. On the contrary, while the impressive array of scholarship on Islamic mythology, theology, history, and culture, could have been more coherently presented, it is nevertheless one of the most erudite, comprehensively-researched critiques of Islam by a former Muslim or indeed by anyone else. According to Ibn Warraq, the claim that the Qur'an is the infallible Word of God cannot be sustained when the techniques of modern Biblical criticism and other critical perspectives are applied to it. The potential consequences for the faith are discussed in other parts of this study.

Another prominent ex-Muslim, Ayaan Hirsi Ali, a Somali-born, Dutch-American public intellectual, author, activist, and former centre-right politician, was named by *Time* magazine in 2005 as one of the 100 most influential people in the world. Ali is particularly critical of those aspects of Islam she regards as oppressive for women and girls, including forced and child marriage, honour killing, and female genital mutilation.[77] Having been a prominent exponent of the New Atheism in the early 2000s, in November 2023, Ali announced her conversion to Christianity. In a Foreword to a recent edition of Ibn Warraq's, *Why I Am Not a Muslim*, she provides six central reasons underlying her own exit from the faith. First, she argues that, devoid of love and compassion, Islam requires total submission to Allah, an abdication of individual responsibility and agency. Second, the faith is utterly reliant upon the alleged revelations of one man (Mohammad) and one book (the Qur'an). Third, it is preoccupied with the afterlife, presented as an erotic and culinary male paradise. Fourth, in sharia-governed states, there is little protection for women or non-Muslims and no social constraints upon the violent enforcement of Islamic law, including in matters of belief, by beheading, amputation, stoning, and flogging on the part of both state and free-lancers. Fifth, adherence to Islam is, in her view, secured through fear of

---

[75] Ibn Warraq, *Why I Am Not a Muslim*.

[76] Ibid., p. 14.

[77] A. Ali, *Infidel: My Life* (Free Press, 2007), *Nomad: A Personal Journey Through the Clash of Civilizations* (Simon & Schuster, 2011), *Heretic: Why Islam Needs a Reformation Now* (Harper, 2015).

adverse consequences in both this life and the hereafter. Sixth, she maintains that Islam emphasises rigid demarcation between believers and infidels, and both assumes and affirms the superiority of the former over the latter.

Conclusion

While Islam is clearly not monolithic, the vast majority of Muslims today nevertheless adhere to Sunni orthodoxy or Shia heterodoxy, neither of which is or has ever been, receptive to liberal, progressive, modern, or reformist perspectives. In fact, each has long histories of brutally suppressing such outlooks and both continue to do so in many parts of the world where they are ascendant. Ironically, given the pervasive assumption that the west is riven with Islamophobia, it is only here that Muslim deviation from orthodox and ultra-orthodox Islam can be expressed in comparative, though not complete safety.

It is difficult to imagine any progressive non-Muslim who would not welcome a more liberal re-interpretation of the faith embraced more widely by the ummah. However, paradoxically, it is precisely naïve and badly informed progressive non-Muslims who are most likely to denounce, as Islamophobic, the inevitable reappraisal of the Islamic tradition this requires, particularly when expressed by much better-informed non-Muslims. Yet, if the attempt to liberalize Islam is to succeed, it must address several significant problems at the heart of which lies the status of the traditional sources of the faith and their implications. Even if the authority of the hadith, sunnah and sharia are downgraded or disregarded altogether, two difficulties remain with the Qur'an itself. First, it includes both liberal and illiberal elements, a fact which should be more honestly acknowledged by all concerned. Second, the case for liberal Islam would be much easier to make if it were conceded that the Qur'an was *inspired* by God rather than directly *dictated* by Him word-for-word. But if this were to be widely accepted it would sound the death knell of traditional Islam as we know it. And even if Turkish Islam is spearheading liberalization of the faith, as Akyol and others maintain, it is not clear how this could or should be applied in other places. Finally, the most challenging problem of all for liberal Islam is that, although it has interested and excited the most open-minded and forward-looking Muslim intellectuals and commentators, it has yet to make much visible headway with the average believer, even in the west. And the environment is a lot less receptive elsewhere.

Chapter 6

Rights and law

Introduction

Before turning to some of the most notorious false accusations of Islamophobic expression, this chapter considers how liberal democratic legal systems, especially in the UK, seek to distinguish between the expression of anti-Muslim hatred and prejudice on the one hand, and lawful criticism of Muslims/Islam on the other. Although the details vary from state to state, each liberal democracy acknowledges a common foundational principle: the right to free expression should prevail unless there are good reasons that it should not. At the global level the most abstract and schematic formulation is found in Article 19 of the Universal Declaration of Human Rights 1948. This simply states: 'Everyone has the right to freedom of opinion and expression; this right includes freedom to hold opinions without interference and to seek, receive and impart information and ideas through any media and regardless of frontiers'. The more detailed version found in the European Convention on Human Rights (ECHR) applies to every state on the continent except Russia – no longer a member of the Council of Europe, the ECHR's parent body, as a result of the full invasion of Ukraine in 2022 – and Belarus which was never a member in the first place. States in the non-European west, including the US, have their own constitutional arrangements based on broadly similar values.

The ECHR is a treaty which binds states internationally. The Human Rights Act 1998 (HRA) – considered further below – made it directly applicable in UK law, but only as far as public authorities are concerned. In other words, while public authorities are legally required to respect the rights in the ECHR, individuals and private bodies are only bound by them if these rights are otherwise provided by national law. However, signatories to the Convention, also have the 'positive obligation' to ensure this happens.

The judgments of the European Court of Human Rights (ECtHR) do not constitute an integrated system of legal doctrine comparable to that of the common law tradition. According to Article 46(1) of the ECHR, they are legally binding only upon the specific state which was party to the litigation in question and amount only to the Court's interpretation and application of Convention rights to the facts of the case before it (typically unique), the arguments presented, and 'cut-and-paste' quotes from its own previous decisions which it is reluctant to modify.

The ECtHR has decided very few cases directly relevant to the issues under discussion in this book. Some general principles have, nevertheless, been established. And although these leave a lot to be desired, the shortcomings could, in theory, be remedied by the Court itself. However, given its unwavering fidelity to its own jurisprudence, this is unlikely to happen. According to s.2(1) of the HRA: 'A court or tribunal determining a question which has arisen in connection with a Convention right *must take into account* any judgment, decision, declaration or advisory opinion of the European Court of Human Rights....'[1] This means that, while UK courts must consider judgments of the ECtHR as authoritative guidance on how Convention rights should be interpreted in cases other than those in which the UK has been party, they are not strictly bound to follow them.

We begin below with a discussion of the core value, the right to freedom of expression provided by Article 10 ECHR, followed by an attempt to summarize its limits, particularly the potential implications for criminal law, which may result in punishment including imprisonment, and civil law which may have other consequences such as lawful dismissal from employment. In recent years the activities of the ECtHR have been criticized in the UK, especially with respect to its intervention in deportation cases, regarded as obstructive particularly by those on the right of the political spectrum. The current policy of both the Conservative party and Reform UK is to address this by withdrawing entirely from the Convention system. But even if this were to occur, it is highly likely that the right to freedom of expression would remain in some form or other in national law. And the view taken here is that it would be difficult to improve upon the formulation provided by the ECHR. The focus on domestic law which follows will be confined largely to England and Wales. Minor differences in relevant arrangements for Scotland and Northern Ireland will be largely ignored.

---

[1] Italics added.

Freedom of expression and its limits

Long the subject of discussion amongst jurists, philosophers and others, freedom of expression has been extolled as vital to a free society by such diverse luminaries of the western intellectual tradition as Milton, Locke, Voltaire, Mill, and Orwell. The case rests on several powerful arguments.[2] First, as social creatures with language and many other forms of self-realization including art, music, literature, dance, and religious ritual, the freedom to express ourselves is vital for our communication, our relationships with each other, our individual wellbeing, our collective and individual identity, and self-governance. Second, the exchange of ideas, the discussion of the methods and evidence upon which they are based, and the giving of cogent reasons for conclusions reached, enables us better to understand ourselves, each other, and our place in the natural and human spheres. But none of this can be fully achieved unless marginal, unfashionable, and unpopular views are included. As George Orwell once famously observed – free speech is pointless if it does not permit telling people what they do not want to hear – especially, it might be added, if they need to hear it. Third, free and frank debate is indispensable if, as a species, we are to have any hope of tackling effectively the problems facing us and life on the planet. Fourth, without adequately protected free expression, other basic freedoms become much less secure because their violation will be more difficult to expose and, therefore, to correct.

However, all credible contributions to the debate recognise that freedom of expression is not absolute and that it not only can, but must, be subject to limits. Philosophers and others have speculated about where relevant lines should be drawn.[3] But the most consequential, real-world distinctions are provided by law. While some have argued for minimum legal restriction, including upon hate speech, this is not the position in the UK.

---

[2] See, eg, K. Whittington, *Speak Freely: Why Universities Must Defend Free Speech* (Princeton University Press, 2019), Chs. 2-3; E. Chemerinsky & H. Gillman, *Free Speech on Campus* (Yale University Press, 2017), Ch. 2; G. Lukianoff, *Unlearning Liberty: Campus Censorship and the End of American Debate* (Encounter, 2012), pp. 18-35.

[3] See, eg, J. Waldron, *The Harm in Hate Speech* (Harvard University Press, 2014); N. Strossen, *HATE: Why We Should Resist it With Free Speech, Not Censorship (Inalienable Rights)* (Oxford University Press, 2018).

As already indicated, the legal anchor for freedom of expression in the UK and throughout the Council of Europe is Article 10 ECHR which provides:

1. Everyone has the right to freedom of expression. This right shall include freedom to hold opinions and to receive and impart information and ideas without interference by public authority and regardless of frontiers. This Article shall not prevent States from requiring the licensing of broadcasting, television or cinema enterprises.

2. The exercise of these freedoms, since it carries with it duties and responsibilities, may be subject to such formalities, conditions, restrictions or penalties as are prescribed by law and are necessary in a democratic society, in the interests of national security, territorial integrity or public safety, for the prevention of disorder or crime, for the protection of health or morals, for the protection of the reputation or rights of others, for preventing the disclosure of information received in confidence, or for maintaining the authority and impartiality of the judiciary.

It has been held by both the ECtHR and by British courts that freedom of expression constitutes one of the essential foundations of a democratic society and is one of the basic conditions for the development of individual self-fulfilment and social progress. The ECtHR and British courts have also affirmed that it is vital for the kind of ideas, views, opinions and outlooks upon which a pluralistic, tolerant, broadminded, progressive, and democratic society depends. In one of its most celebrated judgments, *Handyside v United Kingdom*, the ECtHR famously held that this includes forms of expression that 'offend, shock or disturb'.[4] And as British judge, Lord Justice Sedley, observed in *Redmond-Bate v Director of Public Prosecutions*: 'Free speech includes not only the inoffensive but the irritating, the contentious, the eccentric, the heretical, the unwelcome and the provocative … Freedom only to speak inoffensively is not worth having'.[5] More recently, in dismissing an appeal by the transgender rights charity, Mermaids, against a finding in favour of the respondents, LGB Alliance and the Charity Commission, a UK tribunal

---

[4] *Handyside v United Kingdom*, App. No. 5493/72, Judgment of 7 December 1976, para. 49.
[5] (1999) 7 BHRC 375, para 20.

ruled that there is 'no legal right to be free from criticism by those who disagree with you or to prevent those who hold beliefs that the law recognises as protected from expressing themselves or seeking to persuade others to their point of view'.[6]

Article 10 raises three core questions: What kinds of expression are included, what types of restriction may legitimately be imposed, and under what circumstances?[7] 'Expression' includes the spoken and written word, drama, art, graphics, dress, nudity, symbols and symbolic acts conveying opinions and ideas of a political, social, cultural/artistic or commercial kind, through, for example, graffiti, publications, meetings, broadcasting, theatre, cinema, the internet, and advertising.

The limits to the right to freedom of expression fall into two principal categories. First, certain forms of expression are inherently beyond the scope of Article 10. These include: those hostile towards core Convention values, an invocation of Article 17 which denies the protection of the Convention to anyone engaged in the destruction of any of its rights or their more extensive limitation than the ECHR itself permits; those seeking to deny, belittle, or defend the Holocaust, and possibly in certain circumstances, other clearly established crimes against humanity; and those that incite violence or hatred.

Second, Article 10(2) states that, since exercising freedom of expression 'carries with it duties and responsibilities', it 'may be subject to such formalities, conditions, restrictions or penalties as are prescribed by law and are necessary in a democratic society' with respect to the goals or 'legitimate purposes' stipulated in the second paragraph. The ECtHR has generally sought to identify and specify the 'duties and responsibilities' referred to, according to the characteristics of the applicant. So, for example, journalists, NGOs, and campaigning organizations have an obligation to act with due diligence in seeking to provide verifiably accurate and reliable information and grounded opinion in good faith and according to their professional ethics. Judges and lawyers should maintain the authority and impartiality of the legal process by expressing out-of-court opinions with discretion. Civil servants should refrain from joining extreme political parties and from expressing

---

[6] *Mermaids v Charity Commission for England and Wales and LGB Alliance* [2023] UKFTT 563 (GRC), para. 72.

[7] For a summary of the extensive jurisprudence see, eg, S. Greer, J. Gerards and R. Slowe, *Human Rights in the Council of Europe and the European Union: Achievements, Trends and Challenges* (Cambridge University Press, 2018), Ch. 3.

views that might compromise their neutrality. On the other hand, while politicians have considerable latitude with respect to the opinions they express, in doing so they should show appropriate respect for the democratic process. Employees should also avoid personal attacks when publicly criticizing colleagues or their employers.

The term 'prescribed by law' means not only provided by the positive law of a given state, but also 'compatible with the concept of legality'. In order fairly to warn when sanctions might be applied, this includes the drafting of legal instruments with sufficient precision to exclude arbitrariness and to distinguish clearly between what is lawful and what is not. Subject to a variable 'wriggle room', or 'margin of appreciation' available to states, the 'democratic necessity' test has been held to imply that the limitations are construed narrowly and are proportionate to a 'pressing social need'.

The exceptions found in Article 10(2) are, however, not always easy to distinguish from each other. Nor has the ECtHR always indicated clearly which one or more applies. For example, criminalizing the expression of certain views may be permitted in the context of counterterrorism in the interests of any one or more of the following: national security, public safety, and/or the prevention of disorder or crime. Where an interference is admitted by a respondent state but justification pleaded, the severity of the official sanction will often be the deciding factor in determining whether or not there has been a violation. The ECtHR is, however, generally unsympathetic to blanket bans and is typically most concerned about the proportionality of limits and sanctions, and with the provision of adequate procedural safeguards. It has also repeatedly stated that there is little scope under Article 10 for restrictions on political speech or on debate concerning matters of public interest.[8]

The ECtHR has also emphasised that, in resolving a conflict between the right to freedom of expression and any of the stipulated exceptions, its task is not to assume the role of national authorities but rather to review their decisions, particularly to determine whether, in the light of the case as a whole, the reasons proffered are relevant and sufficient.[9] The criteria which may come into play when achieving an accommodation or 'balance' between

---

[8] *Giniewski v France*, App. No. 64016/00, Judgment of 31 April 2006.
[9] See, eg, *Mamère v. France*, App. No. 12697/03, Judgment of 7 February 2007, para 19; *Lindon, Otchakovsky-Laurens and July v France*, App. Nos. 21279/02 & 36448/02, Judgment 22 October 2007, para 45.

freedom of expression and competing rights and interests include not only whether the particular expression contributed to a debate of public importance but also upon content, context, form, and likely consequences.

The principal Article 10(2) exceptions relevant to the debate about criticism of Muslim beliefs, practices, and conduct are the prevention of disorder or crime, the protection of morals, and the protection of the rights and freedoms of others, particularly freedom of thought, conscience and religion.

Prevention of disorder or crime

In *Otto-Preminger-Institut v Austria,* in 1994, the ECtHR considered how freedom of expression might be restricted in order to prevent disorder or crime and to protect the rights of others.[10]

The applicant, a private, non-profit making, arts cinema in Innsbruck, complained that its freedom of expression under Article 10 of the Convention had been violated by the official seizure and confiscation of a film, *Das Liebeskonzil (Council in Heaven).* This depicted God, Christ, and the Virgin Mary in an unflattering, and sometimes obscene manner, and portrayed them conspiring with the Devil to infect the human race with syphilis as punishment for immorality. Screenings were open to members of the public over 17 years of age, and the cinema's advertising indicated that the film caricatured the Christian creed and explored 'the relationship between religious beliefs and worldly mechanisms of oppression'. The seizure and confiscation were instigated at the request of the Innsbruck diocese of the Catholic church and were based on the offence of 'disparaging religious doctrines' under s. 188 of the Austrian Penal Code. This provides:

> 'Whoever, in circumstances where his or her behaviour is likely to arouse justified indignation, publicly disparages or insults a person who, or an object which, is an object of veneration of a church or religious community established within the country, or a dogma, a lawful custom or a lawful institution of such a church or religious community, shall be liable to up to six months' imprisonment or a day-fine for a period of up to 360 days'.

A majority of the Court (six out of nine judges) held that the cinema's right to

---

[10] App. No. 13470/87, Judgment of 20 September 1994.

freedom of expression had not been violated, while the minority held that it had. Both majority and minority agreed that the interference was in pursuit of the legitimate aim of protecting the right to freedom of thought, conscience and religion of others (considered further below), that the seizure and forfeiture of the film constituted an interference with the right to freedom of expression, and that this was in accordance with both Austrian law and the Convention principle of legality. There was also consensus about the relevant principles, viz. that freedom of expression is one of the foundations of democratic society characterized by tolerance and broadmindedness, that its exercise carries obligations including not to cause gratuitous offence to others, and that, since there is no uniform conception of the importance of religion in member states, there can be no comprehensive definition of what constitutes permissible interference where religious sensibilities are concerned. Subject to Convention supervision, national authorities, therefore, have a 'certain margin of appreciation' in convincingly assessing its necessity and extent. The main difference of opinion was over whether or not the seizure and forfeiture were 'necessary in a democratic society'. The majority thought it was. But the minority disagreed.

The majority also raised the prevention of disorder or crime exception, only to ignore it and to resurrect it later to support its conclusion. Viewed in these terms, the Austrian legislature, police, and prosecuting authorities had a margin of appreciation in deciding whether, and if so how, the presentation of the film should have been prohibited for the sake of public order. However, for this exception convincingly to apply, there should also have been cogent, credible, and concrete evidence that there was such a risk. And no evidence whatever to this effect is offered in the entire report of the Court's decision. Therefore, without it, defining the issue in terms of a clash between the right to freedom of expression and the prevention of disorder cannot be sustained.

Protection of morals

The 'protection of morals' is arguably the most controversial of the Article 10(2) limitations, largely because morality is so nebulous and variable over time and space and there may be little or no European consensus either upon detail or what is necessary and legitimate to protect it. Although the Court has repeatedly affirmed that the right to freedom of expression encompasses views and representations that 'offend, shock, or disturb' it has, nevertheless, invoked both the 'protection of morals' and the 'rights of others' to endorse restrictions upon forms of expression precisely on this basis and typically without distinguishing clearly between these exceptions. The legitimate limits upon the right to express critical, satirical or 'obscene' views about a given religion have also proven difficult to specify clearly. The ECtHR has repeatedly regarded 'gratuitous insult or offence' or 'abusive attacks' upon religion or morality as illegitimate exercises of the right to freedom of expression. But it has failed formally to specify precisely when critique crosses this threshold. As already intimated throughout this study, a great deal hinges upon judgment concerning content, context, style, intention, foreseeable effects, and the relevant public interest.

For example, in *Sekmadienis Ltd v Lithuania*, the applicant advertising company complained to the ECtHR that its right to freedom of expression had been violated by a decision of the Lithuanian advertising standards authority that its advertising campaign breached the national advertising code.[11] The advertisements, in which live models depicted Jesus and Mary, also used the slogans: 'Jesus, what trousers!', 'Dear Mary, what a dress!' and 'Jesus [and] Mary, what are you wearing?!' The advertising authority justified its decision on the grounds that the campaign was contrary to public morals because it distorted the 'main purpose' of religious symbols and constituted their use for inappropriate and 'superficial' ends. However, the ECtHR held that the domestic authorities had failed to strike a fair balance between the applicant's right to freedom of expression, on the one hand, and the protection of public morals and the rights of religious people, on the other. It concluded that, even assuming the majority of the Lithuanian population had found the advertisements offensive, as the respondent state claimed, exercising the right to freedom of expression could not be conditional upon their approval. The applicant's right to freedom of expression had, therefore, been violated.

Defamation

Most complaints to the ECtHR about breaches of Article 10 concern liability for alleged defamation where fine balances typically have to be struck between the right to free expression and the protection of reputations. Although 'reputation' is an express exception to Article 10, the ECtHR also regards it as a limitation implied by the right to respect for private life under Article 8.

---

[11] App. No. 69317/14, Judgment of 30 April 2018.

Ostensibly motivated by combatting the expression of anti-Muslim prejudice, attempts have also been made at the global level to extend the concept of defamation to include religion. For example, on 26 March 2009, the UN's Human Rights Council adopted by 23 votes to 11, with 13 abstentions, a non-binding resolution condemning 'defamation of religion' as a human rights violation.[12]

The Human Rights Council is the UN's principal political human rights-related institution. Unlike the independent expert members of some of the UN's other human rights bodies, its delegates represent the states which appointed them. Thirteen seats are set aside for African countries, thirteen for Asian, eight for Latin American and Caribbean, six for Eastern Europe, and seven in total for Western Europe and the rest. As a result, the Council is dominated by the interests and priorities of Islamic and African countries which control its agenda and generally vote as a block.

The resolution claimed that, since 9/11, Muslim minorities had faced intolerance, discrimination, acts of violence, plus stigmatizing laws and administrative procedures. It called on states to ensure that religious places, sites, shrines, and symbols are protected, to reinforce laws 'to deny impunity' for those exhibiting intolerance of ethnic and religious minorities, and 'to take all possible measures to promote tolerance and respect for all religions and beliefs'. Some 180 secular, religious, and media groups from around the world, warned that the resolution could 'be used in certain countries to silence and intimidate human rights activists, religious dissenters and other independent voices' and ultimately to restrict freedoms.

The adopted text, nevertheless, claimed that 'defamation of religion is a serious affront to human dignity leading to a restriction on the freedom of their adherents and incitement to religious violence' and that 'Islam is frequently and wrongly associated with human rights violations and terrorism'. Speaking for the 56-nation Organization of Islamic Cooperation, the delegate for Pakistan who had proposed the resolution, said a 'delicate balance' had to be struck between freedom of expression and respect for religion. However, the Canadian delegate argued that the text focused too narrowly upon discrimination, and that since 'it is individuals who have rights, not religions', to extend the notion of defamation 'beyond its proper scope would jeopardize the fundamental right to freedom of expression, which includes freedom of

---

[12] https://www.reuters.com/article/idUSTRE52P602/.

expression on religious subjects'. Speaking on behalf of the European Union, this view was supported by the representative from Germany who said that, while all forms of religious discrimination should be taken seriously, it was 'problematic to reconcile the notion of defamation (of religion) with the concept of discrimination'. The delegate added that 'the European Union does not see the concept of defamation of religion as a valid one in a human rights discourse' but 'believes that a broader, more balanced and thoroughly rights-based text would be best suited to address the issues underlying this draft resolution'.

Rights of others

While the 'rights of others' is an express exception to the right to freedom of expression, Article 10 does not specify to which rights it refers. In the context of the present discussion the most likely candidates are the right not to be discriminated against (Article 14, ECHR) and the right to freedom of thought, conscience and religion (Article 9, ECHR). Article 14 provides:

> 'The enjoyment of the rights and freedoms set forth in this Convention shall be secured without discrimination on any ground such as sex, race, colour, language, religion, political or other opinion, national or social origin, association with a national minority, property, birth or other status'.

In this context, 'discrimination' means the direct or indirect allocation of tangible or intangible goods or benefits on an unequal basis without adequate justification by reference to the rights and freedoms of others and/or to legitimate public interests.[13] Criticism of religion alone does not constitute discrimination in this sense. In fact, the reverse is much more likely to be the case because the formal outlawing of 'Islamophobic expression' could constitute discrimination against those who criticize Muslims and/or Islam in an ECHR-compliant fashion.

Article 9 ECHR is in a similar form to Article 10. It provides:

> 1. Everyone has the right to freedom of thought, conscience and religion; this right includes freedom to change his religion or belief and freedom, either alone or in community with others and in public or private, to

---

[13] Greer et al, *Human Rights in the Council of Europe and the European Union*, pp. 186-90.

manifest his religion or belief, in worship, teaching practice and observance.

2. Freedom to manifest one's religion or beliefs shall be subject only to such limitations as are prescribed by law and are necessary in a democratic society in the interests of public safety, for the protection of public order, health or morals, or for the protection of the rights and freedoms of others.

The right to freedom of thought, conscience and religion, therefore, provides a bundle of rights protecting beliefs, their expression, and the right to change them.[14] Like the right to freedom of expression, it is subject only to such limitations as are stipulated by Article 9(2). In principle, the 'rights of others' provided by both Articles 9 and 10, therefore, limit each other. The ECtHR has resolved the apparent conflict this entails by invoking the 'gratuitous insult/offence' test introduced to the jurisprudence in *Otto-Preminger-Institut v. Austria* in 1995. This means that Article 9 does not protect beliefs, or those who hold them, from all criticism but only from that which is gratuitously insulting or offensive, ie which is disrespectful, contemptuous, hateful or scornful and which causes hurt, anger, upset, or embarrassment, without apparent reason, cause, or justification. As the Court held in *Khural and another v Azerbaijan (No. 2)*

> 'A clear distinction must be made between criticism and insult and the latter may, in principle, justify sanctions … The causing of offence may fall outside the protection of freedom of expression if it amounts to wanton denigration … However, the use of vulgar phrases is not in itself decisive in the assessment of an offensive expression as it may well merely serve stylistic purposes. For the Court, style constitutes part of the communication as the form of expression and is as such protected together with the content of the expression'.[15]

Distinguishing between 'criticism' and 'insult' may involve considerable discretion and not all of the Court's judgments are consistent or defensible.[16]

---

[14] Ibid., pp. 168-72.

[15] *Khural and another v Azerbaijan (No. 2)*, App no. 383/12, Judgment of 19 January 2023, paras. 48 & 50.

[16] See, eg *Gunduz v Turkey,* App. no. 35071/97, Judgment of 14 June 2004; *Klein v Slovakia,* App. no. 72208/01, judgment of 31 October 2006; *Sekmadienis Ltd v*

There is also a compelling case for abandoning the 'gratuitous offence or insult' test entirely. In the past half-decade or so, three principal decisions – *E.S v Austria*; *Tagiyev and Huseynor v Azerbaijan*; *and Zemmour v France* – illustrate the challenges raised by criticism of Islam and alleged insult to Muslims. But before considering them, we need to look again at *Otto-Preminger-Institut v. Austria*.

a) Otto-Preminger-Institut v. Austria

As indicated, the main difference of judicial opinion in the Otto-Preminger-Institut case concerned whether or not the seizure and forfeiture of the film were 'necessary in a democratic society'. As far as 'the rights of others' were concerned, the majority of the Court held that the state's margin of appreciation had not been exceeded, and that the criterion had therefore been fulfilled. It came to this conclusion on the grounds that the overwhelming majority (87%) of the population in the Tyrol region were Catholic and, in confiscating the film, the Austrian authorities had acted to prevent an offensive attack upon their religious beliefs and, as discussed in a previous section, to ensure the public peace.

A minority of the Court decided, on the other hand, that while it may be necessary to prohibit violent and abusive criticism of religious groups – since tolerance works both ways and the democratic character of society may be damaged by such criticisms – prohibiting such conduct must be proportionate and this will not be the case if a less restrictive solution had been available but was not used. These judges thought a complete ban on expression would only be acceptable if the behaviour in question reached such a high level of abuse, and came so close to a denial of the freedom of religion of others, as itself to forfeit the right to be tolerated by society. Since, as already noted, the film in question was to be shown at an arts cinema to paying audiences over 17 years of age, and that the public had been warned that it was critical of the Catholic faith, the minority, therefore, concluded that there was little likelihood of any religiously sensitive person being confronted with it unwittingly.

It might be added that allowing the demographics of a particular locality to constrain freedom of expression is open to criticism for three principal reasons. First, if its scope depends upon the tolerance of those criticized it

---

Lithuania, App. no. 69317/14, Judgment of 30 April 2018; *Ibragimov and others v Russia*, App. nos. 1413/08 and 28621/11, Judgment of 4 February 2019.

becomes progressively more limited the less tolerant they are. Second, factoring the demographics of a particular locality into the equation makes the right to freedom of expression contingent upon the will of a regional or local majority, a utilitarian consideration at variance with the non-utilitarian character of the entire contemporary human rights paradigm. Third, where there is no public interest for national authorities to determine, the term 'democratic society' must refer to the character of European, and not to national, much less to sub-national society. Moreover, the concept of 'gratuitous offence/insult' is not found in the text of Article 10 and sits uneasily with the iconic affirmation in *Handyside* that the right to freedom of expression includes the right to 'offend, shock, or disturb'.

b) E.S. v Austria

The applicant in *E.S. v Austria* complained to the ECtHR that her conviction and sentencing to a fine of €480 for 'disparaging religious doctrines' under Article 188 of the Austrian Criminal Code, had violated her right to freedom of expression under Article 10 ECHR.[17] In the autumn of 2009, she had conducted a series of seminars entitled 'Basic Information on Islam' at the right-wing Freedom Party Education Institute in Vienna. In the course of these she had observed, amongst other things, that Muslims regard Mohammad as the perfect man and an example for all male adult adherents to the faith. She also noted that, according to Muslim tradition, at the age of 56, Mohammad had married the six-year-old Aisha, consummating their marriage when she was 9. Rhetorically the applicant had then asked the audience: 'What do we call it, if it is not paedophilia?' On 11 February 2010, she was questioned by the police and prosecuted.

At the end of a hearing on 15 February 2011, the Regional Court convicted the applicant of publicly disparaging an object of veneration of a domestic church or religious society – namely Muhammad, the Prophet of Islam – in a manner capable of arousing justified indignation contrary to Article 188 of the Criminal Code. She was ordered to pay the costs of the proceedings and a day-fine of €4 for a period of 120 days (amounting to €480 in total), or face sixty days' imprisonment in the event of default. Her allegedly repeated infringements were held to be an aggravating factor mitigated by her lack of a previous criminal record.

---

[17] App. No. 38450/12, Judgment of 18 March 2019.

Amongst the statements upon which the court based its verdict were the following:

> 'One of the biggest problems we are facing today is that Muhammad is seen as the ideal man, the perfect human, the perfect Muslim. That means that the highest commandment for a male Muslim is to imitate Muhammad, to live his life. This does not happen according to our social standards and laws. Because he was a warlord, he had many women, to put it like this, and liked to do it with children ... A 56-year-old and a six-year-old? ... What do we call it, if it is not paedophilia? ... And it is still happening today. One can never approve of something like that....'[18]

Having failed to have her conviction overturned on appeal, the applicant applied to the ECtHR on 6 June 2012. The European Centre for Law and Justice, an international NGO, was permitted to submit an opinion as third-party intervener in the proceedings. It maintained that fact-based value judgments, which contribute to public debate and do not imminently incite violence, are permissible under Article 10. It also argued that seeking to protect freedom of religion by recourse to a criminal rather than a civil sanction, was unnecessary in a democratic society and that Article 188 of the Austrian Criminal Code, itself had a 'chilling effect' upon free debate.[19]

However, on 25 October 2018, the ECtHR accepted that the conviction was in accordance with law, that it was necessary in a democratic society because it met a pressing social need and that, subject to a wide margin of appreciation, it pursued, in a proportionate manner, the legitimate aims of 'preventing disorder by safeguarding religious peace' and protecting the religious sensibilities of others. Since the seminars were public, the Court also decided that the applicant could have expected that some members of the audience might have been offended by what she said. It reiterated that, providing any given statement does not 'incite hatred or religious intolerance, a religious group must tolerate the denial by others of their religious beliefs and even the propagation ... of doctrines hostile to their faith'.[20] It, nevertheless, agreed with the domestic courts that what the applicant had said could not be considered as 'contributing to a debate of public interest', but only as an

---

[18] Ibid., para. 13.
[19] Ibid., para. 38.
[20] Ibid., para. 52.

attempt to demonstrate that 'Muhammad was not a worthy subject of worship'.[21]

According to the Court, the applicant must, therefore, 'have been aware that her statements were partly based on untrue facts and apt to arouse (justified) indignation in others' and that she had failed to provide any evidence to the contrary. The ECtHR further endorsed the Regional Court's view that presenting objects of religious worship in a provocative way, capable of hurting the feelings of believers, could be regarded as a malicious violation of the spirit of tolerance, one of the bases of democratic society. It also concluded that the impugned statements were not phrased in a neutral manner aimed at contributing to a public debate about child marriage, but constituted an abusive attack on the Prophet of Islam. Coupled with 'elements of incitement to religious intolerance' they were likely to arouse justified Muslim indignation capable of stirring up prejudice and putting religious peace at risk.

c) Tagiyev and Huseynor v Azerbaijan

In *Tagiyev and Huseynor v Azerbaijan* the ECtHR unanimously held that, by punishing the applicants, two journalists, for inciting religious hatred and hostility in a newspaper article, the Republic of Azerbaijan had violated their right to freedom of expression.[22] Mr Tagiyev was a well-known journalist, and Mr Huseynov was the chief editor of the Azerbaijani newspaper *Sanat Gazeti*. On 1 November 2006, as part of a series entitled *East-West studies*, Mr Tagiyev published, with Mr Huseynor's approval, an article entitled 'Europe and us'. In addition to some reflections on the nature of the 'Azerbaijani man', the author contrasted what he regarded as the laudable achievements of European civilization with their absence in its Islamic counterpart.

A number of religious figures and organizations in Azerbaijan and Iran denounced the article for its negative view of Islam and for the unfavourable comparison drawn with the Western philosophical tradition. There were protests in Iran and an Iranian religious leader issued a fatwa against the author. Based on Article 283 of the Azerbaijani Criminal Code – which outlaws incitement to religious hatred and hostility committed publicly or

---

[21] Ibid.
[22] Application no. 13274/08, Judgment of 5 December 2019.

through the mass media – prosecutions were initiated and the applicants were detained pending trial. Having sought the 'forensic opinion' of 'experts', on 4 May 2007, the Sabayil District Court found the first applicant guilty and sentenced him to three years' imprisonment. The second applicant was sentenced to four years' imprisonment, increased by his official position, for the same offence. Without considering the right to freedom of expression at all, on 6 July 2007, the Court of Appeal upheld the convictions, and on 22 January 2008, the Supreme Court confirmed this verdict. A month prior to this decision, both applicants were released from prison by presidential decree.

The applicants lodged complaints with the ECtHR against the Republic of Azerbaijan on 7 March 2008, claiming their conviction for publishing the article constituted a violation of their rights under Article 10 ECHR. In 2011, while the case was pending, the first applicant was stabbed by an unknown assailant on his way home from work and died in hospital. The Court allowed his wife to pursue the complaint on his behalf.

The domestic courts had found that the applicants' use of the following four remarks in the article rendered them guilty of inciting religious hatred and hostility contrary to the Criminal Code:

(a) 'Europe has always refused and refuses the deceitful humanist ideas of other religions, including Islam. Morality in Islam is a juggling act; its humanism is not convincing'; (b) 'in comparison with Jesus Christ, the father of war fatwas, the Prophet Muhammad, is simply a frightful creature'; (c) 'at best, Islam would advance in Europe with tiny demographic steps. And maybe there would be a country in which Islam would be represented by a few individuals or terrorists living incognito'; and (d) 'the European philosopher does not act as a clown like the Eastern philosopher, is not inclined to Sufism, or madness, stupidity. Yes, the Eastern philosopher is a pure actor; all his activities are decorated with imaginations of miniature ornament for the sake of ideology. The Eastern philosopher says something for the sake of saying something. The aim, the way is unknown, or quite abstract'.[23]

For several reasons, the ECtHR held, on 5 December 2019, that the applicants' right to freedom of expression had been violated. First, the domestic courts relied entirely upon the conclusions of the experts' forensic report, without explaining why the impugned remarks constituted incitement to religious

---

[23] Ibid., para. 8.

hatred and hostility. According to the ECtHR, the domestic courts themselves should instead have examined the statements in the context of the article, the author's intention, the public interest in the matter discussed, and other relevant issues. Second, although states have a margin of appreciation in making such an assessment, when the particular expression involves the freedom of the press to contribute to matters of public interest and debate as the article in question did, its scope is narrow. Third, the national courts did not even try to balance the applicants' right to freedom of expression with the right of religious people not to be gratuitously insulted on the grounds of their faith. Fourth, the derogatory remarks about Islam in the article may have been seen by certain religious people as an abusive attack on the Prophet and upon Muslims living in Europe and could have caused religious hatred. Nevertheless, its core thesis involved a comparison between Eastern and Western values, particularly regarding the role of religion in society, a matter of genuine public interest. Finally, imposing criminal sanctions on the expression of such an opinion would have a chilling effect on the vital role the press plays in democratic society. The Court, therefore, held that the applicants' conviction was disproportionate and not necessary in a democratic society. It, therefore, amounted to a violation of freedom of expression guaranteed under Article 10 of the ECHR. Each applicant was granted €12,000 compensation.

d) Zemmour v France

In *Zemmour v France*, the ECtHR unanimously held that the applicant's freedom of expression had not been violated by his conviction and sentencing for statements made on a television programme which the French courts decided had incited discrimination and religious hatred against Muslims.[24] Zemmour is a controversial French far-right political journalist, pundit, and author of several books. In 2011 he was convicted of provoking racial discrimination, in 2018 of inciting hatred against Muslims, and in 2022 of inciting racial hatred. On 5 December 2019 he applied to the ECtHR arguing that his 2018 conviction breached his right to freedom of expression under Article 10 of the ECHR. On 20 December 2022 the ECtHR held that there had been no violation.

On 16 September 2016, Zemmour had appeared as a guest on the

---

[24] Requête no 63539/19, Arrêt de 20 décembre 2022.

television chat show *Cà vous* ('This is you'), broadcast at 19.00 on Channel France 5, to promote his latest book, *Un quinquennat pour rien* (*A Five Year Term for Nothing*), referenced to the rise in Islamist terrorism in Europe during the five-year term of the then Dutch government. During the live interview he made several statements which prompted the organization *Coordination des appels pour une paix juste au Proche-Orient* ('Coalition for Just Peace in the Near East') to issue proceedings in the Paris Criminal Court under section 24(7) of the Freedom of the Press Act of 29 July 1881 ('the 1881 Act') which makes it an offence to incite discrimination, hatred or violence against a person or group on the grounds of origin or of membership or non-membership of a particular ethnicity, nation, race or religion.

The case against Zemmour focused particularly on five aspects of the interview: (1) His answer 'No' to the suggestion that 'there are Muslims in France who live in peace, who don't take the Qur'an literally and are fully integrated'. (2) His statement that, 'those who wage jihad are seen by all Muslims, whether they say so or not, as good Muslims – they're warriors, soldiers of Islam'. (3) An exchange with the interviewer which went like this: *Interviewer* – 'Terrorism is apocalyptic', *Zemmour* – 'No, it's not terrorism, it's jihadism. So, it's Islam'; *Interviewer* – 'The way you equate jihadism and Islam', *Zemmour*, 'It's the same to me'. (4) 'For 30 years we've been experiencing an invasion, a colonization, which is bringing about a conflagration .... In countless neighbourhoods, on the outskirts of French cities, where many young women are veiled – that's also Islam, that's also jihad, that's also the fight to Islamize a territory which is not, which is in the ordinary course a non-Islamized land, a land of infidels. It's the same thing, it's territorial occupation'. (5) 'I think they ... [Muslims living in France] ... need to be given a choice between Islam and France'. This was followed by, 'So, if they're French, they have to – and this is hard because Islam doesn't lend itself to this – they have to let go of what their religion is'.[25]

On 22 June 2017, the Criminal Court found that these remarks amounted to an offence and fined Zemmour €5,000. On 3 May 2018, the Paris Court of Appeal partly reversed this judgment by deciding that only statements (4) and (5) could be characterised as 'inciting discrimination and religious hatred'. It, therefore, reduced the fine to €3,000. The applicant's appeal to the Court of Cassation was dismissed on 17 September 2019.

---

[25] Ibid., para. 6.

The ECtHR noted that, since the applicant's statements had been made on live TV at peak viewing time, they would have had a wide impact. It also observed that the Criminal Court, the Court of Appeal, and the Court of Cassation had agreed that his controversial remarks had not been confined to criticism of Islam, nor to the rise of Islamic fundamentalism in France, but had equated Islam with terrorism and had effectively called upon viewers to reject and exclude Muslims as a whole. Concluding that the interference with the applicant's right to freedom of expression had been necessary in a democratic society to protect the rights of others, it held that his conduct had not only been discriminatory but had also undermined social cohesion. It concluded, therefore, that the grounds upon which the domestic courts had convicted the applicant had been sufficient and that the fine had not been excessive. There had, therefore, been no violation of Article 10 of the Convention.

e) Reflections

Tagiyev and Huseynor v Azerbaijan, and *Zemmour v France* are easy to defend because in the former the applicants had clearly been engaging in an intellectual criticism of Islam rather than inciting hatred against Muslims. In the latter it was, at least credibly, the other way around. The judgment in *E.S. v Austria* is, however, very unsatisfactory for at least half a dozen reasons. First, the offence with which the applicant was charged, itself ostensibly violates Article 10 ECHR. The ECtHR, therefore, missed a golden opportunity to condemn a violation of the Convention on the part of the Austrian criminal code which, as already indicated, was also the source of controversy in the *Otto-Preminger* case. Second, by accusing the applicant of suggesting that 'Muhammad was not a worthy subject of worship', the Court displayed a staggering misunderstanding of the essentials of the Islamic faith, all mainstream traditions of which regard 'worshiping' the Prophet as heresy.

Third, the Court held that it is not part of the Islamic faith that Mohammad consummated his marriage to Aisha when she was 9 years old. It, therefore, follows that to claim that he did, cannot disparage a genuine Islamic doctrine, with the result that the statement in question falls outside the scope of Article 188 of the Austrian Penal Code. Fourth, the Court concluded that it is a value judgement without a sufficient factual basis to ask if Mohammad's marriage to Aisha means he was a paedophile. However, Article 10 expressly includes 'opinions' without requiring that they be adequately grounded in fact. Indeed, the metaphysical claims of all religions, including Islam rest upon faith and supposition rather than upon demonstrable truth. Fifth, contrary to what the Court held, a claim that there is a long-standing tradition in any contemporary religion which appears to condone sex with children, unquestionably contributes to a vital contemporary public debate. This is especially so if, as in this case, there is no evidence whatever that making such a claim, did in fact, arouse any indignation at all, much less that it jeopardized public order. Finally, although having referred to the 'gratuitous offence or insult' test, the Court conspicuously failed to apply it. Had it done so, the result may have been very different.

The law of England and Wales

Several laws in England and Wales, typically with counterparts in Scotland and Northern Ireland, are relevant to identifying where the line between lawful and unlawful critical engagement with Muslims and Islam lies. However, before considering them, a distinction first needs to be drawn between crimes and civil wrongs. Although private prosecutions are also possible, the detection, prosecution, and punishment of crime, including by imprisonment, are typically the responsibility of the state. Civil wrongs, by contrast, concern unlawful conduct which generally raise only the prospect of legal action on the part of victims for non-criminal remedies such as compensation.

It should be noted that the ECtHR's concept of 'gratuitously offence/insult' has never appeared in the judgment of a British court in any criminal or civil case involving criticism of religion or religious believers. However, the term, 'gratuitously offensive to others' was invoked in the judgment of the Court of Appeal (Civil Division) in *Higgs v Farmor's School and others*, a case involving alleged offence stemming *from* religious convictions.[26] The term disproportionate 'gratuitously insulting behaviour causing alarm or distress' also featured in the High Court judgment in *Percy v DPP* which involved alleged disrespect to the US flag.[27]

However, before turning to the formal legal categories of crime and civil wrongs, something needs to be said about the strange world of 'non-crime hate incidents'.

---

[26] [2025] EWCA Civ 109, paras. 42 & 158.
[27] [2001] EWHC Admin 1125, para. 28.

Non-crime hate incidents

In England and Wales 'hate crimes' are distinguished from 'non-crime incidents' and 'non-crime hate incidents' (NCHIs).[28] Non-crime incidents are those where a concern has been raised with the police about hatred or prejudice – especially but not exclusively towards someone on the grounds of a 'particular characteristic' listed by the Equality Act 2010 (see below) – but where no credible evidence of animosity is found. This may include alleged Islamophobic expression. In such cases the police record the fact that there has been a complaint but not any of the personal details about the alleged perpetrator including their name.

NCHIs, which may also include allegedly Islamophobic expression, lie between hate crimes and non-crime incidents. They originated from the 1999 Inquiry into the racist murder of Stephen Lawrence which recommended that the police should formally log 'racist incidents' which fall below the threshold required for a criminal offence. Other types of hate incident were subsequently added. But it was not until the 2014 Hate Crime Operational Guidance issued by the College of Policing – the professional body establishing and monitoring policing standards in England and Wales – that NCHIs were formally incorporated into policing practice.

In 2021 the Court of Appeal for England and Wales held that, while the mere recording of a speech-related NCHI does not violate Article 10 ECHR, the perception of prejudice by a complainant or any other person is not enough to warrant recording it as such. It also concluded that the guidelines were deficient in several respects. They did not fully acknowledge the importance of the right to freedom of expression, proportionality, necessity, resort to the least intrusive intervention, the need to avoid a 'chilling effect' upon legitimate public debate, and the application of common sense. It was held that proper recognition of these elements would, amongst other things, exclude vexatious complaints and those where there was no evidence of hostility.[29]

Responding to this judgment, in June 2023, and acting pursuant to section 60 of the Police, Crime, Sentencing and Courts Act 2022, the government

---

[28] Home Office, *Statutory guidance – Non-Crime Hate Incidents: Code of Practice on the Recording and Retention of Personal Data (accessible)*, 3 June 2023.
[29] [2021] EWCA Civ 1926; https://www.gov.uk/government/publications/non-crime-hate-incidents-code-of-practice/non-crime-hate-incidents-code-of-practice-on-the-recording-and-retention-of-personal-data-accessible#freedom-of-expression.

introduced a new Code of Practice for the recording of NCHIs, the first time the regime had been placed on a statutory footing. The College of Policing also provided a statement of Authorized Professional Practice (APP).[30] The Code defines an NCHI as 'an incident or alleged incident which involves or is alleged to involve an act by a person ("the subject") which is perceived by a person other than the subject to be motivated – wholly or partly – by hostility or prejudice towards persons with a particular characteristic'.[31] It must also disturb an individual, group or community's quality of life or cause them concern.[32] Officially NCHIs assist the police in identifying conduct, which though not criminal, could become more widespread and which might indicate deteriorating community relations. A 'person other than the subject' includes the alleged victim and any witnesses. And, while 'hostility' is the legal threshold for prosecuting hate crimes, 'prejudice' is sufficient for recording an NCHI. This raises the question – why are the latter not then called 'Non-Crime Prejudiced Incidents' – 'NCPIs'? The distinction between hostility and prejudice is also not clear cut. For example, the Crown Prosecution Service, to whose definition the recording authority must have due regard, understands 'hostility' to include 'ill-will, spite, contempt, *prejudice*, unfriendliness, antagonism, resentment and dislike'.[33]

NCHIs may be recorded without naming the alleged perpetrator. However, where all other relevant criteria are met, their personal information can be lawfully documented, if and only if, the conditions specified in the revised code by the Additional Threshold Test (ATT), are met. These require that the incident in question was motivated by intentional hostility or prejudice causing significant harm or a criminal offence with respect to those with particular characteristics, coupled with a 'real risk of escalation'. The revised guidelines also state that:

> '… recording authorities must note that the majority of speech that expresses political or other opinions, even if offensive or controversial, does not constitute an offence. Fundamentally, offending someone is not, in and of itself, a criminal offence. To

---

[30] College of Policing, 'New Code and guidance for non-crime hate incidents' 2 June 2023.

[31] Home Office, *Non-Crime Hate Incidents,* para. 11.

[32] Ibid., para. 14.

[33] https://www.cps.gov.uk/sites/default/files/documents/victims_witnesses/so-when-is-it-a-hate-crime.pdf. Italics added.

constitute an offence under hate crime legislation, the speech or
behaviour in question must be threatening, abusive or insulting and
be intended to, or likely to, stir up hatred'.[34]

The following examples, relevant to the issues under discussion in this book,
are also provided.

> 'A religious person (the complainant) reports an online post that
> contains an interpretation of their religion that differs from their own
> beliefs. The complainant is offended by the text and asks the police
> to order its removal and speak to the person who posted it. The police
> record the incident as a non-crime incident, but decide that there is
> no evidence of 'hostility' and it is therefore not an NCHI. They notify
> the complainant that they will not intervene. The incident therefore is
> not recorded as an NCHI, and the personal data of the subject is (sic)
> not recorded. The personal data of the subject (in the form of the
> subject's name) that was initially recorded by the call taker is (sic)
> also removed from the policing system'.[35]

Another is as follows:

> 'A police officer witnesses an individual (the subject) express
> hostility towards a Muslim woman and intervenes. The officer's
> judgement that hostility was present is confirmed during the follow-
> up conversation they have with the subject. Whilst the subject's
> behaviour does not constitute criminal activity, the surrounding
> circumstances suggest that the behaviour could potentially contribute
> to or become evidence of a course of criminal conduct – for example,
> harassment. The incident therefore passes the Additional Threshold
> Test. As such, the officer records the personal information of the
> subject, and creates an NCHI record. In accordance with the code, the
> officer notifies the subject that their personal data has (sic) been
> processed in an NCHI record'.[36]

It is likely that over a quarter of a million NCHIs have been recorded, and
despite the revised guidance, the number is rising.[37] Figures from 30 of the 43
police forces in England and Wales showed that, from January to June 2024,

---

[34] Home Office, *Non-Crime Hate Incidents*, para. 43.
[35] Ibid., Example B.
[36] Ibid., Example H.
[37] T. Young, 'When is a crime not a crime?', *The Spectator*, 18 March 2023; 'Free
speech fear as police log more "hate" incidents', *The Times*, 4 September 2024.

11,690 NCHIs were recorded, compared with 11,642 the previous year. Although this constitutes an overall increase of only 0.04%, according to a report by His Majesty's Inspectorate of Constabulary and Fire and Rescue Services: 'There are significant differences in the extent to which forces have responded to the Code and the NCHI APP'.[38] The rate of increase has included, for example, 140% in Staffordshire, 65% in North Yorkshire, 63% in Gwent, and 35% in Suffolk.

There are several problems with NCHIs. First, in spite of revisions to the guidelines, the kind of misconduct required is unclear and also varies significantly between police forces. This has resulted, second, in the recording of incidents as NCHIs, which, at worst, merely involve minor social friction including groundless accusations of racism or Islamophobic expression. For example, an NCHI was recorded in the case of a man who complained that other passengers on a bus had given him 'funny looks', allegedly because of his ethnicity.[39] Third, and most consequentially, NCHIs can show up on enhanced criminal record checks, with for example, potentially negative implications for job applications.

Responses to freedom of information requests have also revealed that NCHIs have been recorded with respect to innocuous, or mildly insulting, remarks with no obvious sign of malice or ill-will.[40] Until recently, the government was divided over the use of NCHIs. The then Home Secretary, Yvette Cooper, appeared, for example, to advocate lowering the threshold, while the Chancellor, Rachel Reeves, was reported to have called NCHIs a 'waste of police time', especially when they involve children.[41]

However, since the autumn of 2025, a campaign to abolish NCHIs has gathered pace.[42] At the beginning of September, several senior figures in the administration of criminal justice called for a more 'common sense' approach. On 7 September, *The Telegraph* reported that Metropolitan Police

---

[38] HMICFRS, *An inspection into activism and impartiality in policing*, 10 September 2024, p. 11.

[39] M. Dathan & B. Ellery, 'Police logging too many hate crimes, watchdog warns', *The Times*, 10 September 2024.

[40] J. Beal, 'Doctors and vicars accused of non-crime hate incidents', *The Times*, 15 November 2024.

[41] Ibid.; C. Hymas, 'Police should use "common sense" when recording non-crime hate incidents, says Yvette Cooper', *The Daily Telegraph*, 19 November 2024.

[42] H. Singh, *The Many Tiers of British Justice: When identity politics and progressivist causes trump impartial policing* (Civitas, 2025), pp. 38-44, 67.

Commissioner, Sir Mark Rowley, planned to present the newly-appointed Home Secretary, Shabana Mahmood, with proposals to change the law 'within weeks' to stop officers over-policing social media. A source close to the Commissioner said: 'Laws that were intended to protect the vulnerable are now tying officers' hands, removing appropriate professional discretion – which some call common sense'. [43] Speaking to the House of Lords Constitution Committee around the same time, Shabana Mahmood said that the police should guard against 'overreach' and should 'focus on the day job' of tackling 'crime in our communities'. [44] Her words were echoed by Sir Keir Starmer at Prime Minister's Questions a few days later.

Prior to the launch of the 2024-25 report of HM's Inspectorate of Constabulary and Fire & Rescue Services, Sir Andy Cooke, HM chief inspector of constabulary, said that NCHIs should be abolished because 'we need to separate the offensive from the criminal' and 'allow people to speak openly without fear that their opinion will put them on the wrong side of the law'. [45] Then, on 21 October 2025 – in the wake of the controversial arrest by five armed police officers, and the 12-hour detention of Graham Linehan, co-writer of the acclaimed comedy sitcom, *Father Ted* and writer of the equally popular sitcom, *The IT Crowd*, for having posted an aggressive gender critical tweet – the Metropolitan Police announced that it would 'no longer investigate non-crime hate incidents'. [46] The statement added that, although these 'would still be recorded and used as intelligence to establish potential patterns of behaviour or criminality', the Commissioner 'doesn't believe officers should be policing toxic culture war debates'. Welcoming the news, Chris Philip MP, shadow home office spokesman, urged the government to 'end non-crime hate incidents entirely and only investigate or record something if it is likely to be an immediate precursor to actual criminality'. [47]

The next day, it was reported that the College of Policing and the National Police Chiefs' Council, planned to advise the Home Secretary that NCHIs should no longer be recorded by any police force in England and Wales.

---

[43] C. Hymas, 'Change law so we can stop policing tweets, demands Met chief', *The Telegraph*, 7 September 2025.

[44] Ibid.

[45] B. Ellery, People must not fear law when they speak out, watchdog says', *The Times*, 10 September 2025.

[46] S. Manning & T. Gould, 'Met to stop investigating non-crime hate after Linehan case', *The Times*, 21 October 2025.

[47] Ibid.

According to Tom Harding, the College's director of operational standards, under an updated system, officers and call handlers would record information only where there was a clear risk of harm.[48] On 24 December 2025 it was reported that ministers were preparing to endorse the conclusions of a review to be published in January 2026 which is likely to recommend that the current system be replaced by a new 'common sense' approach where only the most serious incidents of anti-social behaviour would be recorded.[49]

Criminal Law

The principal criminal offences relevant to the issues discussed in this book include those involving religious hatred, public order, harassment, and malicious communications.

a) Racial and/or religious hatred

There is no generic 'hate crime' offence in the UK. However, hatred of racial, religious, and other minorities may be an element in many other crimes including public order offences and offences against the person or property such as assault and vandalism. Where any given offence is perceived by the victim or a witness to have been motivated by such hatred, this is also likely to constitute an aggravating factor.[50] Both the police and the Crown Prosecution Service (CPS) take 'hatred' to mean, amongst other things, 'ill-will', 'spite', 'contempt', 'prejudice', 'unfriendliness', 'antagonism', 'resentment' and 'dislike'.[51] The CPS states that it only charges any case, whether involving anti-minority hatred or not, where there is sufficient evidence to provide a realistic prospect of conviction and where it is in the public interest to do so. As far as online offences are concerned, only grossly offensive, indecent, obscene or false communications will be liable to prosecution, the potential impact of which upon free speech must also be considered. The guidance states that freedom of expression can only be

---

[48] B. Ellery, 'All police forces poised to stop recording non-crime hate', *The Times*, 22 October 2025.

[49] O. Wright, 'Mahmood backs police plan to end "hate" investigations', *The Times*, 24 December 2025.

[50] https://www.cps.gov.uk/sites/default/files/documents/victims_witnesses/so-when-is-it-a-hate-crime.pdf.

[51] Crown Prosecution Service, *Racist and Religious Hate Crime - Prosecution Guidance*, 3 March 2022.

restricted in very limited circumstances and that prosecutions may only be undertaken when both 'necessary' and 'proportionate'. However, evidence of hostility based on the victim's ethnic or national origin, gender, disability, age, religion or belief, sexual orientation or gender identity will make it more likely that a prosecution will proceed.

Under section 28B(1) of the Racial and Religious Hatred Act 2006, it is also a crime in England and Wales, to use threatening words or behaviour, or to 'display any written material which is threatening', with the intention 'thereby to stir up religious hatred'. Religious hatred is defined by this legislation as 'hatred towards a group of persons characterized by reference to religious belief or lack of religious belief'.[52] The Act also provides that it shall not be interpreted in any way which 'prohibits or restricts discussion, criticism or expressions of antipathy, dislike, ridicule, insult or abuse of particular religions or the beliefs or practices of their adherents, or of any other belief system or the beliefs or practices of its adherents, or proselytising or urging adherents of a different religion or belief system to cease practising their religion or belief system'.[53] In other words, criticizing Muslim or other beliefs, practices, and/or conduct, even in strident and vitriolic terms, is not a crime provided it does not, and is not intended, to stir up religious hatred thus defined. Nine categories, identified by the 2021 Census, are used for the purpose of recording religiously-motivated hate crime: Buddhism; Christianity; Hinduism; Judaism; Islam; Sikhism; other; no religion; unknown.

Prosecutions under section 28B(1) are, however, rare because of the need to prove an intention to stir up rather than merely the likelihood of religious hatred, the requirement that relevant speech should not only be offensive, abusive or insulting but also 'threatening', the defence of freedom of expression, and the fact that prosecutions under this provision require the consent of the Attorney General.[54] Prosecutors tend to rely, therefore, instead upon public order and other offences where anti-Muslim hatred has, or appears to have been an aggravating factor.

What any accused is alleged to have said or done, in what context, and how this is interpreted by the prosecuting authorities and the courts are likely to be decisive in determining their fate. One of the few recorded cases

---

[52] s. 29A.

[53] s. 29J.

[54] S. 29 of the Public Order Act 1986 as amended by s. 1 of the Racial and Religious Hatred Act 2006.

involved Harry Taylor, an atheist, who on three occasions in 2010, deposited leaflets mocking Christ, Islam and the Pope, in the prayer room of Liverpool's John Lennon Airport.[55] Claiming to have been insulted, offended, and alarmed, the airport chaplain reported the matter to the police. Taylor, who had been convicted of similar offences in 2006, was prosecuted for incitement to religious hatred. Having been found guilty by a jury, he was sentenced to a six-month prison term suspended for two years, and a five-year Anti-Social Behaviour Order was also imposed banning him from carrying religiously insulting material in a public place. He was ordered to pay £250 costs and to undertake 100 hours of unpaid community service as well. Distributing anti-religious material is not unlawful per se. But the fact that the leaflets in question were deemed insulting, and that they had been left in a prayer room on three occasions, appears to have convinced the jury that the defendant's conduct amounted to incitement to religious hatred. There is, however, a certain irony in the fact that Taylor's conviction stemmed from incidents in an airport named after John Lennon who once described the Beatles as 'more popular than Jesus' and whose celebrated song 'Imagine' envisages a world without religion.

In the year ending March 2023, in England and Wales (excluding Devon and Cornwall which had introduced a new IT system), 145,214 hate crimes were recorded by the police, a 5% decrease from the year ending March 2022 (153,536 offences), and the first comparable fall since the year ending March 2013.[56] It is thought that the preceding rise may have been largely due to improvements in crime recording and better identification of what constitutes the offence rather than to an increase in offending itself. Ninety-two per cent of hate crimes over this period concerned either public disorder or violence against the person, a pattern consistent with that seen in previous years. As before, the majority (70%, 101,906) were racially motivated. Between March 2022 and March 2023 religious hate crime decreased from 8,602.

In the year ending March 2023, 8,241 religious hate crimes were recorded by the police. Where the perceived religion of the victim was recorded, 44% were against Muslims (3,400 offences). However, as a result of a number of 'carefully worded FOIs' (Freedom of Information requests) Singh discovered that about a quarter of those 'logged as victims of "Islamophobic hate crime"'

---

[55] BBC, 'Atheist guilty over cartoons left at Liverpool airport', 4 March 2010.
[56] https://www.gov.uk/government/statistics/hate-crime-england-and-wales-2022-to-2023/hate-crime-england-and-wales-2022-to-2023.

are non-Muslims mistaken for Muslims on account of their appearance'.[57] The next most commonly targeted group were Jews, targeted in around 19% of religious hate crimes (1,510 offences).

However, the Hamas attack upon Israel on 7 October 2023, and the subsequent wars in the Middle East thereafter, have led to massive increases in both Islamophobic and antisemitic hate crime around the world. In Britain, the *Tell Mama* organization, which monitors Islamophobic incidents, recorded 2,010 cases between 7 October 2023 and 7 February 2024, a 235% increase by comparison with the same four months the previous year. Similarly, the Community Safety Trust recorded 4,103 antisemitic incidents in 2023, a 147% increase from 2022.[58] Other sources claim that the number of recorded Islamophobic incidents has trebled while antisemitic ones have doubled.[59] While official figures for 2025 will not be available until mid-2026 after this book had gone to press, there are no grounds for believing there has been a significant decrease.

b) Public order offences

The principal public order offences relevant to criticism of Muslims and Islam can be found in the Public Order Act 1986. The provisions in question suffer from drafting and other difficulties. Critics have also argued that they are effectively being used to render blasphemy a crime.[60] It is an offence under section 4 for anyone: (a) to use towards another person, threatening, abusive or insulting words or behaviour, or (b) to distribute or to display, to someone else, any writing, sign or other visible representation which is threatening, abusive or insulting. In both cases there must be an intention to provoke immediate unlawful violence or to cause someone else to believe that immediate unlawful violence will be used against them or anyone else. No offence is committed where all relevant parties are inside the same or different dwellings.

---

[57] H. Singh in E. Webb (ed.), *Islamophobia: An Anthology of Concerns* (Civitas, 2019), pp. 39-40.

[58] Community Service Trust Blog, *Antisemitic Incidents Report 2023*, 15 February 2024.

[59] 'Free speech fear as police log more "hate" incidents', *The Times*, 4 September 2024.

[60] G. Scott, 'Challenge to acquittal of man who burnt Quran', *The Times*, 22 November 2025.

It is also an offence under section 4A, if with intent to cause harassment, alarm or distress, someone (a) uses threatening, abusive or insulting words or behaviour, or behaves in a disorderly manner, or (b) displays any writing, sign or other visible representation which is threatening, abusive or insulting, thereby causing that, or another person, harassment, alarm or distress. It is a defence for the accused to prove: (i) that they were inside a dwelling and had no reason to believe that the words or behaviour used, or the writing, sign or other visible representation displayed, would be heard or seen by a person outside that or any other dwelling, or (ii) that the conduct in question was reasonable.

Under section 5 of the Act a person is guilty of an offence if they (a) use threatening or abusive words or behaviour, or behave in a disorderly manner, or (b) display any writing, sign or other visible representation which is threatening or abusive, within the hearing or sight of a person likely to be caused harassment, alarm or distress thereby. An offence under this section may be committed in a public or a private place, but no offence is committed where the words or behaviour are used, or the writing, sign or other visible representation is displayed by a person inside a dwelling and the other person is also inside that or another dwelling. Speech that is merely 'insulting' does not amount to an offence under section 5 if the accused can prove that the conduct in question was reasonable, they had no reason to believe any person likely to be caused harassment, alarm or distress was within hearing or sight, or that they (the accused) were inside a dwelling and had no reason to believe that the words used or the behaviour, or the writing, sign or other visible representation displayed, would be heard or seen by a person outside that or any other dwelling. As for the prosecution, proving intent is not enough. There must also be evidence that somebody, and not necessarily the person targeted, was in fact harassed, alarmed, or distressed as a result.

Section 6 of the Act provides that: 'A person is guilty of an offence under section 5 only if he intends his words or behaviour, or the writing, sign or other visible representation, to be threatening or abusive, or is aware that it may be threatening or abusive or (as the case may be) he intends his behaviour to be or is aware that it may be disorderly'.

Section 29[J] provides a defence in the following terms: 'Nothing in this Part shall be read or given effect in a way which prohibits or restricts discussion, criticism or expressions of antipathy, dislike, ridicule, insult or abuse of particular religions or the beliefs or practices of their adherents, or of any other belief system or the beliefs or practices of its adherents, or proselytising or urging adherents of a different religion or belief system to cease practising their religion or belief system'. This section also provides that, in this Part of the legislation, religious hatred means 'hatred against a group of persons defined by reference to religious belief or lack of religious belief'.

Examples of conduct which could amount to disorderly behaviour under section 5, not necessarily involving an anti-Islam/Muslim dimension, include: causing a disturbance in a residential area or common part of a block of flats; persistently shouting abuse or obscenities at passers-by; pestering people waiting to use public transport or otherwise waiting in a queue; rowdy behaviour in a street late at night which might alarm residents or passers-by; causing a disturbance in a shopping precinct or other area to which the public have access or might otherwise gather.[61]

According to section 31(1)(c) of the Crime and Disorder Act 1998, as amended, a person is guilty of a racially or religiously aggravated public order offence under this section, if they cause harassment, alarm or distress amounting to an offence under section 5 of the Public Order Act 1986 which is racially or religiously aggravated. Section 28(1)(b) of the Crime and Disorder Act 1998 defines a racially or religiously aggravated offence as one motivated (wholly or partly) by hostility towards members of a racial or religious group based upon their membership of that group.

Prosecutions for the kind of public order offences relevant to the themes considered in this book have involved posters, placards and the public immolation of the Qur'an, as illustrated by the following cases.

i) Norwood v DPP

Norwood v DPP was an appeal against conviction under section 5 of the Public Order Act 1986, aggravated by hostility towards a religious group as provided by section 28(1)(b) of the Crime and Disorder Act 1998.[62] Shortly after the 9/11 attacks, the appellant, Mr Norwood, had displayed in the window of his home in a small town in Shropshire, a poster supplied by the

---

[61] Crown Prosecution Service, *Public Order Offences incorporating the Charging Standard,* Prosecution Guidance Public Order and Regulatory Offences, 13 November 2024, section 5.
[62] *Norwood v DPP* [2003] EWHC 1564. On 16 November 2004 the European Court of Human Rights ruled Mr Norwood's application inadmissible, *Decision as to the Admissibility of Application no. 23131/03 by Mark Anthony Norwood against the United Kingdom.*

British National Party of which he was a member. Alongside an image of the blazing Twin Towers, it featured a prohibition symbol superimposed upon the Islamic Crescent and Star accompanied by the phrases 'Islam out of Britain' and 'Protect the British People'. Upon receipt of a complaint from a member of the public, Mr. Norwood was prosecuted and convicted.

The district judge who presided over his trial found that the poster was insulting to Islam and to its adherents, that it was likely to cause harassment, alarm or distress, that displaying it was not objectively reasonable, that the offence was religiously aggravated, and that convicting the appellant was justified under Article 10(2) of the ECHR. On 3 July 2003, endorsing this verdict and reasoning, Lord Justice Auld and Mr Justice Goldring, sitting in the Divisional Court of the Queen's Bench Division, rejected Mr. Norwood's appeal. Delivering the judgment Lord Justice Auld held that:

'The poster was a public expression of attack on all Muslims in this country, urging all who might read it that followers of the Islamic religion here should be removed from it and warning that their presence here was a threat or a danger to the British people ... it could not, on any reasonable basis be dismissed as merely an intemperate criticism or protest against the tenets of the Muslim religion, as distinct from an unpleasant and insulting attack on its followers generally ...(its) ... terms ... and the circumstances and location of its display were, as a matter of plain common sense capable of causing harassment, alarm or distress to those passing by who might see it in the appellant's window ... the prosecution ... (did) ... not have to prove that the display of the poster in fact caused anyone harassment, alarm or distress'.[63]

ii) Ian Sleeper v Commissioner of Police of the Metropolis

In *Ian Sleeper v Commissioner of Police of the Metropolis*, following a complaint from a member of the public received on 23 June 2017, two police officers on foot patrol in central London, later assisted by a third, arrested and detained Ian Sleeper under section 5 of the Public Order Act for causing harassment, alarm, and distress occasioned by 'religious and racial aggravation'.[64]

---

[63] *Norwood v DPP* [2003] EWHC 1564, paras. 33-34.
[64] *Ian Sleeper v Commissioner of Police of the Metropolis* [2003] EWHC 1564; 'Preacher arrested for protesting Islam wins chance to appeal', *Christian Concern*, 20 November 2023.

Mr Sleeper had been engaged in Christian street evangelism outside Southwark Cathedral where an inter-faith community service was about to be held. The evidence indicated that he had chosen the spot with this in mind. On 3 June 2017, two major terrorist attacks had occurred at the nearby London Bridge and Borough Market in which 8 people had been killed and others injured. On 19 June 2017, a van had also been driven into a crowd of worshippers outside a mosque in Finsbury Park, a different part of the capital, and an elderly man had died of a heart attack at the scene. At the time of Mr Sleeper's arrest, the police were, therefore, particularly alert to anything that could be perceived as inciting hatred or violence. In support of his street preaching on the occasion in question, Mr. Sleeper had prominently displayed two handwritten signs in large, easy-to-read, writing. One, placed on the ground facing passers-by, said: 'LOVE MUSLIMS BAN ISLAM THE RELIGION OF TERROR!'. The other, which he held, read: '#LOVE MUSLIMS HATE ISLAM JESUS IS LOVE+HOPE'.

Mr Sleeper's encounter with the police was recorded on officers' bodycam. When they arrived, the arresting officers told him they would have to confiscate and destroy the placards because 'Islam is not a religion of terror, the terrorists make it a religion of terror … you can't display this … it's committing an offence ....' Mr Sleeper said he was 'not attacking people' but 'attacking an idea' and that the placards were legal under human rights law. Having asked the police if there was anything on the placards they did like, a police officer replied: 'Love Muslims, ban terrorists, that's ok … but when you start saying "hate Islam" that's when the problems start'. An officer consulted his sergeant to check the legal position, and then told Mr Sleeper: 'I don't have the power to take these … (signs) … but based on your belief on the law about them not being harmful … I can't guarantee that you won't show them anywhere else, so the only way we can deal with this is that we are going to have to arrest you … the necessity for the arrest is to stop you from re-offending'.[65]

Mr Sleeper was then arrested, taken to a police station in a police van, medically examined, and interviewed in the presence of his chosen solicitor. During the course of questioning, he presented a prepared statement in which he explained that, at the event in question, he had been criticising Islam not Muslims. As a result of failed attempts by the police to reach senior officers

---

[65] Christian Concern, 'Preacher arrested for protesting Islam wins chance to appeal.'

and the Crown Prosecution Service (CPS) to determine whether or not to charge him, Mr Sleeper was held in a cell overnight for 13 hours. He was then released on bail and banned from entering the Borough of Southwark for over six months. On 11 August 2017 he was informed that the CPS had decided not to prosecute.

Mr Sleeper then took legal action against the police, claiming wrongful arrest, false imprisonment, assault, and the violation of his rights under articles 9, 10 and 11 of the European Convention of Human Rights. The trial took place before His Honour Judge Saggerson sitting without a jury at the Central London County Court. A detailed written judgment rejecting Mr Sleeper's case was delivered on 3 April 2023.[66] HHJ Saggerson decided that, although the appellant genuinely held the beliefs he expressed, he had not only intended to start a debate but had meant the message on the 'Ban' placard to be taken literally. The judge also found that, because the 'Hate placard' was abusive and targeted Muslims, the arresting officer had objective and reasonable grounds for suspecting that an offence under section 5 of the Public Order Act had been committed. In the judge's view, the placard message – 'Hate Islam' – would likely have been interpreted as exhorting and inciteful by reasonable members of the public. And there were those in the vicinity who were alarmed or distressed by it.

The judge also held that the 'Hate Islam' slogan did not represent a genuine manifestation of the appellant's religious beliefs since it was not inherently connected to them but was an unnecessary addition reflecting a supplementary opinion which could have been conveyed in more acceptable language. The appellant had argued that the exhortation to 'Love Muslims' mitigated any abusive meaning that might otherwise attach to the words 'Hate Islam'. But, finding this to be facile in this context, HHJ Saggerson concluded that the appellant was in fact inciting hatred towards Muslims as a whole.

The trial judge also held that the appellant's ECHR rights were only relevant in determining whether it was reasonable for the arresting officer to suspect that the words on the placard, in the circumstances in which they were displayed, were protected speech or amounted to an offence justifying arrest. He concluded that this suspicion had been reasonably founded. It was also necessary and proportionate to the legitimate aim of preventing religiously

---

[66] This is summarized in *Ian Sleeper v Commissioner of Police of the Metropolis* [2025] EWHC 151 (KB).

aggravated abuse likely to cause alarm and distress, less intrusive measures had been considered but legitimately excluded, and the placards did not contribute to any public debate.

Mr Sleeper appealed against this judgment to the King's Bench Division of the High Court. Carefully reviewing the decision of the Central London County Court, on 28 January 2025, Mr Justice Sweeting, concluded that, on the evidence, the trial judge had been entitled to find that Mr Sleeper's arrest and detention were lawful. The appeal was, therefore, dismissed.[67]

According to the trial judge, since it would have been difficult for the appellant's behaviour to have been described as 'disorderly', the appeal hinged upon how the terms 'threatening', 'abusive', and 'likely to have caused harassment, alarm or distress' were to be interpreted, and also upon whether or not the conduct in question satisfied them thus understood. Mr Justice Sweeting concluded that the trial judge had not erred in considering that the 'Hate' sign was 'a plain exhortation to others' to hate 'those who practice Islamic ideology and live by Islamic precepts'. In the circumstances, the 'abusive nature of the placard and its attendant risks were ... obvious'.[68] Considering the ordinary meaning of 'abusive', the trial judge had said: 'it includes inflammatory language of an excessive or extreme character or language reasonably likely to be construed as inflammatory to an excessive or extreme degree. It goes beyond that which is "merely" offensive, insulting or rude'.[69]

Nor had the trial judge been mistaken in concluding that it was facile to regard the exhortation '#Love Muslims, Hate Islam, Jesus is Love+Hope' as equivalent to 'hate the sin but love the sinner'. Although, he concluded that this sentiment may be applicable to 'an errant relative or friend', it nevertheless 'easily breaks down when one protests that Muslims (for example) are loved except when they are behaving like practising Muslims in accordance with their Islamic ideologies, customs and teachings' or 'where a person such as the claimant asserts that Islam is "hated" as a religion but not Muslims as people'.[70] Based on the appellant's conduct, including the trial judge's assessment of him as a witness and the overall context of the case, Mr Justice Sweeting held that the trial judge had not been wrong to conclude that

---

[67] Ibid.
[68] Ibid., para. 56.
[69] Ibid., para. 57.
[70] Ibid., para. 64.

the appellant intended to incite hatred towards Muslims and not simply to criticize an ideology.

The appellant's other sign called for a ban on Islam and described it as a religion of terror. According to Mr Justice Sweeting, the presence of this sign, alongside the 'Love Muslims, Hate Islam' placard, provided ample evidence to support the trial judge's conclusion that the appellant was motivated by a desire to incite hatred against Muslims as a group, and not just to express an abstract critique of Islamic ideology. The trial judge had, therefore, been entitled to conclude, on the evidence in the specific context in question, that casting the message on the 'Hate' sign in a paradoxical manner did not preclude it from falling within the conduct at which section 5 of the Public Order Act is aimed. According to Mr Justice Sweeting, HHJ Saggerson found that the appellant's words were likely to be perceived as abusive and to have been likely to incite public disorder, particularly since they were displayed in Southwark shortly after the London Bridge, Borough Market, and Finsbury Park attacks. The 'Hate' sign was not expressed as the appellant's personal view. Its message was not being advocated in a debating chamber or developed in a polemical article. It was set out in headlines and called for those reading to respond by hating Islam just as the other sign called for the banning of the Islamic faith. According to Mr Justice Sweeting, it was not perverse or contrary to the evidence for the trial judge to decide that, in this context, exhorting people to 'Hate Islam' was likely to be perceived as hateful and abusive, that it would cause distress, and that it carried a risk to public order.

iii) Rex v Frost

On 1 February 2025, holding an Israeli flag, Martin Frost (47) live-streamed himself publicly tearing pages from the Qur'an and setting fire to them in front of a crowd of supporters assembled in central Manchester near the Glade of Light memorial to the victims of the 2017 Manchester Arena attack.[71] Frost subsequently pleaded guilty to a single charge of intentionally causing racially or religiously aggravated harassment or alarm to Fahad Iqbal – an on-looker who had attempted to prevent the book burning – by displaying a threatening, abusive or insulting visible representation. The Greater Manchester Police posted a self-congratulatory statement on its X social

---

[71] ITV news, 'Man admits setting fire to Koran near to Manchester Arena memorial', 3 February 2025.

media account including the name and date of birth of the accused. Manchester Magistrates' Court heard that Frost's actions were intended as an act of solidarity with Salwan Momika, murdered in Sweden in January 2025 prior to being tried for publicly burning the Qur'an (see Chapter 8), and that they had also been triggered by mental health problems stemming from the death of his daughter in the conflict in the middle east. Judge Margaret McCormack told the defendant that, although, she was sorry for his bereavement: 'The Qur'an is a sacred book to Muslims and treating it as you did is going to cause extreme distress. This is a tolerant country, but we just do not tolerate this behaviour'. Frost's case was remitted to the Crown Court for sentencing.

iv) Rex v Coskun

On 2 June 2025, Hamit Coskun (50) – a Turkish atheist of Kurdish and Armenian extraction who had spent ten years as a political prisoner in Turkey – was convicted of a public order offence by District Judge, John McGarva JP, at Westminster magistrates' court.[72] Shouting 'Fuck Islam!', 'Islam is religion of terrorism!', and 'Qur'an is burning!', on 13 February 2025, Coskun had publicly set fire to a copy of Islam's holy book (purchased specifically for the purpose) outside the Turkish consulate in London. He claimed this was a protest against the government of Turkey which, in his view, had turned the country into a base for radical Islamists and was attempting to establish a sharia regime. His social media account had announced his intention to stage his protest at the time, date and place in question.

From a property adjacent to the Turkish consulate, a man, later identified as Moussa Kadri, emerged. He accused Coskun of being a 'fucking idiot', to which the defendant repeatedly replied: 'fuck you' and 'fuck Islam'. Saying he was going to kill Coskun, Kadri returned to the building from which he had come and, re-emerging with a knife, launched a savage attack upon him. Kadri was later charged with possessing a knife and of causing bodily harm. In September 2025, describing Kadri's behaviour as 'disgraceful', though triggered by a loss of temper occasioned by seeing Coskun set fire to 'the holy Koran', Judge Adam Hiddleston sentenced him to 20-weeks imprisonment, suspended for 18 months, plus 150 hours of unpaid work and 10 days of

---

[72] B. Ellery & D. White, 'Row over Quran burning conviction', *The Times*, 3 June 2025.

rehabilitation, a lenient punishment for what was a serious and potentially life-threatening assault.[73]

Coskun was also kicked by a passing delivery driver. The police arrived and took Coskun to hospital where his injuries were found not to be serious. He was then arrested. At the police station, a tee-shirt emblazoned with the slogans: 'Islam is a terrorist ideology', and 'The Quran should be banned', was found in his rucksack. He was then interviewed under caution in the presence of a lawyer. Because his command of English is less than perfect, he was granted an interpreter.

Coskun faced two overlapping charges. One was that – contrary to section 5 of the Public Order Act 1986 – in a disorderly manner, and within the hearing or sight of a person likely to be caused harassment, alarm or distress, he had set light to a copy of the Qur'an while holding it aloft and shouting the slogans to which reference has already been made. The other charge included the same components but added that – contrary to section 31(1)(c) of the Crime and Disorder Act 1998 and section 5 of the Public Order Act 1986 – his behaviour had been motivated (wholly or partly) by hostility towards Muslims.

The judge made clear that the defendant had been charged with disorderly conduct, not with criticism of Islam which is not itself an offence nor necessarily disorderly. He added that it is not necessarily disorderly either, to burn a religious book, although doing so may be offensive to some. The key question, therefore, was whether the defendant had crossed the line between lawful criticism of Islam and unlawful abuse of Muslims. Judge McGarva concluded that he had. He found that Coskun's conduct was disorderly because of the timing and location of the book burning, his abusive comments, some things he said to the police, and the reaction of his two assailants. Coskun was fined £240 plus a statutory surcharge of £96.

Since the incident, Coskun has received death threats and has been moved to a safe house. Following the verdict, he said in a statement issued through the Free Speech Union (FSU):

> 'This decision is an assault on free speech and will deter others from exercising their democratic rights to peaceful protest and freedom of expression. As an activist I will continue to campaign against the

---

[73] M. Evans', Prosecutors urged to review case of Muslim who attacked Koran burner', *The Telegraph*, 24 September 2025.

threat of Islam. Christian blasphemy laws were repealed in this country more than 15 years ago and it cannot be right to prosecute someone for blaspheming against Islam. Would I have been prosecuted if I'd set fire to a copy of the Bible outside Westminster Abbey? I doubt it'.[74]

Free speech and secularist campaigners agreed. Claiming the verdict was wrong, shadow justice secretary, Robert Jenrick, said that it 'revives a blasphemy law that parliament repealed'.[75] Others denounced the conviction as 'a concerning capitulation to Islamic blasphemy codes'[76] and vowed to appeal 'all the way to the European Court of Human Rights, if necessary'.[77] The FSU said:

> 'We are supporting Hamit, not because we're anti-Islam, but because we don't think people who don't believe in a particular religious faith should be compelled, under threat of prosecution, to respect the blasphemy codes of its believers. Religious tolerance requires people of faith to tolerate those who criticise and protest against their religion, just as their values and beliefs are tolerated'.[78]

On 10 October 2025, Coskun's conviction was overturned by Mr Justice Bennathan, presiding over Southwark Crown Court. The judge began by saying that, while burning the Qur'an might be something 'many Muslims find desperately upsetting and offensive', the right to freedom of expression 'must include the right to express views that offend, shock or disturb'.[79] He added:

> 'We live in a liberal democracy. One of the precious rights that affords us is to express our own views and read, hear and consider ideas without the state intervening to stop us doing so. The price we pay for that is having to allow others to exercise the same rights, even if that upsets, offends or shocks us'.[80]

---

[74] B. Ellery & D. White, 'Man who burnt Quran says conviction is an assault on free speech', *The Times*, 2 June 2025

[75] Ibid.

[76] D. Shipley, 'England now has a blasphemy law', *The Spectator*, 2 June 2025.

[77] Ellery & White, 'Man who burnt Quran says conviction is an assault on free speech.'

[78] Free Speech Union, 'Hamit Coskun Fund Raiser: Help Us Oppose the Backdoor Blasphemy Law', 2025.

[79] *Rex v Coskun, Crown Court*, 10 October 2025, para. 2.

[80] Ibid., para. 3; 'Man who burned Quran wins free speech appeal', *BBC*, 10 October 2025.

Mr Justice Bennathan addressed seven factors at the heart of the appeal. First, since the defendant's conduct was not aimed at anyone in particular, it was less likely to constitute a section 5 offence than if it had been directed at a specific person or people. Second, it occurred outside the Turkish Consulate, a building likely to be secured against protest. Third, a crowd will typically be more intimidating than one man by himself and in this case, although one or two other people were around at the material time, the only person involved in the protest was Coskun himself. Fourth, since it was daylight, passersby could clearly see that the defendant was alone and empty-handed except for the book to which he then set light. Fifth, the longer a potentially distressing protest occurs, the greater the likelihood that it will harass, alarm or distress someone. However, the defendant's protest lasted only two or three minutes. Sixth, although the character of any such occasion is not determined by the reaction of those present at the time, their response nevertheless provides some indication of the 'sound, feel and appearance of the impugned conduct'.[81] Section 5 criminalises the effect of conduct likely to occur, not that which actually does. The three or so minutes of recorded video footage showed that several people wandered by, and that as things developed, two or three stopped to watch. They saw a man by himself on a fairly empty pavement, shouting and setting fire to a book. There was no sense that any of them felt sufficiently alarmed to hurry away or even to cross the road.

Seventh, although Kadri and the delivery cyclist may have felt insulted, offended and angered by the defendant's conduct, this is not the same as being harassed, alarmed or distressed. It is, therefore, irrelevant to the section 5 offence. Further, courts should be wary of allowing the criminal reaction of one person to turn an exercise of free speech into an offence on the part of others. The defendant's conduct cannot, therefore, be said to have been disorderly, or within the hearing or sight of a person likely to be harassed, alarmed or distressed by it.

Lord Young, Director of the FSU, said that the overturning of Coskun's conviction sent a message that 'anti-religious protests, however offensive to true believers, must be tolerated' and that

> 'had the verdict been allowed to stand, it would have sent a message
> to religious fundamentalists up and down the country that all they
> need to do to enforce their blasphemy codes is to violently attack the

---

[81] *Rex v Coskun, Crown Court*, 10 October 2025, para. 40.

blasphemer, thereby making him or her guilty of having caused public disorder. Instead, the crown court has sent the opposite message – that anti-religious protests, however offensive to true believers, must be tolerated'.[82]

Describing Coskun's protest as a 'lawful act of political dissent', the National Secular Society hailed the judgment as 'an important victory for freedom of expression'.[83] Not everyone agreed, however. For example, *5 Pillars*, a conservative Muslim news website critical of Western and secular liberal values, carried the following headline: 'An atheist Islamophobe who was fined for burning a copy of the Holy Quran outside the Turkish consulate in London has won an appeal against his conviction following a right-wing backlash, raising fears of future anti-Islam hate protests on British shores'.[84]

The quashing of Coskun's conviction did not, however, end the saga. On 22 November 2025, it was reported that the CPS had been granted leave to appeal to the High Court on the grounds that his conduct had been disorderly and therefore constituted a public order offence.[85] The appeal was, however, dismissed. Lord Justice Warby and Ms Justice Obi reminded all concerned that their task was not to re-hear the case and to reach their own conclusions about the facts and legal merits of the charge against the respondent. It was rather, 'an appeal by case stated, in which the court below sets out the facts it found and its decision and identifies a question of law for the opinion of the High Court'.[86] The question posed by the Crown Court was: 'On the evidence we received, were we entitled to conclude [1] that the Respondent's conduct was not "disorderly", and [2] that it was not "likely" to have caused a person within the hearing and sight of it the necessary "harassment, alarm or distress?"' Answering both questions in the affirmative, the judges held:

> 'We are not persuaded that the court left any material factor out of account or relied on any immaterial factor. The evaluation of the facts, their relevance, and their weight, was a matter for the Crown Court.

---

[82] C. Quinn, 'Man who burnt Koran outside Turkish consulate wins appeal against conviction supported by Jenrick', *London Broadcasting Company*, 10 October 2025.
[83] National Secular Society, 'Success! Court upholds right to free speech in Quran burning appeal', 10 October 2025.
[84] R. Carter, 'Quran burner Hamit Coskun wins conviction appeal', *5 Pillars*, 10 October 2025.
[85] Scott, 'Challenge to acquittal of man who burnt Quran.'
[86] *DPP v Hamit Coskun* [2026] EWHC 427 (Admin), para. 2.

We do not consider its reasoning contained any logical flaw .... We are satisfied that the conclusions arrived at were rationally open to the court'.[87]

Other incidents involving alleged desecration of the Qur'an are considered in Chapter 8.

c) Harassment

The crime of harassment was created by the Protection from Harassment Act 1997 and should not be confused with harassment as proscribed by the Equality Act 2010 discussed below. Under the 1997 Act, harassment involves a course of conduct, and not a single or a couple of isolated incidents, repeatedly causing unreasonable and oppressive alarm or distress of sufficient gravity to amount to a crime. The fewer the occasions, and the wider they are spread over time, the less they are likely to constitute such misconduct.

Section 1 of the Act states that a course of conduct amounts to harassment if the person in question, knows or ought to know that it would have this effect. They ought to have known that this would be the case, if a reasonable person in such a position would regard it as such. An element of objectivity is, thereby, introduced to the test. Speech that amounts to unlawful harassment under the Act is not 'within the law' and is not, therefore, protected by the right to freedom of expression. As already indicated, most court cases involving the alleged harassment of Muslims have been based upon public order or offences aggravated by religious hatred. Few, if any, have turned directly upon the 1997 Act itself.

d) Malicious Communications

The Malicious Communications Act of 1988 and the Communications Act of 2003 give the police power to arrest people for what they say online. An average of 30 are arrested every day for such offences.[88] But there have been few prosecutions leading to conviction on this basis alone. One involved 78-year-old evangelical pastor, James McConnell, charged under the 2003 Act with the improper use of a public electronic communications network and

---

[87] Ibid., para. 32.
[88] Lord Lebvedev, 'The right to free speech means nothing if it does not mean the right to offend', *The Standard*, 17 July 2025.

of causing a grossly offensive message to be sent by these means.[89] In a sermon delivered at Belfast's Whitewell Metropolitan Tabernacle on 18 May 2014, and broadcast on the internet, Mr McConnell had described Islam as 'heathen', 'satanic', and as 'a doctrine spawned in hell'. He had also characterized all Muslims, whom he said he did not trust, as potential terrorists on account of their faith. However, in January 2016, Pastor McConnell, who later apologized for causing a public outcry, was acquitted at Belfast Magistrates' Court. District Judge Liam McNally held that, although the remarks could be considered offensive, he did not regard them as 'grossly' offensive as required by the legislation. He added that 'the courts need to be very careful not to criticise speech which, however contemptible, is no more than offensive. It is not the task of the criminal law to censor offensive utterances'.

Civil law

The most relevant civil wrongs for the issues discussed in this book are defamation and harassment under the Equality Act 2010.

a) Defamation

An illustration of the difference between defamation and legitimate criticism of Muslims and Islam under UK law can be found in the case of *Versi v Husain*.[90] The claimant, Miqdaad Versi – formerly director of media monitoring at the Muslim Council of Britain and a campaigner against Islamophobia – complained that he had been defamed in a tweet posted on 21 November 2020, by the defendant, Ed Husain, a Muslim author, academic, and adviser to western governments on Islamist extremism, terrorism and national security. In a twitter thread, the defendant had quoted a tweet posted by the complainant which said: 'Why does Fraser Nelson, a man who as editor is accountable for so much anti-Muslim hate propagated in the Spectator, think it is appropriate to explain Islamophobia to a Muslim woman? And why would citing a pro-Saudi pro-Netanyahu person who works with Richard Kemp, help? [person shrugging emoji]'. The defendant had then replied: 'Pipe

---

[89] A. Rutherford, 'Belfast pastor James McConnell not guilty: "I want to assure Muslims I love them, what I am against is their theology,"' *Belfast Telegraph*, 5 January 2016.
[90] [2023] EWHC 482 (KB).

down, you pro-Hamas, pro-Iran, pro-gender discrimination, pro-blasphemy laws, pro-sectarian, anti-Western "Representative" of an Islamist outfit'. No evidence was submitted to substantiate any of these accusations.

Reviewing the law on defamation, particularly how a hypothetical reasonable reader would interpret any given text in its specific context, the judge held that the natural and ordinary meaning conveyed by the tweet was defamatory since:

> '... right thinking members of society generally would deplore those who express views in support of Hamas, as a militant Islamist group with known links to violence. It is also contrary to the common or shared values of our society to express extremist views that are so objectionable as to undermine the legitimacy of the claimant's own participation in public debate. Attributing such views to the claimant would lower a person in the estimation of "right-thinking people generally." The imputation is one that would tend to have a substantially adverse effect on the way that people would treat the claimant, and their attitude towards him'.[91]

b) The Equality Act 2010

In order to consolidate, update, supplement and strengthen anti-discrimination law in the UK, the Equality Act was passed in 2010. On the basis of nine 'protected characteristics' – age, disability, gender reassignment, marriage and civil partnership, pregnancy and maternity, race, religion or belief, sex, and sexual orientation – it seeks to protect people from discrimination, harassment or victimization in employment and in the delivery of private and public services. In any given case more than one of these may be implicated in the prohibited conduct. With limited exceptions the Act does not apply to Northern Ireland which has its own customized arrangements.

The Act also requires public authorities, in the exercise of their functions, 'to have due regard to the need to ... eliminate discrimination, harassment, victimization and any other conduct that is prohibited by or under this Act', to 'advance equality of opportunity', and to 'foster good relations' between 'persons who share a relevant protected characteristic and those who do not' (the Public Sector Equality Duty – PSED).[92] Providers and relevant constituent institutions must recognise the desirability of achieving the aims set out above. They are also

---

[91] Ibid., para. 61.
[92] Equality Act 2010, s. 149.

obliged to be clear about the equality implications of their decisions, policies, and practices. The PSED does not otherwise restrict or regulate freedom of expression.

In order to qualify as a protected characteristic for the purposes of this legislation, a given religion or philosophical belief must attain a certain level of cogency, seriousness, cohesion and importance, and be genuinely held. It must also amount to something more than a transient opinion or viewpoint, be weighty and referenced to a substantial aspect of human life and behaviour, be worthy of respect in a democratic society, consistent with the fundamental rights of others, and not be incompatible with human dignity.

Recent court cases have affirmed that the PSED does not lawfully justify censoring those who hold a particular religious or philosophical belief – such as anti-Zionism or the view that sex is biological rather than socially constructed – merely because the perspective in question gives rise to lawful criticism of other protected beliefs.[93] On the contrary, it has been confirmed that it would be unlawful for the expression of controversial, though lawful views to be censured by employers who must also actively endeavour to protect employees from vilification, harassment, and victimization including by preventing the initiation of disciplinary processes which would threaten lawful free speech. Employers themselves must also refrain from officially contesting or supporting protected though controversial points of view.

It has also been made clear that criticism of Islam is a lawful belief protected by the Act.[94] Following a series of posts on X, and after a four-year disciplinary process, in April 2025, Patrick Lee, a 61-year old actuary and atheist, was found guilty of misconduct by an Institute and Faculty of Actuaries' (IFoA) Disciplinary Tribunal Panel. Amongst other things, Lee had described Islam as 'backward', 'a dangerous cult', a '1,300-year-old con trick'. He had also called the Prophet Mohammed a 'monster'. In September 2020, an unnamed executive officer at the regulator had referred his social media conduct to the IFoA for investigation. A month later, the Islamophobia Response Unit, a UK charity, also lodged a complaint. The IFoA Disciplinary Tribunal Panel concluded that 42 of his posts criticising Islam, including calling the Prophet Mohammed a 'monster', were 'either offensive or inflammatory or both', and that 29 were 'designed to demean or insult Muslims'.[95] It decided, therefore, that he had breached the 'integrity

---

[93] See, eg, *Miller v University of Bristol*, Bristol Employment Tribunal, 5 February 2024; *Phoenix v Open University*, Watford Employment Tribunal, 22 January 2024.

[94] J. Eastham, 'Right to criticise Islam is protected under British law, judge rules', *The Telegraph*, 8 November 2025.

[95] Institute and Faculty of Actuaries Disciplinary Tribunal Panel Hearing, 7 May 2025, para. 29.

principle' of the Actuaries' Code by having 'failed to show respect for others…
in circumstances where [his] conduct could reasonably be considered to reflect
upon the reputation of the actuarial profession as a whole'. In spite of having been
a member of the IFoA for 34 years, including serving on its council and being
involved in management, Lee was expelled from the organization for two years
and ordered to pay nearly £23,000 in costs.

However, in a written judgment delivered on 3 November 2025, employment
tribunal Judge David Khan held that Lee's view qualified as a protected
philosophical belief under the Equality Act. This was because his claim that
'Islam, particularly in a traditional form – rather than a reformed, modernised,
moderate and Westernised form – is problematic and deserving of criticism', was
directed at religious doctrines and practices and not against 'individual followers
of Islam or to the Islamic faith/religion at large'. The judge also accepted that Mr
Lee believed 'these doctrines and/or their interpretation require urgent reform'.

Whether Lee's tweets were an appropriate manifestation of this belief, and
whether the regulator discriminated against him, will be decided at a final hearing
in February 2026. The judge has, nevertheless, already accepted that they might
be. He held: 'I find that the claimant's evidence in relation to these tweets, that he
was inveighing against the offending doctrines and practices because they
continued to be treated as authentic and officially sanctioned by Islamic leaders,
was not inconsistent with the pleaded belief'. Mr Lee also told the employment
tribunal that his belief was based on 'reasoned analysis rather than prejudice', and
cited his record of substantial charitable donations to causes helping
predominantly Muslim communities as evidence that he is not anti-Muslim.

This verdict, welcomed by free speech and secular campaigners, is the first
in which a court or tribunal has ruled that 'Islam-critical' beliefs are protected
under the Equality Act 2010. Although only a first-tier tribunal decision and
therefore not binding, it is nevertheless likely to be persuasive in other cases. It is
now also clear that the PSED requires those to whom it applies to have due regard
to the elimination of unlawful discrimination, harassment and victimisation
against those who criticize Islam. As Lord Young, Director of the FSU, said:

'this landmark judgment will make it much harder for the
Government to roll out an official, state-approved definition of
"Islamophobia" … After this judgment, how can the Government
hope to prohibit "Islamophobia" or "anti-Muslim hatred," given that
its definition, however tightly drawn, is bound to include describing
Islam as "backward," "a con trick," "a dangerous cult," "the root of
evil" and calling the Prophet Mohammed a "monster"? … Treating
everyone with respect is something few people would disagree with,

including me. But that is not the same as respecting their beliefs and the sooner we grasp that distinction, the better'.[96]

Section 26 of the Equality Act also requires providers to protect their staff from harassment. In this context this means unwanted conduct that has the purpose or effect of violating a person's dignity or creating an intimidating, hostile, degrading, humiliating, or offensive environment for them because of, or connected to, one or more of their relevant protected characteristics, not including marriage, civil partnership, pregnancy and maternity. In deciding whether or not any conduct fulfils these criteria, it is necessary to take into account the perception of those targeted, other relevant circumstances including legal rights or duties, and whether it is reasonable to expect the behaviour in question to have such an effect. The last point is particularly important because the perception of anyone allegedly harassed is not the only relevant consideration in determining whether unlawful harassment has in fact occurred.

Public authorities may also need to consider whether, in cases of alleged harassment, the alleged perpetrator was exercising any of their other Convention rights including freedom of expression. Providers or constituent institutions are not required to take reasonable steps to secure speech on the part of an employee which amounts to unlawful discrimination or harassment.

Most organizations in the UK and elsewhere, including businesses, schools and universities, have codes of conduct prohibiting discrimination, harassment, victimization, and other forms of misconduct, which in principle operate as rules governing membership of the organization concerned. Break them and you may be disciplined, sacked, or required to resign. However, as the following three chapters of this book observe, managers and others in many controversial cases have failed, wilfully or otherwise, to understand that disciplining those subject to their authority for breach of good conduct codes is only lawful if the code is itself lawful and the breach unlawful. The simple fact is that this is not necessarily the case with respect to all such codes or breaches. There is, for example, a world of difference between, for example, a maths lecturer peppering her lectures and seminars with derogatory comments about Muslims being 'untrustworthy, corrupt, intolerant, prone to violence' etc, and a law professor referring students to the authoritative

---

[96] T. Young, 'Criticism of Islam is a Protected Belief, Judge Rules', *Daily Sceptic*, 9 November 2025.

literature which examines contemporary Islam, including the extent to which it is compatible with post-Second World War human rights norms. Managers also need to be much better informed about the difference between the expression of unlawful prejudice against minorities, on the one hand, and lawful criticism of beliefs, practices, and the conduct of any social group, on the other. The following are just a few examples of how this has operated in practice.

The appellant in *Thomas v Surrey and Borders Partnership NHS Foundation Trust and another* claimed he had been unfairly dismissed as an agency worker by the respondent because of his commitment to 'English nationalism'.[97] His complaint was rejected by an employment tribunal, a decision upheld on appeal. The judges in question decided that, while English nationalism could be a 'philosophical belief' protected by section 10 of the Equality Act, the appellant's particular conception of it was not, because by advocating the exclusion and removal of Muslims from Britain, he infringed the fundamental rights of others. His many social media tweets included the following: 'Soldier was asked where do you stand on Muslims? The windpipe usually does the trick he replied'; 'Lets "Trump Muslims" in England with a complete temporary ban also'; plus various references to the hashtag *BanTheBurka* coupled with the suggestion that a woman wearing a headscarf was not welcome in the UK.[98] The Employment Appeal Tribunal added, that while the appellant was not prohibited from holding the views to which he subscribed, he could not complain of allegedly employment-related discrimination under the Equality Act because of them.

In another case, *Mr Z Kioua v Lainston House Ltd*, an Employment Tribunal found that the complainant, a Muslim employed by the respondent and known to be teetotal, had been the victim of harassment resulting in 'injury to feelings' relating to religion or belief contrary to section 26 of the Equality Act. A bottle of cognac Mr Kioua won in a staff raffle had been swapped for a box of 'cheap' chocolates and accepted by another employee in his absence.[99] A manager later told the appellant that to have given him the

---

[97] *Mr S Thomas v 1) Surrey and Borders Partnership NHS Foundation Trust 2) Ms A Brett* [2024] EAT 141.

[98] Ibid, para. 19.

[99] *Mr Z Kioua v Lainston House Ltd*, Employment Tribunals, Case No. 1403090/2018, 21 August 2020; S. Morris, 'Muslim man wins UK tribunal case over Cognac raffle switch', *The Guardian*, 24 September 2020.

cognac would have been akin to giving nuts to someone with a nut allergy. In April 2019 Mr Kioua resigned from the respondent's employment. Rejecting other claims regarding alleged harassment, direct discrimination, failure to make reasonable adjustments, victimisation and constructive dismissal, the tribunal nevertheless held that:

> 'A nut allergy is an illness, a life-threatening illness ... It is not an acceptable point of comparison. It minimises the importance of Mr Kioua's beliefs and practices. The point is that it should not have been said, just as the decision should not have been made to change Mr Kioua's prize ... both are offensive and caused him distress'.[100]

The respondent was ordered to pay the claimant £2,294 in respect of injury to feelings.

In *Mr A Ali v (1) Heathrow Express Operating Company Ltd (2) Redline Assured Security Ltd*, the appellant, a Muslim employee of the first respondent, claimed harassment and discrimination on the part of his employer and the second respondent, the latter of whom was responsible for carrying out security checks at Heathrow Airport and at the airport's Heathrow Express stations. These included conducting tests on how security officers responded to suspicious objects.[101] In August 2017 such a test was conducted using a bag containing a box, some electric cable and a piece of paper bearing the clearly visible Arabic words 'Allahu Akbar'. The appellant was among a group of employees of the first respondent who received an email reporting the results of the test which included images of the bag and note. An employment tribunal rejected the appellant's claim that the second respondent's conduct amounted either to direct discrimination or harassment related to religion under the Equality Act. An Employment Appeal Tribunal rejected his appeal solely on the harassment issue.

The tribunals agreed that the use of the phrase 'Allahu Akbar', widely invoked by those carrying out terrorist attacks in the UK and elsewhere, was intended to add to the sense of suspicion created by the package and had not been chosen gratuitously in order to upset Muslims. It did not inherently associate Islam with terrorism, nor did it stereotype the vast majority of Muslims as terrorists or terrorist sympathisers. They added that it was not reasonable for the appellant to be offended by it in this context, nor to claim

---

[100] *Kioua v Lainston House Ltd*, paras 6.107-108.
[101] [2022] EAT 54.

that it violated his dignity or created an intimidating, hostile, degrading, humiliating or offensive environment for him.

Conclusion

They key to understanding the legal and human rights issues relevant to this study lies in recognizing that criticism of Muslims and Islam is protected by international human rights and domestic law. But not in all circumstances. States typically regard religious hatred as an aggravating factor in crimes such as assault and vandalism. Incitement to religious hatred is also widely criminalized. But the distinction between this offence and non-criminal criticism of religion, though clearcut in principle, is not always so sharp in practice. A great deal depends upon precisely what has been said, the context in which this occurred, and how all relevant factors are interpreted and evaluated.

International human rights law also protects the rights to freedom of thought, conscience and religion, to respect for reputation and privacy, and to be free from discrimination. The ECtHR has, for example, sought to reconcile the friction this may cause by recognising a right on the part of religious believers to be free from deliberate gratuitously offensive or insulting criticism, an approach which sits uneasily with the iconic *Handyside*, 'offend, shock, or disturb' criterion.

Since the Court rarely departs from its own long-standing formulae, the 'gratuitously offensive' test is, therefore, unlikely to be easily abandoned either by the Court itself or by any institution seeking to remain faithful to its jurisprudence. However, at the very least, greater specificity about what it means would be welcome because, as it stands, it permits more official discretion than is warranted. Several additional refinements would, therefore, be appropriate. First, the 'gratuitous insult or offence' should be serious or significant and not merely trivial or minor. Second, it should be caused intentionally or recklessly. Third, it should be of a kind likely to cause serious insult or offence to any religious believer of reasonable tolerance, fortitude, and forbearance. Fourth, there should be concrete evidence, and not mere speculation, that this has occurred. A final requirement, more a matter of conceptual thoroughness than clarifying the scope of the relevant discretion, would involve identifying more clearly the rights allegedly adversely affected by the alleged offence or insult.

As for UK criminal law, the defendant's remarks in *McConnell* arguably lay on the borderline between 'offensive' and 'grossly offensive' as required by the Malicious Communications Act 2003. But, for the courts in *Norwood* and *Sleeper,* a combination of the statements both these defendants made, and the specific circumstances – including the fact that each followed closely in the wake of a terrorist outrage or outrages – contributed to interpreting them as an unlawful breach of public order. However, as a result of *Frost* and *Coskun,* it is not clear if and when public Qur'an burning amounts to a public order offence. If the right to free expression cannot justify what has been said, but no crime has been committed, in England and Wales a 'non-crime hate incident' or a 'non-crime incident' may nevertheless have occurred. At best these concepts have an uncertain future.

Civil law consequences stemming from criticism of Muslims/Islam may including action for defamation and disciplinary action for harassment including possible dismissal from employment. But being critical of the faith or faithful is not enough. The criticism must also have the purpose or effect of violating a person's dignity or creating an intimidating, hostile, degrading, humiliating, or offensive environment for them. Relevant factors which should be considered include the circumstances of the case, the perception of anyone allegedly harassed, and whether it is reasonable or not to expect the behaviour in question would have a harassing effect.

Chapter 7

Artistic expression

Introduction

This chapter, and the next two, seek to demonstrate that accusations of 'Islamophobic expression' – and action motivated by the fear of being denounced as an Islamophobe ('Islamophobia-phobia') – are both widespread and increasing in Britain and elsewhere across a range of sectors and activities. Over 50 notorious and well-documented cases – likely to represent only the tip of a much bigger iceberg – are reviewed. Most of those considered in this chapter involve artistic expression, broadly conceived. However, before considering them we should note allegations that ostensibly accidental resemblances between certain objects and iconic Islamic images, plus the 'inappropriate' use of the name 'Mohammad', are also 'Islamophobic'. In 2005, for example, Burger King in the UK issued an apology and, at considerable commercial expense, withdrew its ice cream packaging in response to a complaint, which also threatened 'jihad', that a graphic depicting a spinning ice cream cone was 'sacrilegious' because it resembled the Arabic word for 'Allah'.[1] And in 2013, having received complaints from Muslim community leaders in Austria, Lego withdrew the Jabba Palace model in its Star Wars collection because it was said to resemble the Hagia Sophia in Istanbul.[2] This iconic building was originally built as a church in the 6th century by the Byzantine emperor Justinian, converted to a mosque in 1453, re-purposed as a museum in 1935, and re-consecrated as a mosque in 2018. When the complaint was made, it had not been a place of worship for Muslims or anyone else for nearly 80 years.

In April 1963, the eminent economist J. K. Galbraith, then US

---

[1] 'Burger King recalls "sacrilegious" desserts', *The Scotsman*, 17 September 2005.

[2] D. Murray, *Islamophilia: A Very Metropolitan Malady* (Self-published, 2013), pp. 7-8.

Ambassador to India, was accused of having insulted Muslims by permitting his children to name their cat, 'Ahmed', a diminutive form of 'Mohammad'. Galbraith, who claimed the cat's full name was 'Ahmedabad', the capital of Gujarat, nevertheless changed its name to 'Gujarat' in response.[3] On another occasion the atheist society at a British university pinned the name 'Mohammad' to a pineapple displayed on its Freshers' Fair stall. Condemning the students, the university's Muslim society also denounced the pineapple itself as Islamophobic, the 'world's first fruit-based accusation of Islamophobia'.[4]

However, an accusation, with much more significant repercussions concerned the 'Sudanese teddy bear blasphemy case'.[5] In 2007, British schoolteacher Gillian Gibbons, who taught children of middle-class Muslim and Christian families at Unity High School in Khartoum, Sudan, was arrested, tried, and convicted under s. 125 of the Sudanese Criminal Code, for 'insulting religion' by allowing her class of six-year-olds to name a teddy bear 'Mohammad'. The complaint was filed by the prosecution's key witness, Sara Khawad, an office assistant at the school, said to have had a grievance against the head teacher. On 29 November 2007, Gibbons was sentenced to 15 days' imprisonment followed by deportation. The next day, in the wake of denunciations by imams during Friday prayers, some 10,000 protesters took to the streets of Khartoum demanding her execution. Witnesses reported government employees inciting the protests. Fearing reprisals, Gibbons was moved for her own safety to a secret location and the school was closed until January 2008. Convinced that the teacher had not intended to cause any offence, many Muslim organizations in other countries, including the Muslim Council of Britain, publicly condemned her punishment. On 3 December, during a meeting between the President of Sudan, Omar al-Bashir, and two British Muslim peers – Lord Ahmed and Baroness Warsi – it was announced that Gibbons had been granted a Presidential pardon and would be released. Upon her return to Liverpool she issued a written statement saying, 'I have a great respect for the Islamic religion and would not knowingly offend anyone'. One of the strangest aspects of this case, and that of Galbraith's cat, is that naming a cherished teddy bear and a beloved pet after the Prophet could

---

[3] *New York Times*, 20 April 1963.

[4] Murray, *Islamophilia*, p. 7.

[5] H. Fisher, 'The Great Sudanese Teddy Bear Controversy', *Liberty*, July/August 2008.

more plausibly be deemed indicators of affection and admiration than insult. But cool reflection is rarely a feature of charges of Islamophobic blasphemy.

The following discussion begins with Salman Rushdie's novel, *The Satanic Verses*, the seminal case which ignited the campaign against allegedly Islamophobic expression in both the artistic and other contexts. This is followed by reviews of similar accusations against other writers and their work, and against films and cartoons.

Writers and their work

Militantly atheistic commentators and writers, such as Richard Dawkins and Sam Harris, have frequently been denounced as 'Islamophobes' for criticising monotheism, including Islam. However, others, such as Sir Salman Rushdie, Michel Houellbeq, Sherry Jones, Martin Amis, and Sebastian Faulks have faced similar denunciations for much less systematic critique.

The Satanic Verses by Salman Rushdie

As already indicated, 'Islamophobia' did not become a widely-used term until the late 1980s when Indian-born British Muslim author Salman Rushdie published a novel entitled *The Satanic Verses*.[6] As Chapter 3 explains, the phrase 'Satanic Verses' refers to an alleged episode in the early history of Islam when, in an attempt to convert the Meccans, the Prophet is said to have received a divine revelation permitting their three most important female deities, Allatt, al-Uzza, and al-Manat, to intercede with the Almighty. Rapidly realizing how incompatible this was with the radical 'oneness of God', the foundational precept of Islam, Mohammad is said swiftly to have recanted, attributing the event to Satanic deception.

Blending contemporaneous events and characters with the life of the Prophet in a magic realist format, Rushdie's novel involves fictional actors Gibreel Farishta and Saladin Chamcha, expatriates of Indian Muslim background who survive the detonation of a bomb by Sikh separatists on a plane over the English channel. In a miraculous transformation, Farishta, who develops symptoms of schizophrenia and occasionally manifests a halo, takes

---

[6] K. Malik, *From Fatwa to Jihad: How the World Changed: The Satanic Verses to Charlie Hebdo* (Atlantic, 2010); M. Ruthven, *A Satanic Affair: Salman Rushdie and the Rage of Islam* (Chatto & Windus, 1991).

on the personality of the Archangel Gabriel, while Chamcha assumes the form of a devil, growing horns and goatlike legs.

The story – which has many twists and turns including two murders by Farishta who commits suicide at the end – features a number of dream sequences, one of which recounts the original Satanic Verses episode. In it, a thinly disguised 'Messenger', called 'Mahound', is opposed by a heathen priestess, Hind, and the sceptical satirical poet, Baal, who hides in an underground brothel where the prostitutes assume the identities of the Prophet's wives. One of the Prophet's companions also claims that, doubting the authenticity of the Messenger's revelations, he has subtly altered portions of the Qur'an. Mahound has Baal and the prostitutes executed. It is also implied that Hind's supernatural powers caused Mahound to succumb to a fatal illness.

Initially, reaction to Rushdie's novel was confined to literary circles. But, a massive global controversy erupted in February 1989 when the Ayatollah Khomeini, Supreme Leader of the Islamic Republic of Iran, issued a religious edict (fatwa) condemning not only Rushdie to death, but also anyone associated with the novel's publication. Around the world many non-Muslims in the west defended Rushdie. However, others, including Israel's chief Ashkenazi Rabbi, Avraham Shapira, Cardinal John O'Connor of New York, Cardinal Albert Decourtray of Lyons, and the Archbishop of Canterbury, Dr George Carey, condemned him for causing offence. Some Muslims denounced the fatwa. Yet others, regarding the book as blasphemous and insulting to them and their faith, demanded that its author should be punished. And when asked if the Iranians were within their rights to kill Rushdie, University of California Los Angeles Director of the university's Near East Studies Centre, Professor Georges Sabbagh, simply replied: 'Why not?'.[7] Similarly, when asked if he would consider attending a demonstration where an effigy of Rushdie was burned, Yusuf Islam (the former pop singer known as Cat Stevens) replied: 'I would have hoped that it would be the real thing'.[8]

Book burnings and mass protests were staged in the UK and elsewhere. British Labour MP Keith Vaz led a march through Leicester calling for the authorities to ban the book, while former Conservative Party Chairman, Norman Tebbit, upbraided Rushdie for betraying his upbringing and his

---

[7] R. Spencer, *Islamophobia and the Threat to Free Speech* (Centre for Security Policy, 2021), p. 10.
[8] 'Geoffrey Robertson's Hypotheticals', *ABC Commercial*, 9 March 2015.

religion. Abroad, several people were killed including Hitoshi Igarashi who translated the work into Japanese. The novel was banned in India as hate speech yet won the 1988 Whitbread Award and was shortlisted for the 1988 Booker Prize. Several attempts were made to murder Rushdie who was placed under 24-hour police protection. He was later knighted by Her Majesty Queen Elizabeth II. By 2022 the author concluded that the threat to his physical safety had all but vanished. Yet that August, at the age of 75, he became the target of a vicious knife attack at a public event in the US, which though narrowly failing to end his life, nevertheless cost him an eye and the use of a hand.

The Satanic Verses controversy prompted some Muslims in Britain to campaign for the offence of blasphemy – which then covered only the Christian faith – to be extended to include Islam. The campaign failed. Instead, some two decades later, the offence of blasphemy was itself abolished. The controversy nevertheless galvanized, united, and empowered both the typically more traditional older generation of British Muslims and their more westernized offspring. It also led to the establishment in Britain of several institutions. These included the Muslim Parliament, *Jam'iat Ihyaa Minhaaj Al-Sunnah* (JIMAS 'Movement of the Revival of the Prophet's Way') – a UK-based conservative Muslim charity dedicated to improving understanding of Islam particularly among young people – and a British branch of *Hizb ut-Tahrir* ('Party of Liberation') – an international jihadi terrorist organization founded in 1953 and dedicated to the establishment of a global Islamic caliphate governed by the sharia. According to Pantucci, it is difficult not to conclude that, in the 1990s, JIMAS and Hizb ut-Tahrir 'played an important role in the radicalization of British Muslim youth', not least through the influence the latter had with university Islamic societies.[9]

Decades later, in July 2025, there was a curious twist to *The Satanic Verses* controversy when a Scottish employment tribunal rejected claims by a Muslim biology teacher, Rabi Ihsan, of Pakistani heritage, alleging direct and indirect discrimination, harassment on grounds of race, religion and sex, and constructive unfair dismissal on the part of her colleagues and employer.[10] According to Ms Ihsan, in October 2022, two teachers had a staff-room conversation in her presence. Ms Gardiner had asked her colleague, Ms Lagan,

---

[9] R. Pantucci, *'We Love Death as You Love Life': Britain's Suburban Terrorists,* (Hurst, 2015), pp. 96, 167.

[10] *Ihsan v Renfrewshire Council and others*, Glasgow Employment Tribunal, 8 July 2025, para. 289.

to recommend an audiobook she could download. Ms Lagan told Ms Gardiner that, having heard about the attempted assassination of Salman Rushdie, she had decided to sample *The Satanic Verses*. Both Ms Gardiner and Ms Lagan claimed not to have been aware that the book had anything to do with religion. When Ms Ihsan told the other two teachers that the novel was 'offensive to Islam', the conversation about it stopped. Ms Ihsan nevertheless described the incident as 'an attempt to provoke me, incite hatred and create a hostile environment'.

According to Attenborough, in 2021, eleven years after she started working at the school, Ms Ihsan enrolled on an Education Scotland course on 'Building Racial Literacy', which encourages participants to embed critical race theory, inspired 'anti-racism', and 'decoloniality' into the curriculum. As a result, she developed an action plan — approved by her head teacher and shared with Education Scotland — which was framed in this vocabulary and which also included an 'Islamophobia awareness' programme.[11]

Ms Ihsan also claimed to have been 'very upset' when, in September 2022, staff in the science department removed, and later destroyed, a creationist book disputing the theory of evolution, the cover of which bore Arabic script and a representation of the holy seal of the Prophet Muhammad. This occurred when teachers discovered that the author had been convicted of serious sexual offences against children. Ms Ihsan had not been present at the time but later told colleagues that the destruction of the book had caused her distress because the cover included a representation of the holy seal. She alleged that the teacher in question had 'displayed aggression' towards her 'protected characteristics and beliefs through expressing statements and destroying a book on Creationist beliefs and evolution', and that the behaviour of other colleagues amounted to 'a series of microaggressions' constituting 'covert Islamophobia'.

Judge Muriel Robison concluded that the conversation about *The Satanic Verses* was neither targeted nor malicious. She held that 'even if it could be said that raising this matter was unwarranted conduct related to religion which made the claimant feel uncomfortable ... it was not reasonable for her to conclude that it had the proscribed effect [of harassment], particularly when the subject was dropped when she raised her concerns'. The judge added that there was no evidence of any conspiracy against the claimant nor that the

---

[11] F. Attenborough, 'Rushdie-ing to judgement', *The Critic*, 7 August 2025.

conversation in question had been intended to upset her. 'To emphasise', she added: 'nothing was said or done "because of" the claimant's religion'. The tribunal also expressed 'concern' that the creationist book had been destroyed but accepted that the teacher involved, citing both its content and the author's criminal history, had acted out of 'genuine concerns'.

Michel Houellebecq

French writer, Michel Houellebecq – described as France's 'greatest living writer' and the 'undisputed star, and *enfant terrible*, of modern French literature' – is one of the most high-profile writers to be accused of Islamophobia.[12] Although he accepts the charge, the French courts have agreed that he has not acted unlawfully. In 2001, remarks Houellebecq made in an interview for the literary magazine *Lire* about his critical and commercially successful novel, *Plateforme* ('Platform'), prompted France's Human Rights League, the Mecca-based World Islamic League, and the mosques of Paris and Lyon to initiate incitement to racial hatred charges. The novel, a first-person romance, ends with a fictional terrorist attack on a sex tourism venue, later compared to the Bali bombings which occurred the following year. In the interview Houellebecq described Islam as the 'dumbest religion' and said that 'when one reads the Qur'an one is crushed, just crushed'.[13] He also claimed that:

> 'Islam is a dangerous religion, and has been from the moment it appeared. Fortunately, it is doomed. On one hand, because the God of Islam does not exist, and even if someone is an idiot, he will eventually realize that. In the long run, the truth will triumph. On the other hand, Islam is undermined from the inside by capitalism. We can only hope that it will triumph rapidly. Materialism is a lesser evil. Its values are contemptible, but nevertheless less destructive, less cruel than those of Islam.[14]

At his trial the prosecution maintained that Houellebecq's books demonstrated a deep hatred of Islam. In his defence the novelist acknowledged that he felt

---

[12] A. Chrisafis, 'Michel Houellebecq: "Am I Islamophobic ? Probably, yes,"' *The Guardian*, 6 September 2015; 'A selection of France's best contemporary writers', *Deutsche Welle*, 11 October 2017.

[13] 'Houellebecq acquitted of insulting Islam', *The Guardian*, 22 October 2002.

[14] M. Aïssaoui, 'Houellebecq et Plateforme: "La religion la plus con, c'est quand même l'islam,"' *Le Figaro*, 30 Decembre 2014.

contempt for Islam and that Christianity, Judaism, and Islam were each based upon scriptural 'texts of hate'. But he also claimed that he had never despised Muslims and argued that criticising a religion did not mean insulting its followers. Declaring that expressing his opinions was protected by the right to freedom of expression, the three-judge Parisian court acquitted Houellebecq on 22 October 2002. A civil action brought by a civil-rights group was also rejected by another court on similar grounds.

Sherry Jones

Other novelists and novels have also been accused of Islamophobia for dubious reasons. This includes *The Jewel of Medina*, an historical novel by Sherry Jones recounting the life of Aisha, Mohammad's favourite wife, scheduled for publication by Random House on 12 August 2008. However, before this occurred, the publisher solicited an appraisal from Denise Spellberg, professor of History and Middle Eastern studies at the University of Texas. Professor Spellberg was said to have described the book as 'incredibly offensive' and a 'very ugly, stupid piece of work' and to have warned that its 'explosive' content could inspire violence from radical Islamist groups.[15] As a result, Random House cancelled publication. On 4 September 2008, British publishing house Gibson Square announced that it would publish the novel. However, on 27 September, the London home of Martin Rynja, the publisher's founder, was firebombed. Three men were later convicted of conspiracy recklessly to damage property and to endanger life. Radical Islamist cleric, Anjem Choudhary, warned of further attacks. Gibson Square then postponed publication indefinitely. Nevertheless, by the following year the novel had been published by several publishers in over a dozen countries.

Martin Amis

The cases of Martin Amis and Sebastian Faulks – described as representing 'the elite of the British literary class' and of portraying themselves as 'truth-tellers … fearless in their depiction of the darker recesses of our, and earlier, times' – illustrate a familiar sequence of events.[16] An

---

[15] A. Nomani, 'You Still Can't Write about *Mohammad*', *The Wall Street Journal*, 6 August 2008.
[16] Murray, *Islamophilia*, p. 41.

author publicly criticizes Muslims or Islam. He or she is then denounced as an Islamophobe. In most cases, including these, a public retraction is rapidly issued, almost certainly prompted by fear of violent reprisals.

Referring to Islamist terrorism in an essay entitled 'The Age of Horrorism', published in September 2006, Amis stated that:

> 'The Muslim community will have to suffer until it gets its house in order. What sort of suffering? Not letting them travel. Deportation - further down the road. Curtailing of freedoms. Strip-searching people who look like they're from the Middle East or from Pakistan ... Discriminatory stuff, until it hurts the whole community and they start getting tough with their children....'[17]

It is difficult not to regard this as an outburst of visceral anti-Muslim prejudice. Amis should not have said it. But having done so, he should have apologised in the most unequivocal and contrite terms. However, the self-confessed agnostic went far beyond this. Launching instead into full-throated Islamophilia, he said:

> 'We can begin by saying, not only that we respect Mohammad, but that no serious person could fail to respect Mohammad – a unique and luminous historical being. He remains a titanic figure, and, for Muslims, all-answering: a revolutionary, a warrior and a sovereign, a Christ and a Caesar, "with a Koran in one hand," as Bagehot imagined him, "and a sword in the other." Judging by the continuities that he was able to set in motion, Mohammad has strong claims of being the most extraordinary man who ever lived'.[18]

Sebastian Faulks

In 2009, another British novelist, Sebastian Faulks, also made an abject apology for the expression of less extreme criticisms of Islam, Mohammad, and the Qur'an. Promoting his new book, *A Week in December* – featuring home-grown would-be Islamist suicide bombers – he told a *Sunday Times* interviewer that he found the Qur'an, which contained 'the rantings of a schizophrenic ... a depressing book ... very one-dimensional ... [and] ... very

---

[17] T. Eagelton, 'Rebuking obnoxious views is not just a personality kink', *The Guardian*, 10 October 2007.

[18] M. Amis, 'No, I am not a racist', *The Guardian*, 1 December 2007.

disappointing from a literary point of view'.[19] He added that, although he thought Christian prophets such as John the Baptist had also probably been mentally ill, unlike the New Testament, the Qur'an had 'no new plan for life'. Referring to the 'barrenness' of its message he claimed that Jesus 'proposed a revolutionary way of looking at the world: love your neighbour; love your enemy; the meek shall inherit the earth'. But 'Mohammad had nothing to say to the world other than, "If you don't believe in God you will burn forever."'[20]

Unlike the remarks by Amis which proposed subjecting Muslims to discriminatory mistreatment, everything Faulks said is simply an opinion about a religious figure and the religion he founded. This includes an arguably insensitive quip about Mohammad's 'schizophrenia' which, as Chapter 3 records, has been debated by scholars and others since the early 20th century. However, following the predictable spate of 'author-risks-Muslim-backlash' newspaper reports, Faulks issued what he called a 'simple but unqualified apology to my Muslim friends and readers for anything that has come out sounding crude or intolerant'. But he then went on to say that, while conducting research for his novel, he had 'ended with high regard for Islam which seems to me more spiritually demanding than Judaism or Christianity'. He added that readers would see how he had 'shown the positive effects of the Qur'an on a kind and typical Muslim family'.[21]

Jack Gantos

Another, allegedly graphic novel, *A Suicide Bomber Sits in the Library*, by the Newbery medal-winning author Jack Gantos, illustrated by artist Dave McKean, and due to be released in May 2019, was withdrawn by Abrams, its publisher, following accusations that it was 'steeped in Islamophobia and profound ignorance'.[22] The book was originally part of *Here I Stand*, a 2016 young adult anthology for Amnesty International, which said at the time that the story – featuring a young, brown-skinned, would-be terrorist who enters a library wearing a hidden explosive vest – 'celebrates the power of books to transform lives'. Captivated by this unfamiliar environment, from which his illiteracy excludes him, the would-be suicide bomber has second thoughts

---

[19] Murray, *Islamophilia*, p. 37.
[20] Ibid.
[21] Ibid., p. 40.
[22] A. Flood, 'Graphic novel "steeped in Islamophobia" pulled after protests', *The Guardian*, 26 November 2018.

about his mission. An open letter to Abrams from the Asian Author Alliance, signed by more than 1,000 writers, teachers and readers, claimed that 'the biggest terrorist threat in the US is white supremacy' and that the novel was 'wilfully fear-mongering and spreading harmful stereotypes in a failed attempt to show the power of story'. McKean, one of the UK's most acclaimed comic illustrators, initially responded by saying that it was 'firmly on the side of literacy, empathy and non-violence'. In a tweet he claimed its premise was that 'a boy uses his mind and faith to decide for himself that violence is not the right course'. However, McKean later changed his mind on account of doubts about such a story coming 'from outside the community involved, and the arguments on Twitter'.[23]

Abrams announced that, with the support of Gantos and McKean, it had withdrawn the book because, while the intention behind the novel 'was to help broaden a discussion about the power of literature to change lives for the better, we recognise the harm and offence felt by many at a time when stereotypes breed division, rather than discourse'. In response, the Asian Author Alliance said that Abrams still 'has far to go in addressing the internal processes that allowed such a book to be green-lit ... We hope they'll somehow show the public that they are working to be better (for example a public pledge to have more inclusive hiring practices) so such problematic stories can be flagged before they cause harm to the community'.[24]

Films

Allegations of Islamophobic expression have been levelled against at least five films: *Submission: Part 1; Fitna; Innocence of Muslims; American Sniper;* and *Lady of Heaven.*

Submission: Part 1

Submission: Part 1 is a 10-minute film, written by ex-Muslim Somali politician and critic of Islam, Ayaan Hirsi Ali, and directed by Dutch director Theo van Gogh. In graphic and controversial terms, it criticizes the alleged mistreatment of women by Islam.[25] Theo van Gogh was named after his

---

[23] Ibid.
[24] Ibid.
[25] S. Castle, 'Life in jail for brutal killer of Dutch film-make Van Gogh', *The Independent*, 27 July 2007.

paternal uncle, a resistance fighter executed during the Nazi occupation of the Netherlands in World War II. The uncle's great-grandfather was also the brother of painter, Vincent van Gogh. A well-known critic of multiculturalism and Islam, particularly after the Iranian Revolution and 9/11, Theo van Gogh's last book, *Allah weet het beter* ('Allah Knows Best', 2003) strongly condemned Muslim beliefs, practices, and conduct. *Submission: Part 1*, the English translation of 'Islam', features four abused Muslim women. Clothed in semi-transparent veils which partially cover texts from the Qur'an written in henna on their otherwise naked bodies, they tell their stories of abuse as they kneel in prayer.

On 2 November 2004, while cycling to work, van Gogh was shot several times, and had his throat slit, by 26 year-old, Mohammed Bouyeri, a Dutch-Moroccan Islamist who objected to the 'Islamophobic' content of *Submission: Part 1*. Referring to the Egyptian Islamist organisation, *Jama'at al-Muslimin*, the murderer then pinned a note with a knife to van Gogh's body, threatened western countries and Jews, and issued a death threat to Hirsi Ali. Bouyeri was tried, convicted, and sentenced to life imprisonment with no prospect of parole, not only for van Gogh's murder, but also for the attempted murder of several police officers and bystanders, illegal possession of a firearm, and for conspiring to murder others.

The police made several other arrests and the Dutch Complaints Bureau for Discrimination on the Internet (MDI) received many complaints about websites allegedly praising the murder and making death threats against other people. Apparent retaliation included four attempted arson attacks on mosques, an arson attack which destroyed a Muslim primary school, a bomb which exploded at another Muslim primary school, and other violent assaults upon Muslim targets. Christian churches were then also subjected to arson and vandalized. While van Gogh's murder was universally publicly condemned, the film also polarized Dutch opinion. Some argued fiercely for his right to criticize Islam in the way he had, while others expressed concern that the right to free speech had been abused to stigmatize a vulnerable minority.

In December 2004, Van Gogh's previous film, *06/05* – a dramatization of the assassination of his friend, Pim Fortuyn (see Chapter 8) – was released, a month after van Gogh's own death, and two years after Fortuyn's.

Fitna

On 27 March 2008, Dutch politician, Geert Wilders, launched on the internet, a 17-minute film, *Fitna*, an Arabic word meaning 'disagreement or dispute' or 'a test of faith in times of crisis'.[26] Together with claims about the influence of Islam in the Netherlands, the film intersperses selected excerpts from the Qur'an with media clips and newspaper cuttings depicting acts of violence by Muslims worldwide. It also maintains that the holy book of Islam mandates Muslims to hate anyone who violates its commands and that it encourages, amongst other things, terrorism, antisemitism, violence against women, subjugation of minorities, and Islamic supremacism. It provoked predictable outrage from some Muslims, including fatwas against Wilders by Al Qaeda, and attempts by some Muslim majority countries to censor it. On 1 April 2008, the controversy was debated by the Dutch parliament and, on 12 February 2009, Wilders was denied entry to the United Kingdom after having been invited by Lord Pearson of the UK Independence Party to show his film in the House of Lords. However, the exclusion was successfully appealed and Wilders arrived in the UK on 16 October 2009 describing the overturning of the ban as a 'victory for freedom of speech'.[27] In June 2011, he was acquitted in the Netherlands of having criminally insulted religious and ethnic groups and of inciting hatred and discrimination.

Innocence of Muslims

Innocence of Muslims is a 14-minute trailer for a full-length film about the Prophet Mohammad, the latter said to have been shown only once to a ten-person audience in Holywood, USA. Written and produced by Nakoula Basseley Nakoula (aka Sam Bacile), a 55 year-old Coptic Christian living in California, the trailer was uploaded to YouTube on 1 July 2012.[28] It opens with scenes portraying the alleged persecution of Coptic Christians and other alleged human rights abuses in contemporary Egypt, and then cuts to cartoonish representations of the Prophet as a child of uncertain parentage, a buffoon, a womanizer, a homosexual, a rapist, a paedophile, and a greedy, bloodthirsty thug. Demonstrations against the video were held on 11 September 2012 in Egypt before spreading to other Arab and Muslim states and some western countries. Hundreds were injured and over 50 killed.

---

[26] G. Crouch, 'Dutch Film Against Islam Released on Internet', *New York Times,* 28 March 2008.

[27] BBC News, 'Dutch MP hails UK visit "victory,"' 16 October 2009.

[28] D. Nissenbaum, J. Oberman & E. Orden, 'Behind Video a Web of Questions', *Wall Street Journal*, 13 September 2012.

Fatwas were issued, and Ghulam Ahmad Bilour, a government minister in Pakistan, offered a bounty of \$100,000 for Nakoula's murder. Claiming they were 'extremely upset' about having been 'taken advantage of by the producer' – and duped by a script originally about life in Egypt 2,000 years ago with the working title, *Desert Warrior* – the film's entire 80-member cast and crew stated that they were also 'deeply saddened by the tragedies that have occurred'.[29]

A *Vanity Fair* article described the video as 'exceptionally amateurish, with disjointed dialogue, jumpy editing, and performances that would have looked melodramatic even in a silent movie'.[30] It added that the clip was 'clearly designed to offend Muslims, portraying Mohammed as a bloodthirsty murderer, Lothario and paedophile with omnidirectional sexual appetites'. Reuters claimed that the video portrayed 'Mohammad as a fool, a philanderer and a religious fake ... shown in an apparent sexual act with a woman'.

On the evening of 11 September 2012, the US diplomatic compound in Benghazi, Libya, was stormed by members of the militant Islamist group, *Ansar al Sharia* and early the following day a different unit of the same organization launched a mortar attack against a CIA facility about a mile away. The US ambassador, three other US officials, two contractors for the CIA, and an unknown number of assailants were killed. Ten others connected with the CIA site were also injured. Although Islamist hostility to the US is both visceral and pervasive in the Muslim middle east and elsewhere, and the fact that the attacks occurred on the anniversary of 9/11, *Innocence of Muslims* was widely seen as having provoked them.

This was endorsed by US President Obama, who condemned the film, and Secretary of State, Hillary Clinton, who told Charles Woods, the father of one of the service personnel killed in the Benghazi attack, that the film maker, 'responsible for the death' of his son, would be arrested and prosecuted.[31] Anthea Butler, a Professor of Religious Studies at the University of Pennsylvania, agreed on the grounds that denigrating a religion in film should result in the imprisonment of the film maker if other people react violently to it. She added that, 'while the First Amendment right to free expression is important, it is also important to remember that other countries and cultures

---

[29] Ibid.

[30] M. Gross, 'The Making of The Innocence of Muslims: Cast Members Discuss the Film that Set Fire to the Arab World', *Vanity Fair*, 27 December 2012.

[31] Spencer, *Islamophobia and Free Speech*, p. 43.

do not have to understand or respect our right'.[32] As Spencer observes, this amounts to saying that Muslims do not have to respect the right to free speech but non-Muslims must respect Islamic blasphemy law.[33] This is also the gist of remarks Mrs Clinton made to the Organization of the Islamic Conference (OIC) High Level Meeting on Combating Religious Intolerance on 15 July 2011. She said that, in order to smooth out 'ripples of intolerance' without directly criminalizing free speech, 'some old fashioned techniques of peer pressure and shaming' should be employed 'so that people don't feel that they have the support to do what we abhor' – cancellation, in other words.[34]

In a similar vein in his annual address to the UN General Assembly two weeks after the events in question, President Obama said that 'the future must not belong to those who slander the prophet of Islam. But to be credible, those who condemn that slander must also condemn the hate we see in the images of Jesus Christ that are desecrated, or churches that are destroyed, or the Holocaust that is denied'.[35] On 27 September 2012, US federal authorities stated that Nakoula had been arrested in Los Angeles for allegedly violating the terms of his probation relating to convictions in the 1990s on bank fraud charges and for manufacturing methamphetamine. On 7 November 2012, he pleaded guilty to four of the charges and was sentenced to a year in prison plus four on supervised release.

The White House also asked YouTube to consider whether continuing to host the video was consistent with the company's policy. YouTube said the video fell within its guidelines as, although it was against Islam, it was not directed against Muslim people, and they did not consider it hate speech. On 26 February 2014, by a 2–1 majority, the United States Court of Appeals for the Ninth Circuit ordered YouTube to remove the video from its website. But in May 2015, the Ninth Circuit unanimously reversed this decision. Four years after the controversy began, Nakoula was discovered unemployed and living in a homelessness shelter. According to Timmerman who wrote a book about

---

[32] A. Butler, 'Opposing View: Why Sam Bacile Deserves Arrest', *USA Today*, 12 September 2012.

[33] Spencer, *Islamophobia and Free Speech*, p. 95.

[34] Ibid., p. 50.

[35] President Obama, 'Remarks by the President to the UN General Assembly', *Whitehouse.gov (speech)*, 25 September 2012.

the affair,[36] he was 'the first victim of Islamic Sharia blasphemy laws in the United States'.[37]

American Sniper

In April 2015, two showings of *American Sniper* were scheduled at Eastern Michigan University, USA. The film, based on the memoir of Chris Kyle, said to be the deadliest marksman in US military history, received six nominations at the 87th Academy Awards including for Best Picture, Best Adapted Screenplay, and Best Actor, and ultimately won the award for Best Sound Editing. The first screening was disrupted by four protesters who climbed on to the stage denouncing the film as 'Islamophobic'. They were briefly arrested and the second showing was cancelled.[38]

Lady of Heaven

Following protests outside some cinemas in Bolton, Birmingham and Sheffield, UK, in June 2022, Cineworld cancelled all UK screenings of the *Lady of Heaven* film about Fatima, the daughter of the Prophet Muhammad.[39] Cineworld claimed its decision was made in order 'to ensure the safety of our staff and customers'. Over 120,000 people also signed a petition for screenings to be cancelled on the grounds that the Prophet, and several revered figures in early Sunni Islam, had been depicted. There was, however, no suggestion that these were negative. The Bolton Council of Mosques denounced the film as 'blasphemous' and 'underpinned with a sectarian ideology'. Meleagrou-Hitchens claims that the Pakistan-based extremist Barelvi movement, *Tehreek-e-Labbaik Pakistan*, was involved in orchestrating the cancellation campaign.[40] Describing the protesters as 'fringe groups', the film's director Malik Shlibak, himself a Shia Muslim, said that

---

[36] K. Timmermann, *Deception: The Making of the YouTube Video Hillary and Obama Blamed for Benghazi* (Post Hill Press, 2016).

[37] H. McKay, 'Blamed for Benghazi: Filmmaker jailed after attack now lives in poverty, fear', *Fox News*, 12 September 2016.

[38] Spencer, *Islamophobia and free speech*, p. 89.

[39] BBC, 'Cineworld cancels "The Lady of Heaven" film screenings after protests', 8 June 2022.

[40] See, eg A. Meleagrou-Hitchens, *Understanding and Responding to Blasphemy Extremism in the UK* (Commission for Countering Extremism – Rethinking Extremism, 2024), p. 22-24.

'no one should dictate for the British public what they can and cannot watch or discuss'.[41]

Cartoons

Cartoons, a perennial source of Islamophobia-related controversy, have led to a number of deaths including twelve employees of the French satirical magazine, *Charlie Hebdo*, and the French school teacher Samuel Paty. This tragic sequence of events also resulted in a teacher at Batley Grammar School in England and his family being driven into hiding, considered in Chapter 9. The cartoon series, *South Park* and cartoonist Molly Norris have also been in the firing line.

Jyllands-Posten

Headlined 'Muhammeds ansigt' ('The face of Mohammad'), on 29 September 2005, *Jyllands-Posten*, a Danish centre-right newspaper, published twelve cartoons of the Prophet Mohammad, including one with a bomb in his turban. There is a long tradition of political and religious satire in Denmark and in the past *Jyllands-Posten* has also caricatured Christian figures. The following text, written by the paper's culture editor, Flemming Rose, and published with the cartoons, indicated that the objective was to contribute to the debate about criticism of Islam and self-censorship:

> 'Modern, secular society is rejected by some Muslims. They demand a special position, insisting on special consideration of their own religious feelings. It is incompatible with contemporary democracy and freedom of speech, where one must be ready to put up with insults, mockery and ridicule. It is certainly not always attractive and nice to look at, and it does not mean that religious feelings should be made fun of at any price, but that is of minor importance in the present context. ... we are on our way to a slippery slope where no-one can tell how the self-censorship will end. That is why *Morgenavisen Jyllands-Posten* has invited members of the Danish editorial cartoonists union to draw Muhammad as they see him'.[42]

The publication of the cartoons sparked an international storm. There were diplomatic repercussions, a consumer boycott of Danish products, and

---

[41] BBC, 'Cineworld Cancels Lady of Heaven film.'
[42] *Jyllands-Posten*, 29 September 2005.

protests around the world, including in Denmark itself. Violence, riots, and attacks upon churches and Christians, and upon Danish and other diplomatic missions, also occurred in some Muslim majority countries. Some 250 deaths were reported and several murder plots against key *Jyllands-Posten* staff were foiled. In the west, opinion about the appropriateness of the publication of the cartoons was also divided. Some condemned what they saw as pandering to 'racist stereotyping'. Others expressed their support for what, in their opinion, was a lawful and legitimate exercise of the right to freedom of expression. As a news story, and/or in the spirit of journalistic solidarity, or scandalized condemnation, the cartoons were reprinted by news outlets around the world. Seeking to build a global campaign, four Danish imams compiled a dossier which included the cartoons plus other images. One, which allegedly featured Mohammad as a pig, was later proven to be a photo of a contestant in a French pig-squealing contest which made no reference whatever to Mohammad, Muslims or Islam.[43] In February 2006, *Jyllands-Posten* published an apology for the offence the cartoons had caused but defended its right to publish them. Rose also later explained to the *Washington Post* that, contrary to being exclusionary, the cartoons indicated that *Jyllands-Posten* accepted that Islam was part of Danish society and was, therefore, as open to satire as any other religion.

The Danish Criminal Code prohibits disturbing public order by publicly ridiculing or insulting the dogmas or worship of any lawful religious community. It also criminalises insult, threat or degradation of natural persons, by publicly and with malice attacking their race, skin colour, national or ethnic origins, faith, or sexual orientation. In assessing whether an offence had been committed in the *Jyllands-Posten* case, the Regional Public Prosecutor noted that freedom of expression must be exercised with proper respect for other human rights, including the right to be protected from discrimination, insult, and degradation. The criminal investigation was, however, discontinued on the grounds that the cartoons were connected to a matter of public interest, a defence to the charges recognised by Danish law. The Danish Director of Public Prosecutors agreed.

---

[43] 'Billede fra grisefestival i imamers mappe' (Picture from pig contest in imam's folder), *DR.dk*, 7 February 2006.

Charlie Hebdo

The publication of cartoons satirizing aspects of the faith, practice, and conduct of Muslims did not end with the *Jyllands-Posten* affair. On 9 February 2006, much more scurrilous renditions, with much more serious consequences for those involved, appeared in the French satirical magazine, *Charlie Hebdo* ('Charlie Weekly'), an anti-racist, sceptical, secular, libertarian, left-wing, and anti-clerical magazine which features cartoons, reports, polemics and jokes. Beneath the banner headline 'Mahomet débordé par les intégristes' ('Mohammad overwhelmed by fundamentalists'), the front page showed a cartoon of a weeping Mohammad saying, 'C'est dur d'être aimé par des cons' ('It's hard being loved by jerks'). Inside, the twelve *Jyllands-Posten* cartoons were reprinted plus some of *Charlie Hebdo's* own.[44] Circulation rose from 100,000 to 160,000 and outrage ensued. President Jacques Chirac condemned 'overt provocations' which could inflame passions.[45]

However, other prominent politicians including François Bayrou, three-times centrist Presidential candidate, and future president François Hollande expressed their support for freedom of expression. Claiming the cartoons were racist, the Grand Mosque of Paris, the Muslim World League, and the Union of French Islamic Organisations (UOIF) initiated legal proceedings. Nicolas Sarkozy, a prominent politician who later also became President of France, sent a letter to the court which tried the issue to express his support for the historic French satirical tradition. On 22 March 2007, exonerating *Charlie Hebdo's* executive editor, the court held that two of the three cartoons were not an attack on Islam, but on Muslim terrorists, and that given the orientation of the magazine in question, the third featuring Mohammad with a bomb in his turban, should be interpreted as a critique of religious fundamentalism.

On 3 November 2011, the cover of *Charlie Hebdo's* 'Charia Hebdo edition', published in response to the introduction of sharia law in Libya and the election of an Islamist party in Tunisia, featured a cartoon of Mohammad saying, '100 lashes of the whip if you don't die laughing'. Claiming Mohammad was 'guest editor', the magazine portrayed him as the good-natured voice of reason, stating that Islam is compatible with humour, decrying the electoral victories of Islamist parties, and calling for the

---

[44] *Charlie Hebdo*, 9 Fevrier 2006.
[45] 'Culte Musulman et Islam de France', *CFCM TV*, 22 March 2007.

separation of politics and religion. Focusing on the sharia, the issue in question discussed, in particular, the oppression of women, domestic violence, mandatory veiling, burqas, restrictions on freedom, forced marriage, oppression of gays and dissenters, and practices such as stoning, flogging, hand/foot/tongue amputations, polygamy, and the indoctrination of young children.[46] Prime Minster of France, François Fillon, and Claude Guéant, Minister of the Interior, expressed their support for *Charlie Hebdo*. However, later that month, the magazine's offices were fire-bombed and its website was hacked. Four times the usual number of copies were distributed in response.[47]

In September 2012, days after a series of attacks on US embassies in the Middle East, ostensibly in response to the film *Innocence of Muslims*, discussed above, the magazine published another set of cartoons, one of which depicted a naked Mohammad on all fours with a star covering his anus. Another showed him in the nude, bending over and begging to be admired. Riot police surrounded the *Charlie Hebdo* offices in Paris to protect it from possible attacks while French embassies, consulates, cultural centres, and international schools were closed in about 20 Muslim countries and security increased in others. This time there was more criticism of the magazine from the French political establishment. Defending freedom of expression, Foreign Minister, Laurent Fabius, nevertheless, questioned the wisdom of publishing such cartoons particularly in the aftermath of an 'absurd video' and asked: 'Is it really sensible to pour oil on fire?'.[48]

The crisis deepened when two heavily armed French Muslim brothers of Algerian descent, Saïd and Chérif Kouachi, burst into *Charlie Hebdo's* offices on 7 January 2015. Shouting in Arabic, '*Allahu akbar*' (God is great') and 'the Prophet is avenged', they discharged a hail of bullets killing twelve and injuring eleven, four seriously. The attackers, who fled the scene, later identified themselves as members of Al-Qaeda in the Arabian Peninsula, which claimed responsibility for the attack. On 9 January, following a massive manhunt, the brothers were killed by the GIGN (*Groupe d'intervention de la Gendarmerie Nationale* – National Gendarmerie Intervention Group). The *Charlie Hebdo* shooting was also followed by several related Islamist terrorist

---

[46] *Charlie Hebdo*, 3 Novembre 2011.

[47] J. Boxel, 'Firebomb attack on satirical French magazine', *Financial Times*, 2 November 2011.

[48] N. Clark, 'French magazine publishes cartoons mocking Muhammad', *New York Times*, 19 September 2012.

attacks across the Île-de-France between 7 and 9 January 2015. This included a siege at a kosher supermarket in which a French-born Malian Muslim took hostages and murdered four people (all Jews) before being killed by French commandos. The day after the attack on its premises, *Charlie Hebdo's* remaining staff announced that the next edition of the magazine would be published as normal but with a print run of one million, rather than the standard 60,000. In the event, 5 million copies went on sale. The magazine also received nearly €1 million from the French government, €250,000 from the *Fonds Google–AIPG pour l'Innovation Numérique de la presse* (Digital Innovation Press Fund), partially bankrolled by Google, and £100,000 from The Guardian Media Group.

Over the next few days a series of rallies took place across France in support of freedom of expression and in honour of the victims of the attack. The phrase 'Je suis Charlie' ('I am Charlie') was also adopted by protesters there and around the globe. Elsewhere there were violent anti-*Charlie Hebdo* protests in which churches were burned and people killed. The Islamic Human Rights Commission, a British pro-Iran NGO, awarded *Charlie Hebdo* international 'Islamophobe of the Year 2015', while the National Secular Society, another British organisation, declared the *Charlie Hebdo* staff 'Secularists of the Year 2015'. Many cartoonists and journalists expressed solidarity with the murdered *Charlie Hebdo* staff. But not all. Receiving a lifetime achievement award from the George Polk Awards in Journalism three months after the massacre, acclaimed *Doonesbury* cartoonist, Gary Trudeau, criticised the murder victims for 'having wandered into the realm of hate speech'. He then proclaimed that free speech had become 'its own kind of fanaticism'.[49] Responding to criticism of these remarks on the *Meet the Press* programme, Trudeau said that he was not blaming the *Charlie Hebdo* staff for their own murders, that he 'should have made it a little clearer' that he was 'as outraged as the rest of the world at the time', and that he mourned the victims deeply. He added that it was 'not really for us to decide' whether or not Mohammad should be criticised or mocked.[50]

In April 2015, six members of the prestigious US writers' organization, 'Poets, Essayists and Novelists' (PEN), condemned it for honouring two of the surviving members of the *Charlie Hebdo* staff, Gerard Biard and Jean-

---

[49] G. Arana, '*Charlie Hebdo* "Wandered into the Realm of Hate Speech" Says Doonesbury Cartoonist Gary Trudeau', *Huffingdon Post*, 10 April 2015.
[50] Spencer, *Islamophobia and free speech*, pp. 67-68.

Baptiste Thoret, with its annual Freedom of Expression Courage Award.[51] According to one of the complainants, Peter Carey, although 'a hideous crime' had been committed, PEN was, nevertheless, seemingly blind to 'the cultural arrogance of the French nation, which does not recognize its moral obligation to a large and disempowered segment of their population'. As Spencer points out, the murderers themselves displayed their own form of cultural arrogance by killing the journalists according to their own conception of Islamic blasphemy law.[52] Salman Rushdie also declared that PEN was right to honour the *Charlie Hebdo* staff without these 'disgusting buts'. He added that: 'The issue has nothing to do with an oppressed and disadvantaged minority' but 'everything to do with the battle against fanatical Islam, which is highly organized, well-funded, and which seeks to terrify us all'.[53] Rejecting the view of Rushdie and others, 204 other writers then joined the six in protesting against the award to the *Charlie Hebdo* journalists, claiming it valorized 'selectively offensive material ... that intensifies the anti-Islamic, anti-Maghreb, anti-Arab sentiments already prevalent in the Western world'.[54]

In 2009, Yale University Press published an account of the cartoon controversy, *The Cartoons That Shook the World*, by Danish author Jytte Klausen. This included numerous illustrations but none of those which had caused the furore in the first place. British journalist Christopher Hitchens described this 'capitulation' as 'the latest and perhaps the worst episode in the steady surrender to religious extremism – particularly Muslim religious extremism – that is spreading across our culture'.[55]

In September 2020, the day before the beginning of the trial of those suspected of involvement in the January 2015 attack, *Charlie Hebdo* republished the controversial cartoons. French President Macron defended their right to do so. While several leaders of European countries supported him, some Muslims called for French products to be boycotted. A few weeks later, two people were stabbed and critically injured outside what had hitherto been the magazine's office. The perpetrator, later identified as

---

[51] Ibid.

[52] Ibid.

[53] A. Flood & A. Yuhas, 'Salman Rushdie Slams Critics of PEN's Charlie Hebdo Tribute', *The Guardian*, 27 April 2015.

[54] G. Greenwald, '204 PEN Writers (Thus Far) Have Objected to the Charlie Hebdo Award – Not Just 6', *The Intercept*, 30 April 2015.

[55] C. Hitchens, 'Yale Surrenders', *Slate*, 17 August 2009.

Zaheer Hassan Mehmood, a 25-year-old allegedly from Pakistan, claimed he had acted to avenge the republication of the cartoons and was unaware that the magazine had moved elsewhere. Relations between France and Turkey also deteriorated when Turkish President, Recep Tayyip Erdoğan, discovered that, in a front-page caricature accompanied by the caption – 'Erdogan: He's very funny in private' – *Charlie Hebdo* had depicted him in his underwear, drinking alcohol, and lifting the skirt of a woman dressed in a hijab to reveal her buttocks.[56]

South Park, Molly Norris, and The Gleaner

In April 2010, the cult US TV cartoon series, *South Park*, featured a character in a bear costume, referred to as 'Mohammad' by other characters. The extremist website *Revolution Muslim*, promptly posted the New York address of the show's distributor, Comedy Central, and its California production studio, together with a picture of the partially decapitated body of Dutch filmmaker Theo van Gogh (see above), declaring that the animators Trey Parker and Matt Stone might suffer a similar fate. In response, Seattle-based cartoonist, Molly Norris, posted her own cartoon of Mohammad and proposed 20 May 2010 as 'Everybody Draw Mohammad Day'.[57] A dedicated Facebook page attracted 101,870 participants. However, 106,000 protested against it. As publicity mounted, Norris and the creator of the original Facebook page dissociated themselves from the event. On her own website Norris also stated that she had been seeking to defend rights not to disrespect religion. The affair sparked a global controversy. A block on Facebook by Pakistan was lifted when the social media platform agreed to prevent site access to users in Pakistan and India. Western commentators both applauded and criticized the Draw Mohammad Day event.

On 11 July 2010, it was reported that the al-Qaeda cleric, Anwar al-Awlaki, had added Norris's name to a hitlist. Having been warned that the FBI considered this a 'very serious threat', Norris changed her name and went into hiding where she remains to this day. The March 2013 edition of the Al Qaeda magazine *Inspire* included Norris with eleven others in a pictorial

---

[56] France 24, 'Charlie Hebdo sparks Turkish fury with cartoon of Erdogan, 27 October 2020.
[57] Spencer, *Islamophobia and free speech*, pp. 25-28.

spread entitled, 'Wanted: Dead or Alive for Crimes Against Islam', and captioned, 'Yes We Can: A Bullet A Day Keeps the Infidel Away'.[58]

A curious aspect of the South Park/Molly Norris affair is that, in the past, *South Park* has depicted God as a giant rodent. The TV cartoon series *Family Guy* also imagined a sequel to Mel Gibson's film, *The Passion of the Christ*, featuring the resurrected Jesus – recognized by Islam, together with Moses and Mohammad, as one of the three Messengers of God – in a thrilling car chase with bullets flying and embalming bandages unravelling. Readers must make up their own minds about why, by contrast with the furore over depictions of Mohammad, these ostensible 'blasphemies' against God Himself, and another revered Islamic figure, have caused no known protest or adverse reaction from any Muslims at all.

The 5 April 2026 issue of *The Gleaner*, the student paper of Rutgers University-Camden, USA, published a cartoon of Mohammad, the Buddha, and Jesus in a bar.[59] Two weeks later, the 19 April issue carried a letter from the Muslim Student Association (the Muslim Brotherhood organization on campus) claiming the image was offensive, not only to Muslims but also to Christians and Jews (though not apparently to Buddhists), and asked for the 5 April issue to be re-published and circulated without it. The paper agreed. Since no copies of the controversial issue survive, it is impossible to comment upon the cartoon. But it is yet another example of campus censorship at the behest of offended Muslim students.

The LeMan 'Mohammad' cartoon

In July 2025, chanting slogans such as 'Kemalist infidels will be held accountable', violent protests erupted in Istanbul against the satirical magazine, *LeMan*, for having published a cartoon allegedly depicting the Prophet Mohammad shaking hands with Moses over a bombed-out city in apparent reference to the Israel-Iran conflict.[60] On charges of having 'publicly insulted religious values', the cartoonist was arrested. Warrants were also issued for the arrest of three editors, and the offending issue was withdrawn from circulation. Turkey's interior minister, Ali Yerlikaya, condemned the

---

[58] Ibid.
[59] Ibid., pp. 91-92.
[60] M. Muzaffar, 'Journalists at satirical magazine in Turkey arrested over Prophet Muhammad cartoon', *The Independent*, 1 July 2025.

cartoonist as 'despicable', while the director of presidential communications, Fahrettin Altun, denounced the publication as an 'immoral attack' upon national values. *LeMan* is known for its provocative satire, including cartoons relating to the failed coup in 2016 and iconic figures such as the 13th century poet Rumi. Apologizing to readers who felt offended by the cartoon, the magazine claimed that it had sought to portray 'the righteousness of the oppressed Muslim people by depicting a Muslim killed by Israel' and that denigrating religious values had never been intended. Tuncay Akgun, one of the editors-in-chief, told the AFA news agency that the 'Mohammad' in question was not the Prophet but a fictionalized figure, killed in the Israeli bombing who also represented the more than 200 million men and boys in the Islamic world bearing his name. As already noted in this study, in order to discourage idolatry, visual representations of the Prophet are widely forbidden in the Muslim world. In recent years, Turkey has frequently cracked down on satirical publications and also consistently ranks low in league tables for freedom of expression and press freedom.

Conclusion

Most of the examples cited in this chapter lack any obvious intention to insult or offend. Others, particularly those involving satire and humour, have been deliberately provocative. Indeed, this is the whole point. But, of itself, this does not necessarily make the expression in question unlawful, illegitimate, or 'Islamophobic'. Only the incident involving the pineapple named Mohammad fails to engage in any obvious public debate. Nevertheless, it could and should more charitably be regarded as a whimsical, if ill-judged, student prank rather than anything particularly malicious or offensive. Apart from the intemperate remarks by Martin Amis, whose 'excessive' back-tracking has been criticized, all the other examples seek either to raise issues, to educate, or to contribute to debates about current or historic affairs, sometimes in particularly arresting terms. None of this is 'Islamophobic'.

Chapter 8

Contemporary public debate

Introduction

Social media and the internet are awash with every kind of viewpoint imaginable including visceral and unreasoned prejudice for and against Muslims and/or Islam. This field is, however, much too vast to be thoroughly considered here. Instead, this chapter discusses the most prominent controversial accusations of Islamophobic expression across a range of other public sectors and activities, including posters, leaflets, politics, protest, Christian proselytism, public service, broadcasting, the media, and debates about wrongdoing and Islam.

Posters and leaflets

The following are amongst the better documented cases in which posters and leaflets have been denounced as Islamophobic. In 2007, in order to advertise the screening of the film *Obsession: Radical Islam's War with the West,* student Republicans put up posters at the University of Florida, USA, declaring – 'Radical Islam Wants You Dead'.[1] The text began with the following disclaimer:

> 'This is a film about radical Islamic terror. A dangerous ideology, fuelled by religious hatred. It's important to remember most Muslims are peaceful and do not support terror. This is not a film about them. This is a film about a radical worldview, and the threat it poses to us all, Muslim and non-Muslim alike'.

Patricia Telles-Irvin, the University's Vice-President for Student Affairs, nevertheless, sent an apologetic message to the entire student body which

---

[1] R. Spencer, *Islamophobia and the Threat to Free Speech* (Centre for Security Policy, 2021), pp. 93-94.

claimed that the posters 'reinforced a negative stereotype … and contributed to a generalization that only furthers the misunderstanding of the religion of Islam'. The Attorney General for Florida rebuked the university for having 'chilled free speech' and stated that it was essential, if the war being waged by radical Muslims against the west was to be properly understood, that it was appropriately labelled as the film sought to do.

In September 2016, a chapter of Young Americans for Freedom (YAF), a conservative libertarian movement, put up posters around the campus of Saddleback College advertising their '9/11: Never Forget Project' which marked the 15th anniversary of the events of that fateful day. Margot Lovette, a Professor of Gender Studies ripped them down on the grounds that they should only have been posted in one of the college's 'free speech areas'. Thomas Columbus, spokesman for the Saddleback YAF declared that this was a blatant infringement of the chapter's First Amendment rights. Others pointed out that the First Amendment made the entire US a 'free speech area'.[2]

In March 2018, Canadian alt-right, libertarian, YouTuber, activist, and commentator, Lauren Southern, received a lifetime ban from entering the UK. This followed a six-hour interview under counterterrorist legislation at the French port of Calais as she tried to cross the English Channel by ferry in order to interview far-right British activist, and founder of the English Defence League, Tommy Robinson. A British security official, who spoke to the *Daily Mail* on condition of anonymity, said Southern had been denied permission to enter on the grounds that her 'presence in the UK was not conducive to the public good'. The previous month, she had handed out leaflets from a stall in Luton, England, which proclaimed 'Allah is gay' and 'Allah is trans'. The then 22-year-old claimed she had been conducting a 'social experiment' which sought to explore how people would react to LGBTQ+ statements relating to Mohammad compared with ones involving Jesus and Christianity. She claimed that the experiment highlighted 'a double standard in Western societies' and asked: 'Why is it racist to say Allah is gay, but not Jesus is gay?'[3]

Gaining lawful entry to any country, including the UK, is conditional upon satisfying certain conditions, typically including not being likely to

---

[2] Ibid., pp. 95-96.
[3] C. Roundtree, 'Canadian far right activist who claimed "Allah is gay" gets lifetime ban from coming to the UK', *Mail On Line*, 26 March 2018.

cause trouble. This aside, Southern's question – more plausibly rendered as 'why is it Islamophobic to say Allah is gay but not "Christianophobic" to say Jesus was gay?' – nevertheless requires an answer especially since the possibility that Jesus was gay has been publicly debated, including by Christians, for centuries.[4]

Politics

For present purposes, two senses of 'politics', broad and narrow, can be distinguished. The broad sense includes every contribution to every debate with a political dimension and is also much too vast to be surveyed here. The following discussion is, therefore, confined to the 'narrow' sense – controversial allegations of Islamophobia levelled against individual politicians.

Some of the more recent eye-brow-raising accusations in British politics include those made against the following unlikely recipients of the 'Islamophobe of the Year' award, announced at an annual ceremony staged by the London-based, pro-Iranian, Islamic Human Rights Commission: Sadiq Khan, the (Muslim) Mayor of London; Sajid Javid, the then (Muslim) Home Secretary; former Islamist turned critic of jihad, Maajid Nawaz; the *Charlie Hebdo* magazine, a mere two months after 12 of its staff had been murdered by Islamist terrorists; and US President Barack Obama. A guest speaker at the ceremony awarding Obama this dubious accolade was also involved in crafting the APPG's definition of Islamophobia discussed in Chapter 10.[5]

Other controversial accusations of Islamophobia, occurring in the aftermath of the Hamas invasion of Israel on 7 October 2023 and the subsequent wars in the region, have included: criticism of the then First Minister of Scotland, (Muslim) Hamza Yusif, who donated £250,000 to the UN Gaza agency UNRWA, accused of links with Hamas, against the advice of his officials who advocated giving £100,000-£200,000 to UNICEF, the UN agency for children, instead; calls by a Muslim MP to declare that the terrorist organization Hamas should scale down its campaign in Gaza; a proposal to light Wembley Stadium's famous arch with the colours of the national flags of countries, including Israel, which have suffered armed attacks; proscribing

---

[4] See, eg, P. Oestreicher, 'Was Jesus gay? Probably', *The Guardian*, 20 April 2012.

[5] K. Mahmood, J. Jenkins & M. Frampton, *A definition of Islamophobia? Old problems remain as new problems emerge* (Policy Exchange, 2024), p. 8.

the Islamist organization Hizb-ut-Tahrir as a terrorist organization; the suspension of a non-Muslim MP for telling a rally: 'We won't rest until we have justice. Until all people, Israelis and Palestinians, between the river and the sea ... [often interpreted as a call for the destruction of Israel] ... can live in peaceful liberty'; Sir Keir Starmer for having called, while visiting a mosque, for the release of hostages taken by Hamas on 7 October 2023; prohibiting children from wearing Palestinian symbols at school; the Speaker of the House of Commons for justifying a controversial departure from Parliamentary procedure on account of threats to MPs following post-7 October pro-Palestinian protests; the use of the term 'Islamist'; the sacking of the (Muslim) president of the National Union of Students, Shaima Dalalli, for having allegedly made antisemitic comments; defences of the rule of law, equality, freedom and rights; and protests in London sparked by the death in police custody of Mahsa Amini in Iran for having failed to wear her head scarf properly.[6]

In the British general election of July 2024, Labour candidates in constituencies with significant Muslim minorities, including sitting MPs with large majorities, were accused of what might be called 'passive Islamophobic expression' for allegedly not having denounced the war in Gaza, nor to have called for a ceasefire, in strong enough terms. This included Khalid Mahmood, (Muslim) Labour MP for Birmingham Perry Bar for more than twenty years, who also defended his seat in the 2019 general election with a majority of 15,000. But, despite having advocated a ceasefire in Gaza, he lost it in 2024 by 507 votes to Ayoub Khan, an independent pro-Palestinian candidate. Posters, shared on social media, with the logo of The Muslim Vote, which mobilized pro-Palestinian sentiment, denounced Mahmood as an Islamophobe for allegedly having failed to defend the Palestinians with sufficient vigour.

One of the most prominent and controversial allegations of Islamophobic expression against a politician led to his murder. Wilhelmus Simon Petrus Fortuijn, known as 'Pim Fortuyn', was a politician, author, civil servant, businessman, sociologist, commentator, professor at the Erasmus University of Rotterdam, and founder of the political party Pim Fortuyn List (Lijst Pim

---

[6] Ibid., pp. 12-19.

Fortuyn or LPF) in 2002.[7] Openly gay and a supporter of gay rights, Fortuyn had been a Marxist, sympathetic to the Communist Party of the Netherlands, but joined the Dutch Labour Party in the 1970s. However, in the 1990s his views began to change. Supporting tougher measures against crime, a more limited state bureaucracy, and a reduced Dutch financial contribution to the European Union, he also criticised national multicultural and immigration policy, particularly with respect to Islam. An admirer of US president John F. Kennedy, Fortuyn fiercely rejected the 'far-right populist' label attached to him by his opponents and the media. He expressly distanced himself, for example, from Hans Janmaat of the Centrum Democraten – who in the 1980s wanted to remove all foreigners from the Netherlands and was repeatedly convicted of offences relating to discrimination and hate speech – and from other prominent European far-right politicians at the time including Filip Dewinter in Belgium, Jörg Haider in Austria, and Jean-Marie Le Pen in France. He also endorsed a number of liberal positions – including Holland's permissive drugs policy, same-sex marriage, and euthanasia – and regarded Article 7, the free speech provision of the Dutch constitution, as more important than Article 1, the anti-discrimination clause. Throughout his political career Fortuyn also expressed support for the state of Israel, and in the last months of his life had grown closer to the Catholic Church.

Fortuyn is quoted as having said many controversial things relating to Muslims and to Islam.[8] He maintained, for instance, that he did not object to Muslim immigrants because of their race or ethnicity, nor was he against multi-racial society, but that he opposed what he saw as the lack of Muslim integration and their unwillingness to adapt to Dutch standards of modernity and social liberalism. If it were legally possible, he said, he would close the borders to prospective Muslim immigrants and that he favoured a cold war with Islam which he saw as an extraordinary threat and a hostile religion, fundamentally intolerant of, and incompatible with, western values. He claimed he wanted to live together with Muslim people but their culture had

---

[7] P. Fortuyn, *Tegen de islamisering van onze cultuur* (A.W. Bruna, 1997); K. Lang, 'Pim Fortuyn – obituary', *The Guardian*, 7 May 2002; See also, 'P. Fortuyn, Tegen de islamisering van onze cultuur (Opposed to Islamization and for the preservation of our culture)' https://www.pimfortuyn.com/images/media/pim %20fortuyn-opposed_to_islamization_of_our_culture.pdf, April 2009.
[8] https://www.pimfortuyn.com/images/media/pim%20fortuyn-opposed to islamization of our culture.pdf.

never been modernized and still failed to accept democracy and the rights of women, gays, and minorities. Although he did not hate Islam as such, he said he regarded it as backward.

In an interview on the Dutch talk show *Jensen!*, broadcast shortly before his death, Fortuyn accused members of the Dutch government and political establishment of putting his life in danger through repeatedly demonizing him and his beliefs. And, on 6 May, during the 2002 Dutch national election campaign, then aged 54, he was shot dead in Hilversum, North Holland, by Volkert van der Graaf, a left-wing environmentalist and animal rights activist. At his trial, the accused said he killed Fortuyn to stop him from scapegoating Muslims and from targeting 'weak members of society' in his quest for political power. Excluding the Second World War, this was the first notable political assassination in the Netherlands since 1672.

Protest

All kinds of protest have been labelled 'Islamophobic'. As in other contexts, this field is much too broad to be considered fully here. Attention will, therefore, focus upon the more prominent and well-documented controversies, including public desecration of the Qur'an.

We begin with one of the most recent. In August 2025, Simon Pearson, a teacher at Preston College posted that, although her behaviour was 'obviously wrong', Lucy Connolly 'should not have been jailed'.[9] He also questioned what he saw as inconsistencies in how the criminal justice system has responded to inflammatory speech, contrasting Connolly's treatment with the apparent tolerance shown towards 'certain sections of society calling for the genocide of Jews', who, he claimed, were 'free to express their opinions and make Jewish people afraid to walk the streets'. At the end of July 2024, riots had erupted in several English towns following the savage murder of three young girls in the English seaside town of Southport on 29 July 2025 by an assailant wrongly suspected of being an asylum-seeker. Hotels accommodating asylum-seekers were also attacked and, in some cases, set on fire.

Lucy Connolly, the wife of a Conservative councillor on West Northamptonshire district council, tweeted: 'Mass deportations, now, set fire

---

[9] J. Iqbal, 'Sacking of Preston teacher is chilling blow for free speech', *The Times*, 5 August 2025; F. Attenborough, 'Teacher sacked after criticising "two-tier justice" in Lucy Connolly case', *Free Speech Union Newsletter*, 4 August 2025.

to all the fucking hotels full of the bastards. While you're at it take the treacherous government politicians with them'. But, in spite of having deleted it three-and-a-half hours later, the tweet had already been viewed over 300,000 times. Connolly later pleaded guilty to inciting racial violence and was sentenced to 31 months in prison with release on licence after having served 40%. In spite of the absence of any reference to Muslims or Islam, a Muslim representative on the National Educational Union complained that the post was 'Islamophobic' and 'racially discriminatory'. Shortly afterwards Pearson was dismissed on the grounds that his conduct violated college policy, was likely to harm its reputation, and damaged professional relationships. He has since lodged legal claims for wrongful and unfair dismissal, harassment, and discrimination under the Equality Act 2010.

Desecration of the Qur'an

Orthodox Muslims revere, not just the message of the Qur'an, but also the physical book itself, which they insist, must be protected from damage and not placed beneath any other book or object. Certain respectful conduct should also be observed when it is being read. However, since the Qur'an does not itself specify how to dispose of worn or defective copies, different traditions have developed about how to do so. These include wrapping them in cloth and burying them in holy ground or burning them privately and respectfully. Most Muslims consider intentional desecration of the Qur'an blasphemous. In some Muslim majority states, this may result in imprisonment or execution. Although also a form of expression, the deliberate public burning of the Qur'an is deeply provocative, disrespectful, and hostile. But, as noted in Chapter 6, whether or not this is unlawful has not been fully settled by British courts.

a) The Kettlethorpe affair

In late February 2023, four pupils were suspended from Kettlethorpe High School in Wakefield, West Yorkshire, England for having accidentally caused minor damage to the Qur'an.[10] The copy in question had apparently been brought into the school by a 14-year-old autistic year 10 pupil as a forfeit for having lost an online video game. Head teacher, Tudor Griffiths, said that

---

[10] BBC News, 'Four Wakefield pupils suspended after Quran damaged at school', 25 February 2023.

there had been 'no malicious intent' and that, apart from a slight tear to the cover and smears of dirt on some pages, the damage was not significant. He added that reports claiming the book had been burnt or destroyed were untrue and that 'we have made it very clear that' the students concerned 'did not treat the Qur'an with the respect they should have. So those involved have been suspended and we will be working with them to ensure they understand why their actions were unacceptable'.[11]

Claiming to have been contacted by others requiring more information, independent councillor for Wakefield East, Akef Akbar, met with 'community leaders'. Death threats were also received by the pupils involved in the incident. According to Meleagrou-Hitchens, as with the Batley affair discussed in the following chapter, the Pakistan-based extremist Barelvi movement Tehreek-e-Labbaik Pakistan, was influential in orchestrating the protest.[12] Apologizing for her child's 'disrespectful' behaviour and seeking forgiveness from the community, the mother of the boy at the centre of the controversy appeared at a news conference in the local mosque alongside police. The episode was recorded as a 'non-crime hate incident' (see Chapter 6). But the police were said to have declined to investigate the death threats against the school children concerned.

Commenting upon both the Batley and Kettlethorpe incidents in his 292-page report, *Protecting our Democracy from Coercion*, published in May 2024, Lord Walney, the UK Government's independent adviser on political violence and disruption, stated: 'The so-called blasphemy rows in secondary schools in the north of England and the implicit threat of violence associated with such allegations exercised a form of veto over what is taught in British classrooms and inappropriately involved religious institutions in internal school issues'.[13] Recommendation 25 states:

'The Government should issue statutory guidance on managing blasphemy-related incidents in schools. This should include commitments to upholding teachers' freedom of expression and not automatically suspending teachers involved in such incidents or revealing their identity. While schools are required to engage with

---

[11] Ibid.

[12] A. Meleagrou-Hitchens, *Understanding and responding to blasphemy extremism* (Commission for Countering Extremism, 2024), pp. 22-24.

[13] Lord Walney, *Protecting our Democracy from Coercion*, May 2024, HC 775, p. 175.

parents on developing Relationships and Sex Education for example, the guidance should set out that schools are not required to engage with local community groups or religious institutions in managing blasphemy-related incidents or other tensions'.[14]

b) Public Qur'an burning as protest

Towards the end of Christopher Marlow's play, *Tamburlaine Part Two* (1587), the eponymous Central Asian and ostensibly Muslim tyrant, challenged Mohammad, 'if thou have any power, come down thyself and work a miracle'. He then burned a copy of the Qur'an and other Islamic texts. Two scenes later he is dead. In the west in recent years, Qur'an burning has undergone a revival as a form of protest against Islam. And, like Tamburlaine, some have paid for it with their lives.

As indicated in Chapter 6, the legality of public Qur'an burning as protest has not yet been authoritatively settled by the British courts. However, in November 2024, in response to a question, the Prime Minister, Sir Keir Starmer, described the desecration of religious texts as 'awful' and urged it to be 'condemned across the house'.[15] Recent episodes abroad include a Qur'an burning event supervised by Terry Jones, pastor of the Christian Dove Outreach Centre in Gainesville, Florida, on 20 March 2011. Twelve people died in rioting in Afghanistan as a result. In Europe, public Qur'an burning has also been particularly prevalent in Scandinavia. While it is not illegal in Norway, protests in which this has been announced in advance have, however, been banned on 'security' grounds.[16] Following the repeal of its national blasphemy law, public desecration of the Qur'an became lawful in Denmark. However, after a spate of such incidents, in December 2023, the Danish Parliament passed a new law making it illegal to burn, soil, trample on, or to cut, recognised religious scriptures such as the Bible, the Torah, and the Qur'an. Sweden does not have a law against blasphemy, and it is generally assumed that the legal prohibition of incitement to ethnic or racial hatred only applies to hostility towards the adherents of any given faith but not to critique of any given religion or desecration of its objects of veneration. But the

---

[14] Ibid., p. 288.

[15] J. Walters, 'Starmer refuses to rule out new UK "blasphemy laws" as free speech row erupts over demand to protect Koran', *GB News*, 27 November 2024.

[16] 'Norway police ban Koran burning protest after Turkey summons Oslo envoy', *Reuters*, 2 February 2023.

consequences of doing so can nevertheless be fatal.

On 29 January 2025, thirty-eight year-old Salwan Momika was shot dead during a live TikTok broadcast at his home in Södertälje, Sweden, hours before a pending court verdict connected with Qur'an burning.[17] Various figures and organisations in the Islamic world welcomed his murder, while some European politicians condemned both it and the background circumstances which had led to it. Five suspects were arrested but were subsequently released due to lack of evidence.

An ethnic Assyrian raised as a Syriac Catholic, Momika had served in pro-Iranian and pro-Kurdish militias fighting ISIS in Iraq. Having registered in Sweden as an Iraqi refugee in April 2018, he became well-known as an anti-Islam demonstrator, organizing live-streamed public demonstrations where he desecrated and burned the Qur'an. As a result of his death, the charges against him were dropped. However, on 3 February 2025, 50-year-old Salwan Najem, a Swedish citizen of Iraqi origin, who had participated in Momika's desecrations, was convicted by Stockholm District Court of 'agitation against an ethnic group'. He received a suspended sentence and was fined 4,000 krona. The court held that, although burning the Qur'an does not itself constitute a hate crime, Najem had been guilty of hate speech because, on four occasions during the video-recorded demonstrations, he had 'expressed contempt for the Muslim ethnic group because of their religious beliefs'. As already indicated elsewhere in this study, Muslims are a religious minority in Sweden and elsewhere, but they are not an 'ethnic group' anywhere.

Christian proselytism

Responding to complaints from the public, some British Christian street preachers have been arrested for allegedly Islamophobic and racist remarks. In addition to the Sleeper case discussed in Chapter 6, the following are amongst the better-documented.

Dia Moodley

In February 2024, Avon and Somerset Police admitted that issuing a 'community protection warning' (CPW) to black Bristol preacher, Dia

---

[17] 'Iraqi man who sparked riots with Koran burnings shot dead in Sweden', *Sky News*, 30 January 2025; 'Salwan Momika dead? Why Iraqi refugee, who burned Quran, is trending?', *The Economic Times*, 2 April 2024.

Moodley, had been 'disproportionate'.[18] In his street sermons Mr Moodley had mocked followers of other religions for their failure to acknowledge 'God's truth', criticized Hindus, Muslims and atheists, and had displayed 'graphic material', including images purporting to show mutilated or aborted foetuses, and placards proclaiming 'abortion is murder', 'all lives matter', and 'God created them male and female'.[19] In 2020, claiming that officers had stood by and done nothing while members of the public spat at him, destroyed his signs, and told him to 'go back home', Mr Moodley arranged a meeting with his local police team. However, the police issued him with a CPW on the grounds that his conduct had been the subject of complaints for several years, and the fact that crowds were becoming 'hostile' and responding 'aggressively' to him was detrimental to the 'quality of life' of other Bristolians. A police spokesman explained that the order had been imposed as a result of having balanced the pastor's right to free speech with the rights of the general public to work and shop in the city without undue distress.

The CPW also imposed other conditions. When preaching or playing recordings of his sermons in Bristol, Mr Moodley, or anyone doing so on his behalf, was required to refrain from using an amplifier or speaker system. Mr Moodley was also prohibited from displaying graphics or images allegedly of mutilated or aborted foetuses, and was permitted to deliver only a single one-hour sermon per day, the content of which had been approved in advance by the police. Nor was he allowed to use 'any words or language that could be considered to negatively affect public health or morals or have the effect of inciting crime and disorder'.[20] He was also banned, 'while in a public area', from passing comment on other religions or from comparing them to Christianity, and from commenting upon 'beliefs held by atheists or those who believe in evolution whilst addressing the public'.[21]

With the support of the Free Speech Union (FSU) and the Alliance Defending Freedom International, Mr Moodley took legal action. In November 2023 the case was settled out of court. Avon and Somerset Police agreed to pay his costs and accepted that some of the restrictions in the initial CPW were disproportionate. Reacting to the news, Mr Moodley said: 'This

---

[18] F. Attenborough, 'FSU helps street preacher fight back against "disproportionate" police gagging order', *Free Speech Union Weekly Roundup*, 8 March 2024.
[19] Ibid.
[20] Ibid.
[21] Ibid.

creeping culture of censorship is detrimental to all of us in society, whatever we believe, and we must challenge it wherever we see it'. Commenting upon the case the FSU's Chief Legal Counsel, Dr Bryn Harris, said:

> 'The state does not hold a monopoly on truth and the ability to discuss and debate ideas, including religious ideas. This is the lifeblood of any genuinely free society. Yet, repeatedly, we see this principle violated by unaccountable police officers and local councils who aggressively pursue their own ideological causes rather than using scarce public resources to tackle real crime'.[22]

Oluwole Ilesanmi

In 2019, following complaints about alleged 'Islamophobia' in his preaching, London street evangelist, Oluwole Ilesanmi, was summarily arrested by the police outside Southgate tube station in London for an alleged breach of the peace.[23] His Bible was confiscated and he was driven four miles in a police car before being released without charge at the side of the road. In a video posted online, the pastor is seen asking police at the time of his arrest not to take away his Bible and proclaiming that: 'Jesus is on the way'. The arresting officer can be heard replying: 'I appreciate that, but nobody wants to listen to that. They want you to go away'. When Mr Ilesanmi refused to relinquish his Bible, an officer said: 'You should've thought about that before being racist'.

Mr Ilesanmi admits describing Islam as an 'aberration' but said he was expressing his point of view as a Christian rather than denigrating Muslims. Sometime later he delivered a 38,000 signature petition to the Home Office, asking for greater protection for street preachers. Recovering £2,500 from the Metropolitan Police for wrongful arrest and for humiliating and distressing treatment, he said: 'I'm glad that the police have recognised that it was not right to arrest me for preaching from the Bible. It was traumatic being arrested. But I'm determined to get back to Southgate and start preaching the gospel again'.[24] Superintendent Neil Billany stated:

> 'The Met respects and upholds the rights of all individuals to practice

---

[22] CBN News, 3 May 2024.
[23] J. Halliday, 'Christian preacher accused of racism gets wrongful arrest payout', *The Guardian*, 28 July 2019.
[24] Ibid.

freedom of speech, and this includes street preachers of all religions and backgrounds. However, if the language someone uses is perceived as being a potential hate crime, it is only right that we investigate. That is the role of the police, even if a decision is subsequently made that their actions are not criminal. In this case, it was deemed appropriate to remove the man from the area'.[25]

Hatun Tash

Hatun Tash is a British ex-Muslim Christian preacher, known for her vocal public criticism of Islam at Speakers' Corner in Hyde Park, London, for displaying cartoons of the Prophet Mohammad, and for brandishing a copy of the Qur'an drilled with holes to dramatize her view about the gaps in its message.[26] Having emigrated to the UK from Turkey, Ms Tash became a student of Christian apologist, Jay Smith, at the Oxford Centre of Christian Apologetics, who later founded the Defend Christ Critique Islam (DCCI) organisation.

She has been arrested twice by the Metropolitan Police at Speakers' Corner. On the first occasion, in December 2020, this followed an assault by a group of Muslim men for wearing a tee-shirt featuring a picture of the Prophet Mohammad. The second time, in May 2021, was for violating COVID-19 regulations.

Ms Tash has also been the victim of several other assaults. In July 2020 she was dragged to the ground by a mob, punched in the face in October 2020, and in May 2021, she was surrounded by other mobs 'screaming for her blood'. In July 2021, suffering wounds to her face and hands, she was stabbed several times by an unknown assailant during another appearance at Speakers' Corner. In September 2022, Muslim convert, Edward Little then under surveillance by MI5 for having plotted to attack Queen Elizabeth II's funeral – was arrested for attempting to purchase a gun with which he intended to kill Ms Tash. In October 2022, the police apologised to Ms Tash for having fallen 'below standards' and awarded her £10,000 in compensation and costs. In December 2023, Little was sentenced to a minimum of 16 years imprisonment. In September 2024, Ms Tash received a further £10,000 in damages and costs

---

[25] 'Met Police payout after Southgate preacher's wrongful arrest', *BBC*, 28 July 2019.
[26] Brendan O'Neill, 'The plight of Hatun Tash shames Britain', *The Spectator*, 23 September 2024; 'Preacher wins payout after arrest for damaging her own Qur'an', *Christian Concern*, 20 September 2024.

from the Metropolitan Police after having been arrested, strip searched, and unlawfully imprisoned for wearing a Charlie Hebdo T-shirt and having her property stolen at Speakers' Corner in London in June 2022.

Public service

No British politician has yet been murdered or physically harmed for allegedly Islamophobic expression. However, on 14 May 2010, 21-year-old British student and Al Qaeda sympathiser, Roshonara Choudhry, attempted to murder Stephen Timms, the Labour MP for East Ham in London by stabbing him. She later claimed this was in retaliation for him having voted in favour of the British and US invasion of Iraq in 2003. In 2021 Conservative MP Sir David Amess was murdered by Islamist Ali Harbi for having voted, several years before, in favour of the bombing of Syria by the UK which, in the event, did not go ahead. Although each of these attacks was motivated by the victims' alleged hostility towards Muslims and Islam, neither involved Islamophobic expression as such.

Lord Austen

On 16 February 2024, having been accused of Islamophobia, Lord Austin was suspended as chairman of the Midland Heart housing organisation which provides affordable homes across the Midlands and receives millions of pounds in public funding.[27] The peer, who was adopted and raised by a Holocaust survivor, served as Labour MP for Dudley North before resigning over Jeremy Corbyn's handling of the party's antisemitism crisis in 2019. He was later made a non-affiliated life member of the House of Lords by Prime Minister Boris Johnson.

Ridiculing claims by the UN Relief Works Agency (UNRWA) that it was unaware of Hamas tunnels underneath its main headquarters in Gaza, Lord Austin posted on X (formerly Twitter): 'Everybody, better safe than sorry: before you go to bed, nip down and check you haven't inadvertently got a death cult of Islamist murderers and rapists running their operations downstairs. It's easily done'. The post was denounced by, amongst others, Muslim Engagement and Development (MEND) as 'Islamophobic' because, by using the word 'Islamists', it could 'plausibly be seen to be talking about

---

[27] F. Attenborough, 'Housing association suspends peer over Hamas "murderers" comment', *The Free Speech Union*, 7 February 2024.

some Muslims in Britain'.[28] Speaking to the *Daily Telegraph* about this experience, Lord Austin said:

> 'The word "Islamists" is very clearly a reference not to Muslim people but to extremists. I have said and written repeatedly that the vast majority of Muslims are just as appalled by racism and extremism as anyone else … I am really shocked and disappointed that this has happened as a result of politically motivated bullies orchestrating a malicious campaign on social media to smear me by deliberately misinterpreting my comments and trying to undermine a lifetime's work fighting racism'.[29]

Gary Mond

In 2023 Gary Mond, a Cambridge-educated accountant, former member of the advisory board of the Conservative Friends of Israel, and chair of the advisory board for the National Jewish Assembly, lost his post as trustee of the Jewish National Fund UK as a result of temporary disqualification by the UK's Charity Commission.[30] Allegedly 'Islamophobic' historic social media posts and 'likes' – which the Commission thought could damage the reputation of the charities with which he was associated – had been revealed.[31] Having spent some £60,000 of his own money attempting to clear his name, a First-tier Tribunal (Charity) decided in February 2025 that the decision of the Charity Commission was unlawful.

One of Mond's posts expressed concern that, if a significant number of Labour MPs were Muslim, 'the Britain that we knew will have gone forever'. In another, he stated that 'civilisation' was 'at war with Islam', a comment Mr Mond later claimed was intended to refer to 'Islamic fundamentalism' rather than to the Islamic faith itself. The tribunal acknowledged that, although some of Mond's posts could have been 'perceived as anti-Islam', the content of his social media activity from 2014 to 2021 did not render him unfit to serve as a trustee. His disqualification was, therefore, unlawful because it constituted a disproportionate and unnecessary interference with his right to freedom of expression. Mr Mond's case is the first in which a disqualification order by

---

[28] https://www.mend.org.uk/lord-ian-austin-suspended/.
[29] Attenborough, 'Housing association suspends peer.'
[30] E. Croft, 'Charity boss cancelled for "Islamophobia" wins legal battle in victory for free speech', *Daily Telegraph*, 8 February 2025.
[31] Ibid.

the Charity Commission has been overturned.

Broadcasting and the media

Accusations that UK broadcasters, particularly GB News, are 'racist' or 'Islamophobic' are commonplace, typically when a story, justified or otherwise, has criticized Muslims. In July 2025, for example, a UK-based Muslim community radio station, Salaam BCR, run by the charity Markaz Al Huda, denounced Ofcom – the government-approved regulatory and competition authority for the UK's broadcasting, internet, telecommunications and postal industries – as Islamophobic. Salaam BCR had been fined £3,500 for hate speech relating to a 38-minute broadcast by Shujauddin Sheikh, ten days after the 7 October Hamas-led invasion of Israel, which included the accusation that 'from killing prophets to only protecting their own interests' the Jews were 'the biggest enemies of humanity'.[32]

Trevor Phillips

Prominent public figure, Trevor Phillips is an unlikely Islamophobe.[33] Currently a television presenter and a columnist on *The Times*, he was formerly, amongst other things, Chair of the London Assembly, head of the Commission for Racial Equality, and Chair of the Equality and Human Rights Commission (EHRC). In 2016, he said, on his own Channel 4 documentary, *What British Muslims Really Think*, that the 1997 report of the Runnymede commission, *Islamophobia: A Challenge For Us All* (see Chapter 10), to which he had contributed, had correctly recognised that antagonism towards British Muslims is a reality. But he added that 'we got almost everything else wrong'. The results of an extensive survey of Muslim opinion conducted for the programme also showed that 23% supported the introduction of sharia law in the UK, 39% believed that wives should always obey their husbands, 31% agreed that bigamy was unacceptable, 47% were opposed to gay people ever being allowed to teach in schools, and 52%

---

[32] M. Dathan, 'Ofcom is racist claims radio station', *The Times*, 17 July 2025.
[33] See, eg T. Dieppe, *Banning Islamophobia: Blasphemy Law by the Backdoor* (Free Speech Union briefing, March 2024), pp. 31-34; M. Frampton, J. Jenkins & K. Mahmood, *The Trial: The Strange Case of Trevor Phillips – How the accusation of Islamophobia is used to stifle free speech* (Policy Exchange, 2020).

thought that homosexuality should be illegal. Phillips declared that he found these findings 'extremely worrying'.[34]

The broadcast polarized opinion. Calling Islamophobia a 'fraudulent concept', Douglas Murray praised Phillips for his willingness to 'break taboos which too many liberals in the UK are keen to continue enforcing in the face of all available evidence'.[35] James Delingpole, said Phillips had been 'brave and honest', and that the British public know that 'large numbers of Muslims don't want to integrate' and that 'their views aren't remotely enlightened'.[36] Others condemned the documentary as Islamophobic. Simon Woolley, founder of Operation Black Vote, complained, that by treating Muslims as a monolithic group and providing 'no historical or social/political context', Phillips had pandered to prejudice.[37] Peter Osborne accused Phillips of employing a double standard by criticizing the alleged social conservatism of British Muslims by reference to views held in the country generally, rather than to those of other religious groups in Britain, many of whose adherents were, he alleged, at least equally socially conservative.[38] Phillips replied by asserting that his reference in the documentary to a 'nation within a nation' was not to Muslims as a whole, but to a significant minority.[39] He also pointed out that the Channel 4 programme had acknowledged the diversity of British Muslims and that, far from suggesting Muslims are collectively in some way at fault, the rest of Britain also needed to re-examine its own norms and behaviour.[40]

However, in March 2020, Phillips was suspended from the Labour Party pending investigation into alleged Islamophobia. His alleged 'misconduct' included citing the survey which found, amongst other things, that a third of UK Muslims preferred their children to be educated separately from non-

---

[34] A. Doyle, *The End of Woke: How the Culture War Went Too Far and What to Expect from the Counter-Revolution* (Constable, 2025), p. 191-2.

[35] D. Murray, 'Trevor Phillips is finally discovering the pitfalls of the term "Islamophobia,"' *The Spectator*, 11 April 2016.

[36] J. Delingpole, 'An inconvenient truth', *The Spectator*, 16 April 2016.

[37] S. Woolley, 'Trevor Phillips's Muslim report: Panders to prejudice', *Operation Black Vote*, 11 April 2016.

[38] P. Osborne, 'The double standards of Trevor Phillips', *Middle East Eye*, 15 April 2016.

[39] D. Barrett, 'British Muslims becoming a nation within a nation, Trevor Phillips warns', *Daily Telegraph*, 11 April 2016.

[40] T. Phillips, 'What do British Muslims really think?', *The Times*, 10 April 2016.

Muslims, that a quarter were sympathetic to the motives of the *Charlie Hebdo* murderers, and that 'Muslims see the world differently from the rest of us', an observation open to positive, negative, or neutral interpretations. Describing these developments as 'pure political gangsterism', Phillips claimed that: 'In essence, I am accused of heresy, and I am threatened with excommunication'.[41] Muslim Labour MP Khalid Mahmood defended Phillips claiming that the 'charges are so outlandish as to bring disrepute on all involved in making them'.[42] Phillips' suspension from the Labour Party was lifted in June 2021.

Lord Singh of Wimbledon

While the print media in the UK are notoriously partisan, their counterparts in broadcasting are required by law to be impartial. This includes not censoring references to attested historical fact merely in order to avoid causing offence. Yet this is precisely what the then 87-year-old Lord Indarjit Singh of Wimbledon claimed happened to him.[43] Lord Singh is a cross bencher in the House of Lords, a respected inter-faith activist and former adviser to the Commission for Racial Equality. He has also represented Britain's 423,000 Sikhs on national occasions such as Remembrance Day services at the Cenotaph and at the coronation of King Charles in 2023. For 35 years he was also a regular contributor to 'Thought for Today', which offers 'reflections from a faith perspective on issues and people in the news', on the BBC's Radio 4 Today programme. This had enabled him to explore universal or common spiritual and moral issues, questions, challenges, and dilemmas, from a Sikh perspective.

However, accusing the BBC of 'prejudice and intolerance' and a 'misplaced sense of political correctness', Lord Singh renounced this role in October 2019. He claimed that the previous November, the BBC had tried, at the last minute, to alter his intended reflections upon the example set by Guru Tegh Bahadur. Although his scripted remarks contained no criticism of contemporary Muslim beliefs, practices, or conduct, he was told Muslims

---

[41] T. Dieppe, 'Trevor Phillips and the Islamophobia indictment', *Christian Concern*, 10 March 2020.

[42] H. Singh, 'Trevor Phillips's fate should terrify us all', *The Spectator*, 10 March 2020.

[43] D. Kennedy, 'Sikh peer leaves BBC Radio 4 show with swipe at "thought police,"' *The Times*, 4 October 2019.

might nevertheless have been upset. Guru Tegh Bahadur, the 9th of the 10 founders of the Sikh faith, is honoured by Sikhs and revered as a martyr for having championed the right to religious freedom for all, and in particular, for objecting to and refusing to comply with Mughal Emperor Aurangzeb's policy of forced conversion to Islam. He was beheaded in Delhi in 1675 as punishment. Having threatened to leave the slot empty rather than have the teachings of his religion 'insulted in this way', Lord Singh was permitted by the BBC to present this Thought for the Day as intended.[44] There is no evidence that any listeners were offended.

Lord Singh then lodged an official complaint with the Corporation alleging that the broadcast about Guru Tegh Bahadur was only one of several occasions upon which the BBC had tried to block his reflections on topics of both importance to Sikhs and relevant to Thought for the Day. On one of these he said he wanted to include the words 'the one God of us all', central to Sikh teachings, but was told not to do so 'because it might offend Muslims'. Although Sikhs are monotheistic, they do not directly share the Abrahamic roots of Islam, Christianity, and Judaism.

Having conducted a review, Lord Singh's complaint was rejected by the BBC's director of radio, James Purnell, who said: 'We disagree with Lord Singh and don't recognise his characterisation of Thought for the Day'. A spokesman for the BBC maintained that 'Lord Singh has been a respected contributor for many years and remains so, but given our commitment to increasingly feature a range of voices from Sikh and other communities, we can't agree to his request for a guaranteed number of appearances'.[45]

According to Lord Singh: 'The aim of Thought for the Day has changed from giving an ethical input to social and political issues to the recital of religious platitudes and the avoidance of controversy with success measured by the absence of complaints'. He added that, 'the need for sensitivity in talking about religious, political or social issues has now been taken to absurd proportions, with telephone insistence on trivial textual changes right up to going into the studio, making it difficult to say anything worthwhile'.[46]

---

[44] Ibid.
[45] Ibid.
[46] Ibid.

The Centre for Media Monitoring

Gilligan and Perry's 2025 report, *Bad Faith Actor*, raises serious concerns about the role played by the Centre for Media Monitoring (CfMM) in falsely accusing the British media of Islamophobia.[47] Ostensibly established to promote 'fair, accurate and responsible reporting', and to help 'change the narrative' about Muslims and Islam, the CfMM was founded in 2018 by the Muslim Council of Britain (MCB), a conservative organization claiming to speak for all Muslims in the UK.[48] However, since 2009, successive British governments have refused to engage with the MCB, primarily due to concerns about its extremism, lack of representativeness, and its links with controversial groups or positions. Claiming that the British media are amongst 'the biggest drivers of Islamophobia in the country', the CfMM alleges that 60% of news stories about Muslims are negative, which, in its view, demonstrates that 'misrepresenting Muslims, misusing terminology or misinterpreting Islamic beliefs and practices' are commonplace.[49]

The CfMM pursues its objectives by publishing thematic reports, denouncing individual journalistic items it considers unfair, inaccurate, or biased, hosting events attended by other editors and reporters, and engaging with journalists, editors, regulators and policymakers. The claim that it delivers masterclasses to journalism students at 'all the top universities' in the UK is, however, difficult to substantiate.[50] Gilligan and Perry found that while some editors, executives and journalists have been persuaded about the Centre's allegations, others remain sceptical. They also acknowledge that while the CfMM has indeed exposed false and harmful stories and secured corrections, this has happened only in a few cases. *Bad Faith Actor* also claims that the CfMM's own reports suffer – to an extent that would not be tolerated by any genuinely professional news outlet – from the same kinds of problem it complains about in others – particularly inaccuracy, unfairness, bias, and a lack of transparency and rigour.

According to Gilligan and Perry, the CfMM has, for example, criticised TV dramas for including Muslim characters who reject the hijab, drink

---

[47] A. Gilligan & D. Perry, *Bad Faith Actor: A study of the Centre for Media Monitoring (CfMM)* (Policy Exchange, 2025).

[48] https://cfmm.org.uk/about-us/.

[49] https://cfmm.org.uk/wp-content/uploads/2023/09/CfMM-Submission-to-Editors-Code-2023.pdf.

[50] Gilligan & Perry, *Bad Faith Actor*, p. 7.

alcohol, or who are gay. It has also openly sided with angry Muslim mobs staging banned anti-gay demonstrations outside primary schools. Its published glossary includes contentious interpretations of key terms, such as 'Islamism' and 'extremism'. The CfMM claims to support free speech and denounces those 'insinuating that we wish to censor and limit criticism'.[51] Yet it also campaigns for 'insults' against Islam to be discouraged by press regulators. Nor, it says, should the media be allowed – as in the case of the grooming gangs controversy discussed below – to suggest that fear of being accused of racism or Islamophobia may have contributed to the failure of relevant authorities to investigate alleged wrongdoing by Muslims.

Gilligan and Perry also accuse the CfMM of pressurizing journalists to downplay or to ignore violent Islamism and of seeking to attack, suppress or downplay fair and accurate media reporting about extremism. Indeed, the CfMM maintains that journalists should never use terms such as 'Islamism', 'Islamic extremism' or 'Muslim extremism' at all, nor should they describe terrorist organizations, including Hamas, as 'Islamist'. According to the CfMM, in order to be regarded as 'unbiased', any report of an Islamist terror attack must also avoid any reference to the culprit's faith or motivation because it claims that, by definition, no genuine Muslim could be a terrorist. The CfMM has also suggested that moderate Muslims, who do not share its particular brand of conservative Islam, may be liberals or government spies. Alternatively, it claims, they may have, at the very least, shed their 'religious identities' in favour of a version of the faith 'sanctioned by the state'.[52]

Gilligan and Perry conclude that the CfMM's purpose is not simply to challenge factual errors or to correct stories about Muslims. As the CfMM itself puts it, the objective is to 'take control of the narrative about Islam' and to pressurise journalists both to avoid any kind of negative Islam-related story, however true, and to accept the partisan views held by the MCB and its acolytes. The *Bad Faith Actor* report claims that this places it at the heart of the current campaign in Britain to confer official public recognition upon the concept of 'Islamophobia' with the ultimate goal of outlawing it. In a foreword, veteran journalist and broadcaster, Andrew Neil, says that the report:

'shows how CfMM has been accepted, without much scrutiny, by

---

[51] https://cfmm.org.uk/wp-content/uploads/2021/11/CfMM-Annual-Report-2018-2020-digital.pdf.
[52] Gilligan & Perry, *Bad Faith Actor*, p. 7.

some senior figures in the media and the press regulator, Ipso; how it has gained influence in their organisations; and how, as a result, it may be succeeding in some of its aims .... CfMM is part of a wider campaign for legal restrictions on what you can say about Islam, with fundamental implications for free speech'.

Islamophobia-phobia and wrongdoing by Muslims

Islam has been invoked in two contrasting ways with respect to alleged wrongdoing by its adherents. One, arguably a form of Islamophilia, concerns attempts to find a justification or excuse in certain elements of Muslim culture.[53] As Bruckner observes, 'unreserved praise for cultural particularities can also conceal a neo-colonial paternalism'.[54] For example, in March 2007, a German judge, Christa Datz-Winter, refused a fast-track divorce to a 26-year old Muslim mother of two – allegedly beaten repeatedly and threatened with death by her husband – on the grounds that domestic violence is permitted by the Qur'an.[55] The judge said that, since the couple came from a 'Moroccan cultural environment in which it is not uncommon for a man to exert a right of corporal punishment over his wife … that's what the claimant had to reckon with when she married the defendant'.[56] Datz-Winter also responded to an objection from the claimant's lawyer by invoking Qur'an 4:34: '... as to those on whose part you fear desertion, admonish them and leave them alone in the sleeping places and beat them'. Commentators and politicians criticised the decision on the grounds that the Qur'an is not part of German law. Germany's Central Council of Muslims also stated that: 'Violence and abuse of people are of course naturally reasons to warrant a divorce in Islam ....' Following a national outcry, Ms Datz-Winter was replaced for this trial by another judge.

Similarly, in 2013 a British Muslim was spared jail after having been convicted of raping a thirteen-year old girl. Concluding that the accused was 'very naïve and immature when it comes to sexual matters', and ignoring the doctrine that 'ignorance of the law is no defence', the judge accepted his plea

---

[53] See T. Dieppe in E. Webb (ed.), *Islamophobia: An Anthology of Concerns* (Civitas, 2019), p. 31.

[54] P. Bruckner (trans. by S. Rendell and L. Neal), *An Imaginary Racism: Islamophobia and Guilt* (Wiley, 2018), p. 20.

[55] K. Connolly, 'German judge invokes Qur'an to deny abused wife a divorce', *The Guardian*, 23 March 2007.

[56] Ibid.

that, as a result of his religious upbringing, he was unaware that child rape was illegal.[57]

On 26 March 2018, in a strange mirror-image of the German case, a British judge, Justice Haddon-Cave, lectured Ahmed Hassan, a teenage Iraqi asylum-seeker, on the peacefulness of Islam and the Qur'an when sentencing him to 34 years imprisonment for having planted a homemade bomb on a rush-hour London tube train which partially exploded at Parsons Green injuring 50 people. He said: 'You will have plenty of time to study the Qur'an in prison in the years to come. You should understand that the Qur'an is a book of peace, Islam is a religion of peace. You have violated the Qur'an and Islam by your actions, as well as the law of all civilised people. It is to be hoped that you will come to realise this one day'.[58]

By contrast, the other side of the coin involves denouncing as Islamophobic, any suggestion that certain elements of Muslim culture, however wayward from the mainstream, may be linked to particular kinds of wrongdoing. The relevance of a Muslim identity in this context will depend crucially upon whether it is integral to, or is merely a contingent characteristic of the wrongdoing itself. And, as with many of the issues discussed in this book, this distinction lies on a continuum. Like the rest of us, Muslims do wrong, including committing crime, which may or may not have any connection with their putative religious faith. For example, depending upon background factors including motive, it may or may not be appropriate to refer to the fact that an assailant, who fatally attacked someone in the street with a knife, was Muslim. It would not be relevant if the assault was, for example, drugs-related, motivated by robbery, or stemmed from mental illness or personal vendetta. So, in such circumstances, reporting and debating the fact that the offender was Muslim, could be seen as an expression of anti-Muslim prejudice.

However, the picture changes fundamentally if, as he knifed the victim, the assailant was heard to shout, 'Allahu Akbar! (God is Great!)' – the iconic Muslim call to arms – or anything else which might suggest the attack had been motivated by Islamist terrorism. In these circumstances reporting and debating the fact that the attacker was Muslim would be entirely appropriate.

---

[57] P. Bentley, 'Muslim abuser who "didn't know" that sex with a girl of 13 was illegal is spared jail', *Daily Mail*, 25 January 2013.

[58] 'Judge shouldn't have interpreted Islam when sentencing bomber', *National Secular Society*, 27 March 2018.

The motive for the offence should also be recognised and factored into the criminal charges, trial, and sentence. But responsible reporting should also observe that Islamist/jihadi terrorism derives from an interpretation of the Islamic faith rejected by mainstream orthodox Islam to which most Muslims in Britain and the wider world subscribe.

There are plenty of examples of the minefields in this domain. Four of the most significant controversies in the recent past concern Islamist terrorism, Pakistani child sex grooming gangs and the so-called Trojan Horse affair in England, and an alleged mass sexual assault in Cologne, Germany.

Islamist terrorism

It has been claimed that it is Islamophobic to describe jihadi terrorism as 'Islamist', or perpetrated by 'Muslim extremists'.[59] It has also been alleged that the UK's counterterrorist Prevent programme – which attempts to identify those at risk of being drawn into terrorism of any kind, and with their consent, to steer them away from it – is Islamophobic and racist.[60] However, this claim rests on very shaky ground for three principal reasons. First, it is not clear how the programme can be inherently Islamophobic and racist when it is based on a model pioneered against Islamists in Saudi Arabia and subsequently adopted and customized by many other states, including Muslim ones such as Indonesia, Libya, Malaysia, the Maldives, Tajikistan, Uzbekistan and Yemen, plus other, non-Muslim countries, such as Australia, Denmark, Germany, India, the Philippines, and Sri Lanka.[61]

Second, for several years, Prevent has been deployed more against white, non-Muslim, right-wing, and other forms of extremism, than their Islamist counterpart. This shift in focus has been criticised by the government-appointed independent reviewer of the Prevent programme, Sir William Shawcross, as detrimental to effective counterterrorism in the UK because the Islamist threat is the more serious.[62] Third, it is also difficult to credit the claim

---

[59] W. Shawcross, *Independent Review of Prevent*, HC 1072, 8 February 2023. p. 85.
[60] See S. Greer, *Falsely Accused of Islamophobia: My Struggle Against Academic Cancellation* (Academica Press, 2023), pp. 130-34.
[61] C. Baker-Beall, C. Heath-Kelly & L. Jarvis (eds.), *Counter-Radicalization: Critical Perspectives*, (Routledge, 2015), Chs. 4, 5 & 13; R. Gunaratna, J. Jerard & L. Rubin (eds.), *Terrorist Rehabilitation and Counter-Radicalization: New approaches to counter-terrorism*, (Routledge, 2011).
[62] Shawcross, *Independent Review of Prevent*, paras. 1.5, 1.12.

that the 'Muslim community' objects to the allegedly anti-Muslim character of Prevent when scientific polling shows that very few Muslims have even heard of it. And, when it is explained to them, the overwhelming majority immediately appreciate the justifications.[63]

Debates sparked by a spate of terrorist incidents in France provide another example. On the evening of Friday, 13 November 2015, a series of coordinated Islamist attacks took place in central Paris and its northern suburb of Saint-Denis. Having failed to gain entry to the Stade de France, where an international football match was in progress, three suicide bombers struck outside the stadium. Another unit, one of whose members also detonated an explosive killing himself, then opened fire indiscriminately on crowded cafés and restaurants in central Paris. A mass shooting accompanied by hostage-taking also occurred at an Eagles of Death Metal concert attended by 1,500 people at the Bataclan theatre. When the police arrived, the attackers either detonated suicide vests or were shot dead. In total, the events that evening left over 130 dead, including 90 at the Bataclan plus seven of the attackers, with over 500 injured, 100 critically.

In addition to the widespread expression of revulsion and condemnation, some also sought to blame the culture of the victims rather than that of the perpetrators. [64] According to Blais Wilfert-Portal, for example, French pavement cafés are one of the most 'explicitly aggressive forms of chauvinism'. Sociologist Geoffrey de Lagasnerie explained that they are also 'one of the most intimidating' and 'traumatizing places' for 'young people from ethnic minorities'.[65] Philosopher Michel Onfray blamed the killings on the 'Islamophobic policy' of the French state which 'alongside the United States' is 'reaping what it sowed'.[66] In July 2016, similar sentiments were expressed following the massacre in Nice of 86 people mown down by an Islamist in a truck. On 18 July, Jean-Luc Nancy stated in Liberation, for example, that: 'We have to blame ourselves, our universal quest for power that is never satisfied'.[67]

---

[63] J. Clements, M. Roberts & D. Foreman, *Listening to British Muslims: policing, extremism and Prevent* (Crest Advisory, 2020), p. 11.
[64] Bruckner, *Islamophobia and Guilt*, pp. 58-61.
[65] Ibid.
[66] Ibid.
[67] Ibid.

Pakistani child sex grooming scandals

A number of child sex grooming scandals, involving mostly Pakistani male perpetrators and thousands of mostly vulnerable white, working-class, under-age female victims many of whom were in care, came to light in several English towns in the 2010s. Some claimed that 'toxic masculinity' and other factors, including opportunities presented to the predominantly Pakistani taxi drivers working in the 'night-time economy', were at the heart of the problem. According to this view, the ethnic and religious identity of the perpetrators was, therefore, irrelevant and was invoked to 'stigmatize Muslim communities'.[68]

Others, including some Pakistanis and other Muslims, maintained that the cultural background of the abusers was relevant for three main reasons. First, it was said to be linked to certain relevant assumptions, particularly the lack of respect for women in general, compounded by contempt for the victims as 'white *kuffar* trash' seen as fair game for sexual exploitation. One survivor stated that: 'As grooming victims, my friends and I were called vile racist names such as "white trash" and "kafir girl" as we were raped. Our Sikh and Hindu friends who were also targeted by Muslim Pakistani gangs were disparagingly called "kafir slags" too'.[69] Second, every dimension of the controversy, including the cultural identity of the abusers, needs to be addressed if similar problems are to be effectively tackled elsewhere. A third reason for considering cultural and religious background concerns the allegation that the failure of relevant authorities to confront the problem in question could be attributed, at least partly, to the fear of being accused of racism and/or Islamophobia. Or, if attention were drawn to the religion/culture of the culprits, of triggering prejudice and hostility in others. As Parveen Qureshi, director of the United Multicultural Centre in Rotherham, said in 2014, the problem of Asian men abusing white girls had been known 'for a long time'.[70]

According to Dr Taj Hargey, Imam of the Oxford Islamic Congregation, 'race and religion were inextricably linked to the recent spate of grooming

---

[68] T. Khan, *Muslim Actually, How Islam is Misunderstood and Why it Matters* (Atlantic, 2022), p. 15.

[69] H. Singh in Webb (ed.), *Islamophobia*, p. 42.

[70] M. de Graaf, '"Muslim leaders fully aware of problem but did nothing": Pakistani community worker makes explosive claims on Rotherham's religious leaders who "talked in mosques but not to police,"' *Mail On Line*, 28 August 2014.

rings in which Muslim men have targeted under-age white girls'.[71] This is because, he claimed, some Islamic preachers encourage their followers to believe that the women in question were 'habitually promiscuous, decadent, and sleazy—sins which are made all the worse by the fact that they are *kuffars* or non-believers' who 'deserve to be punished … by being exploited and degraded'. Hargey also blamed the agencies of the state, including the police, social services and the care system, for their apparent eagerness 'to ignore the sickening exploitation that was happening before their eyes. Terrified of accusations of racism, desperate not to undermine the official creed of cultural diversity, they took no action against obvious abuse'. In October 2018, the then Home Secretary, Sajid Javid, a British-born Muslim whose parents came from Pakistan, said: 'It is a statement of fact – a fact which both saddens and angers me – that most of the men in recent high-profile gang convictions have had a Pakistani heritage'.[72]

In 2015 Dame Louise Casey's report into Rotherham Council detailed a culture of institutional denial surrounding grooming gang offences committed primarily by men of Pakistani heritage, where 'so-called political correctness' had 'cast its shadow' over decision-making with staff across the town pressurized to 'suppress, keep quiet or cover up' concerns. [73] These observations were echoed in the Jay and Telford inquiries. In her 2016 report on opportunity and integration, Dame Louise also observed that: 'Too many public institutions, national and local, state and non-state, have gone so far to accommodate diversity … that they have ignored or even condoned regressive, divisive and harmful cultural and religious practices, for fear of being branded racist or Islamophobic'.[74] For example, Labour MP, Ann Cryer, amongst the first to raise the cultural/religious aspect of the scandal, was denounced as racist and Islamophobic by the Islamic Human Rights Commission. In 2017, the same dubious honour was bestowed upon Dame Louise and, the following year, upon Labour MP, Sarah Champion.

In January 2025 the grooming gang controversy was revived in an

---

[71] H. Dixon, '"Imams Promote Grooming Rings" Muslim Leader Claims', *Daily Telegraph*, 16 May 2013.

[72] Dieppe in Webb (ed.), *Islamophobia*, p. 32.

[73] L. Casey, *Report of an Inspection of Rotherham Metropolitan Borough Council* (HM Government, 2015).

[74] L. Casey, *A Review Into Opportunity and Integration: Executive Summary* (Department for Communities and Local Government, 2016), para 67.

unexpected series of social media interventions by Elon Musk, then the world's wealthiest man. A debate ensued about whether the problem – said to remain unresolved in spite of a string of criminal convictions over the previous decade – should be addressed by local investigations or by a national inquiry. Initially the government opted for several government-backed local inquiries plus a separate three-month national audit into grooming gangs, including 'cultural and societal drivers', to be conducted by (the now) Baroness Casey of Blackstock. But, in June 2025, the Prime Minister announced that Baroness Casey would conduct an audit to determine if a full statutory inquiry was necessary.[75] The announcement coincided with the awarding of an MBE in the King's birthday honours, for 'services to integration, cohesion and to British society', to Muhbeen Hussain. In October 2015, when the Rotherham grooming scandal was exposed, Hussain led a boycott of South Yorkshire Police for having attempted to 'scapegoat' and 'demonize' Muslims by claiming that the police had themselves failed to act for fear of being accused of racism/Islamophobia. He also claimed that, by dint of their criminality, the perpetrators could not be described as 'Muslim'.[76]

Andrew Norfolk, the award-winning correspondent from *The Times* who originally broke the story in the 2010s, said that it was 'difficult to talk about' the fact that the grooming gangs in question were predominantly Pakistani and their victims, vulnerable white girls, 'without being accused of being Islamophobic' and that 'left wing academics still attack me' for this reason.[77] And, in January 2025, Lord Singh of Wimbledon wrote to the Home Secretary on behalf of the Network of Sikh Organizations UK, urging that the review should consider race and religion 'as contributing factors in these terrible crimes'. He added:

> 'Although much of the focus on victims has rightly been those from vulnerable white working-class communities … this stain on British society has also impacted the Sikh and Hindu communities too … We cannot shy away from the irrefutable truth that non-Muslim girls are considered fair game by some perpetrators by virtue of the fact they

---

[75] C. Mason & I. Allen, 'PM announces national inquiry into grooming gangs', *BBC*, 14 June 2025.

[76] G. Pogrund, 'MBE for man who led Muslim boycott of police after grooming scandal', *The Sunday Times*, 13 July 2025.

[77] F. Hamilton, 'National inquiry "shied away from finding cause of grooming gangs,"' *The Times*, 8 January 2025.

are *kuffars* (a derogatory term for non-Muslims). Until we are honest about this admittedly uncomfortable factor, we will be no further forward in addressing cases which involve racially and religiously motivated targeting of vulnerable girls from all our communities'.[78]

Some prominent Muslims echoed these sentiments. For example, writing in her personal capacity in *The Sunday Times*, Baroness Falkner of Margravine, Chair of the Equality and Human Rights Commission, noted that the 'anti-white racism shown towards the victims was mirrored by a kind of hands-off racism towards the offenders'. Acknowledging that, in the UK, the majority of sex abusers in general are white and that demonizing a whole community should be avoided, she also asked: 'why does it appear that Pakistanis, or a subset of Pakistani men, are so overrepresented in gang rape outrages?' Partially answering it she added:

'I'm a first-generation female migrant from Pakistan who naturalized as a British citizen. I'm a secular Muslim and I've grown up, lived and worked in Muslim-majority countries, so I am well versed in the cultural and religious mores of those countries. It is obvious that there are regressive attitudes towards women, especially non-Muslim white girls, in parts of the south Asian diaspora in the UK'.[79]

However, the Muslim Council of Britain said that 'despite persistent racist narratives, recent data ... show that perpetrators come from all backgrounds and that most group-based offenders are white'.[80] It is certainly true that the problem of men sexually preying upon women and girls, either alone or in groups, is much wider than the Pakistani grooming gangs scandal. But, several features of the scandal are relevant to the themes of this book. First, according to the mostly young white victims, their abusers referred to them in derogatory language derived from the Muslim faith, indicating that, applying a distorted ethno-religious lens, the perpetrators saw their prey as inferior 'others' to whom the norms of decent, moral behaviour did not apply. Second, those who pointed out these characteristics were instantly denounced as racist and Islamophobic. Yet, it is highly likely that, if any child sex grooming gang scandal involved white non-Muslim men abusing non-white Muslim girls,

---

[78] F. Hamilton, 'Sikh girls treated as "fair game" by grooming gangs', *The Times*, 27 January 2025.

[79] K. Falkner, 'If honour and shame matter to our community, where is the outcry?', *The Sunday Times*, 19 January 2025.

[80] Hamilton, 'Sikh girls treated as "fair game."'

these features would be quickly recognised and resoundingly condemned by those who deny their relevance when the ethno-religious identity of victims and perpetrators is the other way around. Finally, fearful that being more proactive would have resulted in contributing to racist and Islamophobic stereotypes, and themselves being denounced as racist and Islamophobic, the authorities failed to address the problem with sufficient application and rigour. Sadly, a review commissioned by the Surrey Safeguarding Children Partnership, concluded in November 2025, that similar fears had featured in the tragic murder of 10-year-old Sara Sharif after a life of abuse by her father and stepmother.[81]

On 9 December 2025, it was announced that Labour peer, Baroness Longfield, the former children's commissioner, would lead a full statutory inquiry with the power to compel witness testimony, into 'how ethnicity, religion and culture in responses at national and local level, as well as other issues of denial' have been connected with grooming gangs.[82] The inquiry will begin in March 2026 and will also supervise relevant local investigations. The assumptions underpinning these developments clearly conflict with the hostility displayed towards the view, to which reference has been made in this section, that the grooming gangs scandal has had nothing to do with these issues. Prima facie any investigation predicated on such assumptions would amount to 'Islamophobia' according to the All-Party Parliamentary Group's widely-criticized definition, nevertheless endorsed amongst others by the Labour Party, considered further in Chapter 10.

The Trojan horse controversy

The Trojan Horse controversy involved an alleged plot to introduce an intolerant Islamic ethos to several secular state schools in Birmingham, 30% of the population of which is Muslim, significantly higher than the figure of 6.5% for England and Wales as a whole.[83] The affair began in March 2014 with the leaking to the press of an anonymous letter, sent to Birmingham City Council some months before, which both described how to take control of a

---

[81] B. Ellery, '"Race sensitivities hid Sara abuse,"' and 'Lessons Not Learnt', *The Times*, 14 November 2025.

[82] M. Dathan, 'Victims criticise choice of chair to lead national grooming gangs inquiry', *The Times*, 10 December 2025.

[83] D. Perry & P. Stott, *The Trojan Horse Affair: A Documentary Record* (Policy Exchange, 2022).

Birmingham school for the purpose of instituting a conservative Muslim agenda and speculated about how this might also be achieved elsewhere. Aimed at installing a new leadership more sympathetic to conservative Muslim values, the letter, amongst other things, encouraged parents to make false accusations about the school's leadership regarding sex education, forced Christian prayer, and mixed physical education. The author, who claimed to have been instrumental in installing a new headteacher at four Birmingham schools, also identified twelve other schools in the city which could be easy targets due to large numbers of Muslim pupils and poor inspection reports. Having disclosed that it had received the letter, Birmingham City Council also revealed that there had been hundreds of similar allegations including some dating back over 20 years.

The Department for Education (DfE) initially responded by banning, from the teaching profession for life, 14 teachers and Tahir Alam, who in protest against the allegations, had resigned as chair of the Park View Educational Trust which ran three of the schools concerned. Between 2016 and 2017 the bans against the teachers were overturned, dropped, and/or dismissed by the courts. But in December 2017 the DfE revealed that a tribunal had ruled against a challenge made to his ban by Mr Alam.[84] Government funding was withdrawn from three of the schools involved. Claiming that the schools in question had staged a 'cover-up', Prime Minister David Cameron also announced proposals to send Ofsted (the regulator) without warning to any school. The Education Secretary, Michael Gove, also stated that in future all British schools would have to promote British values of tolerance and fairness and that teachers would be banned from the profession if they allowed their schools to be infiltrated by extremists.

Public reaction to the Trojan Horse controversy split along predictable lines. Some instantly accepted the allegations at face value. Though reserving judgment, others thought they were sufficiently credible to warrant official investigation. Yet others, including the Muslim Council of Britain, accused the authorities of an 'Islamophobic' witch hunt based on an elaborate hoax.[85] Having conducted their own inquiries, a number of British newspapers and

---

[84] 'Ruling on ex-chair of governors at "Trojan Horse" school kept under wraps', *TES Magazine*, 2 January 2018.

[85] Muslim Council of Britain, 'Who was behind the National Hoax? Muslim Council of Britain Calls for Independent Public Inquiry into "Trojan Horse" Affair', Press Release, 10 February 2021.

The New York Times, each concluded that the original letter, which sparked the controversy in the first place, was a forgery.[86]

An investigation headed by Peter Clarke – former senior Metropolitan Police officer and ex-head of the Counter Terrorism Command – was commissioned by the DfE. His report concluded that, although there had been no conspiracy as such, there had been 'co-ordinated, deliberate and sustained' attempts 'by a number of associated individuals, to introduce an intolerant and aggressive Islamic ethos' to 'a few schools in Birmingham'.[87] This was characterized by anti-Western rhetoric, 'segregationism' (dividing the world into 'us' and 'them', with the latter including all non-Muslims plus Muslims who disagree with this perspective), intolerance of difference (towards secularism, other Muslims, or other religions), attempts to impose conservative Muslim views and practices upon others, and claims of a worldwide conspiracy against Islam.

Amongst other things, the Clarke inquiry heard that, in some schools, the curriculum and education plans had been changed to increase the faith component, that the choice of modern languages had been restricted to the study of Arabic or Urdu, that reference to terms such as 'condom' and 'the pill' had been banned, that creationism was taught as fact in school assemblies and science lessons, that children were banned from playing musical instruments, and that the curriculum no longer included drama lessons. At several schools the inquiry also found evidence of intolerance toward gay, lesbian, bisexual and transsexual people, and that governors and staff exhibited openly homophobic behaviour.

Former head teacher, Ian Kershaw, was also appointed by Birmingham City Council to conduct an inquiry.[88] Like the Clarke investigation, Kershaw found no evidence of a conspiracy as such. But the inquiry nevertheless concluded that there was evidence of a concerted attempt to change how the

---

[86] S. Shackle, 'Trojan horse: the real story behind the fake "Islamic plot" to take over schools', *The Guardian*, 1 September 2017; H. Syed & B. Reed, 'What went on inside the Trojan Horse scandal?', *The Times*, 10 February 2022 and 'The Trojan Horse Affair', *The New York Times*, 3 February 2022.

[87] P. Clarke, *Report into allegations concerning Birmingham schools arising from the 'Trojan Horse' letter July 2014*, HC 576, 22 July 2014, p. 15.

[88] *Report of Ian Kershaw of Northern Education for Birmingham City Council in Respect of Issues Arising as a Result of Concerns Raised in a Letter Dated 27 November 2023 Known as the 'Trojan Horse' Letter*, Birmingham City Council, 14 July 2014.

Islamic faith was presented. It also concluded that school governors and teachers had tried to promote and enforce radical Islamic values and that there was evidence of extremism in 13 schools. Kershaw attributed the council's slow response to allegations in the letter – that there was a culture of avoiding difficult issues and problems with school governance – to the fear of incurring accusations of racism or Islamophobia, a view endorsed by the then (Muslim) Labour MP for Birmingham Perry Barr, Khalid Mahmood. However, launching the protest movement 'Hands Off Birmingham Schools', Salma Yaqoob, a former Birmingham City Councillor and prominent Muslim spokesperson, claimed the controversy was motivated by a climate of political and media hysteria.

Whether or not the original letter was a hoax, and irrespective of the veracity of what the Clarke and Kershaw inquiries had been told, it is certainly not Islamophobic to raise and debate the wider issue – attempts to promote conservative Islam in secular state schools in England and Wales – because there is ample evidence that this has occurred and is still occurring. For example, having inspected 21 schools in Birmingham in 2014, Ofsted found evidence of an organised campaign by conservative Muslims to target certain schools, and that head teachers had been 'marginalised' or forced out of their jobs in order to be replaced by others more sympathetic to this agenda.[89] As a result some schools had been placed under special measures, including for failing to take adequate steps to safeguard pupils against extremism, an accusation also levelled at Birmingham City Council by the head of Ofsted, Sir Michael Wilshaw, who received the Islamic Human Rights Commission's award of 'Islamophobe of the Year' for his investigations into the Birmingham Trojan Horse affair. Leader of Birmingham City Council, Sir Albert Bore, also claimed that the council had been in touch with authorities in Manchester and Bradford, in the latter of which issues similar to those raised in Birmingham were also said to have arisen.[90]

Senior DfE sources have claimed that coordinated attempts to undermine and supplant head teachers have occurred in Bradford, Manchester, and the London boroughs of Waltham Forest and Tower Hamlets. The National Association of Head Teachers has also expressed similar concerns about

---

[89] A. Sparrow & B. Quinn, 'Ofsted finds "culture of fear and intimidation" in some schools', *The Guardian*, 9 June 2014.
[90] 'Trojan Horse: 25 schools probed over alleged takeover plot', *BBC*, 14 April 2014.

schools in parts of East London and other large cities around the country. On 10 June 2014, the Labour MP for the London constituency of Poplar and Limehouse, Jim Fitzpatrick, warned of a 'Trojan Horse'-style Islamist plot to infiltrate councils in London and the risk of racial politics taking hold.

The Cologne New Year's Eve 2015 mass sexual assault

Another example of wrongdoing allegedly linked to religious/ethnic identity, concerns claims by over 500 women that they were sexually assaulted in Cologne on New Year's Eve 2015 mostly by groups of young men of north African origin. Prominent leftists were quick to denounce, as racist and Islamophobic, any possible connection between the attacks and the cultural identity of the assailants. As French socialist feminist Caroline De Haas tweeted: 'those who tell us that the sexual attacks in Germany are due to the arrival of migrants: go dump your racist shit somewhere else'.[91] Commenting upon such stark denials, Bruckner states:

> 'The male in rut is guilty only if he is white, heterosexual, and Western. The others are exculpated in advance, out of post-colonial remorse … When German women are raped, it seems to some people more urgent to denounce the possible racism of those who name the aggressors than to provide help to the women who have been attacked'.[92]

On 31 January 2016, Algerian writer, Kamel Daoud, published an op-ed in the Paris daily, *Le Monde*, about the incident, attributing such events to the collision between sexual attitudes in many Muslim countries and the cultural shock experienced by young men from such places when they encounter women in the west freely walking the streets which, they wrongly assume, makes them sexually available.[93] Although Daoud was not the only one to make this claim, a Salafist imam in Algeria issued a fatwa calling for his murder. In February 2016, a number of historians and commentators also published a petition in *Le Monde* denouncing Daoud as an Islamophobe.[94] According to Bruckner, this represents an inversion of the appropriate

---

[91] Bruckner, *Islamophobia and Guilt*, p. 48.
[92] Ibid., pp. 49.
[93] Ibid. p. 22.
[94] Ibid., pp. 22-23.

priorities by the multicultural left: 'respecting cultures is more important than respecting persons'.[95]

Conclusion

According to the legal standards discussed in Chapter 6, those who were accused of Islamophobia/racism in most, if not all the controversies discussed in this chapter, sought to raise legitimate concerns about wrongdoing or thorny neglected problems, publicly to bear witness to their non-Muslim faith, to educate, or to contribute to debates about current or historic affairs, albeit sometimes in strident and robust terms. By accidentally damaging the Qur'an, the school kids in the Kettlethorpe incident clearly had no intention to insult or offend. Yet they were pilloried and forced to face a humiliating investigation. The circumstances in which public desecration of the Qur'an constitutes a public order offence remain unclear. But there are grounds for arguing that, at least in some cases, it should not.

---

[95] Ibid., p. 23.

Chapter 9

Academic controversy

Introduction

In addition to the education-related issues discussed in previous chapters, other false charges of Islamophobic expression, coupled with institutional Islamophobia-phobia, are fuelling a deepening crisis for academic freedom across the western world. Some of the less serious examples include the historian Sylvain Gugenheim being denounced, in 2008, by Alain de Libera as an 'erudite Islamophobe'. Gugenheim's offence was expressing the academic opinion in his book, *Aristote au mont Saint Michel: Le racines grecques de l-Europe chrétiennne* ('Aristotle at Mont-Saint-Michel: The Greek Roots of Christian Europe'), that contrary to the prevailing wisdom, the Arabs played a marginal role in transmitting the knowledge of the ancient Greeks.[1] Other less censorious scholars, such as Jacques Le Goff, regarded Gugenheim's book, as 'interesting but debatable'.[2] In 2016, at a conference hosted by the Massachusetts Institute of Technology, a more jaw-dropping claim was made by University of Melbourne Professor of Anthropology, Ghassan Hage, who said that Islamophobia is accelerating global warming because both emanate 'from a similar mode of being, or enmeshment in the world, what is referred to as "generalized domestication."'[3]

A particularly bizarre example of academic-related Islamophobia-phobia also occurred on 25 November 2024 when a preliminary draft of this book was confiscated by Parliamentary security in London. The Head of Campaigns at the National Secular Society, Megan Manson – to whom a copy

---

[1] P. Bruckner (trans. by S. Rendell and L. Neal), *An Imaginary Racism: Islamophobia and Guilt* (Wiley, 2018), p. 27.

[2] Ibid.

[3] 'Is Islamophobia Accelerating Global Warming', *MIT Global Studies and Languages*, 9 May 2016.

had been sent for comment – had it in her bag when she visited the Palace of Westminster with her colleague, Stephen Evans, NSS's Chief Executive Officer, in connection with their professional responsibilities. As a result of the routine search which every visitor to Parliament is required to undergo, the document was seized on the grounds that it was not 'the right sort of politics' and that it 'could be deemed offensive'. Most of the rest of what Megan had in her possession in connection with her job was also confiscated. The 'offending items' were only returned when Stephen and Megan appealed to the MP they were scheduled to meet. Having lodged a formal complaint, an apology was received from the Parliamentary authorities.

However, the most serious cases in this field concern the consequences of discussing the *Charlie Hebdo* cartoons in class. In the others, rather than defending the right to academic freedom, relevant institutions in France, the United States, Canada, and the UK have often chosen instead to side with those making the false accusations of Islamophobia against their staff. This has had inevitable negative consequences for those concerned – vilification, victimization, cancellation, trauma, fear, vulnerability to physical attack, demands for apology and/or dismissal, ostracism from colleagues and others, disciplining or dismissal by employers, and irreparable damage to employment, career, and reputation. Self-censorship on the part of others has also been an inescapable consequence.

The Charlie Hebdo cartoons in the classroom

The most savage consequence of allegations of Islamophobia in an educational context concern the presentation of the *Charlie Hebdo* cartoons for discussion in a class. This led to the murder of Samuel Paty, a French school teacher, and to a teacher in England being forced into hiding with his family.

The murder of Samuel Paty

In October 2020, complying with the French national curriculum, Samuel Paty, a secondary school teacher in the Paris suburb of Éragny-sur-Oise, sought to illustrate a discussion about freedom of expression. Having warned Muslims in advance and granted them permission to leave the room if they wished, Paty showed a class taking a moral and civic education course at least one *Charlie Hebdo* caricature of Mohammad. A student later claimed that the cartoons had featured in lessons every year since the *Charlie Hebdo* shooting in 2015.

A few days later, on 16 October, Paty was stabbed to death and then beheaded outside his school by Abdoullakh Abouyezidovich Anzorov, an 18-year-old Chechen Muslim refugee. In an audio message delivered in Russian just before he was fatally shot by police, Anzarov proclaimed his readiness to die a 'shahid' (martyr), and claimed he had murdered Paty for having 'shown Allah in an insulting manner' and to 'avenge the prophet'.[4] It later transpired that Anzorov had been in touch with two unidentified jihadists in Syria. Paty's murder was also the climax of a hostile social media campaign which began when one of his students, a Muslim girl who had not been present at the material time, told her father that the *Charlie Hebdo* cartoon of a naked Mohammad with his genitals exposed had been presented in class.

Brandishing placards declaring 'Je suis Samuel' and 'Schools in mourning', thousands joined by politicians and other prominent people, took to the streets in rallies in Paris and other French cities in protest against the murder. On 21 October a national memorial for Paty, posthumously awarded the *Légion d'honneur* by President Macron, was held at the Sorbonne. The French Council of the Muslim Faith, the principal body liaising between Muslims and public authorities in France, condemned Paty's murder and provided imams with a text for use in Friday prayers. However, the Grande Mosque de Pantin, north of Paris, was closed for six months by order of the Ministry of the Interior for having published videos inciting violence against the murdered teacher. Expressing 'regret' for the videos, the mosque later removed them from its website and publicly condemned the 'savagery' of Paty's killing. Two Muslim NGOs, *Collectif contre l'islamophobie en France* (Collective Against Islamophobia in France, CCIF) and Barakacity, accused of taking part in a social media campaign against the teacher, were also dissolved. Ten people including an imam, the father of the student whose allegations had prompted the social media campaign, and two students who had identified Paty to Anzorov, were charged with conspiracy to and assisting with murder.

The killing of Samuel Paty prompted fresh soul-searching in France about how Muslims, particularly those recently arrived from abroad, might be better integrated. An opinion poll conducted by *Institut français d'opinion publique* (Ifop) found that 87% of respondents thought the national commitment to

---

[4] 'L'assassin était en contact avec un djihadiste russe', *Le Matin*, 22 Octobre 2020.

secularism (*Laïcité*) was under threat and 79% agreed that Islamists had declared war on France.[5] In December 2023, six teenagers, convicted of various offences in connection with the murder, were each given short or suspended prison sentences, including requirements relating to school attendance or work and having regular medical checkups. Almost exactly a year later, at the end of November 2024, the Muslim schoolgirl, then aged 13, who claimed Paty had ordered Muslim students to leave his class while he showed the *Charlie Hebdo* caricatures, admitted in court to having lied. In tears, she apologised to his family.[6] It turned out that she had falsely claimed to having attended the class in question in order to deflect repercussions from her parents for having been suspended from school for two days for bad behaviour. Her slanderous allegations, which ultimately led to Paty's murder, earned her an 18-month suspended sentence. Four of her five co-defendants – all of whom were aged 14 or 15 at the relevant time and had faced charges of criminal conspiracy with the aim of preparing aggravated violence – received suspended sentences. The sixth, who had identified Paty to Anzarov, was required to wear an electronic tag for six months. The girl's father, Brahim Chnina, was sentenced to 13 years imprisonment for associating with a terrorist organisation and of launching the online harassment campaign which prompted Anzarov to kill Paty. Several other adult co-defendants were sentenced to terms of up to 15 years imprisonment for a range of related offences.

The Batley Grammar School affair

The ripples from the Charlie Hebdo affair spread far and wide. These included a religious studies teacher at Batley Grammar School (BGS) in Yorkshire, England, being forced into hiding with his family in 2021 following protests calling for his dismissal.[7] On 22 March, in a lesson with Year 9 (13/14-year-olds) on religious freedom and freedom of expression, the

---

[5] 'Le regard des Français sur la menace terroriste et l'islamisme', *IFOP*, 22 Octobre 2020.

[6] D. Averre & E. Savlvoni, 'Muslim schoolgirl admits lying that her teacher was Islamophobic - which led to him being decapitated by a jihadist - because she was suspended for two days and worried her parents would be angry', *Mail On Line*, 26 November 2024.

[7] See S. Khan, *Threats to Social Cohesion and Democratic Resilience: A New Strategic Response*, March 2024, pp. 71-85.

class had been shown the *Jyllands-Posten* cartoon of the Prophet Mohammad with his turban partially concealing a bomb (see Chapter 7). According to an investigation, later conducted by Dame Sara Khan – then Independent Adviser to the UK Government for Social Cohesion and Resilience upon whose report the following account, including quotes, is based – the lesson in question had been taught in this manner for two years. Its content, including representations of the Pope and Jesus plus the Mohammad cartoon, had been approved by the school's senior leadership team.

In an all-too-familiar sequence of events, later on the day in question, a parent of one of the pupils called the teacher to complain and warned of 'repercussions'. On 23 March, senior leadership at BGS sent a letter to all parents and guardians apologising for the image used. A few days later dozens of protesters gathered outside the school gates demanding that the teacher be sacked. It has been claimed that the extremist movement *Tehreek-e-Labbaik Pakistan* was influential in orchestrating the protest.[8] Others have argued that some South Asian Muslim immigrants and their offspring have also eagerly joined such British 'anti-Islamophobia' protests in order to demonstrate, particularly to those in their countries and places of origin, that the UK's liberal and secular social environment has not diluted their fidelity to faith, family, and clan.[9]

In the wake of the protests the teacher received threats on social media. Pictures of him, his wife, home, and car were shared on Instagram, Snapchat, and Facebook. On WhatsApp others were encouraged to 'defend the Prophet'. Threatening messages, such as 'watch your back', 'let's sort this out for the Prophet', and 'he should be scared for his life', were shared on Facebook. A local Muslim charity, 'Purpose of Life', also published an open letter including the teacher's name.

Dr Abdul Shaikh, a local academic and Muslim activist, told the PA news agency: 'I was shocked like many Muslims in the town that Muslim school children's religious sensitivities were completely ignored by the school teacher who decided to show an offensive image that lampooned the noble Prophet Mohammed'. A mother said she might consider removing her

---

[8] A. Meleagrou-Hitchens, *Understanding and responding to blasphemy extremism* (m, 2024), pp. 17-21.

[9] See, eg, T. Modood, *Muslims, race and equality in Britain: Some post-Rushdie affair reflections*, (Third Text, 4:11, 1990), pp. 127-134; P. Nash, *British Islam and English Law* (Cambridge University Press, 2022), Chs. 2 & 8.

child from the school because the material used was 'out of order and unacceptable'. However, another parent told BBC Radio Leeds that, although she was upset by the cartoons, she did not agree with the protests which she found 'quite scary and intimidating'.

Head teacher, Gary Kibble, also issued an 'unequivocal' apology for the incident, and stated that the member of staff concerned, who had been suspended pending inquiries, also offered his 'most sincere apologies'. The head added that teaching had been 'immediately withdrawn … on this part of the course' and that 'we are reviewing how we go forward with the support of all the communities represented in our school'.

Having called the police and been disappointed by their apparent lack of concern, the teacher then fled his home with his partner and family. They remain in hiding to this day. The National Education Union (NEU), to which the teacher belonged, initially declined his request for assistance on the grounds that, having been suspended from the union he could not, therefore, communicate with its staff. However, the Khan review found that it later offered support. By this stage, the story was being covered by the national media. At a televised press conference following a meeting with a number of stakeholders and others – including a local Muslim activist involved in the protest but with no children at the school – senior school managers issued yet another apology and announced an inquiry. Tracy Brabin, then Labour MP for Batley and Spen, issued a statement declaring that 'the upset and offence … caused is understandable but … also predictable'. She also said she was 'pleased that the school has recognised that it was inappropriate and has apologized for the offence caused'. Later she added that, although 'no teacher should be facing intimidation or threats, there is no excuse for that', she welcomed the 'school's apology and recognition of the offence this has caused'.

A Department for Education spokesperson said that 'it is never acceptable to threaten or intimidate teachers', and that while dialogue between schools and parents should be encouraged when controversial issues emerge, 'the nature of the protest we have seen, including issuing threats … are completely unacceptable and must be brought to an end'. The spokesperson added that, subject to their obligation to ensure political balance, schools are free to include in the curriculum, a full range of issues, ideas and materials, including those which are challenging or controversial. But in deciding which material to use in the classroom 'they must balance this with the need to promote respect and tolerance between people of different faiths and beliefs'.

The school was then closed and classes were held online as protests continued outside its gates. Two other teachers who had used the same teaching materials as their vilified colleague, were also suspended pending an investigation. The Charity Commission stated that it was aware of the letter from Purpose of Life and that it had been in touch with the school's trustees seeking further information relating to regulatory issues. Although the protests ended just before the Easter break on 29 March, more were threatened for the summer term.

In May 2021 a review conducted by the Batley Multi Agency Trust concluded that the lesson in question had been conducted ...

> 'in line with national guidance and local Authority area agreements. Difficult issues such as blasphemy are included ... as ... a key part of the national curriculum and are important learning points for all our young people. The image in question was used on 22 March as part of the "controversial issues" topic in the RS scheme of work for Year 9 ... to initiate discussion about the meaning of "blasphemy" within the secure confines of a classroom setting ... teaching staff who developed and delivered the lesson genuinely believed that using the image had an educational purpose and benefit, and that it was not used with the intention of causing offence'.[10]

In March 2023 an online survey of over 1,000 teachers in Britain, conducted by YouGov and the think tank Policy Exchange, found that 16% of respondents had consciously self-censored since the events at BGS. Fifty-five per cent said they would not have used an image of the Prophet Mohammad in the classroom in any case. Forty per cent also claimed that their schools did not have any formal guidance about the use of teaching materials that might cause offence.[11] According to another Policy Exchange report, through its proxy, the Islamic Centre of England, Iran is increasingly involved in anti-blasphemy protests in Britain.[12]

The Grenoble cases

In March 2021, a mere five months after the murder of Samuel Paty, three

---

[10] Ibid.

[11] D. Perry, *'Blasphemy' in Schools: Self-Censorship and Security Fears Amongst British Teachers* (Policy Exchange, 2023).

[12] P. Stott, *Tehran Calling: The Iranian Threat to the UK* (Policy Exchange, 2024).

professors at the University of Sciences Po Grenoble, were placed under police protection as a result of death threats stemming from Islamophobia allegations.[13] Those against two, identified in the French press only as Claire M. and Vincent T., are unclear. However, the controversy surrounding the third, Klaus Kinzler, an associate professor of German language and culture from Stuttgart, is better documented. Together with caricatures, the names of Vincent T and Professor Kinzler were plastered on banners at the entrance to the university accompanied by the words: 'Fascists in our lecture halls. Klaus Kinzler and Vincent T. Resign. Islamophobia kills'. Although removed in the afternoon, photos of the slogans were circulated on social networks and a student union, UNEF, also posted them online.

The affair began in December 2020 when the proposed title of a planned seminar on equality – 'Should Islamophobia be included together with antisemitism and racism?' – was being discussed by students and teachers. Kinzler, who is married to a Muslim, argued that Islamophobia was not comparable to antisemitism and that the title should therefore not include it. As a result, he was excluded from the email discussion. Another professor who supported his position was then also targeted by UNEF.

Reacting to these developments, France's interior minister for citizenship, Marlene Schiappa, said that the campaign against the professors was 'a particularly disgusting act' and that UNEF had actively put their lives 'in mortal danger'.[14] Having temporarily suspended Kinzler, Professor Sabine Saurugger, director of Sciences Po Grenoble, told the *Times Higher Education* that this was based only on the fact that he had described Sciences Po Grenoble as a 'political re-education camp' and that his colleagues were indoctrinating their students.

Responding to these developments, the president of the Auvergne-Rhône-Alpes region, Laurent Wauquiez, announced that 'all funding and all cooperation' had been suspended with respect to the university over its 'unacceptable ideological and communitarian drift'. Regional funding, which covers activities such as lifelong learning and exchange programmes, was said to be worth about €500,000 (£418,000) a year.

Others, however, condemned the suspension of funds. For example,

---

[13] B. Upton, 'Islamophobia row puts French campuses in crossfire as poll looms', *Times Higher Education*, 10 January 2022.
[14] Ibid.

Simon Dawes, a media lecturer at Université de Versailles Saint-Quentin-en-Yvelines said:

> 'For an individual politician to cancel funding to a university based on the unfounded allegations of a disgruntled employee is a significant and worrying development. It is a political act and a violation of the principle of academic freedom. The way that this case has been appropriated by others for political ends is yet another example of universities being instrumentalised in a culture war that may well lead to the end of academic freedom'.[15]

The French government and others, have expressed concern that French universities are creating an intellectual breeding ground for terrorism by viewing society through the lenses of ethnicity, religion, and gender, rather than the republican ideal of equality. Former students of Dr Kinzler also published an open letter in the newspaper, *Le Journal du Dimanche*, calling for his reinstatement, criticising the student protesters, and demanding that Sciences Po Grenoble be reformed in order better to protect the political balance among staff and students. One of the signatories, Christophe Gaudin, assistant professor of political science at South Korea's Kookmin University, who studied under Dr Kinzler's tutelage in Grenoble from 1999 to 2003, said: 'No matter how quickly some academic controversy may escalate, nothing is more crucial than keeping it civil, within the walls of the university'.[16] In February 2021 Frédérique Vidal, the French science minister, announced plans to create an inventory of research in higher education to make sure there was 'pluralism of ideas'.

The United States

Cancel culture is rife in the United States. In the academy itself it is largely practiced by the illiberal left, while elsewhere it is conducted against very different targets by the illiberal right. Two particularly egregious false accusations of Islamophobia concern Erika López Prater and Nicholas Damask.

---

[15] Ibid.
[16] Ibid.

Erika López Prater

In April 2023, Dr Erika López Prater, an adjunct instructor in art history at Hamline University in Minnesota, was told that, as a result of complaints, her teaching contract would not be renewed. The complaints were prompted by Dr Prater having shown, and discussed in an art class, celebrated paintings of Mohammad by a devout Muslim artist widely regarded as classic examples of medieval art.[17] The syllabus for the course alerted students to this prospect. Immediately prior to presenting them, Dr Prater also reissued the warning to the class, which included Muslims, and advised anyone who did not want to see the pictures to look away or leave the room. A Muslim student, nevertheless, complained that her faith, which she claimed forbids representations of the Prophet, had been disrespected.

Defending the decision not to renew Dr Prater's contract, Dr Fayneese Miller, Hamline's President, and David Everett, Associate Vice-President of Inclusive Excellence, sent a note to staff saying that 'respect for the observant Muslim students in that classroom should have superseded academic freedom'. Each side of the controversy attracted support and even split the Council of American-Islamic Relations (CAIR), a Muslim civil rights and advocacy organization, whose stated mission is to enhance understanding of Islam, protect civil rights, promote justice, and empower American Muslims. While the Minnesota chapter supported Dr Miller, the national movement defended Dr Prater. The university's full-time faculty overwhelmingly voted against Dr Miller's decision. Dr Prater then sued Hamline for defamation, religious discrimination, and infliction of emotional distress. The results of a representative opinion survey published in March 2024 indicated that 52% of Muslim respondents in Britain thought showing a picture of the Prophet Mohammad should be illegal.[18]

Nicholas Damask

Dr Nicholas Damask is a professor of political science at Scottsdale Community College (SCC), in Arizona, and a former Salvatori Fellow at the Heritage Foundation, a US conservative think tank. Having taught a

---

[17] P. Basken, 'Hamline president to leave amid Islam dispute', *Times Higher Education*, 4 April 2023.

[18] Henry Jackson Society, *British Muslim and general public attitudes polling*, March 2024, p. 7.

course on 'Islamic terrorism' for 26 years without incident, in April 2020 he received a brief email from a Muslim student, Mohammad Sabra, who claimed to have been 'offended' in an unspecified way by the class content.[19] Damask replied that the intention of the course was to explore what motivated tens of thousands of young men, many from privileged backgrounds, to fight for terrorist groups, including ISIS, in Syria and Afghanistan.

The aggrieved student, who declined to make a formal complaint, then uploaded quiz questions from the unit to the Instagram account of a Canadian Muslim with a social media following in the hundreds of thousands. These were: 'Q. Who do terrorists strive to emulate? A. Mohammad. Q. Where is terrorism encouraged in Islamic doctrine and law? A. the Medina verses. Q. Terrorism is …. in Islam. A. Justified within the context of jihad'. Hostile messages, including from as far afield as Malaysia, Pakistan, and the Palestinian territories, immediately began to pour into SCC's Instagram account. Some threatened the college with a school shooting or bombing, while others proposed that Damask should have his throat slit. Professor Damask and his family fled their home, only returning when it had been made sufficiently secure.

The quiz questions and answers are crude and presumptuous. As Chapter 4 of this study indicates, terrorism can be justified by reference to Islamic doctrine only when the latter is twisted and distorted beyond anything the mainstream tradition would accept. But since this is precisely what jihadi terrorists do, it is not Islamophobic to discuss the connection between terrorism and the Muslim faith. In the circumstances some clarification along these lines was required. But, as is common in cases of this kind, SCC instead threw Damask to the wolves. On a new Instagram post, the college asserted that the student was correct, Damask was wrong, and that Sabra would receive full credit for all the quiz questions related to Islam and terrorism.[20] College officials then issued an apology to the student and to the 'Islamic community'. The professor, they said, would be required to apologize for the 'Islamophobic' questions which would be permanently removed from the assessment, and that, before resuming teaching the class, he would probably

---

[19] R. Spencer, *Islamophobia and the Threat to Free Speech* (Centre for Security Policy, 2021), pp. 77-82.
[20] Ibid., p. 78.

be required to have his course material approved by an Islamic scholar and to take a class taught by a Muslim.

From the outset, Damask was supported by the advocacy group, the US Foundation for Individual Rights and Expression (FIRE), and by the college's district chancellor. Following an investigation, he was resoundingly exonerated. The online furore also eventually died down. But in June 2020, the Council on American-Islamic Relations (CAIR) took both SCC and Damask to a federal court demanding an injunction to prevent his claims being presented both in class and the entire college district.

CAIR claimed that, as a public employee, Damask had established a 'state-sponsored' course 'disfavouring religion, specifically Islam'.[21] This was, in other words, no less than a plea for a 'defamation of Islam exception' to the First Amendment to the US Constitution, the freedom of religion and free speech clause. CAIR also argued that no reasonable public employee would countenance defaming Islam in the course of their employment, and that by including an image of Mohammed in his lecture slides, Damask had also 'insulted the prophet'.[22] The district judge dismissed the claim on the grounds that it was much more likely that Damask merely wanted to shed some light upon the ideological roots of contemporary jihadi terrorism. And even if his primary message had really been to express disapproval of Islam, this was entirely consistent with the US Constitution which protects religious believers from unequal treatment but which does not require curricula to avoid conflicts with a student's religious beliefs.

Undeterred, in August 2020, CAIR appealed to the Ninth Circuit Court of Appeals which upheld the original decision and also chastised the appellants. While the lawsuit wended its way through the judicial system, two of Damask's colleagues who teach, respectively, religion and sociology contacted him admitting that they had excised discussion of Islam from their syllabuses for fear of being sued and that the prevailing intimidatory atmosphere in higher education was chilling debate. Damask not only continues to teach his course but, as a result of his ordeal, has added additional material to it.

------

[21] Ibid.
[22] Ibid.

Canada

Institutions in Canada are also suffering from Islamophobia-phobic reactions to false charges of Islamophobia in academic contexts. Two of the most notorious cases concern Stuart Kamenetsky and Collin May.

Stuart Kamenetsky

The deadly attack by Hamas upon Israel on 7 October 2023, the subsequent invasion of Gaza by the Israel Defence Forces, and the ensuing war on several fronts, have prompted a significant increase in reported incidents of both antisemitism and anti-Muslim hatred around the world, including on university campuses in the west. However, not everything said in support of, or against, Israel or the Palestinians necessarily counts as either antisemitism or Islamophobia. There is, in fact, much more scope for 'distasteful' and 'offensive', though legitimate and lawful comment on both sides, than many are prepared to accept.

A disturbing example of false accusations of anti-Arab prejudices with undercurrents of alleged Islamophobia connected with this crisis erupted at the University of Toronto (UofT).[23] On 16 October 2023, a shadowy, hitherto unknown group, calling itself 'Students Against Discrimination' (SAD), launched a petition demanding that the university investigate, and take 'appropriate disciplinary action' against one of its academic staff, Dr Stuart Kamenetsky, a Professor of Psychology, for posts SAD claimed violated UofT's Code of Conduct. According to the petition, these were 'offensive', 'misleading', and 'discriminated against Arab students', painting 'us as violent terrorists and savages – a gross misrepresentation that fosters an environment of fear and hostility'.[24] UofT's Prohibited Discrimination and Discriminatory Harassment policy, which follows the Ontario Human Rights Code, states that behaviour including 'threatening or offensive comments', may violate the right to equal non-discriminatory treatment by creating a poisonous environment in the workplace. Academic and non-academic administrators at UofT are also required to create and nurture a learning space free from discrimination and harassment. The petition, promoted on a student Reddit page and 'Fire Kamenetsky' hashtag, garnered nearly 2,500 signatures

---

[23] S. Kamenetsky, 'Universities in Crisis | Opinion: There is no academic freedom for Jewish faculty at the University of Toronto', *Fathom*, November 2023.
[24] Ibid.

in a month. Kamenetsky claims also to have received 'threatening' voicemails and emails. And, in a ten-item list, students involved in a walkout, staged on 29 January 2024 by pro-Palestinian groups, demanded that he be officially investigated by the UofT.

Since 2013, Kamenetsky's personal Facebook account has included expressions of support for Israel. However, the more recent controversy was triggered by a screenshot of a LinkedIn post he shared, featuring a cartoon from *Charlie Hebdo*, the satirical French magazine. A bald man with a long black beard, wearing a gown or robe and a green headband, stands with blood-stained hands in front of an empty washbasin. The speech bubble says: 'Such barbarians!' and the headline caption reads: 'Israel has shut off water supply to Gaza'. In an op-ed, published in November 2023 by the journal *Fathom* – which promotes 'a deeper understanding of Israel and the region' – Kamenetsky claimed that the cartoon was a 'caricature of a Hamas terrorist (typical green headband for clear identification with Islamic extremism) attempting to wash his bloody hands'. In an email to *The Varsity*, he also said that his posts were not directed at Arabs or Muslims in general but specifically at 'Hamas, terrorism, authoritarian regimes and media bias'. He claimed as well that, having been asked by Muslim students to remove the controversial posts, he had done so. *The Varsity* confirmed that it had not found any on his Facebook page.

Kamenetsky further stated that he values all lives, that he has been promoting human rights for his entire career, and that his 'heart bleeds' for 'all innocent lives lost in any conflict'. Describing the petition as a 'witch hunt consistent with cancel culture trying to silence me', he claimed that there had been a 'nuanced conversation' about the post on the Reddit platform. He also repeated his complaint that the UofT lacked commitment to academic freedom for staff expressing support for Israel particularly those who are themselves Jewish. While Kamenetsky acknowledged that the Hamas cartoon could be seen as 'distasteful', he argued that ultimately it was part of an important dialogue that the university should protect. In an email to *The Varsity*, a UofT spokesperson stated that the university is committed to supporting all members of its community impacted by Kamenetsky's posts and by the current violence in the Middle East. It encouraged those affected to get in touch if they needed support.

Professor Kamenetsky has not been investigated nor denounced by the UofT. He has instead simply been shunned. This has included an absence of any replies from senior university administrators to emails notifying them about the social media campaign demanding that he be investigated. Little official support has been forthcoming from his own department either, although he says the chair 'finally stepped up' after a Palestinian student complained that, in spite of never having met him, she felt unsafe taking any of his classes. Having contacted Kamenetsky, campus police provided protection for the first few weeks of the spring term 2024 including when the walkout was in progress. But, apart from ongoing social media animosity towards him, there were no other incidents. Having received legal advice that there were no grounds for litigation against either the UofT or the campaigners, Professor Kamenetsky has taken no further official action. The controversy, therefore, appears to have run its course. But as he said in an email to the author of this study – echoing sentiments that would be shared by most if not all in his position – 'something died inside of me with respect to my (adult) life-long relationship with the University and even my colleagues. With the exception of the Jewish ones and relatively few non-Jewish colleagues, none of whom were from my department, they failed to offer any support including, whatever their politics, on a personal level as colleagues and friends'.

Collin May

In September 2022, following an accusation of Islamophobia, Collin May was dismissed from his post as Director of the Alberta Human Rights Commission and Tribunal (AHRC).[25] In common with many of those against whom such allegations are made, May is an unlikely Islamophobe. He is a fully qualified lawyer, Adjunct Lecturer in Community Health Sciences at the University of Calgary, and a human rights activist focussing on LGBTQ+ rights, health equity issues relating to indigenous and elderly people, and academic freedom. He also has degrees in political philosophy, religion – specializing in medieval Islamic, Jewish and Christian thought – and in law, from Harvard University, the École des hautes études en sciences sociales (Paris), Dalhousie Law School, and the University of Alberta. From 1997 to 2002, he worked with the United Nations International Telecommunications Union and then the Geneva-based International Committee of the Red

---

[25] G. Brahm, 'Bibliophobia: The Cancellation of Collin May, an Interview', *Telos*, 19 January 2024; AHA Foundation, 'Fired Over a Book Review: What the Collin May Case Reveals About Academic Freedom', 21 July 2025.

Cross/Red Crescent. In addition to the AHRC, he also served on several boards and other tribunals including the Board of Directors of the Canadian Institute of Workplace Harassment and Violence which seeks to protect members of minority communities and women from bullying and violence at work.

The campaign to unseat May, an openly gay conservative, began in the spring of 2022 not long after he was appointed by Alberta's Premier, Jason Kenney, of the United Conservative Party (UCP), as Chief of the AHRC. The left-wing Alberta New Democratic Party (NDP) was quick to denounce the appointment as an attempt by the UCP to further its political agenda. That July, Duncan Kinney, an NDP-affiliated blogger, publicized a review by May, published in 2009, of *Islamic Imperialism: A History* (Yale University Press, 2006), by Efraim Karsh, a distinguished though controversial history professor at King's College London. As May, a serious student of Islam who denies being an Islamophobe, states: 'Both my review and Professor Karsh's book were characterized as being "Islamophobic," racist, and hate speech. My review was even linked to violence against black Muslim women in hijab in Alberta more than ten years after its publication'.[26]

He adds that in the review:

> 'I noted that Professor Karsh, in his own non-orientalist approach, referred to Islam as a highly imperialist and militaristic religion. The NDP-affiliated blogger who wrote the first piece on my review wrongly attributed this view to me while ignoring the context and nuances of my review. Indeed, he ignored the very next sentence following my statement of Karsh's position, which started with the words: "But we need to be careful here . . . ." As it turns out, none of my critics were even remotely careful when it came to attacking me'.

As Chapter 2 of this study demonstrates, views such as that expressed by Karsh and many others have been endorsed by scholars and commentators in a centuries-old debate featuring Muslims, ex-Muslims and non-Muslims.

Denunciation of May from Canadian Muslim leaders soon followed. Faisal Bhabha, a law professor at Toronto's York University, questioned his commitment to 'combating Islamophobia', while Imam Sadique Pathan of Edmonton's Al Rashid Mosque, accused him of 'binary thinking' and of

---

[26] Brahm, 'Bibliophobia.'

engaging in 'Islamophobia or outright racist views towards Muslims'.[27] May also complained to the University of Calgary, University of Alberta, and Mount Royal University about derogatory statements relating to his sexuality and competence made by a minority of faculty. Citing 'academic freedom', he says, nothing was done about it. Joining the pile-on, the University of Calgary Muslim Student Association (UCMSO) signed a letter calling for his dismissal from the AHRC. Claiming that the review was 'stereotyping' and 'hurtful', the National Council of Canadian Muslims (NCCM), an Islamist organization, also demanded that May be dismissed. As required by Premier Kenney, May agreed to meet them to discuss their concerns. But he refused to apologize. In September 2022, he was sacked from the AHRC ostensibly for having failed to prioritize meetings with the Muslim community and for threatening to sue his critics for defamation.

In 2024 May described the impact of the Islamophobia accusation in the following terms:

> 'Shortly after I was terminated, my partner and I lost our home, and each developed health issues. That my partner had worked for former NDP Premier Rachel Notley for four years and that I personally knew many of the Alberta NDP MLAs who were now calling me racist and a purveyor of hate speech, made the betrayal all the more bitter. Added to this was the sheer injustice of the experience'.[28]

He added that his determination to fight back had been boosted by the support he received from many quarters including Jews, Muslims, immigrants, and the LGBTQ+ community. For example, in a press release, Raheel Raza, president of *Muslims Facing Tomorrow*, a Muslim organization dedicated to fighting Islamism, condemned the NCCM's actions and called for May to be reinstated as AHRC chief.

Represented by the Lawfare Project, and law firm Zacharias Vickers McCann LLP, May is suing the government of Alberta for unfair dismissal, plus the NCCM and Duncan Kinney for defamation. He claims that the accusations are part of a broader campaign to silence individuals who criticize Islam even in a scholarly context. Benjamin Ryberg, Chief Operating Officer of the Lawfare Project, emphasized that the lawsuit is not simply intended to

---

[27] *The Hub*, 28 June 2024.
[28] J. George, 'Ex-Human Rights Chief Sues Canadian Muslim Organization for Defamation', *Focus on Western Islamism*, 1 May 2025.

restore their client's reputation, but is also 'crucial in defending the integrity of public discourse and ensuring that scholarly and intellectual freedom are not undermined by defamatory accusations of Islamophobia designed to intimidate and silence'.[29]

In a press release Ryberg added that, if the claim were to proceed to trial, it was likely that critical scrutiny would be brought to bear upon the term 'Islamophobia' which, he said, critics maintain has been weaponized by Islamist groups to discourage scrutiny of their agenda and their allegedly questionable financial practices. On 21 May 2025, it was announced that Collin May had been appointed Senior Fellow at the Frontier Centre for Public Policy, an independent Canadian centre-right public policy think tank.

The United Kingdom

In her review of threats to social cohesion, Dame Sara Khan found that:

'In recent years, public debate over freedom of speech in higher education has intensified. Some argue that there is now a climate of censorship in UK universities, with others believing that universities struggle to know how to protect free speech while also upholding equality legislation, preventing discrimination and restricting hateful narratives that can threaten cohesion … In the cases we heard, the institutional response to threats and censorship was either entirely lacking or too slow to be of any real effect. Academics repeatedly reported feeling left on their own by their employers due to weak leadership, a lack of support from their institution and no knowledge of where to turn for support. Instead, they were often left to deal with the consequences of finding themselves being cancelled or harassed'.[30]

Amongst the most prominent false accusations of Islamophobia in this context are those concerning Maryam Namazie, Kate Smurthwaite, Jordan Peterson, a proposed Centre for the Study of Political Islam at the University of Bradford, and the author of this study.

No-platforming

In 2015, ex-Muslim secularist, human rights campaigner and long-term

---

[29] Ibid.
[30] Khan, *Threats to Social Cohesion,* p. 150.

critic of political Islam, Maryam Namazie, joined the long list of invited speakers 'no-platformed' by student unions. In her case this occurred at the University of Warwick and it was on the grounds that her talk could 'incite hatred' against Muslim students. [31] Later that year, during a lecture at Goldsmiths College London, members of the Islamic Society disrupted Ms Namazie's presentation by heckling, turning off her slides – which included a *Jesus and Mo* cartoon – and creating what she described as a 'climate of intimidation'. One of those in attendance made a gesture resembling a death threat. After the event, describing Namazie as a 'known Islamophobe', Goldsmiths' Feminist and LGBTQ+ Societies issued statements in solidarity with the protestors. [32]

A charity performance by feminist comedian Kate Smurthwaite at Goldsmiths was also sabotaged by an organised boycott. Opponents booked all available tickets in advance then failed to attend. The protest was justified online as a response to her 'transphobic, whore-phobic and Islamophobic' views. As Smurthwaite noted, 'Every time this comes up I say, "Send me an example." Their example of Islamophobia is when I have quoted the Council of Ex-Muslims of Britain'. [33]

The proposed Bradford Centre for the Study of Political Islam

In 2015, the University of Bradford decided to establish a Centre for the Study of Political Islam in its world-renowned Department for Peace Studies and International Development. Trailed as an exercise in seeking to understand political Islam in the context of peace and reconciliation, a full consultation was carried out, funding was pledged, and approval was received from the University's senior management. The launch was scheduled to take place in the House of Lords in the UK parliament in December that year. [34]

However, within a week of the despatch of invitations, local Muslim 'community leaders' expressed their opposition to the project, particularly the

---

[31] 'Maryam Namazie secular activist barred from speaking at Warwick University over fears of inciting hatred against Muslim students', *The Independent*, 28 September 2015.

[32] 'Goldsmiths Islamic Society students disrupt human rights activist's speech', *Evening Standard*,

[33] 'Feminist comedian's charity gig sabotaged by opponents', *Mail Online*, 31 March 2016.

[34] Khan, *Threats to Social Cohesion*, pp. 47-8.

use of the term 'political Islam'. In response, the University organised an event to which local Muslim activists were invited. The aims and objectives of the proposed centre were fully explained. It was also pointed out that 'political Islam' is an entirely legitimate field of academic study and research. Many who attended the meeting were satisfied with this information. But others remained opposed to the establishment of the Centre.

A campaign of intimidation and fear quickly followed. Leaflets were distributed in Bradford mosques, and messages were posted on social media sites and WhatsApp, calling for a boycott of the University on the grounds that the proposed centre would 'demonize, stereotype and alienate' Muslims. Flyers threatened that if the University continued with its 'Islamophobic ideology', protests would be organised at, ironically, its Peace Garden. Activists encouraged others to write to one of the senior female academics involved with the Centre, who later told the Khan Review that the protesters 'did not appreciate' that the Centre was 'an academic endeavour'. Having found her name, photo, and details had been published on a flyer widely distributed to local Muslim communities, she was told that a British-based Islamist extremist group 'had her contact details' and that she 'should be very careful'.[35] As a precaution, she started to arrive for work at different times and to park her car in different parts of the campus. The academic chosen to lead the Centre also received threats and hostile phone calls from anonymous callers. He too changed his working hours and had signs removed from his office door so that his whereabouts could not easily be discovered. Another senior member of staff involved with the project told the Khan Review that some Muslims in Bradford supported and welcomed the proposed Centre and disagreed with the complaints of the so-called 'community leaders', who, they claimed, 'acted like they owned the University'.

Concerned about the possibility of harm to staff, damage to the University's reputation, and the prospect of on-going noisy protests disrupting life and safety on campus, the University's senior management team decided not to establish the Centre after all. Those involved with the proposal told Dame Sara Khan that they were deeply disappointed by the lack of support from local political leaders and institutions who had failed publicly to defend the University and the right to academic freedom.

---

[35] Ibid.

Jordan Peterson – the Cambridge controversy

Jordan Peterson – a Psychology Professor at the University of Toronto, author, and media commentator, who describes himself as a classical British liberal and traditionalist – began to receive attention in the late 2010s for his 'anti-woke' views on cultural and political issues. While these mostly concern sex and gender he has also been accused of Islamophobia.

For example, in March 2019, the University of Cambridge cancelled a two-month Visiting Fellowship Peterson had been offered by its Faculty of Divinity during which he planned to write lectures on stories found in the Old Testament Book of Exodus. His appointment had prompted protest from Cambridge students and academics opposed to his views. However, the decision to revoke the Visiting Fellowship was expressly taken because the Faculty had seen a photograph of Peterson with his arm around a supporter wearing a tee shirt stating: 'I'm a proud Islamaphobe (sic)'. This may either have been a defiant assertion by the person wearing the tee-shirt, of genuine anti-Muslim prejudice, or an ironic reference to the fact that any criticism of Muslims or Islam is currently likely to be regarded as Islamophobic. But, however it may be interpreted, there is no evidence that Peterson endorsed the slogan. Nevertheless, the Faculty of Divinity declared that such sentiments were 'antithetical to the work of a Faculty that prides itself in the advancement of inter-faith understanding'.[36] However, in 2021 it was reported that the University had revoked the cancellation of Peterson's Visiting Fellowship and that he would, after all, spend between 10 days and two weeks there attending seminars, talks and other engagements.[37]

That September, Professor Stephen Toope, the Vice-Chancellor of the University of Cambridge, announced that he would resign in 2022, five years into what was expected to have been a seven-year term, ostensibly to spend more time with his family. The Peterson affair was only one of a number of controversies which caused division in the Cambridge academic community leading to criticism from outsiders.[38]

---

[36]   https://www.cam.ac.uk/news/rescindment-of-visiting-fellowship-statement-from-vice-chancellor-professor-stephen-j-toope.

[37] B. Moss, 'Controversial professor Jordan Peterson to return to Cambridge after being disinvited in 2019', *Varsity*, 1 October 2021.

[38] D. Murray, 'Farewell to Cambridge's disastrous Vice-Chancellor', *The Spectator*, 20 September 2021.

In 2023, an Ontario court upheld a ruling from the College of Psychologists of Ontario that some of Peterson's public statements were unprofessional. As a result, he was required to undergo social media training. Peterson has undeniably made some critical remarks about Islam and Muslims. Nevertheless, on 13 July 2022, he released a 6-minute video on YouTube entitled 'Message to Muslims', which encourages them to strive to make their faith a model for humanity, to heal the divisions with each other, and to reach out to Christians and Jews. To facilitate this, he suggests the construction of a dedicated website.[39]

The BRISOC scandal

The BRISOC scandal provides yet another illustration of the relationship between false accusations of Islamophobia and Islamophobia-phobia, fully documented in my book, *Falsely Accused of Islamophobia: My Struggle Against Academic Cancellation.*[40] The controversy began in mid-February 2021 when the University of Bristol Islamic Society (BRISOC) launched a potentially life-threatening social media campaign to have me sacked as Professor of Human Rights at the University of Bristol Law School. Multiple counts of Islamophobic expression in my teaching and other public output were alleged. Accompanied by my photo, BRISOC's online petition which eventually garnered over 4,000 signatures, demanded that I apologise 'to all Muslim students'. And if I refused, the University was called upon to discipline me, including by dismissal. BRISOC also insisted upon the scrapping of the Islam, China, and the Far East module on my Human Rights in Law, Politics and Society (HRLPS) course, each of which I had been teaching for nearly a decade and a half with the full approval of the Law School and the consistent praise of students and external examiners. As one Muslim commentator put it: 'In the name of fighting *Islamophobia* and discrimination ... (BRISOC) .... basically want to stop any critical discussion of the Islamic tradition, both from within and without'.[41] After an exhaustive five-month official University inquiry, I was unequivocally exonerated of all charges, a verdict unanimously upheld on appeal in October 2021. The

---

[39] https://www.youtube.com/watch?v=7pd0HLeYKsE
[40] Academica Press, 2023.
[41] A. Alam, 'Controversy over Bristol University Professor Steven Greer's "Islamophobia": Why Critical Discussion of Islamic Tradition Should Not Be Snubbed', *New Age Islam*, 26 February 2021.

University of Bristol nevertheless succumbed to a bout of Islamophobia-phobia considered further below.

As the University's inquiry was being conducted, BRISOC's social media campaign – which, in spite of my retirement in September 2022, has yet officially to end – augmented the list of bogus accusations made in their official complaint, including several manifest lies. The latter included the allegation that I regard the Chinese repression of the Uighurs as merely 'superficially discriminatory' when the relevant Powerpoint slide clearly indicated the opposite.[42] They also claim that I had mocked and laughed at the Qur'an when it was in fact an extract from the *Analects of Confucius* that prompted some laughter from the class.[43]

These issues aside, the principal allegations in BRISOC's formal complaint were that it is Islamophobic to claim, as they alleged I had, that: 1. Islam lacks a single institution to interpret the faith; 2. the Qur'an is non-narrative, non-systematic, and non-chronological and was originally addressed, in an elusive and elliptical style, to people already familiar with its message; 3. Islam spread rapidly through war, conquest, trade, and conversion; 4. Islamic law is uncompromisingly individualistic and is fundamentally based on submission and the performance of obligations not rights; 5. the source of political authority in Islam is revelation not reason; 6. jihadi terrorism is 'Islamist'; 7. Islam is hostile to the modern conception of democracy; 8. historically Islam was a progressive faith insofar as it was open to all; 9. the *Charlie Hebdo* massacre illustrates how the traditional Islamic death penalty for blasphemy can be exacted by self-appointed executioners; 10. Britain's counterterrorism programme Prevent is not Islamophobic or racist.[44]

Statements 1-6 are simply statements of fact universally acknowledged in the authoritative literature as recounted in previous chapters of this study. As such, none expresses anti-Muslim prejudice. The remainder are matters of opinion. But not mine. They are opinions widely discussed in the authoritative literature and by other responsible commentators. It is particularly bewildering how item 8, which is complimentary about Islam, could possibly be regarded as Islamophobic. Using the *Charlie Hebdo* massacre as an

---

[42] Greer, *Falsely Accused of Islamophobia*, p. 261.
[43] Ibid., p. 43-44.
[44] Ibid., Ch. 3.

illustration of the potentially fatal consequences of blasphemy in traditional Islam, cannot credibly be regarded as Islamophobic either for two reasons. As Chapter 4 discusses, blasphemy has long been, and still is, punishable by death in many parts of the Muslim world, including by mobs and free-lancers claiming no authority but their own. Second, how such conduct may be regarded by the various streams and schools of Islam is also precisely the kind of question an undergraduate lecture might justifiably flag up for further exploration in a seminar, as was my purpose.

BRISOC claims my analyses of jihadi terrorism and the UK's counterterrorist Prevent programme are also Islamophobic and racist. I do indeed maintain that jihadi terrorism is Islamist by nature and not by Islamophobic attribution, and that Prevent is not systematically discriminatory, racist, Islamophobic, or anti-democratic, nor does it systematically violate human rights. I also maintain that anyone, and not just Muslims, should be targeted by Prevent if evidence-based concerns arise that they may be vulnerable to recruitment into terrorism. These issues are not only addressed earlier in this chapter but are also thoroughly discussed in my book, *Tackling Terrorism in Britain: Threats, Responses and Challenges Twenty Years After 9/11*.[45]

BRISOC also alleges that I was guilty of Islamophobia for having claimed that Islam and human rights are incompatible. This is simply untrue. I have, in fact, publicly distinguished three positions about the relationship between Islam and human rights: the human rights ideal is western, un-Islamic, and does not fit a Muslim context at all well, a view held both by some western commentators and by conservative Muslims; an Islamic conception of human rights was revealed to Muslims by God long before the west manufactured its deviant version, a view held only by some Muslims; and Islamic and non-Islamic approaches to human rights, though different, are not inherently irreconcilable, the view I personally take.[46]

Instead of defending me from these false allegations, and in spite of my unequivocal exoneration, the University of Bristol nevertheless chose to curry favour with BRISOC when it should instead have disciplined those involved in their potentially life-threatening campaign. In September 2021, the Islam,

---

[45] Routledge, 2022.

[46] 'Islamofauxbia – The Smearing of Steven Greer', *Concrete Milkshake*, 22 February 2021.

China and the Far East module was removed from the syllabus of HRLPS, expressly to avoid further student complaints. Following the unanimous rejection of BRISOC's case, in October 2021, the University then publicly acknowledged my vindication. But, in doing so, it nevertheless undermined the verdict of its own inquiry by stating that it 'recognised' BRISOC's 'concerns' and that HRLPS needed to be revised in order, amongst other things, to respect the sensitivities of students taking it.[47] The University has, however, signally failed to explain how and why these 'sensitivities' became more acute in 2020-21 and thereafter, than at any other point in the previous decade and a half, particularly since nothing of substance had changed over the relevant period and that the unit had been positively audited on an annual basis by students and external examiners.

Instead of having capitulated to BRISOC's demands, the University should have swiftly rejected the formal complaint on any of the many procedural and substantive defects from which it suffered, publicly announced this result, and warned the students involved that there would be disciplinary consequences in the event of a campaign against this outcome and/or against me.

As a direct result of the BRISOC scandal, in the autumn of 2021, I became Visiting Research Fellow, and later Research Director, at the Oxford Institute for British Islam, an independent progressive Muslim think-tank. In 2023 the publication of my book, *Falsely Accused of Islamophobia*, and my story were also reported by media outlets with a global readership/audience of 231 million. Amongst other things, this led to a call from Labour MP, Barry Sheerman, for the Vice-Chancellor of the University, Professor Evelyn Welch, and the entire senior management team, to resign. Needless to say they declined to do so.

It had been my intention to lodge a formal complaint about the University's mishandling of the BRISOC scandal with the Office for Students (OfS, the universities' regulator) under a new scheme due to come into operation in August that year. Following the election of a Labour government in 2024, its introduction was, however, delayed by Bridget Phillipson, the newly appointed Secretary of State for Education. Responding to considerable protest, Ms Phillipson, however, reversed this decision. As a result, a pared

---

[47] University of Bristol, 'University statement regarding complaint against Professor Steven Greer', 8 October 2021.

down version, eventually including a revived individual complaints process, will be introduced after all. But it is unlikely to come into operation until the end of the decade. In April 2025, the OfS fined the University of Sussex £585,000 for governance and managerial failures which led, in 2021, to Professor Kathleen Stock being hounded out of her job by an angry mob which accused her of 'transphobia'. On 16 June 2025, twelve free speech and minority religious organizations[48] referred the BRISOC scandal to the OfS on the grounds that it bears a striking resemblance to the Sussex case and that there are no good reasons for the OfS not to treat them in the same manner.

In common with most if not all student Islamic societies, the University of Bristol Islamic Society (BRISOC) is affiliated with the Federation of Islamic Student Societies (FoSIS). Concerns have been raised that FoSIS is financially supported by foreign Muslim activists including states hostile to the west. On 18 October, Arif Ahmed, Director of Academic Freedom and Free Speech at the OfS told *The Times Higher* that universities should take 'very strong steps' to address such interference, including by imposing 'very severe sanctions on students' found to be involved in it.[49] The University of Bristol did precisely the opposite in the BRISOC case, the self-censoring reverberations of which continue uncorrected and unabated. There is, therefore, not only an unanswerable case for the OfS to investigate the BRISOC scandal, but there are also compelling reasons for it to investigate the activities of FoSIS as well.

Conclusion

All the false accusations of Islamophobia discussed in this chapter involved teachers or academics seeking to engage in legitimate and lawful discussions with their students and others about Muslims and Islam which would not have raised an eyebrow had they been about any other faith or its adherents. They each follow a familiar pattern. Baseless accusations are amplified by self-appointed 'Muslim representatives' and others demanding

---

[48] Academics for Academic Freedom, Alumni for Free Speech, Committee on Academic Freedom, Council of Ex-Muslims of Britain, Christian Concern, Don't Divide Us, Free Speech Union, Network of Sikh Organizations, Oxford Institute for British Islam, Oxford Islamic Congregation, Project Resist, Global Hindu Federation.
[49] J. Grove, 'Students caught spying should face "severe sanctions," says Ahmed', *Times Higher Education*, 17 October 2025.

on social media, apology and/or disciplining, potentially creating risks to the life and physical safety of those concerned. Insinuating that the charges are valid, the institution in question, rapidly issues an abject apology, instigates an investigation and suspends the hapless victim. Other institutions with responsibilities to protect those exposed to the ire of vicious online mobs, including the police, typically either fail to take the issue seriously, distance themselves from it, publicly disown the victim who is then left struggling to survive with little or no hope of rebuilding a ruined professional life. In most cases, those wrongly accused are also ostracised and shunned by their colleagues who, at best, conveniently look the other way rather than rising to their defence. Some may even join the baying mob. And even if, and when, exoneration eventually arrives, a great deal of irremediable and enduring personal harm will have been caused both to the direct victim and to their nearest and dearest. The resulting climate of intimidation also deters others from taking the risk of finding themselves in the same position. These should be matters of grave concern for anyone who takes academic freedom and free speech seriously.

Chapter 10

Defining Islamophobic expression

Introduction

It is said that the term 'Islamophobia' was first coined by French colonial officials in the 19th century and appeared later in an essay by Alain Quellien in 1910.[1] But it did not gain much traction until *The Satanic Verses* controversy in 1988, discussed more fully in Chapter 7. Strictly speaking, a 'phobia' is not just an aversion, but a clinically observable anxiety disorder defined by recurrent and excessive fear of an object or situation. The suffix has, however, been appended to a range of nouns indicating individual and/or collective prejudice towards various minorities – for example, homosexuals (homophobia), foreigners (xenophobia), transexuals (transphobia), and Islam/Muslims (Islamophobia).

In addition to sloganized and highly partisan contributions from campaigning organizations, there is now a substantial and expanding academic literature on 'Islamophobia'. At least one journal and numerous books are devoted to the subject.[2] These tend to rest upon three key assumptions. First, the west is, and has always been, hostile towards Muslims and Islam.[3] Second, this is the result of deeply entrenched racism and prejudice in a symbiotic relationship with imperialism and colonialism. Third,

---

[1] P. Bruckner (trans. by S. Rendell and L. Neal), *An Imaginary Racism: Islamophobia and Guilt* (Wiley, 2018), pp. 2-5. A. Doyle, *The End of Woke: How the Culture War Went Too Far and What to Expect from the Counter-Revolution* (Constable, 2025), p. 156.

[2] See, eg, J. Esposito & I. Kalin (eds.), *Islamophobia: The Challenge of Pluralism in the 21st Century* (Oxford University Press, 2011); N. Massoumi, G. Mills & D. Miller (eds), *What is Islamophobia?: Racism, Social Movements and the State* (Pluto Press, 2017); P. Morey, A. Yaqin & A. Forte (eds), *Contesting Islamophobia: Anti-Muslim Prejudice in Media, Culture and Politics* (I. B. Taurus, 2018).

[3] See eg, T. Hussain, *Muslim Europe: A Journey in Search of a Fourteen Year History* (Viking, 2025).

following the events of 9/11, hostility towards Muslims and Islam has been turbo-charged by the 'war on terror'.[4]

However, as indicated in previous chapters, for several reasons, this is a contested thesis.[5] For one thing, as noted in Chapter 1, it is highly unlikely that there would be a debate in the contemporary west about Islamophobia at all had it not been for the visceral reaction of some Muslims and others to the publication of *The Satanic Verses* in 1988, the onset of jihadi terrorism and its consequences particularly since 9/11 in 2001, the explosion of 'cancel culture' in the west over the past decade or so, the growing public controversy in the UK about immigrants and asylum-seekers most of whom come from predominantly Muslim countries, and the sharp rise in anti-Muslim and antisemitic hatred since the wars in the middle east erupted in the aftermath of the invasion of Israel by Hamas on 7 October 2023.

Those who claim that Europe's 'intrinsic Islamophobia' is encoded in its DNA, fuelled by western imperialism and colonialism, typically fail to observe several inconvenient truths. First, in its heartlands, Islam has itself been deeply imperialistic for much of its history. As also already noted, some Muslims have criticized the more conservative interpretations of their own faith, not infrequently in terms which would be denounced as Islamophobic if expressed by anyone else. Non-Muslim contributions to the centuries-old debate about the pros and cons of Islam have also spanned a spectrum between hostility at one end, and admiration at the other, with various more nuanced positions, including 'active curiosity' and 'respectful engagement', in between. For centuries, some Muslims have themselves harboured racial and other social prejudices. According to Said ibn Ahmad, an 11th century judge, for example, Europeans are closer to beasts than humans and lack 'keenness of understanding and clarity of intelligence and are overcome by ignorance and apathy, lack of discernment and stupidity'. Also in the 11th century, Avicenna, amongst other things, the father of modern medicine, believed that

---

[4] See, eg E. Said, *Orientalism* (Penguin, 2003) and *Covering Islam: How the Media and the Experts Determine How We See the Rest of the World* (Vintage, Fully Revised Edition, 1997); L. Fekete, *A Suitable Enemy: Racism, Migration and Islamophobia in Europe* (Pluto, 2009); D. Kumar, *Islamophobia and the Politics of Empire:20 years after 9/11* (Verso, 2021).

[5] K. Malik, *From Fatwa to Jihad: How the World Changed: The Satanic Verses to Charlie Hebdo* (Atlantic Books, 2010); Bruckner, *An Imaginary Racism*; G. Kepel, *Jihad: The Trail of Political Islam* (I.B.Taurus, 2009). F. Halliday, *Islam and the Myth of Confrontation: Religion and Politics in the Middle East* (I.B.Taurus, 2003).

Africans are 'slaves by nature' and according to Ibn Khaldun, one of the greatest medieval philosophers, they are comparable to 'dumb animals'.[6] Antisemitic tropes are also commonplace in the contemporary Arab world including the mainstream media.[7]

Numerous definitions of Islamophobia, typically inadequately distinguished from 'Islamophobic expression', have also been offered.[8] Up to 2025, the most influential ones in Britain were those provided by the Runnymede Trust in 1997 and 2017, and by the All-Party Parliamentary Group on British Muslims in 2018. Various factors, not least the electoral challenge posed in several Labour held constituencies arising from controversy about the invasion of Israel by Hamas on 7 October 2023, prompted the government to seek yet another definition in 2025.

Several observations can be made about the dozen or so other contenders. Terms such as 'hatred', 'dislike', 'fear', 'prejudice', 'aversion', 'provocation', 'intolerance', and 'hostility' are often employed to characterize the negativity involved. Some definitions add the qualifier that this should be 'contrived', 'irrational' or 'exaggerated'. Others include certain manifestations beyond mere expression, such as 'abusive behaviour', 'threats of violence', 'damage to and desecration of property', 'assault', 'extreme violence', 'nullifying or impairing the recognition, enjoyment or exercise, on an equal footing, of human rights and fundamental freedoms in the political, economic, social, cultural or any other field of public life', 'unequal treatment', 'exclusion from major political and social spheres', 'bias', 'discrimination', 'marginalization from social, political, and civic life', 'threatening conduct', 'harassment', 'incitement', and 'intimidation'. More than half link Islamophobia to racism.

However, even the most influential definitions of the narrower accusation of 'Islamophobic expression' suffer from several fatal flaws. None offers a clear statement of the essentials of contemporary mainstream Muslim beliefs, practices and conduct against which the offending expression could be assessed. Each also conspicuously fails to consider the legal and human rights landscape which any official, particularly a legal definition should observe.

---

[6] J. Marozzi, 'Does Europe have "anti-Muslim DNA,"' *The Times*, 13 December 2025.
[7] R. Mazza, 'Muslim Attitudes to Jews and Israel – edited by Moshe Ma'oz' (2011) 20 *Digest of Middle East Studies*, 132-135.
[8] See H. Singh, *Islamophobia' revisited* (Civitas, 2023), pp. 22-24; All Party Parliamentary Group on British Muslims (APPG), *Islamophobia defined: The inquiry into a working definition of Islamophobia*, 27 November 2018, pp. 23-25.

And, while lip service is typically paid to the fact that not all criticism of Muslims and Islam is Islamophobic, there has also been little attempt to identify clearly where the line should be drawn. Plenty of examples of alleged Islamophobic expression have been offered but little if any regarding lawful and legitimate critique. Nor do any of the current definitions consider the developing crisis involving false accusations of Islamophobic expression or how the 'lived experience' of ex-Muslims should be accommodated. Those definitions which include hostility towards non-Muslims misidentified as Muslim, are also massively over-inclusive, confused, and particularly unhelpful because, typically, it is not clear if the antagonism in question stems from the religion, or some other characteristic of the victim, their appearance, for example.

The Runnymede definitions

In 1997 the Runnymede Trust, a British racial equality and civil rights think tank, published a 70-page consultative report by the Commission on British Muslims and Islamophobia, *Islamophobia: A Challenge For Us All.* [9] This, the first sustained exploration of the then relatively newly-identified phenomenon, was launched that November by Labour Home Secretary, Jack Straw. In 2017, coinciding with the 20th anniversary, Runnymede published an updated report, *Islamophobia: Still a challenge for us all.* [10]

The 1997 report

The 1997 report, the bulk of which concerns Islamophobia-by-deed rather than by-word (see Chapter 1), is serious, thoughtful, and sincere. Many of its recommendations – including those concerning outlawing religious discrimination, making incitement to religious hatred an offence, and that the offence of blasphemy should be reviewed – have since been implemented. A welcome distinction is also drawn between 'prejudice' and 'discrimination', the latter typically a tangible consequence of the former. Of considerable importance for present purposes, the authors also acknowledge that it is 'not

---

[9] G. Conway, *Islamophobia – A Challenge For Us All: Report of the Runnymede Trust Commission on British Muslims and Islamophobia* (Runnymede, 1997).
[10] E. Ehahi & O. Khan (eds.), *Islamophobia: Still a challenge for us all* (Runnymede, 2017).

intrinsically phobic or prejudiced ... to disagree with or to disapprove of Muslim beliefs, laws or practices', not least because adherents to other religions, as well as 'agnostics and secular humanists', have long done so.[11] Nor is it Islamophobic robustly to criticise and to oppose the attitude of some Muslims towards the west, the policies and practices of Muslim states and regimes (particularly regarding the position of women and on other democratic and human rights grounds), or to condemn movements and organizations claiming Islamic justifications for terrorist campaigns. Significantly, and as noted in Chapters 2-5 of this book, the report reminds readers that such debates, arguments and disagreements take place between Muslims as they do between Muslims and others.[12]

Having acknowledged this, the discussion about how Islamophobia should be defined also begins well. Recognising that the term is 'not ideal', and drawing a parallel with how the concept of 'antisemitism' evolved, the authors state that 'Islamophobia' refers to 'a new reality' of 'unfounded hostility towards Islam', including 'unfair discrimination against Muslim individuals and communities, and to the exclusion of Muslims from mainstream political and social affairs'.[13] But, as Hasan points out: 'If the term is not ideal, it was irresponsible to use it and a more suitable alternative – such as anti-Muslim prejudice/discrimination – should have been adopted' instead.[14]

The authors of the 1997 report also frame the central issue with respect to allegedly Islamophobic expression in precisely the same terms as this study: 'How, then, can one tell the difference between legitimate criticism and disagreement on the one hand and Islamophobia, or unfounded prejudice and hostility, on the other?'.[15]

a) Open and closed views

Regrettably, the report fails to provide a convincing answer. This is not lease not least because it is based upon the problematic distinction between 'open' and 'closed' views of Islam according to the following criteria:

---

[11] Conway, *Islamophobia*, p. 4.
[12] Ibid.
[13] Ibid., p. 4,
[14] R. Hasan, *Does 'Islamophobia' Curtail Free Speech?*, IEA Discussion Paper No. 12, September 2022, p. 8.
[15] Conway, *Islamophobia*, p. 4.

1. Monolithic/diverse; 2. Separate/interacting; 3. Inferior/different; 4. Enemy/partner; 5. Manipulative/sincere; 6. Criticism of West rejected/considered; 7. Discrimination defended/criticised; 8. Islamophobia seen as natural/problematic.[16]

'Open' views, exhibiting the following features, are said to include 'legitimate disagreement and criticism' plus 'appreciation and respect':[17]

'1. Islam seen as diverse and progressive, with internal differences, debates and development; 2. Islam seen as interdependent with other faiths and cultures – (a) having certain shared values and aims (b) affected by them (c) enriching them; 3. Islam seen as distinctively different, but not deficient, and as equally worthy of respect; 4. Islam seen as an actual or potential partner in joint cooperative enterprises and in the solution of shared problems; 5. Islam seen as a genuine religious faith, practised sincerely by its adherents; 6. Criticisms of 'the West' and other cultures are considered and debated; 7. Debates and disagreements with Islam do not diminish efforts to combat discrimination and exclusion; 8. Critical views of Islam are themselves subjected to critique lest they be inaccurate and unfair'.[18]

According to the report, 'phobic dread of Islam is the recurring characteristic' of 'closed' views which, in the following terms, the authors 'equate' with Islamophobia:

'1. Islam seen as a single monolithic bloc, static and unresponsive to new realities; 2. Islam seen as separate and other – (a) not having any aims or values in common with other cultures (b) not affected by them (c) not influencing them; 3. Islam seen as inferior to the West – barbaric, irrational, primitive, sexist; 4. Islam seen as violent, aggressive, threatening, supportive of terrorism, engaged in 'a clash of civilisations'; 5. Islam seen as a political ideology, used for political or military advantage; 6. Criticisms made by Islam of 'the West' rejected out of hand; 7. Hostility towards Islam used to justify discriminatory practices towards Muslims and exclusion of Muslims from mainstream society; 8 Anti-Muslim hostility accepted as natural and "normal."'[19]

---

[16] Ibid., p. 5.
[17] Ibid., p. 4.
[18] Ibid., p. 5.
[19] Ibid.

While the report does not regard Islamophobia as a species of racism, it, nevertheless, refers to Islamophobia as being 'mixed with racism', claims that a closed view of Islam has the effect of justifying racism, and that anti-Muslim sentiment tends to be combined with hostility towards immigrants and Asians.[20]

The authors' conception of Islamophobia, and the distinction between the 'open' and 'closed' perspectives in particular, are deeply flawed for several reasons. First, there is no attempt to state what Muslims in fact believe, how they practice their faith, and how they might otherwise behave. While this is common in contributions to the debate which seek to defend Islam from widely held criticisms, including in the authoritative literature,[21] it leads to a third problem – the failure to distinguish between Islamic orthodoxy, heterodoxy, and heresy. The report also subtly commits the very error of which the closed perspective quite rightly stands accused – treating Islam as a monolith, implicitly characterized by a westernized version marginal to the global faith and far from ascendant in Britain or any western country. This corresponds neatly to Shyrock's stereotype of the 'good Muslim' which, as he maintains, is as much a stereotype as the bad Muslim invoked by the Islamophobe. According to Shyrock the 'good Muslim':

> 'as a stereotype has common features: he tends to be Sufi (ideally one who reads Rumi); he is peaceful (and assures us that jihad is an inner, spiritual contest, not a struggle to "enjoin the good and forbid the wrong" through force of arms); he treats women as equals, and is committed to choice in matters of hijab wearing (and never advocates the covering of a woman's face); if he is a she, then she is highly educated, works outside the home, is her husband's only wife, chose her husband freely, and wears hijab (if at all) only because she wants to. The good Muslim is also a pluralist (recalls fondly the ecumenical values of medieval Andalusia and is a champion of interfaith activism); he is politically moderate (an advocate of democracy, human rights, and religious freedom, an opponent of armed conflict against the U.S. and Israel); finally he is likely to be an African, a south Asian, or, more likely still, an Indonesian or Malaysian; he is less likely to be an Arab, but as friends of the "good Muslim" will

---

[20] Ibid., pp. 9-10.
[21] See, eg T. Khan, *Muslim, Actually: How Islam is Misunderstood and Why it Matters* (Atlantic, 2022).

point out, only a small proportion of Muslims are Arabs anyway'.[22]

As recounted elsewhere in this study, Shyrock's 'good Muslim' is not typical of those who adhere to the mainstream faith, particularly beyond the west. Orthodox Islam is deeply conservative and, contrary to what Runnymede's open list assumes, not at all 'progressive'. Nor are all versions of the faith – especially those espoused by contemporary Islamist movements such as Al Qaeda, ISIS/DAESH, Boko Haram, Al Shabab etc – 'equally worthy of respect', or viable potential partners in 'joint cooperative enterprises', and/or in the 'solution of shared problems' with non-Muslims.[23] Critical views of Islam are also more likely to be denounced as Islamophobic by those who entertain the 'open' view, than as the report naively expects, 'subjected to critique lest they be inaccurate and unfair'.[24]

It can readily be conceded that, as far as specifics are concerned, any non-Muslim who endorses all the positions the Runnymede report characterizes as 'closed', particularly item 7, may well be regarded as an 'Islamophobe'. But not every item on this list is necessarily indicative of prejudiced hostility. Adhering to the sentiments in items 1, 2 and 5, as they stand, may involve factual errors. But, as Chapters 2-5 of this study demonstrate, it is not inconsistent with scholarly and wider debates to regard particularly the mainstream orthodox interpretation of Islam as 'static and unresponsive to new realities'.[25] Orthodox Islam has unquestionably been, and remains, expressly and consistently hostile to innovation, particularly regarding matters of belief and practice. After all, the Qur'an is said to be God's final, perfect, and unalterable revelation to humanity. It is also entirely compatible with the informed debates to observe that at least some of the values of orthodox Islam are difficult, if not impossible, to reconcile with western commitments to democracy, human rights, and the rule of law, nor to note that, in the core of the Muslim world, Islam has always involved a fusion of religion, politics, law, morality, and culture. Throughout history, orthodox and other Muslims have also clearly used Islam for political and/or military purposes, including enslavement and empire building.

---

[22] A. Shryock, *Islamophobia/Islamophilia: Beyond the Politics of Enemy and Friend* (Indiana University Press, 2010), pp. 9-10.
[23] Conway, *Islamophobia*, p. 5.
[24] Ibid.
[25] Ibid.

The distinction between 'open' and 'closed' views is also much too binary to capture the fact that positive and negative attitudes towards Islam and Muslims lie on a continuum which reflects degrees of appreciation and hostility, as well as many ways in which positivity and negativity can be held and expressed. A particular howler is that endorsing item 2, and the 'clash of civilizations element of item 4 on 'the closed' list, would make ultra-orthodox Islam itself 'Islamophobic'. In spite of the lip service paid to freedom of expression, 'it has never been made clear' by the report or by anyone else for that matter, 'what the threshold of acceptable criticism is'.[26] Another of the report's pervasive assumptions is that negative views about Muslims and Islam are both ubiquitous and at least prima facie Islamophobic – 'Islamophobic discourse, sometimes blatant but frequently subtle and coded, is part of the fabric of everyday life in modern Britain'.[27] And, as one critic of the Runnymede analysis points out, since 'the report does not allow for well-founded hostility or a *rational* basis for a fear .... its thrust is that *any* hostility towards Islam and Muslims is deemed unfounded and *ipso facto*, Islamophobic'.[28] This makes it difficult to determine precisely what kinds of critical comment would not be Islamophobic. Crucially, the report fails to provide even a single one.

b) The media

Another issue raised by the 1997 Runnymede study, and a perennial one in the British debate, concerns the media. Assuming, but failing to demonstrate, that the media is deeply afflicted by negativity towards Muslims and Islam, greater responsibility on its part is recommended, including more sensitive and positive representations. The report also encourages greater willingness on the part of the public to call the media to account through appropriate regulatory channels, and that the media themselves should be more alert to anti-Muslim and anti-Islam stereotypes. Two particular challenges in this context are, however, either ignored or downplayed.

One concerns the scale of the alleged problem of anti-Muslim/Islamic expression in the media. Even in 1997, before the proliferation of contemporary electronic platforms, it was impossible accurately to assess the

---

[26] Hasan, *Does 'Islamophobia' Curtail Free Speech?*, p. 6.
[27] Conway, *Islamophobia*, p. 11.
[28] Hasan, *Does 'Islamophobia' Curtail Free Speech?*, p. 8. Italics in original.

dimensions of this alleged problem for two main reasons: the sheer volume of output and the lack of consensus about whether or not, in any given instance, a specific branch of the media had, in fact, been guilty of this particular prejudice. Unsurprisingly, as the regular host of all kinds of insulting stereotypes, the tabloid press was, and remains, an obvious target for complaint. However, the claim that the more serious press, and the broadcast media, were and remain seriously and routinely afflicted by Islamophobic expression is more difficult to prove and to accept. Welcome authoritative light was shed on this matter when, in 2012, Lord Leveson stated in his inquiry into alleged media misconduct more generally: 'The evidence demonstrates that sections of the press betray a tendency, *which is far from being universal or even preponderant*, to portray Muslims in a negative light'.[29] The internet, where many, particularly young people, now get their news, has made it impossible to measure the public expression of any kind of prejudice. It can reliably be assumed that cyberspace is awash with negative and positive images of Muslims and Islam just as it is replete with every conceivable negative and positive image of everything else.

The second challenge concerns the fact that, by contrast with, for example academic discourse, one of the most powerful and most potentially controversial modes of expression employed by the media is the cartoon. By their very nature, cartoons are caricatures which typically seek to express the essence of a particular perspective on any given issue or controversy, often in deliberately crude, stereotypical, and sometimes shocking ways. This is precisely the point. Distinguishing between cartoons which express anti-Muslim prejudice from those which present lawful and legitimate, though perhaps unflattering critiques is, prima facie, much more difficult than with respect to most other forms of public expression and also much more subjective. A cartoon which provokes both protest and acclamation may even be said to have fulfilled its purpose. But expecting a significant reduction in representations of Islam and Muslims which Islamophiles find distasteful is simply a non-starter in any state with a genuinely free press.

The 2017 report – Islamophobia as racism

In spite of its manifest deficiencies, Runnymede's 1997 conception of

---

[29] Lord Justice Leveson, *An inquiry into the culture, practices and ethics of the press*, Volume II, , 29 November 2012, Ch. 6, para. 8.45. Italics added.

Islamophobia remained the gold standard for over two decades. The report's 20th anniversary provided the opportunity for an update, *Islamophobia: Still a challenge for us all*,[30] which takes the form of a collection of essays from a range of authors on different topics. The following review is brief for three main reasons. First, the account in the report of how Islamophobic expression should be defined is also very short. Second, the report never gained the traction of its predecessor, largely because, third, it was effectively superseded the following year by the report of the All Party Parliamentary Group on British Muslims, *Islamophobia defined: The inquiry into a working definition of Islamophobia*, considered further below.

The 2017 report is, nevertheless, worthy of critical scrutiny, especially because of the confusion it has added to the debate about how Islamophobia should be defined, particularly its assertion that it is a type of racism. The report notes that domestic and global contexts have changed fundamentally since 1997, adding that, as a result of 9/11 and 7/7, Muslims have been framed by policymakers 'largely in terms of terrorism or as a civilizational threat', a conception which, though centuries old is said to have re-emerged in new and toxic ways.[31] No evidence is provided to support this view. Like the 1997 report, the bulk of the 2017 version concerns Islamophobia-by-deed rather than by-word. In common with its predecessor, the 2017 report also accepts that, as a system of beliefs, Islam can and should be subject to criticism.[32] However, it fails abjectly to specify where the line between acceptable criticism and Islamophobic expression should be drawn.

Claiming to endorse the conception of Islamophobia found in the earlier version, the 2017 report characterizes this in three propositions: 'unfounded hostility towards Islam; practical consequences of such hostility in unfair discrimination against Muslim individuals and communities; and exclusion of Muslims from mainstream political and social affairs'.[33] It then offers both a short and long definition of Islamophobia. The former simply states: 'Islamophobia is anti-Muslim racism'.[34] But, as Sir Trevor Phillips notes: 'when we finalized the Runnymede report in 1997, we specifically rejected

---

[30] Ehahi & Khan (eds.), *Islamophobia*.
[31] Ibid., p. 5.
[32] Ibid., p. 10.
[33] Ibid., p. 7.
[34] Ibid.

the notion that Muslims should be characterized as a racial grouping'.[35] The longer version is as follows:

> 'Islamophobia is any distinction, exclusion or restriction towards, or preference against, Muslims (or those perceived to be Muslims) that has the purpose or effect of nullifying or impairing the recognition, enjoyment or exercise, on an equal footing, of human rights and fundamental freedoms in the political, economic, social, cultural or any other field of public life.[36]

The 2017 report also states that its focus is upon 'naming anti-Muslim prejudice so that it can be identified and acted against'.[37] Yet this will be impossible without a clearer distinction between such prejudice and lawful and legitimate criticism of Muslims and Islam. However, apart from maintaining that the focus on ideas has 'obscured what instead should be a focus on people', and that 'too many criticisms of Islamophobia suffer from bad-faith literalism',[38] not a single example of non-Islamophobic criticism of Islam or Muslims is provided.

In only a few pages, for three main reasons, the report also urges, particularly the government, to adopt its definition of Islamophobia as anti-Muslim racism. First, it claims this fits with contemporary sociological understandings of racism.[39] There is, however, no critical engagement with these deeply flawed approaches themselves, the most significant of which is the elision of colour-based prejudice with those stemming from cultural and other stereotypes. More about this later. Second, it states that 'as with many Black and minority ethnic groups, Muslims experience disadvantage and discrimination in a wide range of institutions and environments, from schools to the labour market to prisons to violence on the street'.[40] Probably. But this does not mean that it happens equally to these diverse groups or in the same ways. Third, according to the report, 'policies to tackle Islamophobia should be developed in line with policies to tackle racial discrimination more

---

[35] T. Phillips, 'Foreword' to J. Jenkins, *Defining Islamophobia: A Policy Exchange Research Note* (Policy Exchange, 2018), p. 5.
[36] Ehahi & Khan (eds.), *Islamophobia*, p. 7.
[37] Ibid., p. 10.
[38] Ibid., p. 7.
[39] Ibid.
[40] Ibid., p. 8.

generally, with the focus also on the real effects on people'.[41]

The All-Party Parliamentary Group's definition

On 27 November 2018, the All Party Parliamentary Group on British Muslims, chaired by MPs, Anna Soubry (Conservative) and Wes Streeting (Labour, and since July 2024, Secretary of State for Health and Social Care), published a 72-page report entitled *Islamophobia defined: The inquiry into a working definition of Islamophobia*. All Party Parliamentary Groups (APPGs) are informal, cross-party associations, independent of Government, with no official status and no powers granted by Parliament or any of its committees. Composed of self-selecting members of both Houses, they are more likely to attract those already convinced that the given focus concerns a problem that needs addressing than those who are not. It is clear that the APPG on British Muslims was dominated by those who already believed that the state and society in Britain present more of a problem for Muslims than the other way around. APPGs often produce thoughtful and authoritative reports. Regrettably *Islamophobia defined* is not one of them.

There are five basic components to the report's core thesis. Islamophobia is a form of racism. It is a serious problem in contemporary Britain. It manifests at virtually every sector and level of society including education, employment, public service, the media, culture etc, and in a range of ways from microaggressions to murder. In the interests of both victims and society in general, something needs to be done about it forthwith. The key lies in defining it in a 'legally binding' manner.

According to the APPG, the definition it proposes is 'required in order to bring about a transformation in social etiquette' by preventing 'negative attitudes that would not be classed as crimes by police'.[42] Of particular relevance to this study is the claim that the definition would establish 'tests… for ascertaining whether contentious speech is indeed reasonable criticism or Islamophobia masquerading as "legitimate criticism."' It would also set 'appropriate limits to free speech', and would expose the fact that the 'supposed right to criticize Islam results in nothing more than another subtle

---

[41] Ibid.

[42] APPG, *Islamophobia defined: the inquiry into a working definition of Islamophobia* (APPG, 2018), pp. 33, 32.

form of anti-Muslim racism'.[43] The report claims that a 'legally binding definition … is not advocated in an effort to create a protective umbrella that can shield Islam from any form of criticism, rather to demarcate clearly and definitively the boundaries between legitimate criticism and anti-Muslim racism'.[44]

However, by any credible standard, the APPG has manifestly failed to achieve this objective, not least because, as repeatedly noted in this study, not a single example of legitimate criticism has been provided. In spite of protestations to the contrary, the sentiment underpinning the APPG's report is that, as Hasan puts it, 'pretty much all criticism of Islam is illegitimate'.[45]

The APPG's proposals were promptly condemned by a wide range of critics, including human rights activists such as Peter Tatchell and Index on Censorship, secularist campaigners, and many Muslims themselves.[46] The report was also rejected by the then Conservative government which embarked upon its own attempt to define Islamophobia, an exercise directed by Imam Qari Asim, dismissed in 2022 because of his controversial views especially for supporting the campaign against the screening of the Lady of Heaven film (see Chapter 7).[47] A letter drafted by the National Secular Society, and published on 9 December 2018, warned that the APPG's definition:

> 'will clearly render legitimate commentary and debate about Islam beyond the bounds of reasonable debate. Far from combatting prejudice and bigotry, erroneous claims of "Islamophobia" have become a cover for it. LGBT rights campaigners have been called "Islamophobes" for criticizing the views of Muslim clerics on homosexuality. Meanwhile, ex-Muslims and feminist activists have been called "Islamophobes" for criticizing certain Islamic views and practices relating to women. Even liberal and secular Muslims have been branded "Islamophobes."'[48]

In May 2019 the then Home Secretary, Sajid Javid (himself a Muslim)

---

[43] Ibid., pp. 32, 11, 36.

[44] Ibid., p. 42.

[45] Hasan, *Does 'Islamophobia' Curtail Free Speech?*, p. 12.

[46] K. Mahmood, J. Jenkins & M. Frampton, *A Definition of Islamophobia? Old problems remain as new problems emerge* (Policy Exchange, 2024), p. 7.

[47] T. Dieppe, *Banning Islamophobia: Blasphemy by the Backdoor* (Free Speech Union briefing, 2024), p. 30.

[48] M. Amin, p. 86, and National Secular Society, p. 91, in E. Webb (ed.), *Islamophobia: An Anthology of Concerns* (Civitas, 2019).

received an open letter, entitled *APPG Islamophobia Definition Threatens Civil Liberties*, signed by over 40 prominent Muslims, Christians, Sikhs, Hindus, atheists, Parliamentarians, journalists, activists, and academics.[49] The signatories' principal complaints were that the definition offered is vague, expansive, and confused especially regarding the conflation of race and religion, and that the APPG's concept of 'Muslimness' (see below) will fall to self-appointed representatives to define, and, therefore, would be likely to exclude those not considered to be 'sufficiently Muslim'. The signatories to the letter also express concern, that by creating a climate of self-censorship, Islamic beliefs and even extremists will be shielded from criticism and that open discussion about matters of public interest will be shut down.[50] This has been confirmed by reliable surveys which have found, for example, that British non-Muslims tend to self-censor more about issues related to Islam than with respect to other faiths, and that Muslims in Britain are also 'more likely than average to think that people should be careful not to offend when talking about Islamic topics'.[51] The signatories also claim that the APPG's report is, in fact, already being used to silence legitimate debate, especially on the part of ex-Muslims, feminists, those campaigning for LGBT+ rights or against the hijab and halal slaughter, journalists investigating Islamism, Muslims working in counter-extremism, plus schools and Ofsted (the regulator) enforcing gender equality. They predict that it will undermine social cohesion, aggravate community tensions and will fuel the very bigotry against Muslims which it is designed to prevent. As they maintain, the law already protects individuals against anti-Muslim hatred and unlawful discrimination without the need for an anti-blasphemy law which would protect Muslims and Islam, but not any other faith or its adherents, from hostility or criticism.

The APPG's report has, nevertheless, been uncritically adopted by the Labour Party, the Liberal Democrats, the Scottish National Party, the Scottish Conservatives, Plaid Cymru, the Green Party, at least 52 local councils, more

---

[49] https://www.civitas.org.uk/content/files/islamophobiaopenletter.pdf.

[50] See also National Secular Society, 'Islamophobia definitions threaten free speech at 20+ universities', 23 November 2023.

[51] Respectively 38% for 'Islamic topics' compared with 17% for 'Christian topics' (p. 13) and 71% compared to 31% overall (p. 36), Commission for Countering Extremism, *CCE Freedom of Expression Survey Findings Report*, June 2025.

than 20 universities, major trade unions, numerous NHS trusts, police bodies, public-sector employers, student unions and advocacy groups.[52]

The many problems with the APPG's report, therefore, deserve deeper and more systematic examination according to the following principal categories: method; omissions; assumptions and reasoning; definition; and examples.[53]

Method

The report's principal methodological flaw, common in studies of this kind, is the failure to employ scientifically valid procedures for the collection and analysis of relevant information. Since making a submission to the APPG was largely a self-selecting process, unsurprisingly the bulk of the 43 cited come from those who are already committed to the view that a legally binding definition of Islamophobia is required. As Jenkins states: 'Many questions need to be asked about how the report was compiled … [including] … whether due diligence was carried out on its authors and their sources ….'[54] Several have highly suspect credentials and few of those who contributed are not convinced that a legally binding or indeed any definition of Islamophobia is necessary at all.[55] And as Jenkins also observes: 'while the APPG quotes much evidence of Islamophobia uncritically, it goes out of its way to attack the position of the Southall Black Sisters'.[56] Evidence submitted by the National Secular Society and Lord Singh of Wimbledon, was also selectively cited merely to be summarily rejected.[57]

Omissions

The report's principal omissions are as follows. In spite of having

---

[52] Singh, *Islamophobia' revisited*, pp. 13-25, 26-36. Lord Young, S. Armstrong, F. Attenborough, B. Harris & L. Maby, *Why Labour's Definition of 'Islamophobia' Will Have a Chilling Effect on Free Speech: The Free Speech Union's response to the Government's consultation on a proposed definition of 'anti-Muslim hatred/Islamophobia'*, Free Speech Union Briefing, July 2025, p. 18.

[53] See particularly the contributions from thirteen commentators assembled in E. Webb (ed.), *Islamophobia*.

[54] Jenkins, *Defining Islamophobia*, p. 8.

[55] APPG, *Islamophobia Defined*, p. 31; Hasan, *Does 'Islamophobia' Curtail Free Speech?*, p. 2, & P. Patel in Webb (ed.), *Islamophobia*, p. 48.

[56] Jenkins, *Defining Islamophobia*, p. 11

[57] E. Webb in Webb (ed.), *Islamophobia*, p. 6.

complained about 'institutional Islamophobia' and the 'lack of institutional and/or individual understanding about Islam...',[58] in common with the Runnymede reports, the APPG fails to provide even the briefest account of the Islamic faith and of how Muslims understand and practice it. This may well have been because of the fear that exploring the details might expose it itself to accusations of Islamophobia. This failure is, however, critical, since the difference between legitimate critique and anti-Muslim prejudice hinges upon the extent to which Muslims and Islam are properly understood and accurately and dispassionately depicted.

The APPG's definition has also been criticized for its failure to include 'intra-Muslim' prejudice, ie that between members of certain Muslim sects against other Muslims on theological, ethnic, or other relevant grounds.[59] Without any discussion or explanation, the issue is side-stepped in favour of designating this as a type of sectarianism.[60] But, if Islamophobia were to be outlawed as the APPG proposes, prima facie this would mean that any hostility thus designated would be unlawful when expressed by a non-Muslim, but not when expressed in precisely the same terms by a Muslim.

The APPG also fails to consider several potentially negative effects of what it proposes. Four in particular stand out. First, particularly remiss on the part of legislators, is the absence of even a rudimentary account of the current law relating to anti-Muslim hatred and prejudice. In fact, the APPG's report suffers from a staggering lack of appreciation that the relevant legal and human rights landscape in the UK is governed by the European Convention on Human Rights, the Human Rights Act 1998, and the Equality Act 2010, as discussed in Chapter 6. The result is that the report fails to explain why the current regime is defective or inadequate, or anything beyond the most vague and unconvincing account of how a legally binding definition of Islamophobia would operate in practice, the difference it would make, or why it is needed only for Muslims but not for adherents to any other faith.[61]

Relevant legal instruments expressly frame unlawful hostility towards, and discrimination against, minorities in generic terms. As Pragna Patel of

---

[58] APPG, *Islamophobia defined*, p. 45.
[59] 'Hard line groups are "weaponizing" Islamophobia, Government's counter-extremism tsar warns', *Daily Telegraph*, 15 September 2018.
[60] APPG, *Islamophobia defined*, p. 41.
[61] K. Falkner, 'If honour and shame matter to our community, where is the outcry?', *The Sunday Times*, 19 January 2025.

Southall Black Sisters puts it:

> 'our research and casework has shown that ... the solution to the problem of racism, inequality and oppression lies not in adopting a religious framework as a countering mechanism, but through the endorsement and application of universal equality and human rights-based laws and norms'.[62]

It is not clear either if the APPG intends all forms of Islamophobia to become what it calls 'civil offences' creating an entitlement to non-criminal remedies, or if just some, and if the latter, which this should be. The report also fails to recognise that, as Chapter 6 also discusses, a deepening problem with the Equality Act is how conflicts between any two or more of the characteristics the legislation protects, particularly religious and secular belief, should be reconciled.

Second, the only (very limited) discussion of the implications of its own proposals the APPG entertains for counterterrorism concern quotes from two anonymous sources which allege that British policy in this field is itself Islamophobic. According to one: '... Islamophobia is perpetuated in political rhetoric and a broad range of policy measures ... [including] ... in counter-terrorism, in community cohesion, in integration, in immigration debates, and worst of all, in the continuous racialization of criminality'.[63] Another claimed that: 'Islamophobia is felt by the whole Muslim community through institutionalised Islamophobia, through security measures like Prevent'.[64] These sweeping statements, devoid of any supporting evidence, have been challenged by other commentators on the basis of much more reliable information.[65]

Implementation of the APPG's proposals could have a number of potentially dangerous consequences which the report completely ignores. For example, they might expose investigations into Islamist plots to charges of 'institutional Islamophobia'. They could also potentially enable any Muslim at the receiving end of virtually any currently lawful counterterrorist power to mount a legal challenge on the grounds that, motivated by 'perceived

---

[62] Patel in Webb (ed.), *Islamophobia*, p. 49.
[63] APPG, *Islamophobia Defined*, p. 44.
[64] Ibid., p. 44.
[65] See, eg S. Greer, *Tackling Terrorism in Britain: Threats, Responses, and Challenges Twenty Years After 9/11* (Routledge, 2021).

Muslimness', this was Islamophobic and, therefore, unlawful.[66] If successful, such challenges might enable guilty parties to evade justice with all the morale-boosting implications this would have for Islamist extremists and terrorist organizations, deter prosecution and other agencies from enforcing the law, and expose entire sectors of counterterrorist law and policy to the possibility of being declared unlawful. This would also make it more difficult for the authorities to avoid engaging with certain unrepresentative Muslim organizations, and for the police and others to stop young people, like Shamima Begum and her friends, from joining Islamist fighters abroad.[67] Indeed, as Walton and Wilson point out, the APPG's report appears to 'envisage some significant alteration, or even repealing, of existing counter-terrorism and counter-radicalization measures'.[68]

Third, there is also very little discussion in the report about the impact the APPG's 'legally binding' definition of Islamophobia would have upon free speech. What there is, is cavalier and complacent at best when it should have been the centrepiece of the entire exercise. The simple fact is that the APPG's definition of Islamophobia is impossible to reconcile with the right to freedom of expression.[69] The statement that 'recourse to the notion of free speech and a *supposed right to criticise Islam* results in *nothing more* than another subtle form of anti-Muslim racism, whereby the criticism humiliates, marginalizes, and stigmatizes Muslims', speaks volumes about the APPG's conflation of Islamophobic expression with the expression of legitimate critique of Muslims and Islam.[70] As Patel from Southall Black Sisters puts it: 'Our concern is that adopting a religious framework has, amongst other things, consequences for .. [the] … right to challenge practices such as domestic violence which necessarily involves challenging religious and cultural injunctions and values'.[71]

Finally, there is no appreciation of the risk that outlawing Islamophobic expression, but not the equivalents for other faiths and ideologies, is more likely to provoke resentment and anti-Muslim prejudice than to discourage it,

---

[66] R. Walton & T. Wilson, *Islamophobia – Crippling Counter-Terrorism* (Policy Exchange, 2019), pp.15-26.
[67] Ibid., pp. 7, 9, 10, 19 & 25.
[68] Ibid., p. 14.
[69] Hasan, *Does 'Islamophobia' Curtail Free Speech?*, p. 15.
[70] APPG, *Islamophobia Defined*, p. 35. Italics added.
[71] Patel in Webb (ed.), *Islamophobia*, p. 49.

with inevitably corrosive effects upon social integration and cohesion. As, in a different context, Bruckner observes, this derives from the dubious assumption that 'Islam is supposed to deserve special treatment because it is, more than other religions, the "religion of the oppressed."'[72]

Assumptions and analysis

The report makes numerous contentious assumptions and claims unsupported by any credible evidence or argument. It asserts, for example, that Islam is a 'religion' not an 'ideology'.[73] Yet, since religions include ideas, they embody a type of ideology. It also maintains that the concept of 'Islamophobia' is intended to protect Muslims not the Islamic faith.[74] Yet, the clue that the term refers to a faith rather than to a race, ethnicity, or even a group of believers, is in the title – *Islam*ophobia. No one talks of '*Muslim*ophobia'. Contradicting its own assertion that Islamophobia is fundamentally driven by race not belief, the report also claims that 'it is Muslims' religiosity that informs prejudice'.[75]

The APPG also quotes, with apparent approval, the eye-brow-raising assertion by Professor Tariq Modood that, when the Windrush generation came to Britain, 'they thought they were Barbadians, Ghanaians, Jamaicans' and that 'they didn't know they were black. They were told they were black when they arrived in Britain. So, I think racializing is something that is done from the outside ….'[76] To attribute, without evidence, identities to any minority group which they themselves may not endorse, is presumptuous to say the least. It also flies in the face of the widely-held view that black identity is something black people have proudly claimed for themselves rather than having it foist upon them by their white oppressors.

In addition to confusing the distinction between Islam and Muslims, the report also fails to appreciate the difference between Islam and Islamism. As Namazie argues, the purpose of normalizing the term 'Islamophobia' is to 'appease fundamentalists by conflating criticism of Islam and Islamism with bigotry against Muslims in order to restrict free expression, particularly

---

[72] Bruckner, *An Imaginary Racism*, p. 33.
[73] APPG, *Islamophobia defined*, p. 38.
[74] Ibid., p. 42.
[75] Ibid., p. 46.
[76] Ibid., p. 41.

blasphemy and heresy'.[77]

The report also seeks to connect the phenomenon of Islamophobia with antisemitism. Claiming that Islamophobia is 'the same type of racism as antisemitism',[78] the definition of the former follows closely that drafted by the committee on Antisemitism and Holocaust Denial of the International Holocaust Remembrance Alliance (IHRI). But, as Bruckner points out: 'anti-Semitism is racialist by essence, it does not oppose Judaism as a belief but Jews for what they are'.[79] The same is not true of anti-Muslim hatred.

The APPG also claims that, since antisemitism has been defined without negatively impacting upon free speech, the same would be true of an official definition of Islamophobia.[80] There are several problems here. First, the IHRI's definition of antisemitism has not been universally endorsed. On the contrary it has, in fact, been criticized on several grounds.[81] Second, the IHRI's definition has not been enshrined in statute as the APPG maintains should be the case for its definition of Islamophobia, nor does it consider why this is the case. The reason is that, for every relevant legal purpose, antisemitism is a type of prejudice and/or discrimination governed by laws against such conduct framed in universal rather than faith-specific terms. Third, as far as relevant domestic and international human rights law are concerned, antisemitism and genuine Islamophobia are each specific forms of generic religious antagonism which may, amongst other things, prompt the crime of incitement to religious hatred, and motivate other criminal offences such as physical assault, harassment, and vandalism.

The APPG report also compares the minting of the term 'Islamophobia' with the emergence of the term 'genocide'. It states:

> '... just like genocide indicates a "very particular kind of crime against humanity that required public visibility and recognition in the particular historical context of the mid-20th century world" so Islamophobia indicates a very specific kind of racism directed against Muslims'.[82]

---

[77] M. Namazie in Webb (ed), *Islamophobia*, p. 79.

[78] APPG, *Islamophobia defined*, p. 41

[79] Bruckner, *An Imaginary Racism*, p. 70.

[80] APPG, *Islamophobia defined*, p. 37; Dieppe, *Banning Islamophobia*, p. 24.

[81] C. McGreal, 'UN urged to reject antisemitism definition over "misuse" to shield Israel', *The Guardian*, 24 April 2023.

[82] APPG, *Islamophobia defined*, p. 43.

The APPG is not, of course, claiming that the effects or impact of Islamophobia and genocide are similar but merely that there is a certain similarity in the way in which the two terms emerged from the specific historical contexts in question. But even this is remarkably clumsy and insensitive because the similarities are superficial and the differences much greater and much more apparent. And it is, of course, possible to be irrationally hostile to Muslims and/or Islam (and therefore to be an 'Islamophobe') without wanting Muslims to be killed, much less the entire ummah.

However, the most fundamental assumption the report makes is that Muslims in Britain are essentially vulnerable, passive, harmless, and admirable, yet routinely victimized, vilified, persecuted, subjected to systematic prejudice/discrimination, and 'securitized' by state and society.[83] The UK is said to suffer from pervasive 'structural anti-Muslim racism', 'state Islamophobia', and 'institutionalized Islamophobia', that it has an 'Islamophobic environment', that Muslim women are 'feared' and seen as the 'enemy within', that Muslims are routinely dehumanized by the media and political parties, and that Islamophobia is preventing the admission of Muslim applicants to Russell Group universities.[84] These are all serious allegations. Yet no evidence is provided to substantiate any of them. On the contrary, ethnographic studies and reliable scientific polling have consistently demonstrated the opposite.

For example, the dominant picture which emerges from several studies of Muslim communities in Britain is one of diversity, particularly regarding ethnicity, doctrine, and degree of integration/segregation.[85] A 2018 review of survey research on Muslims in Britain also found that:

> 'Muslims have a strong sense of belonging to Britain and of feeling part of British society. In a 2016 survey, for example, 93% said they

---

[83] For a particularly strident statement of this view see S. Warsi, *Muslims Don't Matter* (Bridge Street Press, 2024).

[84] APPG, *Islamophobia defined*, p. 8; Phillips, 'Foreword', p. 7; Jenkins, *Defining Islamophobia*, pp.11-12.

[85] See, eg S. Gilliat-Ray, *Muslims in Britain: An Introduction* (Cambridge University Press, 2010); I. Bowen, *Medina in Birmingham, Najaf in Brent: Inside British Islam* (Hurst, 2014); S. Khan with T. McMahon, *The Battle for British Islam: Reclaiming Muslim Identity from Extremism* (Saqi, 2016); J. Ferguson, *Al-Britannia, My Country: A Journey through Muslim Britain* (Bantam, 2017); S. Warsi, *The Enemy Within: A Tale of Muslim Britain* (Allen Lane, 2017).

felt they belonged to Britain, with more than half saying they felt this "very strongly," and in another survey in 2015, 95% said they feel loyal to Britain ... Indeed, Muslims are more likely than the British public as a whole to say that their national identity is important to their sense of who they are (55% of Muslims say this, compared to 44% of all adults)'.[86]

The review also found that 70% of Muslims feel they are fairly treated by government, and while some believe there is anti-Muslim prejudice in Britain, the majority do not.[87] However, a majority of Muslims from minority ethnic backgrounds (63%) think there is more prejudice against Muslims than against other religious groups. A significant minority, particularly among graduates and youth, also believe that people of their faith do not have the same life chances as others and that prejudice against them is increasing.[88] One in four Muslims (27%) say they have experienced discrimination, a figure which rises to one in three (34%) for graduates and Muslims aged 18-24.[89] Although 26% worry about being physically attacked, less than 14% of Muslims say harassment is a 'very big' or 'fairly big' problem.[90]

The APPG makes another related assumption – that every material disadvantage suffered by Muslims is the result of discrimination. As Chapter 1 indicated, a 'material disadvantage' is an objectively measurable, and by comparison with relevant others, a less favourable differential in access to material benefits, such as income, employment, education, qualifications, health care, plus opportunities and life chances not necessarily deliberately or negligently caused. By contrast, 'discrimination' is a type of disadvantage occasioned by avoidable and unjustified acts or omissions on the part of someone else. However, the APPG's report does recognise most of the more subtle characteristics of discrimination. It may be direct and intentional, or indirect and unintentional. It may stem from acts or omissions on the part of the state or others. It may be systematic /institutionalized – ie occurring on a wide scale though possibly varying from sector to sector – or it may be casual or contingent, ie occurring sporadically and randomly.

---

[86] Ipsos MORI Social Research Institute, *A Review of survey research on Muslims in Britain: Research report of the Aziz Foundation, Barrow Cadbury Trust, the Joseph Rowntree Charitable Trust, and Unbound Philanthropy* (Ipsos MORI, 2018), p. 8.
[87] Ibid., p. 9.
[88] Ibid., p. 10.
[89] Ibid.
[90] Ibid.

The report could also have added that official discrimination can occur in several ways. A law or public policy is 'directly discriminatory' or 'discriminatory by design' if, without justification, it expressly targets a specific social group. However, even if it lacks this characteristic, it may, nevertheless, be indirectly discriminatory particularly because of unintended consequences, including for example, the manner in which it is implemented. In its turn this may either be systemic or the result of deliberate, though contingent, random, or sporadic conduct on the part of a specific official or officials, but not the relevant agency as a whole.

However, although as the APPG claims, there is plenty of reliable evidence that Muslims suffer material disadvantage, it does not follow as the report assumes, that this is all necessarily due to discrimination of any kind. The APPG also fails to distinguish adequately between 'objective' discrimination, typically very hard to prove, and the 'perception of discrimination' which is, in principle, much easier to document, but may not be a reliable indicator of the former. As Hasan points out, the report does not provide 'demonstrable evidence of Muslims being systematically oppressed because nonesuch exists'.[91]

Definition

The most fundamental shortcoming in the APPG's report is, however, its definition of Islamophobia. It asserts that:

> 'Islamophobia is rooted in racism and is a type of racism that targets expressions of Muslimness or perceived Muslimness'.[92]

It then states that, rather than a list of essential features, this conception can be illustrated by a range of guidelines and examples considered further below.

a) Islamophobia as racism

Although the APPG is not alone in regarding Islamophobia as a type of racism, this is a deeply flawed approach for several reasons.[93] First, the report cites a number of definitions of Islamophobia without explaining why those

---

[91] Hasan, *Does 'Islamophobia Curtail Free Speech?*, p. 13.
[92] Ibid., pp. 50 & 51.
[93] See, eg the European Commission Against Racism and Intolerance General Policy Recommendation No. 7, adopted on 13 December 2012, para. 6.

which do not make this assumption are not as worthy as those which do.[94]

The claim that Islamophobia is a type of racism also relies upon the concept of 'cultural racism' which, although having had considerable influence over the past few decades,[95] has also been criticized on several grounds. It ignores the fact that neither 'culture' (shared beliefs, practices, forms of expression etc) nor 'race' (characterised by DNA, skin colour, ethnicity, common ancestry, clan membership, etc) map neatly onto each other. Non-white people do not share the same culture as each other any more or less than whites. Within each of these two categories there are many cultures. Indeed, the terms 'black culture' or 'Asian culture' may themselves be deemed 'racist' because they assume (wrongly) that black people have the same culture and that this is also true of Asians.

Adherents to global proselytizing religions, such as Islam and Christianity, also come from many races. And although racial prejudice is typically triggered by visual cues, religious affiliation is generally less visible without the distinctive names, clothing, or symbols – such as hijabs, crucifixes, or kippahs – which declare, or appear to declare it. Religions also invite reflection and debate, including about their social, political and legal implications, in ways which race does not.[96]

The 'cultural racism' thesis is also typically articulated at a high level of abstraction with little if any attempt to specify the detailed policy implications, particularly those which concern how the distinct prejudices pertaining to each might be tackled.[97] As the great French social theorist Claude Lévi-Strauss observed: 'nothing so much compromises the struggle against racism, or weakens it from the inside, or vitiates it, as the indiscriminating use of the word "racism"' itself'.[98] And, as Bruckner observes, even 'the attempt to escape from it is itself denounced as a racist act'[99] and 'by ceaselessly racializing every form of ethnic, political, sexual, or religious conflict, this

---

[94] Mahmood et al, *A Definition of Islamophobia?*, p. 8; Hasan, *Does 'Islamophobia' Curtail Free Speech?*, p. 12.

[95] See, eg T. Modood, *Essays on Secularism and Multiculturalism* (Rowman & Littlefield, 2019), Part I.

[96] Dieppe in Webb (ed.), *Islamophobia*, p. 30.

[97] Amin in Webb (ed.), *Islamophobia*, p. 87; Hasan, *Does 'Islamophobia' Curtail Free Speech?*, p. 13.

[98] C. Lévi-Strauss (trans J. Neugroschel), *The view from Afar* (Chicago University Press, 1992), p. xv.

[99] Bruckner, *An Imaginary Racism*, p. 25.

kind of "anti-racism" constantly recreates the very curse against which it claims to be fighting'.[100]

However, racial and anti-Muslim discrimination can clearly overlap, particularly in England and Wales where over 90% of Muslims are non-white. According to UK law, and international human rights law, where this occurs, one element may constitute a form of indirect discrimination compounding the direct discrimination arising from the other. The prejudices under consideration are also capable of supplanting each other. For example, antagonism towards immigrants in post-2nd World War Britain, initially manifested and was debated in racial rather than religious terms. Yet, in the case, particularly of Pakistanis, *The Satanic Verses* controversy and the events of 9/11 and 7/7, shifted the focus from colour-based racism, to hostility on religious, ie anti-Muslim grounds, or at least complicated it.[101]

Third, the APPG's definition also appears to assume that the 'racism' in question concerns attitudes and conduct on the part of white non-Muslims against non-white Muslims. Yet, as Phillips notes, this is 'profoundly Eurocentric' because it defines Muslims 'exclusively in terms of their treatment by non-Muslim, mainly white Britons'.[102] But Muslims are not all non-white. And some non-whites, for example those from Hindu and Sikh communities, may also be prejudiced against Muslims and vice versa. It is difficult to see, therefore, how a black non-Muslim discriminating against a black Muslim because of their religion, or a white non-Muslim discriminating against a white Muslim on the same grounds, could credibly be accused of 'racism' because, in each case, perpetrator and victim belong to the same race. Being, or being perceived to be Muslim is clearly a consequence of adhering to, or being perceived as adhering to Islam, an identity derived from faith or ideology not from race or ethnicity. As Dawkins points out with characteristically penetrating insight:

> 'The fact that you can't leave your race means that, if Islam is indeed a race, apostasy is literally impossible. Yet apostasy has to be possible in Islam or it couldn't be punishable by death. So the statement that Islamophobia is a form of racism is more than just

---

[100] Ibid., p. 10.
[101] S. Warsi, *The Enemy Within: A Tale of Muslim Britain*, (Allen Lane, 2017), pp. 21-31.
[102] Phillips, 'Foreword', p. 7.

incorrect. It contradicts a fundamental, and incidentally obnoxious tenet of Islam'.[103]

Finally, British courts have long recognised that, for the purpose of anti-discrimination law, certain religious groups such as Jews and Sikhs, may also constitute an ethnic group if they share a common history, culture, identity and ethnicity in addition to their religion but that this is not the case for Muslims because Islam is a religion that includes many ethnicities and nationalities.[104] Leaked government Equalities Office advice, dated 15 April 2019, also states that the APPG's definition:

> 'is not in line with the Equality Act 2010, which defines "race" as comprising colour, nationality and national or ethnic origins – none of which would encompass a Muslim or an Islamic practice. This means that, over time, there could be tensions between the Act and the official definition of Islamophobia'.[105]

b) Muslimness

The APPG's concepts of 'Muslimness' and 'perceived Muslimness' are also deeply problematic for the following reasons. First, they are not defined, nor is it clear whose perception, that of the alleged victim, the perpetrator, or an independent third party, counts. Nor is it clear how and when this strange characteristic manifests itself. As Chapter 2 noted, converting to Islam merely requires the sincere affirmation of the shahada that there is no God but Allah and that Mohammed is His prophet. So, when and how does the 'Muslimness' of those new converts who affirm the shahada in private – particularly women who are not under any religious obligation to attend the mosque – appear? Third, as Namazie, a spokesperson for the Council of ex-Muslims of Britain puts it:

> 'If you terrorize a primary school in Birmingham to prevent lessons saying that being gay is OK, if you defend sharia courts despite their promotion of violence against women, or legitimize apostates being shunned and killed, then you will automatically pass the Muslimness

---

[103] R. Dawkins, 'Foreword' in Dieppe, *Banning Islamophobia*, p. 4.

[104] *Seide v Gillette Industries Ltd* [1980] IRLR 427 ETA; *Mandla v Dowell-Lee* [1983] 2 AC 548; *Commission for Racial Equality v Precision Manufacturing Services Ltd*, ET, Case No. 4106/9; *R (E) v Governing Body of JFS* [2009] UKSC 15; *Seide v Gillette Industries Ltd* [1980] IRLR 427, EAT.

[105] Quoted in Mahmood et al, *A Definition of Islamophobia?*, p. 10.

authenticity test! Not so much if you are a gay Muslim, or an ex-Muslim, or a feminist who doesn't want to wear the hijab or fast during Ramadan, or a secularist who is opposed to sharia law'.[106]

The concept of Muslimness also 'essentializes religious identity in a way that leaves little room for other forms of identity'.[107] And, although the APPG pays lip service to the fact that there are many forms of Muslim identity, it assumes a very monolithic conception which includes, for example, traditional Muslim female attire.[108] For Patel the term 'Islamophobia' 'also pre-supposes that there is a homogeneous group of Muslims who are defined only by their religion' all of whom 'consent to a singular version of Islam that must be protected from any criticism'. This, she claims, has been 'conveniently used by Muslim fundamentalists and ultra-conservatives to clamp down on any kind of internal questioning or dissent from religious and community norms as defined by the most powerful and dominant illiberal forces in minority communities'.[109] In its turn, this is likely to stifle the development of liberal Islam in the west which many believe is essential to promote Muslim integration and to foster social cohesion.[110] As Phillips states, the vague concept of 'Muslimness' rests on 'the delusion that all adherents of the faith would agree on doctrine, dress and behaviours; this is the "progressive" equivalent of "they all look alike to me."'[111] And, as Khan puts it, such 'a narrow understanding of "Muslimness" leaves behind those Muslims who, because of how they choose to live their lives or practice their religion, do not have a "Muslimness" that other Muslims find acceptable'.[112]

As already noted, the APPG's conception of Muslimness also fails to distinguish between 'Islam', a complex worldwide religion and culture, and 'Islamism', the political project of reviving the Caliphate ideally on a global scale, a vision which the majority of Muslims do not endorse. The result is that criticism of this aspiration is taken to be criticism of Islam itself and, according to the APPG's distorted perspective, is, therefore,

---

[106] Namazie in Webb (ed.), *Islamophobia*, pp. 77-78.
[107] Jenkins, *Defining Islamophobia*, p. 14; Namazie in Webb (ed.), *Islamophobia*, pp. 77-8.
[108] Jenkins, *Defining Islamophobia*, p. 14.
[109] Patel in Webb (ed.), *Islamophobia*, p. 52.
[110] Husain in Webb (ed.), *Islamophobia*, pp. 70-71.
[111] K. Mahmood et al, *A Definition of Islamophobia?*, p. 6.
[112] S. Khan, 'We Are Still Ignoring Victims Of Anti-Muslim Prejudice', *Huff Post*, 3 December 2018. See also Tatchell in Webb (ed.), *Islamophobia*, p. 20.

'Islamophobic'.[113] Finally, as many have pointed out, it is unclear why the term 'Muslimness' is appropriate for Muslims but the term 'Buddhistness', 'Hinduness', and 'Sikhness' are not ,with respect to adherents to these religions.[114]

There can be little doubt, therefore, that the claims 'Islamophobia is a type of racism', and that 'Muslimness is a race', are merely transparent attempts to ensure that the 'sacralization of race' includes Muslim beliefs, practices, and conduct, because if successfully achieved, anyone engaging in criticism of them can then be denounced as having committed the unforgivable sin of racism.

Examples

The APPG claims, that taking into account the overall context, its list of 'contemporary examples of Islamophobia' in public life, the media, schools, the workplace, and in encounters between religions and non-religions in the public sphere could include but is not limited to:

> 'calling for, aiding, instigating or justifying the killing or harming of Muslims in the name of a racist/ fascist ideology, or an extremist view of religion; making mendacious, dehumanizing, demonizing, or stereotypical allegations about Muslims as such, or of Muslims as a collective group, such as, especially but not exclusively, conspiracies about Muslim entryism in politics, government or other societal institutions; the myth of Muslim identity having a unique propensity for terrorism, and claims of a demographic "threat" posed by Muslims or of a "Muslim takeover"; accusing Muslims as a group of being responsible for real or imagined wrongdoing committed by a single Muslim person or group of Muslim individuals, or even for acts committed by non-Muslims; accusing Muslims as a group, or Muslim majority states, of inventing or exaggerating Islamophobia, ethnic cleansing or genocide perpetrated against Muslims; accusing Muslim citizens of being more loyal to the "Ummah" (transnational Muslim community) or to their countries of origin, or to the alleged priorities of Muslims worldwide, than to the interests of their own nations; denying Muslim populations the right to self-determination e.g., by claiming that the existence of an independent Palestine or Kashmir is a terrorist endeavour; applying double standards by

---

[113] Jenkins, *Defining Islamophobia*, p. 15.
[114] See, eg Hasan, p. 18 & Namazie, p. 76, in Webb (ed.)

> requiring of Muslims behaviours that are not expected or demanded
> of any other groups in society, eg loyalty tests; using the symbols and
> images associated with classic Islamophobia (e.g. Muhammed being
> a paedophile, claims of Muslims spreading Islam by the sword or
> subjugating minority groups under their rule) to characterize
> Muslims as being "sex groomers," inherently violent or incapable of
> living harmoniously in plural societies; holding Muslims collectively
> responsible for the actions of any Muslim majority state, whether
> secular or constitutionally Islamic'.[115]

Although potentially undermined by the self-defeating admission that these 'could', but depending upon the context would not necessarily, constitute Islamophobia, these examples – most, by the way, illustrations of alleged Islamophobic expression rather than Islamophobic discrimination – are deeply problematic for the following reasons.[116] First, they appear, like the magician's rabbit pulled from the hat, at the very end of the APPG's report and are not discussed, explained or defended in any way there or hitherto. Second, although the report mentions intention and recklessness as elements in Islamophobic conduct – including by implication expression – neither is included in the definition or examples. Third, in common with the Runnymede reports, not a single illustration of legitimate criticism of Islam and Muslims is provided, nor is there any attempt to identify when the context would result in any of the stated examples not amounting to Islamophobia.[117] This risks, as Holland puts it, 'the ludicrous situation of being able to write without fear of prosecution about the Christian tradition of crusading or antisemitism, but not the Islamic tradition of jihad or the jizya'.[118] Fourth, according to this template, it would be 'Islamophobic' for ex-Muslims to express most of their 'lived experience'.

In fact, very few of the examples constitute genuinely anti-Muslim prejudice which could not be defended in any circumstances. And this makes it impossible to fashion a legally unchallengeable definition of 'Islamophobic expression' in this, or any other, manner. Calling for, aiding, instigating, or justifying the killing or harming of Muslims, or making dehumanizing or demonizing allegations about them, is certainly abhorrent and is likely in most

---

[115] APPG, *Islamophobia Defined*, pp. 56-7.
[116] See, eg Toube in Webb (ed.), *Islamophobia*, 99-102.
[117] Jenkins, *Defining Islamophobia*, p. 13.
[118] Dieppe, *Banning Islamophobia*, p. 17.

circumstances to be unlawful, whether 'in the name of a racist/fascist ideology or an extremist view of religion' or not. But, according to the APPG, conduct of this kind would only be 'Islamophobic' if those concerned were non-Muslim because we should regard those ultra-orthodox Muslims, such as al-Qaeda and ISIS/DAESH, who call for the death of those they regard as heretical Muslims, as 'sectarian' instead.[119] 'Mendacity', ie lying about Muslim beliefs, practices, or conduct would certainly amount to anti-Muslim prejudice if negative. However, positive lies, though objectionable on other grounds, cannot, by definition, be *anti*-Muslim. However, 'stereotyping' – conveying a fixed, oversimplified, and generally negative image – will only be Islamophobic if the image in question is untrue, distorted or misleading. And what counts as a stereotype may be a matter of opinion rather than objective fact. For example, some may think that claiming mainstream Islam is replete with myths and fairy tales invokes 'a derogatory stereotype'. But most secular westerners, and many 'progressive' Muslims such as Hargey whose views were discussed in Chapter 5, regard at least some of the beliefs considered in Chapters 3 and 4 as falling into this category.

It is not clear either that any of the following is necessarily Islamophobic; conspiracy theories concerning 'Muslim entryism in politics, government or other societal institutions'; accusations that Muslims as a group, or Muslim majority states, have invented or exaggerated Islamophobia, ethnic cleansing or genocide perpetrated against Muslims; fears that Muslims pose a demographic threat or a possible political takeover; accusations that Muslim citizens are more loyal to the ummah, the transnational Muslim community, or to their countries of origin, or to the alleged priorities of Muslims worldwide, than to their own nations by birth or adoption. This is because these are all empirical claims, in principle capable of being tested and shown to be true or false according to the evidence and the circumstances. It is not Islamophobic for any of them to be investigated and discussed to establish whether or not they are true. Nor can any conclusion the evidence supports be Islamophobic either.

It is not clear, either, that there is such a thing as a 'myth of Muslim identity having a unique propensity for terrorism', or if there is, who subscribes to, or propagates it. It is certainly true that Muslims do not have a 'unique propensity' towards terrorism because, as a matter of fact, many non-

---

[119] Toube in Webb (ed.), *Islamophobia*, p. 101.

Muslim ideologies have endorsed terrorist tactics, including nationalists of various kinds and those of the extreme secular left and right. But it is also undeniably true that some Muslims have been and remain involved in terrorism conducted in the name of their faith and that this is the principal terrorist threat in the UK, Europe, and the west generally.

Holding Muslims collectively responsible for real or imagined wrongdoing committed by a single Muslim, group of Muslims, or by any Muslim majority state will, or will not, be Islamophobic according to how evidence-based or otherwise the claim is that the activities in question were genuinely mandated, authorized, or permitted by the faith. This complex matter may be up for debate. But it is not Islamophobic merely to consider or to investigate it. It is difficult to know what holding Muslims responsible 'even for acts committed by non-Muslims' means or what might count as an example. A possible illustration might be anti-Muslim hate incidents following acts of Islamist terrorism.

The claim that it is Islamophobic to deny 'Muslim populations the right to self-determination eg by claiming that the existence of an independent Palestine or Kashmir is a terrorist endeavour' is also open to criticism on several grounds. First, it fails to address the vital question of when any given 'Muslim population' has such a right. Would it be available to Muslims in Britain, India, or Russia, for example? Was it available to ISIS/DAESH when they set up their Caliphate in 2014? If not, under what circumstances would such a right arise? Second, any right the Palestinians may have to self-determination is not strictly a right to *Muslim* self-determination since some Palestinians are non-Muslim. Third, if opposing the right to national independence is inherently racist then this must be true of all those who voted against Scottish independence in 2014, and their supporters elsewhere in the UK. Fourth, it is much more the *pursuit* than the *existence* of an independent Palestine or Kashmir which might, depending upon the methods, be described as a 'terrorist endeavour'. As with other assertions in the APPG's definition, whether such a claim is or is not Islamophobic will depend upon the extent to which terrorism is or is not an integral component of the project. Finally, the likely character of any Muslim state seeking independence from an existing state or states also has to be considered. Would it have the right, for example, to constitute itself as an Islamist state bent on territorial expansion including conquering and eliminating neighbouring states? Debating such issues is far from Islamophobic.

Applying any kind of double standard to any group not applied to any other comparable social group will require at the very least a compelling justification. In Britain the debate about loyalty tests has focused much more upon immigrants in general than upon Muslims in particular. To claim that the use of symbols and images associated with classic Islamophobia is Islamophobic is tautological because it assumes precisely what needs to be demonstrated. As already noted in previous chapters, it is said, for example, that Mohammed was a paedophile because he married his favourite wife, Aisha, when she was 6 years old and consummated the marriage when she was 9. However, since it has also been claimed, as Chapter 3 pointed out, that Aisha was in her late teens on the relevant occasion, the issue should be regarded as unproven. Provided all relevant evidence is included in the debate, it is not Islamophobic to engage in it.

As Chapter 2 of this study has clearly demonstrated, far from being Islamophobic, it is an incontestable fact that, in its early history, Islam was indeed 'spread by the sword', and that non-Muslim minorities were legally subordinate in Islamic states and, in some, this remains the case in fact if no longer in law. As Tom Holland has tweeted: 'Military conquest and the subjugation of minority groups have absolutely been features of Islamic imperialism'.[120]

It is an anti-Muslim prejudice to state or to imply that Muslims are *inherently* 'sex groomers', violent or incapable of living harmoniously in plural societies because there is no reliable evidence for it. But, as Chapter 8 considers, this is quite different from observing that Muslims have been involved in, for example, systematic sex grooming scandals and that questions have legitimately been raised about whether or not certain interpretations of their faith and culture may be implicated.

Nor is it clear how accusing Muslims as a whole of being responsible for wrongs committed by a single Muslim, or group of Muslims, or holding Muslims collectively responsible for the actions of a given Muslim state, is necessarily Islamophobic, particularly if the activities in question were carried out in the name of the faith. In such circumstances, there may be scope for debate about the credibility of such claims. But it is not Islamophobic to engage in it.

It may be Islamophobic to accuse *all* Muslims of being more loyal to the

---

[120] Dieppe, *Banning Islamophobia*, p. 17.

global 'ummah' (transnational Muslim community), to their countries of origin, or to the alleged priorities of Muslims worldwide, than to the states in which they are now settled. But it is certainly true of some. As Professor Ekmeleddin Ihsanoglu, a Turkish academic and former Secretary-General of the Organization of Islamic Cooperation once put it, belonging to the ummah means having a 'unique bond ... which transcends all other considerations of allegiance or loyalties or barriers, or nationhood, ethnicity, geography or language'.[121] In a similar vein Wajid Akhter, Secretary-general of the Muslim Council of Britain has said that 'British Muslims should raise their children to identify primarily as Muslim, rather than as British'[122]

This is also palpably the case with the worldwide Islamist movement which is hostile to nationalism and which seeks to create a global Caliphate. As Young et al put it, the implication of the APPG's examples is that attempting to ban consanguineous marriages, which can have serious health consequences for offspring, could be denounced as racist.[123]

In spite of the absence of any examples of legitimate criticism of Islam and Muslims, the APPG report states that it found five tests presented by Professor Tariq Modood, 'compelling and a useful measure for ascertaining whether contentious speech is indeed reasonable criticism or Islamophobia masquerading as "legitimate criticism."' These are: 1. Does it stereotype Muslims by assuming they all think the same and, in particular, does it suggest that all or most Muslims have a blameworthy characteristic which defines them, drowning out any worthy characteristics and ignoring contextual factors? 2. Is it about Muslims or a dialogue with Muslims which they would wish to join? 3. Is mutual learning possible by listening, for example, to those Muslims who think contemporary societies like Britain are oversexualised and encourage sexually predatory and undignified behaviour? 4. Is the language civil and contextually appropriate? 5. Is the criticism sincere or made for ulterior motives? If the answer to any of the five tests is 'Yes', Modood claims we may be dealing with Islamophobia or anti-Muslim racism.[124]

Civility, sincerity, the avoidance of negative stereotyping based upon

---

[121] https://www.youtube.com/watch?v=bDF9mDbVRqU.

[122] A. Gilligan, *The Muslim Council of Britain's New Leadership: A Research Note*, Policy Exchange Briefing, January 2025, p. 4

[123] Young et al, *Labour's Definition of 'Islamophobia'*, p. 26.

[124] APPG, *Islamophobia defined*, p. 36. See also T. Modood, 'Islamophobia and normative sociology' (2020) 8 *Journal of the British Academy* 29-49.

ignorance or deliberate misrepresentation, and a willingness to engage in dialogue and mutual learning, should certainly be features of any legitimate contribution to the debate about Muslim beliefs, practices, and conduct. But it cannot be denied that Muslims 'think alike' at least on some issues – the divine source of the Qur'an for example – otherwise there would be nothing that would justify calling them 'Muslim'. Modood's list would also be more complete if rehearsing criticisms based upon the authoritative literature, and greater latitude with respect to satire and humour, were included. However, the problem lies less with these criteria themselves and more with their application. As already indicated, most of the APPG's examples of Islamophobic expression are, in fact, commonplace observations in the authoritative literature about Muslims and/or Islam. Moreover, false accusations of Islamophobia referenced to the APPG's examples, are not only possible; they are being made with increasing frequency, as Chapters 7-9 show.

The Working Group's Definition

The British debate about Islamophobia rumbled on in the wake of the APPG's report. But nothing of significance happened as far as national public policy was concerned until after the general election in July 2024. Since then, there have been two significant developments. First, although the APPG's definition was originally intended to be 'legally binding', its advocates have since generally downgraded their expectations to securing a 'working definition'. But as Mahmood et al ask:

> 'what *work*, specifically, is this definition meant to be doing? ... On the one hand, its advocates claim that the APPG definition will carry no legal weight; on the other they insist that any failure to adopt the definition will cripple the struggle against Islamophobia. How is this circle to be squared? It is not hard to find the answer. Advocates of an Islamophobia definition have explicitly stated that adoption will be a first step towards its wider operationalization'.[125]

Second, in the 2024 election, Labour lost a handful of seats, including Mahmood's, to independents campaigning on a pro-Gaza ticket, and only narrowly held on to several others, including the Prime Minister's, with

---

[125] Mahmood et al, *A Definition of Islamophobia?*, p. 9. Italics in original.

significantly reduced majorities. The party, therefore, felt under pressure to stem the electoral haemorrhaging by assuaging the discontent. As indicated, it had already endorsed the APPG's conception of Islamophobia not long after it was minted. However, the 2024 Labour manifesto made only a vague commitment to introduce 'a landmark Race Equality Act, to enshrine in law the full right to equal pay for Black, Asian, and other ethnic minority people, strengthen protections against dual discrimination and root out other racial inequalities'. It also promised to reverse 'the Conservatives' decision to downgrade the monitoring of antisemitic and Islamophobic hate'.[126]

On 2 September 2024, in response to a question from Lee Anderson MP asking for a statement concerning the Government's definition of Islamophobia, Angela Rayner, then Deputy Prime Minister and Secretary of State for Levelling Up, Housing, and Communities, told the House of Commons: 'A new definition must be given careful consideration so that it comprehensively reflects multiple perspectives and considers the potential implications for different communities. We are actively considering our approach to Islamophobia, including definitions, and we will provide further updates in due course'.[127] Afzal Khan, Labour MP for Manchester Rusholme, also wrote to Sir Keir Starmer urging the government formally to adopt the APPG's conception.[128]

It is, however, far from clear that most Muslims, including those who campaign against anti-Muslim prejudice, favour making 'Islamophobia' unlawful. For example, Fiyaz Mughal, founder of the Tell Mama organization, which records anti-Muslim hate crime and offers support to those who have experienced it, advocates including agitation against alleged anti-Islam blasphemy as itself a type of Islamist extremism which, he says, presents 'an inherent threat against the democratic and secular values of our country'.[129] In August 2025, Mughal established a campaigning organization, *Keep the Law Equal*, with the single express purpose of opposing the adoption of 'a state-sanctioned definition of "Islamophobia,"' which he claims, although non-statutory, could be used by public and private institutions with

---

[126] *Change: Labour Manifesto 2024*, p. 90.

[127] Hansard, *Islamophobia*, Volume 753, debated on Monday 2 September 2024.

[128] F. Attenborough, 'Is the Labour Government inching closer to adopting a definition of "Islamophobia"?', *Free Speech Union Newsletter*, 5 September 2024.

[129] H. Yorke, 'Extremists "falling between the cracks" as officials accused of underplaying Islamism', *The Times*, 24 November 2024.

detrimental effects upon otherwise innocent parties including employees. This, he says, would be 'unfair, divisive, and dangerous' since nothing comparable is being proposed with respect to any other religion. Mughal also argues that it would introduce an anti-blasphemy law by the back door, exacerbate social division by creating a perception of a two-tier society, and chill public debate particularly about the sharia, traditional female Muslim dress codes, and the role certain interpretations of the Islamic faith may have upon wrongdoing including the activities of grooming gangs.[130]

A particularly powerful contribution to the debate was also made on 4 September 2024 by the Network of Sikh Organisations (NSO). In a letter to Ms Rayner expressing 'grave concerns' about the threat posed to free speech by the APPG's definition, the NSO warned that Sikhs would resist it becoming law.[131] The letter maintains that 'shutting down historical truths about current and historical religious persecution', and outlawing Islamophobia as the APPG defines it, would create a religious hierarchy that would risk exacerbating rather than alleviating intercommunal tensions. Sikhs object particularly strongly to characterising, as Islamophobic, the statement – 'Islam was spread by the sword' – not least because some of their own revered gurus were martyred in Moghul India for refusing to convert to Islam. They also claim, that not only were minority groups subjugated under Islamic rule in the past, but that this continues in some places today. The letter cites, as examples, the 'recent ethnic cleansing' of Hindus and Sikhs in Afghanistan, the massacre of Yazidis by ISIS/DAESH, the 'genocide in slow motion' of Christians in Nigeria, and the 'appalling treatment and persecution of minority faiths' in Bangladesh and Pakistan.

According to the NSO, incorporating the APPG's 'flawed definition into law' would mean that 'discussing the history of the Indian subcontinent and the persecution of minorities across the world' would not only absurdly be equated with racism. It would 'cause disquiet and perversely persecute truth-tellers', censoring and denouncing as racist, discussion of seminal moments in Sikh history. The letter adds that the religious discrimination which would result is 'likely to be subject to legal challenge in the form of a judicial review'. While recognising that the government needs to take steps to tackle

---

[130] https://keepthelawequal.com/; S. Swinford, 'Definition of Islamophobia risks unrest, Muslim campaigner warns', *The Times*, 26 August 2025.
[131] 'Sikhs dub Islamophobia definition "censorship,"' *The Times,* 5 September 2024.

hatred against Muslims and immigrants, the NSO points out that 'targeting criminality with a flawed definition of "Islamophobia" would be counterproductive' and that 'there is no evidence it would reduce anti-Muslim hatred in any case'.

The NSO also affirms that, with respect to relevant challenges, Sikhs 'believe more free speech is the answer, not less', and that although 'there are difficult conversations to have about historical truths, or specific aspects of religion … shutting them down is not the solution'. The letter concludes that 'the British Sikh community will strongly resist any attempt to distort recorded history'. Responding to the Sikhs' intervention, Baron Khan of Burnley, Parliamentary Under-Secretary of State for Social Housing and Faith, announced at the end of September 2024 that the government did not regard the APPG's definition as 'in line' with existing equality law, which he also affirmed, provided adequate protection against Islamophobia.[132]

There has, however, been pushback against these developments. For example, questioning Prime Minister Keir Starmer in the House of Commons on 27 November 2024, Labour MP for Birmingham Hall Green and Moseley, Tahir Ali, asked if he would 'commit to introducing measures to prohibit the desecration of all religious texts and the prophets of the Abrahamic religions'.[133] Responding, the PM undertook to tackle 'Islamophobia in all its forms'. Describing 'desecration' as 'awful', he also urged it to be 'condemned across the house'. Amongst others, the National Secular Society said that, if implemented, Ali's 'deeply alarming' request would amount to the reintroduction of blasphemy laws in the UK. Adding that MPs should 'uphold' and not 'seek to dismantle' the UK's foundational values, concern was also expressed that the PM had offered no defence of the right to free speech. In a separate question, and apparently ignoring Baron Khan's statement in September, Imran Hussain MP – who has previously backed the APPG's 2018 report – called upon the Prime Minister to 'adopt a definition' of Islamophobia.

On 24 December 2024, it was reported that the government had 'shelved

---

[132] O. Wright, 'Free speech fear over definition of Islamophobia', *The Times*, 30 September 2024.

[133] https://www.secularism.org.uk/news/2024/11/nss-mps-call-for-new-blasphemy-laws-deeply-alarming. See also G. Heffer, 'Senior Tories warn against "blasphemy laws" after Labour MP urges Keir Starmer to ban the "desecration" of religious texts and abuse of prophets of Christianity, Islam and Judaism', *Mail On Line*, 27 November 2024.

work on blasphemy laws'.[134] However just over a month later, it was disclosed that, in her role as communities' secretary, Angela Rayner, had nevertheless, decided to establish a working group to assist in drafting an official non-statutory definition of Islamophobia.[135]

Terms of reference and membership

According to its terms of reference, the group had two principal objectives. One was 'to develop a working definition of Anti-Muslim Hatred/Islamophobia which is reflective of a wide range of perspectives and priorities for British Muslims'. The other was 'to provide advice to the Deputy Prime Minister and Secretary of State for the Ministry of Housing Communities and Local Government (MHCLG) on appropriate and sensitive language to describe, understand and define unacceptable treatment, prejudice, discrimination and hate targeting Muslims or anyone who is perceived to be Muslim'.[136] This was to include 'advice regarding the merits of government adopting a non-statutory definition of unacceptable treatment of Muslims and anyone perceived to be Muslim, including what a proposed definition should be'. Evidence-based recommendations were to be made for Ministers 'to consider', and it was stated that all its advice would 'be private for Ministers' and would 'not be made public'. The proposed definition would also be 'non-statutory' and would 'provide the government and other relevant bodies with an understanding of unacceptable treatment and prejudice against Muslim communities'. The terms of reference also required that it must 'be compatible with the unchanging right of British citizens to exercise freedom of speech and expression – which includes the right to criticise, express dislike of, or insult religions and/or the beliefs and practices of adherents'.

Members of the working group were required to abide by the government's published engagement principles and standards, and as they discharged their responsibilities, to inform MHCLG in writing of all external engagements. Any potential or actual conflicts of interest were to be raised

---

[134] G. Scott, 'Work on new blasphemy laws has been put on hold', *The Times*, 24 December 2024.

[135] C. Hymas, 'Angela Rayner to set rules on Islam and free speech', *The Daily Telegraph*, 4 February 2025.

[136] https://assets.publishing.service.gov.uk/media/67e12094d8e313b503358c7c/Anti-Muslim_Hatred_Islamophobia_Definition_Working_Group_Terms_of_Reference_March_2025.pdf

with the Ministry immediately and to be signed off by the departmental Permanent Secretary. Members were also expected to adhere to the 'Code of Conduct for Board Members of Public Bodies, June 2019', including accountability to the public, particularly by submitting themselves to scrutiny, demonstrating openness/transparency and showing willingness publicly to disclose information unless there were clear and lawful reasons for not doing so. Members were expected to spend no more than 5-10 hours per month on the project, and the chair was required to meet bi-monthly with officials to discuss their work. The government also claimed the right to disband the group at any point and without notice if it decided that the exercise no longer met its aims and objectives, or if there was no longer a valid business case for the group to exist. Ministers were to review the group's progress after six months and to confirm next steps.

The terms of reference also stipulated that, in addition to the chair, the other four (non-stipendiary) members of the group, would be 'technical experts', directly appointed by Ministers for their ability to deliver the Group's objectives. However, no criteria for their selection were made public. Dominic Grieve KC, a former Conservative Attorney General who had written a very complimentary foreword to the APPG's 2018 report, was appointed as chair. The others were Professor Javed Khan OBE, Managing Director of the Muslim think tank, EQUI; cross-bencher Baroness Shaista Gohir OBE, CEO of Muslim Women's Network UK; Akeela Ahmed MBE, Co-Chair of British Muslim Network; and Asha Affi, Independent Consultant. Apart from Grieve all the others are Muslim or of Muslim heritage. Given that four of the five are also on record as having endorsed the APPG's 2018 definition of Islamophobia and its underlying rationale, speculation was rife that the working group was likely to produce a very similar report. There was also criticism about the lack of transparency concerning its proceedings and the narrowness of the consultation exercise conducted. A limited and tendentious questionnaire considered below, partially addressed the problem of making unsolicited submissions.

The controversy deepens

As 2025 wore on, the controversy surrounding the working group deepened in several ways. For example, in July 2025, an opinion poll of over 2,000 respondents, conducted by JL Partners, found that the introduction of an official, though non-statutory definition of Islamophobia, would damage

Labour at the ballot box and boost the vote for Reform UK.[137] Before the establishment of the working group had been announced, 29% of voters favoured Labour, with Reform UK trailing at 23%. But having heard about the working group's agenda, Reform UK polled 30% and preference for Labour fell to 20%. If this were reflected in a general election it would give Reform UK a projected parliamentary majority of 106 seats. While forecasting electoral outcomes on the basis of opinion polls is notoriously unreliable, the current public mood appears to be clear.

In November, another poll, also conducted by JL Partners, found that around a third of the 1,500 respondents opposed defining both the terms 'Islamophobia' and 'anti-Muslim hatred.[138] According to the survey, 36% regarded a new definition of 'Islamophobia' as a wholly or somewhat 'bad' thing, while 20% said it was wholly or somewhat a 'good' thing. Thirty-one per cent said that a new definition of the term 'anti-Muslim hatred' was a wholly or somewhat 'bad' thing, while one in five (20%) said it was wholly or somewhat a 'good' thing. James Johnson, co-founder of JL Partners, said: 'Whichever way the proponents of a definition try to spin this, it remains toxic with the British public. Semantics are not going to save the prospect of a new definition from sinking badly with the public'.

Other voices also expressed fresh concerns or endorsed those already articulated. On 10 July 2025, Dominic Grieve briefed Parliamentarians at the House of Lords. Amongst other things he told those present that the working group may conclude that there was no need for the definition in question after all.[139] Afterwards, 37 peers from different parties wrote to him, warning that the attempt to define anti-Muslim hatred/Islamophobia risked chilling free speech and exacerbating community tensions.[140] Acknowledging that harassment and discrimination faced by British Muslims are genuine causes for concern, the letter maintained that the term 'Anti-Muslim Hatred' may not be the best way of describing it, and that 'Islamophobia' and 'anti-Muslim hatred' are not the same thing. The signatories urged the group to abandon the

---

[137] M. Phillips, '"Islamophobia" law is a dangerous obsession', *The Times*, 22 July 2025.

[138] C. Hymas, 'Majority of public "does not want" Labour's Islamophobia definition', *The Telegraph*, 20 November 2025.

[139] T. Scotson, 'Ministers Set To Drop The Word "Islamophobia" From New Definition', *Politics Home*, 20 October 2025

[140] https://order-order.com/2025/07/14/peers-warn-grieve-islamophobia-definition-threatens-free-speech/

term 'Islamophobia' on the grounds that it was 'unhelpful' to imply that 'all criticism of the religion of Islam is motivated by fear and prejudice', and that some of those most vulnerable to hatred from Sunni Muslims are themselves heterodox or 'heretical' Muslims. They also warned of the serious risks which could arise if institutions and disciplinary bodies misapplied whatever definition emerged.

The peers urged the working group to broaden its membership and to postpone arriving at any conclusions until after the report of the public inquiry into the grooming gangs scandal had been published (See Chapter 8). They also recommended that it should 'advise the government that it would be unwise for the state to adopt an official definition' at all, and to make not only the draft definition but the working group's advice public for full Parliamentary scrutiny before the government decided whether or not to adopt it. In July 2025, the Free Speech Union also published a 38-page critique of how the working group had been established and had set about its task, the main points in which are included in what follows.[141]

In September, Conservative MP Claire Coutinho, shadow equalities minister, expressed concern that the working group would deliver a definition privileging one minority over others, and would 'shut down difficult but necessary conversations about grooming gangs, gender equality, and even Islamist extremism' compounding the current 'culture of censorship'.[142] And on 7 December, a week before the new definition was leaked, the former head of the Equality and Human Rights Commission (EHRC), Baroness Falkner, told Sky News's *Sunday Morning with Trevor Phillips* that the new definition would increase restrictions upon free speech. She warned that, in particular, it could be weaponised against women's rights campaigners, who are likely to be 'accused by ethnic-minority men of Islamophobia if they dare say something about how Muslim women are suppressed. I'm a Muslim woman myself. I know all about this'.

Concerns were also raised about alleged conflicts of interest on the part of some members of the group. Dominic Grieve, Baroness Gohir and Ms Ahmed have links with the Aziz Foundation, created and funded by controversial billionaire, Asif Aziz, which financially supports and works

---

[141] Young et al, *Labour's Definition of 'Islamophobia.'*
[142] S. Swinford, 'Labour's Islamophobia definition gives grooming gangs "impunity,"' *The Times*, 22 September 2025.

closely with other controversial organizations.[143] These include the Muslim Council of Britain – spurned by successive British governments since 2009 on the grounds of its questionable representativeness, alleged extremism and links to contentious groups and positions – and Muslim organizations such as Mend, the Islamophobia Response Unit, and Islamophobia Awareness Month, which amongst other things oppose the Prevent counterterrorist programme. The Foundation also funded the Citizens' Commission on Islam, Participation and Public Life, chaired by Dominic Grieve, and the Muslim Women's Network, chaired by Baroness Gohir.

On 21 July 2025, the MHCLG announced that the British Muslim Trust (BMT) – of which Ms Ahmed is CEO – would receive up to £1m a year to monitor incidents of Islamophobia, provide support to victims, 'raise awareness', and encourage greater reporting of hate crime. [144] The announcement coincided with the MHCLG slashing funds to 'Tell Mama', a long-established and widely-respected organization, founded by Fiyaz Mughal an outspoken critic, as already indicated, of any attempt to provide an official non-statutory definition of Islamophobia.

Ms Ahmed also co-chairs the British Muslim Network (BMN), an orthodox Sunni-led organization, launched in February 2025, also funded by the Aziz Foundation. BMN's other co-chair is Qari Asim, dismissed in 2022 by the then Conservative government as an advisor on Islamophobia as noted above. Reformist Muslims, minority and allegedly 'heretical' Muslim sects, such as the Ahmadis, do not appear to have been included in the BMN. According to Dr Taj Hargey, founder of the reformist think tank the Oxford Institute for British Islam: 'This proposed network is going to be meaningless if they only have a bunch of Muslim conservatives and right-wingers part of it and liberals and progressives and others like myself are just ignored'.[145]

Lord Toby Young, director of the FSU, called for Ms Ahmed to step down from the working group on the grounds of a 'clear conflict of interest' because the more broadly the working group's definition, 'the more work

---

[143] J. Jenkins & A. Gilligan, *A Fale Comptromise: Why a definition of 'Anti-Muslim hostility' is as bad as a definition of 'Islamophobia', possibly worse'* (Policy Exchange, 2026), pp.19-22.

[144] C. Hymas, 'Activist advising Rayner over Islamophobia definition sparks conflict of interest row' *The Telegraph*, 21 July 2025.

[145] H. Baldock, 'UK Labour Minister Begs Forgiveness from New Muslim Organization', *Focus on Western Islamism*, 11 April 2025.

there will be for the BMT to do and the more money it will be given by the Government'. He added that the slashing of funds for Tell Mama 'suggests that the Government has already decided to impose a dangerously authoritarian definition, zealously monitoring social media posts for traces of "Islamophobia" and then petitioning Ofcom to take them down, before it has even read any of the consultation responses'.[146]

Claiming that the working group was independent and would submit evidence-based advice to ministers, the government defended the appointment of Ms Ahmed and the BMT as recipients of the Combatting Hate Against Muslims fund, on the grounds that each has 'critical expertise and experience' in the field and that the BMT was appointed 'following a rigorous and transparent application process, in which it was the highest scoring applicant'.[147]

Baroness Gohir was also accused of conduct unbefitting a government adviser. In November she was reported to the parliamentary standards watchdog for having hosted an event in Parliament on 12 November 2025 attended by Haleem Kherallah. In June, Kherallah had been video-recorded with others at his Palestinian restaurant, *Shakeshuka*, in London, apparently celebrating TV broadcasts of Iran's ballistic missile attack on Haifa and Tel Aviv in which 28 Israelis were killed.[148] The baroness said that the parliamentary event had been organized, and the guest list compiled, by the Muslim-led charity, 'Waw Creative Arts', to celebrate the diversity of Muslims in public life.

On 5 September 2025, Angela Rayner resigned both from the government and as deputy leader of the Labour Party. This followed the decision of the PM's ethics adviser, Sir Laurie Magnus, that she had breached the ministerial code by failing, earlier in the year, to pay the appropriate tax on the purchase of an £800,000 flat. It was also revealed that her replacement as Minister for Housing, Communities and Local Government, Steve Reed MP, when Labour shadow local government secretary, had written to all leaders of local

---

[146] W. Jones, 'Activist Advising Rayner Over Islamophobia Definition Sparks Conflict of Interest Row', *Daily Sceptic*, 22 July 2025.
[147] C. Peters, 'Government-backed Islamophobia group linked to foundation that slammed counter-extremism programme', GB News, 22 July 2025.
[148] M. Dathan, 'Questions over guest of Islamophobia peer', *The Times*, 26 November 2025.

authorities urging them to implement the APPG's definition of Islamophobia.[149]

Consultation and transparency

Although the group's terms of reference made no provision for public consultation, on 7 May 2025, Lord Khan of Burnley stated: 'The group will consult with a wide variety of stakeholders to ensure that the voices of all relevant stakeholders are heard and considered'.[150] In June, the Working Group launched its consultation in secret. Invitations were sent privately to only a small group of select consultees. No explanation has been given about how they were chosen.

Following the intervention of the FSU, which wrote to Ms Rayner and to the working group raising serious concerns about the legality of such a highly selective consultation, the exercise was extended by the provision of a short online questionnaire. However, no opportunity was provided for the kind of substantial submissions typically associated with public consultations about proposed public policy. None of the numerous civil society, academic, public interest and faith-based organisations with relevant interests and expertise were encouraged to make submissions, nor was the general public either informed about the consultation or invited to participate. Both the peers' letter and the FSU claim this exposed the working group to the criticism that these choices were made in order to ensure a particular outcome.

The lack of transparency about how the working group would discharge its responsibilities also raised serious questions about whether it would conscientiously assess the evidence it received. While large public bodies often struggle to analyse consultation data effectively, the working group comprised just five members, each operating on a pro bono basis and was expected to devote only five to ten hours per month to the task.

It was also alleged that the failure to provide adequate consultation breached the core relevant legal standards known as the 'Gunning principles'. These require consultation to take place when public policy proposals are at a formative stage, that sufficient information is provided and time allowed for consideration and response by consultees, and that the observations and opinions received are conscientiously taken into account in decision-

---

[149] Swinford, 'Labour's definition of Islamophobia.'
[150] Written Answer to HL6894, House of Lords, Lord Khan of Burnley, 7 May 2025.

making.[151] Yet, with respect to the working group, no draft proposals, definition text, policy options, human rights analysis, or any explanation of how a non-statutory definition might be applied in practice, were offered. Nor was any attempt made to identify the areas in which the right to freedom of expression could be affected. Once the consultation was open to the public, respondents were given less than ten working days to reflect on the complex issues at stake. There was no indication about how responses would be evaluated or if they would be published.

The online questionnaire was also presumptuous and tendentious. For example, it tended to assume that anti-Muslim hatred is racist.[152] Yet, as Communities Minister, Lord Khan had stated, under the Equality Act, hostility toward Muslims falls under the 'religion or belief' and not the 'racial' strand. [153] Assuming that a non-statutory definition of anti-Muslim hatred/Islamophobia would be adopted, the questionnaire also concentrated upon content rather than seeking to make the case for having such a definition at all. Furthermore, by failing to provide open-text fields inviting free-form responses, there was no opportunity for thorough critical engagement. The FSU maintained that, having reduced the consultation exercise to a limited 'call for evidence' with no clear route for deliberation or reply, the public law duty to consider relevant representations may have been breached.

Legality

According to the FSU, there are several potentially fatal legal problems with any official non-statutory definition of anti-Muslim hatred/Islamophobia. First, by adopting and promoting whatever definition the working group proposed, the Secretary of State would be acting *ultra vires* (unlawfully beyond his/her powers) because existing legislation already allocates all relevant fields to other statutory bodies.[154] Any such definition adopted by public bodies, could breach the Equality Act by discriminating against both non-Muslims and Muslims with dissenting, 'heretical' or 'apostate' views. It may also contravene the Public Sector Equality Duty to foster good relations

---

[151] *R v North and East Devon Health Authority ex p Coughlan* [2001] QB 213; *R (Moseley) v Haringey LBC* [2014] UKSC 56.
[152] Young et al, *Labour's Definition of 'Islamophobia'*, pp. 10, 22-25.
[153] Ibid., p. 23.
[154] Ibid., p. 20.

between people with different protected characteristics.[155] Devoid of legal status and authority, such a definition used by a public body to limit freedom of expression, would also breach Article 10(2) of the European Court of Human Rights.[156] These issues are discussed more fully in Chapter 6.

In the autumn of 2025 the FSU and NSO threatened to launch judicial review proceedings to challenge whatever definition emerged from the working group.[157] And, on 22 October 2025, the EHRC announced that *any* attempt to define anti-Muslim hatred/Islamophobia not only risked conflicting with existing legislation leading to confusion for litigants and courts, but that it could also have a chilling effect upon freedom of speech, and could damage community cohesion.[158] A spokesman for the MHCLG disputed the EHRC's claims that, by considering the working group's definition without first consulting the EHRC itself, the government may have acted unlawfully, and that if the endeavour were to proceed there should have been a full public consultation.[159]

Effects

As many have pointed out, and as Chapter 6 of this study shows, the attempt to provide an official non-statutory definition of anti-Muslim hatred/Islamophobia is unnecessary because existing laws already offer adequate protection. The peers' letter also warned that, if the government were to endorse whatever definition the group proposed, it was likely to assume that enough had been done to address the problem and that other, more effective ways of tackling it would, therefore, be neglected.

It has also been observed that, merely because the definition would be 'non-statutory', would not mean that failures to comply with it would be free from adverse consequences for those concerned. Coupled with the likely sanctions, the definition is likely to be embedded in the speech codes of government departments, local authorities, the Courts and Tribunals Service,

---

[155] Ibid., p. 19.

[156] Ibid., p. 20.

[157] M. Kendix, 'Islamophobia definition "risks hindering police,"' *The Times*, 16 September 2025; F. Hamilton, 'Sikhs plan legal challenge to Islamophobia definition', *The Times*, 7 October 2025.

[158] M. Dathan, 'Islamophobia definition risks free speech, says watchdog', *The Times*, 22 October 2025.

[159] Young et al, *Labour's Definition of 'Islamophobia'*, pp. 12-14.

police forces, NHS trusts, museums, galleries, universities, schools, etc, not to mention Ofcom, IPSO and other regulators.[160] According to the FSU, 'a broad and ambiguous definition blurring the line between race and religion is likely to lead to workplace investigations, disciplinary action, reputational harm, and a chilling effect on lawful speech, especially in institutions governed by Equality, Diversity and Inclusion (EDI) policies that prioritise harm avoidance over open debate'.[161] The FSU maintains that it is also likely that an official non-statutory definition would strengthen the hand of the controversial Centre for Media Monitoring considered in Chapter 8, and would increase the incidence of Non-Crime Hate Incidents discussed in Chapter 6. Once established, it is also said that a 'rachet effect' would likely take hold, with government and Parliament pressed to do more.

As the FSU argues, any definition will either add nothing to existing legal protections, or risk unlawful overreach in its application.[162] As it says:

> 'If ministers are determined to adopt a non-statutory definition for use by public bodies, they should rely on the term 'anti-Muslim discrimination' and ensure that any guidance is grounded in the principles and legal thresholds already established under the Equality Act 2010 and other applicable legislation ... (and) ... if a definition is adopted, it should reflect existing law and limit itself to identifying those forms of anti-Muslim discrimination that are already unlawful under current civil and criminal law. Furthermore, the definition should not include advice that falls within the statutory powers or duties of other bodies'.[163]

Definition

In mid-October 2025, the working group submitted its report to the government in secret. The text remained undisclosed to the public until it was leaked and reported by the BBC on 15 December.[164] On 9 March 2026, as part

---

[160] See, eg, M. Kendix, 'Islamophobia definition "risks hindering police."'
[161] Young et al, *Labour's Definition of 'Islamophobia'*, pp. 17-19.
[162] M. Kendix, 'Islamophobia definition "risks hindering police."'
[163] Young et al, *Labour's Definition of 'Islamophobia'*, p. 27.
[164] C. McSorley, 'Ministers finalising definition of anti-Muslim hatred', *BBC*, 15 December 2025.

of a policy paper on social cohesion and resilience,[165] the government officially endorsed an edited version of the leaked text, described by the formal Guidance, as a 'working definition'.[166] The revised formulation reads:

> 'Anti-Muslim hostility is intentionally engaging in, assisting or encouraging criminal acts – including acts of violence, vandalism, harassment, or intimidation, whether physical, verbal, written or electronically communicated – that are directed at Muslims because of their religion or at those who are perceived to be Muslim, including where that perception is based on assumptions about ethnicity, race or appearance.
>
> It is also the prejudicial stereotyping of Muslims, or people perceived to be Muslim including because of their ethnic or racial backgrounds or their appearance, and treating them as a collective group defined by fixed and negative characteristics, with the intention of encouraging hatred against them, irrespective of their actual opinions, beliefs or actions as individuals.
>
> It is engaging in unlawful discrimination where the relevant conduct – including the creation or use of practices and biases within institutions – is intended to disadvantage Muslims in public and economic life'.

The policy paper also promises increased support and funding to programmes that directly tackle anti-Muslim hatred. A Special Representative on anti-Muslim hostility will also be appointed, 'to champion efforts across the UK to tackle hostility and hatred directed at Muslims and those perceived to be Muslim'. The Guidance also affirms that implementing and measuring the success of the 'working definition', will be subject to ongoing monitoring and regular review, and that possible adjustments may be made in response to feedback and other developments. It also encourages public, private and third sectors, to adopt the definition and to consider how it applies in their contexts.

Reaction to the BBC's disclosure and the official announcement has split

---

[165] Ministry of Housing, Communities & Local Government, *Policy paper – Protecting What Matters: Towards a more confident, cohesive, and resilient United Kingdom*, 9 March 2026.

[166] Ministry of Housing, Communities & Local Government, *Guidance – A Definition of Anti-Muslim Hostility: An overview of the government's new non-statutory definition of anti-Muslim hostility, what it seeks to address and its intended application*, 9 March 2026.

along predictable lines. Free speech, secularist campaigners and others have repeated concerns fully rehearsed throughout the debate.[167] The FSU and the Network of Sikh Organizations have renewed their threat to launch litigation. Some Muslim organizations have, however, complained about what they regard as a 'watered down' definition, particularly the absence of any reference to 'Islamophobia'.[168] The Muslim Council of Britain has, for example, advocated the continued endorsement of the APPG's report instead.[169]

Several elements of the new definition and the accompanying Guidance are welcome. First, appearing to reflect the previous three decades of debate and some of the concerns about the working group's deliberations, it is an improvement on what has gone before. The Guidance does not, for example, claim – as the 1997 Runnymede and APPG reports did with respect to Islamophobia – that anti-Muslim hostility is 'systemic' or 'institutionalized' in the UK. Each of the three parts of the new definition also requires, with respect to Muslims, *intentionally* being involved in criminal acts, encouraging hatred through 'prejudicial stereotyping', or engaging in unlawful discrimination.

Nor does the Guidance endorse the assertion that Islamophobia is a species of racism. However, this is compromised by the confusing extension of the concept of 'anti-Muslim hostility' to those mistakenly perceived as Muslim, a process the Guidance claims is 'sometimes described as racialisation'. Strictly speaking, only Muslims can suffer genuine 'anti-Muslim hostility'. However, victimization as a result of being mistaken for a Muslim, might credibly be included where there is clear evidence of such antagonism – words uttered during a hate crime incident for example – rather than mere speculation that this was the motive.

---

[167] Baroness Falkner of Margravine, 'Special protection for Muslims means a two-tier system', *The Times*, 10 March 2026; National Secular Society, 'NSS concerned by leaked anti-Muslim hostility definition', 16 December 2025; M. Thompson, 'Ministers add the finishing touches to long-awaited definition of Islamophobia', Free Speech Union, 16 December 2025.

[168] W. Akhter, 'MCB Warns Against Lack of Transparency And Watering Down Of Islamophobia Definition', *Muslim Council of Britain*, 16 December 2025; H. Tagari, 'UK Government abandons official Islamophobia definition', *5 Pillars*, 17 December 2025.

[169] Muslim Council of Britain, 'MCB Response to Government Proposed "Anti-Muslim Hostility" Definition', Press Release, 10 March 2026.

The Guidance also makes clear that open debate in the public interest is important and must be fully safeguarded, that context matters, and that the following do not constitute 'anti-Muslim hostility':

> 'criticisms of a religion or belief, including Islam, or of its practices, or critical analyses of its historical development; ridiculing or insulting a religion or belief, including Islam, or portraying it in a manner that some of its adherents might find disrespectful or scandalous; criticism of the belief systems or practices of individual adherents of a religion or belief, including Islam; raising concerns in the public interest; contributing to debates in the public interest, including academic and political debate'.

However, there are also problems. First, several related difficulties arise from the most fundamental – the failure to provide an authoritative summary of the relevant law. Neither the definition nor the Guidance recognizes that, subject to one possible exception, the definition is, in effect, a statement of what the law already requires. The exception is that the threshold for 'encouraging' anti-Muslim hatred could be lower than that for 'inciting' it. The Guidance also says that the second paragraph of the definition is 'intended to encompass behaviour that is not necessarily unlawful, but which is reprehensible in this context, because it extends beyond the bounds of protected free speech'. However, 'unprotected' speech is, by definition, unlawful. The Guidance also claims that 'legislation alone is not enough', because 'law can address offences, but a definition can be the foundations of the wider cultural, educational and preventative work needed to stop hatred from taking root'. Yet, even if the official non-statutory definition provided something additional to the law, there is no obvious reason why this should not apply to all forms of anti-social hostility and not just to those which affect Muslims.

A second problem is that no non-legal mechanisms have been provided to challenge mistaken, false or inappropriate applications of the new definition. Most public institutions are likely officially to endorse it. Some may even scrupulously apply it. Yet, even if they have embraced it, others may simply ignore it with impunity when it suits them. Had the new definition been in place at the relevant times, it is unclear what would have happened to any of the relevant controversies discussed in Chapters 7-9. It is unlikely, for example, to have made much difference to those involving threats and intimidation alleging Islamophobia, such as the censorship of some books and films, the Kettlethorpe affair, and the fate of the proposed Centre for the Study of Political Islam at the University of Bradford. The outcome with respect to others is more difficult to imagine.

The lack of even the most schematic account of what Muslims believe and how this might affect their conduct is a third defect. This is crucial, because in its absence, it will be difficult if not impossible to determine if any relevant statement amounts to a stereotypical prejudice intended to encourage anti-Muslim hatred, or is simply an accurate report about Muslim beliefs, practices and conduct, and/or a lawful and legitimate opinion.

A further problem is the assumption that Muslims in the UK are a beleaguered minority suffering widespread anti-Muslim hostility. As the Guidance correctly reports, anti-Muslim hate crime has dramatically increased in recent years. But it also fails to mention that, as noted by this study, reliable opinion polling consistently shows that the vast majority of Muslims in the UK have a strong sense of belonging to this country, regard it as a good place in which to practise their faith, and have not been the victim of anti-Muslim discrimination themselves. Nor does the Guidance address the question of whether some Muslims may be guilty of anti-Muslim hostility against other Muslims, for sectarian reasons for example.

Conclusion

Since the late-1980s, the 'Islamophobia' debate in Britain has been characterised by the meteoric rise in the public profile of the term – as marked by the Runnymede and APPG reports – and by its subsequent fall, though probably not disappearance, as indicated by its absence from the official non-statutory definition of 2026. While its exclusion is welcome, the new definition suffers from several critical defects and may also have a number of negative consequences. Expression hitherto denounced as 'Islamophobic' may simply be rebranded as 'prejudicial stereotyping' intended to encourage anti-Muslim hatred. However, the intentionality requirement, which should have a high evidential threshold, may make bogus complaints on this basis more difficult to sustain. Doubts about the kinds of statement which are, and which are not permitted, may nevertheless, also result in the persistence of self-censorship of lawful and legitimate discussion of Muslims and Islam.[170]

---

[170] G. Scott, '"Self-censorship" risk of anti-Muslim hostility definition', *The Times*, 11 March 2026.

The authority of the new definition is also undermined by the failure to provide a compelling rationale – particularly about why reliance upon the existing law is inadequate – the many defects in the process by which the working group was constituted, the secrecy surrounding its deliberations, and other controversies. As a result, it may, therefore, simply join rather than replace the many alternatives.

There are no obvious grounds either for believing that the new official definition will make a positive contribution to tackling the problem of anti-Muslim hatred itself. As many have argued, the best routes to this destination lie, instead, in an enhanced commitment by both state and society to challenge all forms of overt social antagonism, coupled with the robust enforcement of the existing law in this field, framed as it is in universal rather than faith-specific terms.

Chapter 11

Islamophobia and free speech

A sceptic might argue that the few dozen controversies surveyed in this book indicate that false accusations of 'Islamophobic expression' are, at worst, a minor problem for the west and even less so globally and do not, therefore, amount to a free speech crisis. This would, however, be to misunderstand the issue. For one thing, they have an unwarranted and an enduringly harmful impact upon the direct victims plus an unquestionably chilling and self-censoring effect upon lawful and legitimate debate about Muslims and Islam.

Every attempt to provide an effective definition of 'Islamophobic expression' consistent with the values of right-respecting democracies has failed. The most fundamental substantive defects have been the complete absence of even the most schematic account of relevant legal and human rights norms and the lack of any account of the essentials of the Muslim faith according to its principal interpretations. In Britain, freedom of expression is legally sacrosanct though not absolute. Incitement to religious hatred is a crime. Religious hatred is an aggravating factor where other offences, such as physical assault and vandalism, involve it. Religious harassment is also criminal in certain circumstances. In other contexts, harassment or discrimination on religious grounds may result in other sanctions, including dismissal from employment.

And the difficulties with the definitions do not end here. Many rely upon survey data or 'consultation'. The surveys typically involve self or targeted selection rather than random representative sampling. 'Consultation' also tends to be limited and there are generally other weaknesses in data collection. Unscientific, skewed, and lop-sided analyses often resting upon demonstrably false assumptions, have been the result. A particularly egregious example concerns the conflation of race and religion. Not only is this intellectually incoherent – Muslims come from every race under the sun and do not constitute a race themselves – it openly conflicts with British equality law which regards these as separate and independent protected characteristics, albeit ones which may sometimes coincide in practice.

Most illustrations of allegedly 'Islamophobic expression' provided by those definitions which proffer them would also be perfectly lawful in most circumstances. And, by sharp contrast, no attempt has ever been made by the 'anti-Islamophobic expression movement' to provide a list of legitimate and lawful criticisms of Muslims and Islam. Critique of Islam, a body of ideas, is also typically confused with hostility towards Muslims, a group of people.

Key features of orthodox Islam have, in fact, been critically appraised for centuries, including by Muslims themselves. Even in the west the debate has long featured both positive and negative opinion. According to the received view, the faith began peacefully in the mid-7th century, and having survived an attempt by its Arab enemies to wipe it out, expanded by rapid imperial conquest motivated primarily by the quest for loot, tribute, slaves, territory, and dominion rather than by missionary zeal. Until the early modern period, the civilizations which arose in the core of the Muslim world also conspicuously outstripped the cultural and other achievements of Christendom. This was widely recognised by observers in non-Muslim Europe at the time as it has been by informed opinion ever since. Although Jews and Christians were often well-treated in the Muslim empires, they nevertheless, had formally second-class status, experienced various forms of discrimination including a special tax, and also suffered periodic bouts of official and unofficial persecution including bloody massacre. Other minorities were not so fortunate. And various minorities in many Muslim majority countries continue to face prejudice and discrimination in fact if not in law.

Non-Muslims are at best sceptical about the claim that the Qur'an is the literal word of God, dictated via the Archangel Gabriel to the Prophet Mohammad, and that the other formal sources of the faith also have divine sanction. Critics also claim that the Qur'an suffers from grammatical and other flaws including contradiction. The orthodox 'doctrine of abrogation' itself maintains that later revelations cancel earlier ones. Why God would alter what He had previously revealed has yet to be convincingly explained.

The authority and authenticity of the hadith – anecdotes about the life of Mohammad some of which give rise to obligatory or recommended conduct – have also been called into question. Most non-Muslim experts maintain that many, if not most, were manufactured by competing Muslim factions in the early history of the faith to support rival positions on matters of doctrine linked to the quest for political advantage.

Similar problems are said to arise with Islamic law, the sharia. The assumptions that it has divine status, that it was complete by the Middle Ages, and that it cannot, therefore, be altered or augmented, have also been treated with scepticism by critics. It has been pointed out, for example, that even if the many celebrated Muslim jurists over the centuries agreed on all specifics, this would not prove its divine origin. But the existence of several schools of jurisprudence in both the Sunni and Shia traditions makes the perfect and unalterable divine infallibility of the sharia difficult to defend.

Provided no attempt is made to impose Muslim beliefs about metaphysical matters and devotional practices upon others, no liberal-minded person is likely to object to Muslims subscribing to them themselves. The principal areas of live controversy centre, instead, upon the implications of contemporary mainstream Islam for matters of public policy, most if not all of which are also of concern for progressive Muslims. In addition to the animal welfare implications of halal meat, the following are amongst those most vigorously debated.

Although the Qur'an does not mandate any particular mode of governance – and can even be interpreted as expressing some sympathy for democracy – no genuinely democratic tradition ever developed in the core of the Muslim world. And no contemporary Muslim majority state is fully democratic. Indeed, most fall far short. Mainstream orthodox Islam also raises issues regarding the position of women, sexual and marital relations, crime, punishment, and human rights. The Qur'an clearly assumes, for example, that men are in charge of women, requires wives to obey their husbands, and, as a last resort, permits husbands to strike them if they are disobedient. It also allocates women half the inheritance of a man and accords the testimony of women a status formally equal to half that of a man, at least in financial matters requiring witnesses. Men are also allowed up to four wives simultaneously, Christians and Jews included, while those victorious in war are also permitted to take, as sex slaves, 'the captives that your right-hand possesses'. By contrast, a Muslim woman can have only one (Muslim) husband at any given time. According to the sharia, a man may divorce his wife by simply saying three times 'I divorce you', while a woman can only divorce her husband through formal legal proceedings.

The harsh punishments prescribed by traditional Islam, which remain available in states such as Saudi Arabia, Pakistan, and Iran, are particularly controversial in the west. The most serious offences are apostasy and blasphemy which, in spite of significant differences in how frequently death sentences are passed and carried out, remain capital offences in several contemporary Islamic states such as Pakistan and Iran. Muslim scholars do not see eye to eye about how to deal with either. In jurisdictions where blasphemy is a crime, obtaining a fair trial is also a challenge because it is blasphemous for witnesses, lawyers, judges, reporters and others to repeat what the defendant is alleged to have said. One result is that, not infrequently, mobs and free-lancers exact punishment without any reliable evidence or any opportunity for those accused to defend themselves. Although it is not true that the orthodox Islamic tradition regards terrorism, especially the deliberate targeting of non-combatants, as legitimate, the Salafi-jihadi interpretation of the faith clearly has no such reservations.

Banning, or severely restricting, criticism of what Muslims believe and how they behave would not only be a violation of the right to freedom of expression. It would inhibit attempts to tackle challenges such as those presented by certain types of sex grooming by gangs, jihadi terrorism, and attempts to 'Islamize' school curricula. Those with the courage to discuss these issues may continue to be stigmatized and penalized, socially if not legally, with potentially detrimental consequences for them and for society generally. What started out at the beginning of 2025 as an attempt to provide an official, non-statutory definition of 'anti-Muslim hatred/Islamophobia', ended in March 2026 with a definition of 'anti-Muslim hostility' instead. This is welcome for three main reasons. First, it constitutes the wholesale official retreat from the concept of 'Islamophobia' and its narrower incarnation, 'Islamophobic expression'. Second, it amounts effectively to little, if anything, more than a statement of the current law. Third, it lists the kind of criticism of Muslims and Islam that do not amount to 'anti-Muslim hostility', which it is to be hoped, will soon be more fully fleshed out.

But, for several reasons, it is also open to criticism. It assumes that Muslims generally want, and need, the new definition when there is inadequate evidence that this is, in fact, the case. Breach of its limits is also unenforceable by any non-legal means. It fails to provide an authoritative statement of Muslim beliefs, practices and conduct which would enable lawful and legitimate critical inquiry to be more unflinchingly undertaken. Finally, it may fuel more strident demands on the part of the 'anti-Islamophobic expression movement', disappointed that the 2025-26 exercise produced much less than expected. But one thing can be predicted with considerable confidence: the debate about Islamophobia and free speech is far from over.